America Town

America Town

Building the Outposts of Empire

Mark L. Gillem

University of Minnesota Press
Minneapolis • London

Lyrics from "Big Yellow Taxi" are reprinted in chapter 4. Words and music by Joni Mitchell. Copyright 1970 (renewed) Siquomb Publishing Corporation. All rights reserved. Used by permission.

Parts of chapters 4 and 5 were originally published in "America Town: Planning the Outposts of Empire," *Journal of Architectural Education* 58, no. 3 (February 2005).

Unless otherwise noted, the author took the photographs and created the graphs and maps in the book.

Published by the University of Minnesota Press
111 Third Avenue South, Suite 290
Minneapolis, MN 55401-2520
http://www.upress.umn.edu

Library of Congress Cataloging-in-Publication Data

Gillem, Mark L.
    America town : building the outposts of empire / Mark L. Gillem.
        p.   cm.
    Includes bibliographical references and index.
    ISBN-13: 978-0-8166-4952-5 (hc : alk. paper)
    ISBN-10: 0-8166-4952-9 (hc : alk. paper)
    ISBN-13: 978-0-8166-4953-2 (pb : alk. paper)
    ISBN-10: 0-8166-4953-7 (pb : alk. paper)
    1. Military bases, American—Foreign countries.   2. Military bases, American—Social aspects.   3. Land use—United States—Planning.   4. Land use—Government policy—United States.   5. Suburbs—Public opinion.   I. Title.
    UA26.A2G55   2007
    355.70973—dc22   2007012423

Contents

Acknowledgments

While I alone am responsible for the content of this book, I am deeply grateful for the advice, support, and encouragement of colleagues from around the globe.

I am especially indebted to Nezar AlSayyad. As a gifted designer, active administrator, and inspirational educator, he has found the balance I hope to achieve. He has shown me that the border between academia and practice can be occupied. He supported this research even when I had doubts about capitalizing on my military background.

I am thankful for the advice and guidance of Galen Cranz and Michael Southworth. In our noisy classrooms during the renovations of Wurster Hall on the Berkeley campus of the University of California, in the comfort of her home, and in the cold lecture halls where we taught undergraduate students, Galen opened my eyes to the value of ethnographies and to the sociocultural settings in which architects and planners operate. She reviewed the manuscript with exacting detail, for which I am eternally grateful. Sitting in Michael's office, surrounded by books on planning and urban design, with his window-wall looking out to a beautiful grove of redwoods, I always felt welcomed. He kept me grounded in the physical reality of spatial practice.

In the studios we taught together, Dan Solomon helped me see the linkage between urban policy and urban design. In our walks around San Francisco and in discussions on campus, Allan Jacobs helped me see the value of connecting demographic and spatial data. I am quite thankful for Ananya Roy's elegant analysis and enthusiastic support of my work. Finally, Sam Davis taught me about sociocultural factors from a practicing architect's perspective. In one of his courses, I even lectured about my military experience—a real boundary-blurring event for me and for the students. It never fails to amuse me how quickly students stereotype soldiers, and I hope my example confused them a bit. But the same is true for many of the federal employees I encountered, who, on hearing I was an academic, quickly dismissed me as a left-wing radical. Fear of the unknown, stereotyped "other" is alive and well on the left and on the right.

In the U.S. military, I thank Don Ritenour, Darrell Campbell, and David Duncan for their support of this project. As architects, they have their own opinions on the shape of settlement space. Nevertheless, they were always supportive of my work, even with the knowledge that it would be critical. They agreed to my survey methods and let me speak freely at their conferences. I thank the hundreds of soldiers, sailors, and airmen who took time out of their busy lives to share with me their impressions of living and working on America's overseas outposts. Their graciousness is rarely highlighted in the discussions of military policy. In particular, I thank Tricia Kessler, Kelly Holliday, Anthony Lee, Dale Masin, and Larry Herges for generously sharing their time and ideas. Tricia and I worked together on active duty, and she was willing to listen to my stories and offer her own interpretations. Kelly and Anthony have spent too many nights away from home on military duty, but were always ready to share their discerning thoughts on the planning and design of America Towns. Dale was an early and active supporter of my academic path and challenged me to remain objective throughout this study. Larry, an architect in the Air Force, set me on a route of critique during my earliest days on active duty. "Never accept the status quo," he would say. As a Vietnam veteran, he knows the danger of a military staffed by officers who just report for duty and salute smartly. I also thank Jerry Zekert and Jim Minor for their willingness to let me discuss planning issues in their courses. I became a regular speaker at several events, and the feedback from participants helped me find what I hope is a balanced analysis.

I would like to acknowledge the contributions of many people outside the military who helped move this project into its current form. I am quite thankful for the dozens of residents of South Korea, Italy, and Japan who generously met with me to share their stories. Back in the United

States, comments received from colleagues and students at numerous conferences, colloquiums, and seminars helped me refine the work. While this book was still in its earliest drafts, Valerie Hedrick read and reread every page and challenged my writing and my thinking. At one particularly enlightening retreat in California's Sonoma Valley, Anthony King and Mia Fuller gave me much needed advice and encouragement. The project has also benefited tremendously from the critiques of the manuscript offered by my peer reviewers. They approached the work from a variety of perspectives and made generous recommendations for improvements in both structure and content. At the University of Oregon, my colleagues in the departments of architecture and landscape architecture gave me the time and intellectual space to complete the manuscript. At the University of Minnesota Press, I acknowledge the enthusiastic support of my editor, Pieter Martin, as well as Katie Houlihan and Therese Boyd. Their professionalism and dedication to service have helped bring this book to your hands.

Above all, I thank Sarah, who has endured three residential renovations, six moves, six years of doctoral work, a one-year master's program, and several years of my undergraduate studies in architecture. Without her help making notecards, scanning images, and taking care of our two children when I was ensconced in my office or traveling abroad, this project would have failed. Her careful editing, constructive critiques, and insightful suggestions helped clarify my thinking and writing. Thank you, Sarah.

Acronyms

AAFES	Army Air Force Exchange Service
AFI	Air Force Instruction
AFRC	Armed Forces Recreation Center
AICUZ	Air Installation Compatible Use Zone
AT/FP	Anti-Terrorism/Force Protection
BAH	Basic Allowance for Housing
BRAC	Base Realignment and Closure
BX	Base Exchange
CBO	Congressional Budget Office
DECA	Defense Commissary Agency
DMZ	Demilitarized Zone
DoD	Department of Defense
FAR	Floor Area Ratio
FHA	Federal Housing Authority
GAO	Government Accountability Office
GOJ	Government of Japan
HUD	Department of Housing and Urban Development
ICB	International Competitive Bidding
ITE	Institute of Transportation Engineers
JFIP	Japan Facility Improvement Program
KNHC	Korean National Housing Corporation
LPP	Land Partnership Plan
MAJCOM	Major Command
MFH	Military Family Housing

NATO	North Atlantic Treaty Organization
PACAF	Pacific Air Forces
POV	Privately Owned Vehicle
PX	Post Exchange
Q-D	Quantity-Distance
RFP	Request for Proposals
RIF	Reduction in Force
ROK	Republic of Korea
ROKAF	Republic of Korea Air Force
SACO	Special Action Committee Okinawa
SBF	Sea Based Facility
SOFA	Status of Forces Agreement
USAF	United States Air Force
USAFE	United States Air Forces Europe

Introduction

"Can you drop 500 feet," I asked the pilot.

"Sorry, I can barely hear you," came the muffled reply.

After I adjusted my headset, I tried again. The helmet kept out some of the din, but I could still barely hear the pilot's confirming response, "Okay, entering 2,500 feet."

I felt it, though. The drop and accompanying banking maneuver forced me against the seat. We had lifted off just after sunrise and were hovering near the Pacific coastline. A cerulean sky and still seas would greet the throngs of swimmers and boaters that usually played over the colorful coral reefs. After arriving at the right spot, I opened the side door and pulled a spring-loaded lever; my seat lunged out of the hovering Blackhawk and locked into place with a jerk. I was outside the relative safety of the helicopter and the only thing between the ground and my seat was 2,500 feet of clear air.

With the exterior seat firmly in place, I began the photo shoot. I took the best shots when the helicopter was banking 90 degrees and I was face down above the striking landscape of Kadena Air Base in Okinawa, Japan. Beneath me was the arrogant attitude of America's imperial might sprawled across the verdant landscape of the beautiful tropical island. The most damning views were at the borders where the 11,018-acre base met its Japanese neighbors (see Figure I.1). America's landscapes of consumption had found their way to Okinawa. The base, with its sprawling subdivisions, strip malls, and streets wide enough to land fighter jets, abutted the compact urban fabric of Okinawa-chi, Kadena-cho, and

Figure I.1. Imperial land use: Chatan-cho, Japan, on the left; Kadena Air Base on the right.

Chatan-cho. The golf course stood ready to defend the base at its western edge. The split-level ranch homes had yards big enough to land several Blackhawks. The main shopping center's parking lot was bigger than the dense town center of Okinawa-chi. What was the United States doing building like this in a place so short of land that airports are constructed on artificial islands? How did this happen and what does this tell us about the culture of America's military and the complicity of the "host" nation?

Since September 11, 2001, scholars have published numerous books on empire.[1] Some have even focused on the expanding network of America's overseas bases.[2] Yet, none of these authors addressed questions I posed in the Blackhawk that morning. Their focus has principally been on the strategic implications of the wars in Afghanistan and Iraq. On the political left, these wars testified to imperial hubris. America was acting largely alone without the consent of the global order. On the political right, scholars viewed the wars as a justifiable use of imperial power.[3] Largely missing from these accounts, however, was a discussion of the spatial impacts of projecting imperial might.[4] I am not interested in essentializing American troops as lazy, sex-starved "Imperial Stormtroopers," as some writers have done. Nor am I content with simply quantifying the impact in terms of total numbers of overseas bases. Sheer numbers can mask real issues. As an architect and planner, I am more interested in the actual bases themselves and the processes used in their design and planning. How imperial powers use land is a significant concern. Despite widespread media attention focusing on the tragic stories of rapes, deadly accidents, and environmental damage, surveys of local residents near some of these outposts reveal not so much an all-consuming desire for their demise but disgust, above all, with the excessive use of land by American forces.[5] The excesses of American culture are indeed most evident in the way the U.S. military consumes land.

Imperial powers have extended an imposing reach across the globe, which at a minimum included the establishment of temporary and permanent military outposts used both to project imperial power and to control the occupied territories and populations. From the Peloponnesian wars to the Iraq wars, building military outposts has been a central function of power projection that scholars too often ignore in the imperial debates. This is where I hope to join in. While I am neither a historian nor scholar of empire, nor do I propose to present a comprehensive review of empire's spatial hunger, I do hope to illuminate some of the processes and problems associated with the housing of America's military force. I use the term *housing* in a broad sense to include all the spatial requirements of garrisoning America's soldiers abroad.

In this study, I examine ways that design practices, institutional policies, and actual projects have contributed to the creation of America Towns across the globe. My focus, though, is not on battleships and runways. Rather, I concentrate on the spatial implications of exporting American suburbs—places filled with rambling subdivisions, supersized shopping centers, and lush golf courses. Although many scholars have studied Japantowns, Koreatowns, and Chinatowns in North America, few have looked at America Towns overseas.[6] These places, built by and for expatriates, incorporate familiar building patterns but are also transformed by local conditions. They bring together diaspora communities searching for spatial familiarity. The buildings and neighborhoods both expose and obscure economic, political, and social priorities.

For America Towns, what are the spatial models and what do these places reveal and conceal? I suggest that the spatial model is a low-density suburb, exported from the homeland, replete with auto dependency, isolated uses, and low net densities. It is a model that requires vast tracts of buildable land to give residents a slice of the American Dream. These simulacrums of suburbia are necessarily like gated communities, with guards and walls designed to keep out the troublemakers. And, like many gated communities, they are sited far from urban centers in part to avoid the entanglements of interaction.

One woman living in a gated community in the United States made a comment that applies as much to America's outposts as it does to her middle-class enclave: "The irony is that we are trapped behind our own gates. Unable to exit. Instead of keeping people out we have shut ourselves in."[7] Americans working overseas for the Department of Defense (DoD) are shutting themselves in as well—into well-appointed compounds. While various branches of the military have their own terms for these compounds, and numerous scholars refer to these places in a variety of ways, I use "outpost" here because it refers both to a military site and to the far-off nature of that site.[8]

Touring Empire

In this book, I offer a tour of some of these outposts. The intent is not to analyze grand imperial strategies but to reveal how such strategies play out on the landscape. While the focus of this study is primarily on the reach of the current American Empire (Map I.1) and how this empire has acquired and modified its domain, I begin with a short examination of how previous empires have managed their land holdings. Part I, "Empire's Reach," reveals how empires across time have marked their territories. First, I focus primarily on European powers, arguably the ancestors of America's imperial project. From the Greeks to the Brits, European powers have played the game of empire as rabidly as anyone else has. As imperial reach became increasingly global, design became increasingly regulated. Imperial designers sought order over "disorder" and achieved it through demolition and displacement. These actions, however, were not unilateral. They required consent and complicity among some of the governed. These historical lessons provide insight into the current functioning of empire.

After this brief historical prelude, I look at how imperial attitudes have contributed to a longing for more—more space, more power, more control. But rather than concentrate on the soft power employed by American corporations and boosters, which has been well documented elsewhere, my attention is on the hard power of the U.S. military and its imperial reach as it plays out in and around its outposts.[9] What would

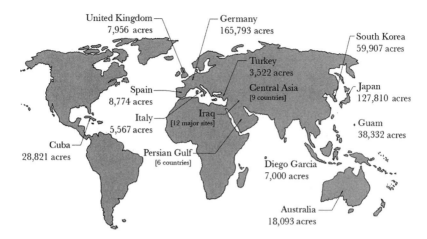

Map I.1. The "new" American empire's reach, ca. 2006. This map shows the published acreage in countries where the United States has a major presence—and the imperial reach is extraordinary. In other locations (including Iraq and countries in Central Asia and the Persian Gulf), the military does not track acreage in its Base Structure Report so only the number of major sites is shown.

Americans think of the United Kingdom, Germany, South Korea, Japan, or Italy stationing troops in the United States? If one considers just South Korea, in 2006 there were ninety-five sites, including forty-seven major outposts, in a nation half the size of the state of Washington. From large air stations to small intelligence sites, as of 2006 the United States had its soldiers stationed in more than 140 countries. In most countries shown in Map I.1, which highlights only those areas with a substantial U.S. presence, the military operated out of permanent buildings rather than tents. In the Persian Gulf area, the Afghan region, and Iraq, the numbers are for "temporary" outposts using a mix of tents and buildings. To support the overthrow of the Taliban regime in Afghanistan, the United States established numerous new bases in and around that troubled nation. Moreover, in the larger "war against terrorism," the United States has substantially increased its presence around the globe. In Iraq, the U.S. Army maintained a force of roughly 150,000 troops over four years after the "fall" of Baghdad.[10] Despite its claims to the contrary, the United States may in fact leave some type of permanent presence in Iraq—it seems that "to the victor go the spoils," from oil contracts to base leasing rights.[11] In 2004, for instance, military analysts identified up to fourteen sites in Iraq that may be "enduring" outposts.[12] This follows America's imperial history. After all, the United States left bases in Japan, Germany, and England following World War II, South Korea following the Korean War, and Saudi Arabia, Kuwait, and Qatar following the first Gulf War.

By focusing on the numbers, which are important, we may miss the more telling story found on the ground, inside the heavily guarded gates of these imperial outposts. The impact of these outposts is not simply a matter of their acreage. The impact involves a complex web of spatial, social, cultural, and political factors not easily addressed by an Excel spreadsheet. While numerous scholars have already documented many of the sociocultural problems presented by these bases, I focus on the spatial ramifications of building America Towns. What are the effects of living under empire's wings? Fighter jets screaming along at Mach 2, bombers accidentally dropping their loads, and fuel tanks leaking into water tables are just a few of the drawbacks we will uncover. I reveal yet another problem with an examination of the sociospatial dimensions of several red light districts in South Korea built to cater to the desires of American soldiers. The Romans had *vicis*. The British had bazaars. The Americans have Hooker Hill. I conclude Part I by suggesting that, despite this wide array of spillover, what receives the least attention in the United States but is perhaps the most significant to those living next to America's outposts is America's gluttonous use of foreign land.

In Part II, "Familiarity on the Frontlines," I ask two questions. What are imperial designers building today, and how do they go about implementing their plans? I first analyze ways in which these bases are like familiar American suburbs: sprawling enclaves of consumption filled with split-level ranch homes and big-box stores that would make Wal-Mart proud. American designers overseas follow a well-honed script for producing their version of suburbia. It is auto-focused, abundantly paved, widely spaced, extensively lawned, increasingly franchised, clearly segregated, and haphazardly ordered. I then look at how designers of these places have exported the suburban ideal to overseas outposts while remaining largely ignorant of the host nation's planning and design practices. Organizational structures and policy directives work together to maintain the sprawling status quo. I also reveal how privatization and policies of fear demand even lower densities resulting in ever more expansive compounds with longer borders that will only be more difficult to defend; an unintended irony.

In Part III, "Outposts under Construction," we travel to three coun-tries to see several outposts under construction. The selected sites are representative of American bases worldwide, where similar environments have emerged out of standardized practices. For consistency, and because I have a level of familiarity with its bases, I have focused on outposts built by one branch of the U.S. military, the U.S. Air Force (USAF). Even so, U.S. Army, Navy, and Marine installations overseas follow similar patterns of development and could easily be substituted for the out-posts I have chosen. To select from the plethora of available locations, I concentrated on outposts that the United States has slated to remain open. Additionally, I wanted to study permanent locations with actual buildings rather than bases filled mainly with tents and temporary build-ings. This ruled out most locations in the Middle East and Central Asia. By looking at "enduring" outposts, we may be able to better understand what might happen in these war-torn regions as "temporary" locations often become permanent.

In this study, Italy, South Korea, and Japan are the destinations. Bring your hardhats. Making the unfamiliar familiar is a work in progress. The first stop is Aviano Air Base in Italy. Here, an ally has struggled to sup-port tremendous expansion at one of the busiest military installations in Europe. Starting in 1996, the North Atlantic Treaty Organization (NATO) has pumped over $500 million into construction at the base. The work-ers have completed a controversial plan called Aviano 2000, which built an American suburb near an Italian hilltown, a Disneyland of consump-tion filled with big-box stores, a bowling alley, and even a Burger King. We will focus on the successes and failures of implementing such a grand plan.

We then head to South Korea, where an ambitious realignment pol-icy fulfills some of the objectives of the Land Partnership Plan (LPP), a joint agreement between South Korea and the United States designed to reduce the number of American bases on the peninsula. While the U.S. military's overall footprint will shrink, the boot comes down hard on already heavily impacted urban areas near Osan and Kunsan air bases. These two bases will be our case study sites.

Finally, we cross the Sea of Japan. Following the rape of a twelve-year-old schoolgirl by three U.S. soldiers, Japan and the United States estab-lished the Special Action Committee Okinawa (SACO) with the goal of reducing bases on the island. The goal of reduction remains elusive; instead, the bases there have grown considerably. We will make a stop at Kadena Air Base in Okinawa to see SACO's impacts.

I end this study with a snapshot of tomorrow's outposts and suggest empire builders are following a new model of avoidance. While the U.S. Navy's fleet has practiced avoidance since its inception, this is largely a new tactic for America's land-based military branches. Rather than hide out in the hinterlands, America's Army and Air Force established major outposts in and around the capital cities of its "allies." Now, however, increasingly isolated in their own enclaves, American military forces overseas are avoiding contact altogether. This withdrawal into an isolated yet, paradoxically, heavily engaged empire presents its own set of contradictions that pose difficult questions for further research. In the end, this study shows how the United States has transported its sociospatial practices to diverse geographical settings, regardless of local concerns. This practice, however, is a common approach for empire. The Romans, for instance, exported their rigid grid plans across the conquered territories. In a similar fashion, America has exported its suburban land-use patterns, its version of home, across the globe, thereby helping engrave the military's incessant focus on command and control on distant landscapes.

Back to the Blackhawk: my ability to requisition a helicopter, to fly over the homes and schools, parks and playgrounds of another country reveals my dilemma. I am both an analyst of and participant in the exercise of imperial power. I come to this research from my scholarly position as a student of empire, from my professional position as a practicing architect and planner, and from my experience as a former active-duty officer in the USAF charged with preparing, analyzing, and critiquing plans for development at bases across the globe. I sit on a three-legged stool and am trying to remain balanced. I leave it up to you to judge if I have tipped the stool too far in one direction. If you read this study from the left, you may call me an apologist for empire because I am not advocating its demise here. If you read this study from the right, you may call me insubordinate for exposing the costs and methods of fulfilling empire's spatial demands. If you read this from the center, you may simply call me indecisive. I look forward to the debate.

PART I
Empire's Reach

> At some very basic level, imperialism means thinking about, settling on, controlling land that you do not possess, that is distant, that is lived on and owned by others.
> —Edward Said, *Culture and Imperialism*

CHAPTER ONE

Empires across Time

How many empires have come and gone? How many people have lived under, fought for, or battled against empire? Every continent has endured the wrath of imperial might. Yet imperial power can liberate just as it can oppress. It can defend just as it can attack. For better or worse, the rise and demise of empire is the rule rather than the exception throughout history. To act, though, empires have required outposts beyond their homeland, places from which they could project their awesome, and frequently gruesome, power. These outposts have existed to support the implementation of power.

Throughout recorded history, empire's reach has covered the globe. China and Japan exemplify the reach of imperial power in Asia. Greek and Roman warriors extended empires across Europe and into Asia and Africa. In the Middle East, Arab Muslims established a new empire in Persia in the seventh century.[1] More recently, Holland, Spain, Britain, Germany, Italy, and France all vied for exclusive imperial power. Since its inception, the United States has been on its own imperial quest for territory, first within the continent and then abroad. The common element in all these endeavors was the establishment of some type of military garrison, outpost, or base in the conquered lands. The actual use and occupation of these outposts varied according to imperial needs. Some were exclusively reserved for military use, and imperial powers relegated civilians to locations outside the perimeter walls. Others included both military and civilian populations within the walls of the settlement. Still others were primarily civilian settlements with designated areas for military use.

Without outposts where empires could rearm, refuel, and recharge their soldiers and their equipment, the global projection of military power would have failed. In looking at the settlement patterns prevalent on the outposts of earlier empires, several themes emerge that will help decode quite similar planning practices currently employed on America's outposts. Other empires heavily regulated the planning and design of their outposts. They displaced local populations and demolished their building stock. They sought order over the seemingly disordered indigenous environments. They gained the consent of some segment of the local leadership. And they officially sanctioned prostitution. While not a comprehensive historical account of imperial planning practices, this chapter helps anchor today's imperial actions to the actions of earlier empires. Many themes presented here will resurface when I discuss the practices of the American military in subsequent chapters.

Displacement and Demolition

Once the first wave of empire-builders identified a suitable site, the next step in imperial planning usually involved the actual acquisition of land. Regarding expropriation of land, practices varied from one regime to the next. The *Laws of the Indies*, in a classic example of government doublespeak, stated in Ordinance 136:

> If the natives wish to oppose the establishment of a settlement they are to be given to understand that the settlers desire to build a town there not to deprive them of their property but for the purpose of being on friendly terms with them. . . . If, after many different attempts have been made to gain their consent the natives still withhold it then the settlers are to proceed to establish their town but are not to take away any of the belongings of the Indians or to do them more hurt than what may be necessary in order to protect the settlers and enable them to build without interference.[2]

At best, one could call this expropriation by coerced consent. If the settlers chose to build on previously developed land, how could this not be considered anything but deprivation of property, regardless of whether or not the indigenous residents had proper paperwork substantiating their claim? Justifying such a scenario as a friendly taking is laughable. The distinction that land, and perhaps one's home on that land, supposedly is not a "belonging of the Indians" begs the question of just what is a belonging? On July 3, 1573, Spain's Philip II published the *Laws of the*

Indies. In addition to justifying expropriation, these rules also specified overall settlement locations (defensible locations with access to water and sources of food were the standard), the use of a grid street network, the location of noxious uses like slaughterhouses and tanneries, and the inclusion of a main plaza. Recognizing the need to construct encampments that supported the well-being of the residents, the *Laws* became a royal endorsement of urban planning.[3]

Several centuries later, the French also used slippery language to their advantage. In Algiers, by using French definitions for land ownership, military engineers expropriated land in the way of expansion regardless of its tenure under tribal and Islamic law and regardless of its use. In the nineteenth and early twentieth centuries, the French military razed schools, mosques, and other public facilities in the way of "progress," a concept defined, of course, by the imperial power. In mid-nineteenth-century Algiers, Marshal Thomas Bugeaud, acting as the lead engineer, instituted his policy of *razzia* that included knocking down as many buildings as needed to insert his cherished grid plan and moving out of the way as many people as he saw fit to implement this French vision of urban order. In the Casbah, the historical center of the city, his demolition crews flattened numerous religious monuments to make way for military buildings and parade grounds.[4] Bugeaud's efforts foreshadowed the work in Paris of Baron Georges Haussmann, the prefect of the Seine from 1852 to 1869. While the work of Haussmann, following plans first sketched out by Napoleon III, is well known, scholars continue to question the military utility of the project.[5] While not discounting the project's practical and economic benefits to Paris, knowing that one of Haussmann's contemporaries was Marshal Thomas Bugeaud in Algiers, it would make sense that military utility was one of the motivating factors for the former just as it was for the latter.[6] These actions link metropole and colony in a way that bears witness to the transnational nature of imperialism.

In British India, expropriation policies were quite similar to those of the French. The British had two policies regarding expropriation—one before and one after the infamous 1857 Indian Rebellion. The worst of the fighting began in early May 1857 in Meerut near Delhi when some members of the Indian Army known as sepoys mutinied. Upset with ongoing annexations, extreme tax assessments, and arrogant British attitudes, the sepoys, with the help of other Indians, killed hundreds of

British officers, their wives, and their children. Across a wide swath of the Indian northwest, the rebellion rapidly gained strength. The sepoys and their supporters besieged barracks and sacked cantonments. At Lucknow's British Residency, only one-third of the occupants survived a nine-month siege.[7]

Britain's retribution was equally violent. Before the rebellion, Britain normally secured land for its cantonments through purchase. Afterwards, the British not only armed themselves with more powerful weapons of destruction but also with more powerful weapons of expropriation. Seizures and dispossession were the new norm.[8] In post-rebellion Lucknow, Lt. Gen. Robert Napier was in charge of the clearing and quite interested in preventing another uprising. Shortly after the fighting subsided, he moved in and expelled the populace, then demolished around 40 percent of the town. To pay for this early form of urban renewal, he distributed the cost among the populace and refused to let them return if their tax bills were in arrears, whether or not their homes survived.[9] This specific policy, repeated elsewhere in Britain's empire, represents the pinnacle of imperial hubris. Napier would justify his approach to expropriation in the now-familiar language of national security. With the memory of Lucknow's siege still fresh, he would establish "security" at any cost—especially if the British did not have to pay. Giving primacy to the military's needs over other concerns, regardless of the potential ramifications, has not ended with Napier.

Ordering "Disorder"

Imperial powers regularly drafted detailed regulations governing the planning of their overseas settlements. To bring order to the newly acquired landscapes, Western European powers implemented planning policies based on cultural norms that stressed consistency, order, and control. In the face of what appeared to them as chaotic and disordered indigenous settlements, filled with possible dangers around every bend, imperial designers brought out the demolition crews in earnest. The impacts were obvious at all levels of planning—from the location of brothels to the destruction of entire neighborhoods. Demolitions were one common tactic used by imperial powers in their quest for ordering the "disordered" colonies. "North African cities," in the words of one military observer at the time, "are constituted without regular design. They are a mass of houses in all dimensions and forms that look more or less the same."[10] Similarly, the Italians in Addis Ababa considered the overall layout of the existing city disordered, unplanned, and haphazard.[11]

This attitude is prevalent among some military planners at U.S. bases over a century later; however, they speak of disorderly Asian cities, not African ones. The conflation of regularized design with order is a cultural value, not a statement of fact. Culture-specific norms shape the built environment in response to a host of social, economic, and political factors. Over time, even the French recognized that the Moroccan medina was a social environment worthy of conservation. The indigenous homes and quarters represented an interconnection between form and social practice.[12] But, when norms come in conflict, the powerful prevail. Demolitions proceed. Displacement ensues. "Order" triumphs.

Following displacement and, if need be, demolition, the next step in imperial planning involved the insertion of a regularizing network of streets. Regularity was the order of the day. Grid plans predominated. For Western European powers, the grid symbolized imperial authority and order as well as simplicity. The grid reaches back in time to the Greeks, who often planned their outposts with straight streets at right angles as they moved across parts of Asia.[13] Next the Romans established forts throughout their expanding empire using the easily replicable grid pattern. This focus on the straight street for the fort became the ordering device for later Renaissance plans by Alberti and Palladio. Alberti considered the straight street or *viae militares* essential for the movement of military regiments. Similarly, Palladio observed that "the ways will be more convenient if they are made everywhere equal; that is to say, that there be no place in them where armies may not easily march."[14] Regardless of cost, either in terms of financial resources or in land use, the consistently wide streets did accommodate the needs of the military first. Since militaries implement the policies of the powerful, it is not surprising that those in power would support planning strategies that called for streets wide enough for a battalion's march. It was, in effect, a symbiotic state of affairs.

The Spanish crown was equally clear in its requirement for broad avenues. In the *Laws of the Indies,* Ordinance 116 gives these awkward instructions: "In cold climates the streets shall be wide; in hot climates narrow, however, for purposes of defense and where horses are kept the streets had better be wide." Given that horses were the main form of locomotion in Spanish colonial settlements and that defense was usually a concern, it is no wonder that the last five words in the ordinance carried the most weight. From Mexico City to Manila, the Spaniards rarely varied from the wide streets prescribed by the *Laws*.[15]

The spatial requirements of the grid's wide streets supported development densities much lower than typically found in the indigenous settlements. Whether in nineteenth-century Indian cantonments or twentieth-century French colonial cities, the pattern was similar. Europeans would occupy verdant, low-density landscapes and the "locals" would inhabit the opposite.[16] In this love affair with low densities, Michel Ecochard's segregated settlements in Morocco resulted in the Moroccan quarter supporting a density fifteen times greater than the European quarters.[17] These densities also disconnected the building fabric and justified the increasingly object-focused nature of architecture over the place-focused nature of urban design. This then allowed for greater freedom in the siting of monumental buildings throughout the conquered world. The French in Pondicherry, India, used the impressive Government House to project their power across the sociocultural landscape, the Italians in Ethiopia designed monumental buildings as powerful political statements, and the British built the Victoria Memorial in the heart of Calcutta as an exemplar of imperial strength.[18] Together with the demand for widely spaced officer housing, elaborate parade grounds, varied recreation areas, and wide security buffers, the spatial requirements of the grid and its streets led to extremely low densities and extensive land consumption. This is another pattern the American military implemented on its own outposts in the late twentieth century.

Using planning and design to maintain separation between the indigenous population and the colonizers became a common tactic in the nineteenth and twentieth centuries. Racial differences translated into spatial practices. In North Africa, the Italians segregated the imperial and indigenous cities.[19] Similarly, in nineteenth-century India, the British government published regulations dictating the planning and security of their cantonments. At cantonments such as Meerkut and Kanpur, the British established distinct and separate zones for bazaars, sepoys' huts, and European quarters. By setting each zone apart, planners juxtaposed Indian "disorder and disease" against British "order and cleanliness."[20] This zoning kept the "unclean" away from imperial forces. Likewise, in Morocco, French planners confined the Muslim section of the city to the central medina with a 250-meter *cordon sanitaire*.[21] These planners hoped that this physical barrier would prevent the diseases of the natives from spreading into the European quarters.[22] Whether in Africa or India, this essentializing of the "other," equating deleterious effects with biological characteristics, resulted in an array of planning solutions.

This common feature of imperial planning highlights the unequal distribution of power. Across the map, imperial powers viewed their subjects through a bifocal lens of race and gender. First, given that the command of imperial military forces was stratified primarily along racial lines, where most officers were white and the rank-and-file armies of the colonized were not, race was a characteristic that played a significant role in the planning policies of empire. Second, given that imperial armies were largely male and their outposts were in settings well outside the moralizing influence of their homeland, gender also played a key role in imperial sociospatial planning policies. On the surface, planners based many of these policies on a fear of disease. While planners knew of some vectors, they guessed at others. For instance, the British in India thought a deadly miasma rather than the ordinary mosquito caused malaria and promulgated policies that dictated the location of cantonments on mountainous sites with cool, dry air. For those cantonments that had to be in the flats, the British were certain that the prevailing winds from the neighboring native towns carried infection-laden air.[23]

The Regulation of Imperial Vice

The most heavily regulated known vector concerned the spread of venereal disease. To combat the rapid spread of disease among soldiers, imperial powers implemented sociospatial regulations governing prostitution. These rules were highly controversial and they link the nineteenth-century British Empire to the actions of the twentieth-century American Empire. Given this link, it is worthwhile to cover in some detail the experience of the British in India. Understanding land use, after all, is not simply about learning who has title or who sets the rules, but also about what goes on in the landscape.

In light of astonishing rates of infection among its soldiers, in 1864 Britain published the Cantonment Acts, which invited women working as prostitutes into their cantonments, and required them to undergo regular medical examinations. Under the auspices of minimizing the possibility of soldiers contracting sexually transmitted diseases, the Acts also led to "public" housing and licensing of these women. In June 1886 the quarter-master general outlined policies for controlling venereal disease that had clear sociospatial implications:

> In the regimental bazaars it is necessary to have a sufficient number of women, to care that they are sufficiently attractive, to provide them with proper houses. . . . If young soldiers are carefully advised in regard to the advantages of ablution and recognize that convenient arrangements exist in the regimental bazaar, they may be expected to avoid the risks involved in association with women who are not recognized by the regimental authorities.[24]

By 1886 this policy, published in an official memorandum as part of the enforcement of the controversial Cantonment Acts, generated widespread condemnation in Britain. The "proper houses" for the "sufficiently attractive" prostitutes were in fact *chaklas* or brothels in the bazaars, which kept the women conveniently out of the barracks but conspicuously close to them as well. The Army required the women to reside in these areas and, using regimental funds, built them dwellings within direct view of the soldiers' tents, which also simplified the cantonment commander's ability to exercise his control over this lustful landscape.

Implicit in the policy is the idea that not only native women, but also native men were the source of illness. The British military attempted to segregate the former from the latter. This is like placing a sign on a water fountain, "For Whites Only." The white men did not want to share the commodified women stationed in their cantonments with the infected "other." Despite these regulations, infection rates did not peak until 1895 at 536 cases per 1,000.[25] Thirty years of increasingly liberal policies toward prostitution, coupled with the segregation of prostitutes for exclusionary commerce, only increased the rate of infection. From a public-health standpoint, it appears that these men were swimming in their own cesspool. Britain's prejudice, namely that local men were a source of infection and hence the policy of isolating chaklas spatially, literally made their soldiers and the local women sick. This government-sponsored prostitution made it easier for them to exchange their meager paychecks for sexual services.

Public distribution of the memo energized Alfred Dyer, publisher of *The Sentinel: The Organ of the Social Purity Movement.* Although the bias dripping from the newsletter's pages is evident from the moral scope of its title, Dyer seemed especially interested in arousing the ire of his largely

Christian audience in Britain; so, in 1887 he traveled to India and published several withering articles recounting his findings. In a grandiose
writing style common for the era and the audience, he exposed some of
the worst abuses. "At Deolali," he writes, "where the English soldier lads
are taken direct on their arrival in India, my heart was deeply stirred as
I stood on the border of this large camp and beheld, planted within a
stone's throw of the school of the Church Missionaries, the official quarters of the licensed prostitutes."[26] He uncovered several damning facts.
The British Army sponsored seventy-five centers of prostitution at cantonments across India. The local commanders ordered the women to
march with the soldiers from camp to camp and even sent women into
the army's cholera camps, sealing their fates. Larger military stations
like Sitapur sponsored multiple bazaars for the "government certified
harlots" at a ratio of one woman for every eleven men. Authorities directed soldiers to patrol the areas to keep order there. Military leaders
used cantonment funds to build homes for each woman. The construction of these home/offices was a serious matter. The 1886 annual report
from the British government in Allahabad stated,

> It is proposed to endeavor to induce a greater number of prostitutes
> to reside in cantonments, by making their residences more attractive.
> Assistance would be given them from cantonment funds, which are in a
> flourishing condition, to enable the women to furnish their houses so as
> to make them convenient both for themselves and their visitors.[27]

Commanders guaranteed this convenience by purposely siting the
chaklas as close as possible to the customers, sometimes within yards of
the dining halls, regimental offices, and gymnasiums. At a cantonment
in Bareilly, for example, Dyer found that the chaklas were sixty-four
yards from the street with nothing else in the way of their doors and
those of the troops. The bulging bank accounts were due to the cantonment's busy bars; profits from the sale of alcohol went into the funds
used to build the dwellings.

Dyers's findings stirred widespread opposition to the Cantonment
Acts. After opponents of the Acts put considerable political pressure on
members of Parliament, in June 1888 the House of Commons condemned
the Acts and called for their repeal. But the British government in India,
with the assistance of the Army's commander-in-chief, opposed the
repeal, claiming the Acts were necessary for the health of the troops.
There was no talk of the health of the women. In light of the military's

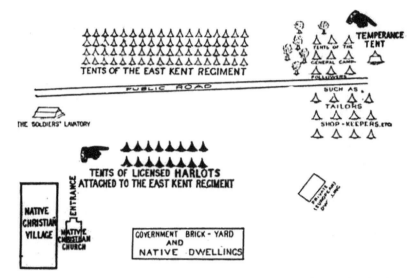

Figure 1.1. "The Government versus the Gospel at Bareilly": Alfred Dyer's sketch and title made "on the spot" during his visit to India in 1887. Reprinted from *Sentinel* 10, no. 3 (March 1888).

opposition, Parliament passed the new Cantonment Acts of 1889, which sidestepped the issue and allowed for removal of any infected individual but did not require compulsory examinations. Of course, identification of infected women required "voluntary" examinations.

In 1887 Dyer drew a sketch of the Bareilly Cantonment (Figure 1.1). Even if we look past Dyers's "hand of authority" that points out the obvious by locating the brothels and the temperance tent just to emphasize the point for his Christian readers back in Britain, this map reveals a spatial narrative that locates powers and priorities on the landscape. The seemingly dueling locations of the tents for the East Kent regiment and the "harlots" attest to their mutually destructive relationship. The supporting roles played by the other camp followers as well as the "native Christian" villagers is cast in place by their locations as well. That the lavatory bridges the gap, but is located on the side of the "natives," reinforces the imperial attitude. It is as if the regimental site designers were saying, "We'll use your women as convenient commodities, and we'll site our excrement on your side to boot." Ironically, the authorities sited the temperance tent inconveniently behind the tents of other "camp followers."

Reports of compulsory examinations and continued housing for prostitutes in the cantonments revealed that the new Acts were less than effective. By continuing the practice of housing prostitutes in the regimental bazaars, the Army was acting in defiance of the new rules. The situation uncovered deep fissures between the homeland and the colony. Two separate bodies investigated the impasse: one established by the Indian viceroy Lord Landsdowne (1888–94), the Indian Commission; and one established by resolution of the House of Commons, the Russell Committee. Unsurprisingly, the Indian Commission supported the viceroy's view that the government of India had attempted as best it could to comply with the rules. The Russell Committee, however, came to a different conclusion and recommended additional legislation for the cantonments. In Britain the secretary of state for India, Lord Kimberley (1882–86, 1892–94) outlined legislation prohibiting the compulsory examination of women and consequently the licensing and housing of prostitutes. Although the Military Committee of the Council of India opposed the new rules because they impaired effective control of the cantonment population, the secretary of state overruled the council and forwarded the policy to India. Reports by Christian missionaries in India of abuses of women by British soldiers, escalating protests against the Cantonment Acts in Britain, and crises in other parts of the British Empire, convinced the secretary of state that the Acts should be repealed and the new policy implemented. In 1895 the Cantonment Amending Bill passed, thus outlawing compulsory examinations and banning prostitutes from living in cantonments.

The story does not end there. One year later, the infection rate remained staggeringly high, 522 per 1,000, and two years later, the rate was still 507 per 1,000. Only 37 percent of British soldiers left India unaffected by venereal disease. Military commanders in India justified their reluctance to abandon the original Cantonment Acts, citing the high rate of infection, which they claimed hampered the military's readiness. When considered in these terms, the debate reopened, and in 1897 the rules changed once again. The British government repealed the revised Acts and approved new rules that allowed for the examination of women when reason for suspicion existed, which essentially gave the military a free hand at conducting inspections. This time, the British government of India ignored protests in Britain under the cover of national security.

While the officially reported rates of venereal disease infection slowly dropped after the Army adopted the new rules, other factors also contributed to the decline. For example, soldiers began self-treating to avoid reporting, and while some cantonments saw increases, others saw decreases. As a result, the statistics used to justify the renewed examinations are unconvincing.[28]

As the debates in Parliament raged on, the British troops eagerly set a flagpole in the middle of the chaklas and would hoist up a flag announcing that the place was open for business. Working under the shadows of empire's flag would be the victims of the imperial appetite, some of the same victims of empires across time: poor women with few options and a finite future. During this period, the boundaries between English and Indian, local and global, male and female became intertwined in a complex narrative of sexual practices, international politics, and hybrid places. The events surrounding the Cantonment Acts and the British Army's experience in India foreshadow empire's sexual politics and the resulting sociospatial exploitation of women on and around military outposts for the next hundred years. Unfortunately, not much has changed.

Among Consenting Adults

Although most imperial powers largely imposed their planning policies unilaterally, their subsequent spatial impacts were felt at all socioeconomic levels of the "host nation," using today's nomenclature. This is an appropriate term because there was a degree of complicity between the colonizer and the colonized. While not necessarily invited in the sense that a host may invite one over for drinks and dinner, locals of all ranks contributed to the imperial endeavor. They provided facilities, services, and political cover for the imperial "guests." From the brothels in Bareilly to the avenues of Algiers, men and women, harlots and shopkeepers, cooks and kings all participated in imperial conquest. Granted, they were not primary roles, nor were all of these participants likely acting out of their own free will, given the pressures empire could bring to bear. Political demands, secret payoffs, and regular paychecks all contributed to indigenous support for a variety of imperial activities.[29]

India is an illustrative case. In addition to the women staffing the chaklas in Bareilly and in seventy-four other locations across the country, bazaars were also home to a variety of shopkeepers, day laborers, and farm hands benefiting from the imperial expense account. Moreover, the British co-opted sepoys to staff the Indian unit of the imperial army. In 1885 the British Army in India had 145,738 members from the "native" populations and 74,040 from the homeland.[30] While some of the sepoys who staffed these positions did revolt (as in Lucknow in 1857), many more often participated in military campaigns of the British army in their own country and abroad. The British also co-opted princes, like His Highness Maharaja Sir Raghubir, to do their bidding. While the local princes would be playing king, the British would set about clearing slums, straightening streets, and "ordering" the built environment.[31] Local rivalries, allowances, and granted power worked together to sustain indirect rule, maintain public order, minimize administration costs, and facilitate tax collections.[32]

The costs of empire are indeed steep and the more help from the locals the better. But for the British, the peak of their colonial power announced the decline of their global leadership. Paying empire's bills, in terms of human lives and financial resources, became a challenge. Death rates in India for enlisted men reached 69 per 1,000, compared to 10 per 1,000 of men of similar age who remained in Britain.[33] As the British were overextending themselves in India and across Africa, another empire was preparing to wage a war near Britain's back yard. World War I required the British Empire to refocus and realign its resources. In just two short decades after the fiery debates about the Cantonment Acts, the British would be mired in a continental war that mobilized over eight million of their imperial troops and, in the victorious end, awarded the Crown with new colonies whose costs nearly drained the queen's coffers. Hence, by World War II, the British could barely afford to hold onto their island nation. In nineteen centuries, the world witnessed the progression from Pax Romana to Pax Britannica. Empires built up their new territories to suit their own needs. They increasingly regulated planning efforts that led to displacement and demolition of those living under imperium. They sought to order the "disorder" of the conquered lands. They sited garrisons, overlaid grids, and established *cordon sanitaires* to reinforce dominance and difference. And they did this with the partial consent of the conquered. Granted, not everyone agreed to empire's demands, but the select few that benefited from the imperial line of credit gave the exercise an imprimatur of acceptance. Next in this progression of empire is Pax Americana.

CHAPTER TWO

Pax Americana: The "New" Empire

Reluctant. Incoherent. Arrogant. Benevolent. Informal. Invited. There are as many titles for today's American Empire as there are scholars of empire. From all points on the political spectrum, there are copious attempts at defining the current phase of Pax Americana. Some terms, like *invited empire* and *informal empire,* are the most absurd.[1] Suggesting that the Japanese, Germans, or Italians "invited" the United States into their homeland to establish hundreds of military bases seriously distorts the definition of "invitation." Moreover, an empire built around detailed legal arrangements and systematic budget authorizations hardly qualifies as informal. The network of military bases that makes up today's empire follows specific, formal planning guidance.

America took on the mantle of a global imperial power beginning with the distribution of the spoils of World War II, which, for the Americans, translated into a new land grab. After the war, America took under its "protection" 76 percent of Germany, 45 percent of Korea, all of Japan, and military bases throughout Italy.[2] The imperial outposts built in these countries extended the saga of colonialism into the late twentieth century.[3] In support of its political, military, and economic objectives, the United States developed a broad network of "America Towns" through complex Status of Forces agreements and intricate basing contracts.[4] The economic justification today, however, reflects multinational rather than monopoly capitalism—a subtle difference ushered in by the rampant capital and information flows associated with processes of globalization. Several authors argue that globalization is an Americanization of world culture.[5] Some suggest it is a more general process where ideas, entities, or cultures extend their reach across the globe.[6] Others see it as a dissolution of distance that polarizes rather than homogenizes.[7] Shared among the many conceptualizations of globalization is the attribute of movement—of goods, services, people, and ideas—across national borders. Supporting this globalized world is military power ready to maintain the flow.

The post–September 11 period is a new phase in America's imperial ambitions. As was the case before September 11, global influence, if not outright control, is still the primary policy objective and the projection of power across the globe to achieve this goal is still an imperial intent. In 1991 the motto of the USAF summed up this intent: "Global Power, Global Reach."[8] The reach allows for the power and the power allows for the reach. However, there are two new attributes of empire. First, the United States has replaced an overwhelming desire for territorial expansion with a quest for the small sites needed to project imperial power. Reaction time, not acreage, is the new metric. The old American Empire wanted territories. The new American Empire wants launch and recovery sites for its F-15s. Today's empire does not so much require vast territories, dependent colonies, or puppet governments. Rather, it needs places for its soldiers to sleep at night and pavement to park its warplanes.

Second, the United States has shifted from containing its enemies to actively seeking them out. In 2002 and again in 2006, the Bush administration's *National Security Strategy* called for preemptive war. The United States, according to the strategy, "will not hesitate to act alone, if necessary, to exercise our right to self-defense by acting preemptively." The presumed security of the United States overrides the sovereignty of another nation. The language followed the logic of the 2001 *Quadrennial Defense Review,* published just over two weeks after the September 11 attacks (a remarkably quick response given typical bureaucratic inertia). This report stated that defending the United States "could include changing the regime of an adversary state or occupation of foreign territory until U.S. strategic objectives are met." These documents in part established the legal basis for the invasion of Afghanistan and Iraq.[9]

Predictably, the global repercussions of this unilateral approach have been intense. In the Iraq War, which was the first substantial test of the doctrine, Germany and France stayed out of the "coalition of the willing" altogether. Longtime ally Turkey refused to let the United States use the bases in its country to prosecute the war despite offers of up to $26 billion in military and economic "aid" from the Bush administration.[10] Millions marched worldwide in condemnation of the war. The Spaniards did not reelect their president who supported the war. Despite these protestations, the United States proceeded with its plans based on the erroneous claim that Iraq was developing weapons of mass destruction.

The United States made this shift to preemption in an era when its troops have been increasingly unwelcome in the very nations hosting them, which requires new investments and new strategies regarding military bases. The United States has mothballed many of its outposts in "recalcitrant" nations like Saudi Arabia and Turkey. The shift now has been to building new bases in Afghanistan, Iraq, and Central Asia.[11] The idea of empire is certainly not new to the United States. Just as the legacy of imperialism led from the British Isles to the eastern seaboard of North America, so too did it march across the continent to the shores of the Pacific and beyond. This march, and the attitudes that support it, are worth reviewing.

Empire's March

The United States did not wait until the end of World War II to begin its imperial quest. Empire building began much earlier. From the founders to the forty-third president, America's leaders have tried to extend the reach of American power. The imperial model inspired Thomas Jefferson and his contemporaries to conquer the continent. These men believed that they were establishing a new empire with ever-expanding frontiers. Not content on the East Coast alone, they set the course for violent expansion to meet the fledgling nation's destiny at the shores of the Pacific. Writing in 1885, John O'Sullivan even argued that it was "our manifest destiny to overspread the continent allotted by Providence for the free development of our yearly multiplying millions."[12] This ideological justification in support of the growing country could relieve the empire-builders of the need to worry about the impacts of expansion. The end, if ordained by Providence, justified the means. As with the European imperialists, displacement of the racially distinct "other" and demolition of their landscape were the norms. The U.S. Army and its supporters either killed or relocated anything indigenous, from Native Americans to buffalos, which stood in the way. They corralled Native Americans that survived the onslaught in reservations. They emptied indigenous cultural landscapes. The Great Plains, for example, became a vast hunting arcade, then a feedlot. In a repeat of the Spanish imperial approach, without a notarized title to the land, which of course was impossible, the land claims of Native Americans were invalid. This imperial model was neither assimilation nor association. Rather, it was annihilation.

In the form of the National Land Survey of 1785 and its relentless grid covering much of America, order was on the way. The pattern continued. "The white settler," in the words of Theodore Roosevelt in 1894, "has merely moved into an uninhabited waste; he does not feel that he is committing a wrong, for he knows perfectly well that the land is really owned by no one."[13] As with the *Laws of the Indies,* the imperial power defined land ownership. If these were waste spaces, then they could only benefit from their date with "democracy." Civilization's virtues were not optional. This bears an uncanny resemblance to the attitude in the 2002 *National Security Strategy,* which calls on the United States to "[e]xpand the circle of development by opening societies and building the infrastructure of democracy."[14] However, to open a society requires some effort and implies some resistance. The U.S. military's role in part has been to act as the pry bar—quelling any resistance—and this has required the use of fortified outposts as bases of operations. In the American West, one of the first signs of "civilization's" arrival was the Army fort. By the mid-nineteenth century, the U.S. Army built over sixty major forts west of the Missouri River, from Fort Leavenworth, Kansas, to the Presidio of San Francisco.[15] The motto could have been "Continental Reach, Continental Power."

Reaching the Pacific, though, did not satisfy the imperial appetite. By the end of the nineteenth century, military strategists called for a broader empire. In 1890 Alfred T. Mahan advocated the taking of the Caribbean, Hawaiian, and Philippine islands for bases to protect U.S. commerce.[16] Eight years later, displeased with Spanish coaling stations in Cuba and angry over the controversial sinking of the USS *Maine* in Cuba's Havana Harbor on February 15, 1898, the United States declared war with Spain on April 25, 1898. While no evidence linked the accused nation to weapons of mass destruction (at the time, mines caused considerable damage to navies worldwide), major media outlets joined the call for action, the public fell in line, and the war proceeded. Does this sound familiar?[17] On May 1, 1898, the U.S. Navy defeated the Spanish fleet in Manila Bay in just six hours and captured Manila three months later. U.S. Gen. Wesley Merritt established a military government in Manila, and he served as the military governor.

In the summer of 1898, the fledgling American empire went global. In just two months, it annexed Hawaii, occupied Cuba, and colonized Puerto Rico, the Philippines, and Guam.[18] Now, with a free hand, the United States could build bases beyond its own borders. As the secretary of the navy at the time, this experience clearly shaped the mind of the future twenty-sixth president, Theodore "Teddy" Roosevelt, who later intervened in Central America to create Panama and finish its canal. The experience also set the prototype for establishing overseas bases: intervene militarily (whether justified or not); win quickly (with overwhelming force if possible); and build extensively (starting first on the adversary's own bases).

Following his uncle's example, Franklin Roosevelt was the next president to expand substantially the American empire. He frequently requested plans for a global network of bases, and his staff proposed that the United States become heirs of empire after World War II.[19] This desire became national policy in 1945 as part of the *Strategic Concept Plan,* which called for "[a]n outer perimeter of bases from which to reconnoiter and survey possible enemy actions . . . and to launch counteractions."[20] In conformance to this plan, the combined efforts of the U.S. Departments of Defense and State led to extensive construction of American bases in Europe and Asia after World War II.[21] In less than fifty years, from 1898 to 1945, the United States went from a continental empire to a global superpower, with only one rival—the former Soviet Union, an empire that would eventually crumble under its own oppressive weight. The foundation for the American expansion rested not only on issues of national security but also on a militaristic mind-set that justified global dominance.

Longing for Empire

"We shall run the world's business whether the world likes it or not."[22] These are the words of San Francisco–based venture capitalist Joshua C. Holroyd, a minor character in *Nostromo,* a novel completed by Joseph Conrad in 1904. Holroyd was a financial backer for a mining endeavor in a fictional South American country called Costaguana, and his words epitomize the imperial attitude: global, unilateral, beneficial. Moreover, they highlight the link between capitalism and empire—both are mutually supportive. Karl Marx realized this in 1848: "The need of a constantly expanding market for its products chases the bourgeoisie over the entire surface of the globe. It must nestle everywhere, settle everywhere, establish connections everywhere."[23]

Over 150 years later, the 2002 *National Security Strategy* reinforced the connection between empire and capitalism and called for the United States to "actively work to bring the hope of democracy, development, free markets, and free trade to every corner of the world."[24] Three out of the four objectives support the needs of the "market." This is an imperial attitude, and it manifests itself in multiple ways; some are glaringly obvious; some are quite subtle. Carpet-bombing and Coca-Cola apparently work together to extend empire's reach. However, following September 11, 2001, the U.S. government largely abandoned a soft-power approach, with its subtle incorporation of quieter means to advance national objectives. While a soft-power approach uses powers of persuasion and example to influence global affairs, a hard-power approach relies on direct military and economic action.[25] Rather than wait for the likes of Nike and NBC to shape an Americanization of the globe, a more aggressive approach relies on the Air Force's B-52s and the Army's Brigade Combat Teams. However, this approach wears on empire's allies, perhaps best exemplified by the words of Thomas Fowler, a character in one of Graham Greene's most well-known novels. In this exchange from *The Quiet American,* set in Vietnam in the early 1950s when the French exercised colonial control, Fowler, a veteran British correspondent ponders the murder of his acquaintance, companion, and competitor, Alden Pyle.

> He was a quiet American. "Have you any hunch," he asked, "why they killed him?" Suddenly I was angry; I was tired of the whole pack of them, with their private stores of Coca-Cola and their portable hospitals and their wide cars and their not quite latest guns.[26]

While Pyle was trying to establish a nominally independent "third force" for the liberation of Vietnam, Fowler was struggling with his own dark view of imperialism. Meanwhile, both men declared their love for the same alluring woman, Phuong, but "always spoke of her ... in the third person, as though she were not there. Sometimes she seemed invisible, like peace."[27] Empires quietly ignore their victims, who may be in violent and outspoken opposition to imperial policies or simply toil away quietly in the shadows, like Phuong, filling the opium pipes, washing the soiled clothing, and servicing the sexual needs of empire's representatives.

Is this attitude of domination and disregard so entrenched that it is inevitable? While it would be easy to essentialize American cultural imperialism, it denies the contested, produced, and hybridized aspects of culture. From the Anti-Imperialist League, formed in 1898 to fight U.S. colonization of the Philippines to today's American Empire Project, Americans of all ranks have expressed opposition to empire's reach.[28] However, regardless of well-organized resistance at home and abroad, driven by the needs of the market, justified using the language of national security, and enforced by military might, America's quest for global dominance continues. The attitude appears to be thus: because America has the right to intervene, it requires the power to do so. Of course, one could reverse this attitude. Because America has the power, it thinks it has the right.

This attitude trickles down to the emissaries of empire. While most are law-abiding, respectful guests, others are less sensitive. Some rape, others buy sex. Some drink to oblivion, others dump toxic waste into rivers. Some drive recklessly, others steal the cars they need. While these things happen in America, too, and the military will inform you that the crime rate per capita is lower for soldiers than national averages in countries like South Korea or Japan, the fact remains that the girl would have been spared, the river would not flow with formaldehyde, and some cars would still be with their owners.[29] The standard of behavior is higher for a guest. After all, if a child acts horribly at the dinner table, that is one thing, but if a guest spits in the host's face that is quite another. Apart from what soldiers do, their underlying attitudes also expose imperial arrogance. Following widespread protests in Japan denouncing the rape of a twelve-year-old schoolgirl by three Marines, many Okinawans called for removal of the U.S. military presence on the island.[30] After prefectural elections in 1998, Keiichi Inamine, a supporter of the bases, ousted Gov. Masahide Ota, a vocal opponent of them. "Most of this is just political," said one military officer. "With the elections over the base issue will die down."[31]

For a military officer to attribute the heartfelt emotions and deep-seated anger about the rape of a young girl to politics is ignorant at best. This attitude relieves the U.S. military of responsibility for the actions of its members. The military is largely relieved of this responsibility any-way due to the Status of Forces agreements governing local consequences for military behavior. These agreements give the United States jurisdic-tion over many criminal actions committed by its members while sta-tioned overseas. Unless the United States agrees to transfer jurisdiction, the accused may transfer home and may or may not face disciplinary action. In effect, the United States transplants its criminal justice system to foreign soil. In addition, the agreements give military members a "free pass" into and out of the host nation. With a flash of a military ID card and perhaps the unfolding of some orders, soldiers can avoid nor-mal immigration procedures—no need for a passport or visa. Where are the lines between "special," "stronger," and "better"?

The agreements raise complex questions of sovereignty that are at the core of the understanding of built form as well. In previous eras of imperial power, the occupier operated largely with a free hand, with little need for any kind of agreement between sovereign nations because the occupied nation effectively ceased to exist. Today, however, the United States stations its bases in sovereign nations. As such, the host nation's rules would normally apply to their territory. However, the U.S. military is an extension of U.S. sovereignty and, according to some scholars, the maintenance of military discipline depends on the applicability of U.S. military laws. So conventions governing everything from military con-duct to the layout of space generally default to the U.S. position regard-less of the concerns, customs, or cultures of the "host nation." The place-ment of the U.S. military above the "law of the land" they are in reinforces an attitude of arrogance among some deployed members of the U.S. military. Their actions leave an unattractive impression of insensitivity among the locals.[32]

The "New" American Empire

Aboard the USS *Abraham Lincoln* shortly after the "collapse" of the formal Iraq resistance in May 2003, U.S. President George W. Bush proclaimed, "Other nations in history have fought in foreign lands and remained to occupy and exploit. Americans, following a battle, want nothing more than to return home."[33] The members of the advance team should get an award for setting the stage for this audacious statement. Facing the president stood the proud men and women of the U.S. Navy. Above him was a colorful banner declaring "Mission Accomplished." He wore a military flightsuit and was clearly invigorated by an extremely brief jet flight from nearby San Diego. While what he said is true for American soldiers wanting to return home, this is certainly not the case for the neoconservative supporters of the new American Empire. Since 2001, these supporters have been quite busy expanding empire's reach through retaliatory raids, preemptive wars, and one-sided realignments. While they justify their actions in national security terms, they also place greater burdens on U.S. soldiers and generate new demands for land. Perhaps recognizing the limits of his version of imperial power, President Bush even acknowledged that U.S. troops will remain in Iraq past January 2009—six years after the banner proclaimed "mission accomplished."[34]

Following the lead of the neoconservatives in Washington, D.C., and despite the rhetoric of the commander-in-chief, the Department of Defense (DoD) is not eager to bring all the troops home either. Over fifteen years after the end of the Cold War, the United States still operates 766 permanent overseas sites, from small intelligence sites to large air bases. As of FY2006 these locations housed a total population of nearly 600,000 soldiers, civilian employees, and family members.[35] Overseas as of FY2006, the DoD controlled 711,418 acres and nearly 300 million square feet of buildings with a replacement value of $117.6 billion. On permanent installations, the total building area and total land area fell through 2001. September 11, 2001, arrested the fall and, in terms of land area, the total began rising once again, albeit slowly (Figure 2.1).

The numbers come from the *Base Structure Report*. The DoD regularly produces the report using the real property records of nearly every installation worldwide. But the report does not include "temporary" bases set up in support of the conflicts in Afghanistan or Iraq, nor does it include overseas locations under ten acres or those with replacement values of less than one million dollars. The DoD calculates this value, known as the Plant Replacement Value, using the cost to replace the current physical plant (facilities and supporting infrastructure) using current codes and construction costs.

While the *Base Structure Report* does not list all installations, it does give a detailed accounting of the largest permanent sites. These are the ones that generate the most controversy—from Kadena Air Base in Okinawa to Aviano Air Base in Italy. Moreover, while some scholars believe

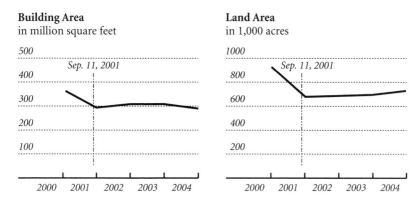

Figure 2.1. The overseas footprint of the U.S. military. The years are fiscal years, October 1 to September 30. From Department of Defense *Base Structure Reports*.

the report understates the impact of the military's global footprint, the report may actually overstate the position.[36] Many of the listed installations, for instance, are actually geographically separated components of a major installation. For example, in Italy, Aviano Air Base has eleven entries, which includes entries for each area of the base as well as the leased housing areas. Around Aviano, the base is seen as one complex, not eleven separate sites.

The real trouble arises in the very definition of a *base*. Within the DoD, each service uses different terms: the Army calls their overseas installations "camps," the Air Force calls them "bases," and the Navy and Marines call many of their sites "air stations." People in the DoD are not the only ones who cannot decide on consistent nomenclature. Military analysts fuss over terminology as well. Robert Harkavy, for example, prefers the technocratic term "facility," C. T. Sandars refers to "bases," and James Blaker uses the cumbersome term "base sites."[37] But these definitions, largely determined by geographical factors, apply equally to military bases in the United States and overseas. Regardless of their label, their impact can be disproportional to their size. Perhaps the two most contentious locations today do not even qualify as "large." Using the language of the *Base Structure Report* for consistency, the 1,184-acre Marine Corps Air Station Futenma, in Okinawa, Japan, has a plant-replacement value of $690.1 million, which makes it a "small installation." The 638-acre Yongsan Garrison, in the heart of Seoul, has a replacement value of $1.36 billion, which makes it a "medium installation," but it is barely more than half the size of Futenma. In both places, dense urban development surrounds the installations and they have been at the center of major diplomatic initiatives that have involved presidents of the United States and South Korea and the prime minister of Japan.[38]

This imperial reach comes with a shocking price tag. To support its permanent and temporary installations, in fiscal year 2007 alone, the DoD budget authorization for military construction projects totaled $12.4 billion.[39] This does not include the billions of dollars contributed by the host nations and allied militaries. As the British found out, building, staffing, and maintaining an empire is expensive. America, however, has decided to charge it. The U.S. defense budget is now roughly equal to the combined defense spending of the rest of the world—all 192 countries.[40] In fiscal year 2006 alone, defense-related spending totaled $419.3 billion, consuming roughly 20 percent of the federal budget. This bloated spending occurred in an era of recordbreaking federal budget deficits, $390 billion in 2006.[41] This is a "mortgaged empire." At least one thing comes cheaply—the land America's outposts occupy. Following historical precedent, the United States does not directly pay for using another nation's land. Rather, the nation "lucky enough" to host the United States must foot the bill. The justification is that the United States should not have to pay rent since the host nation is "benefiting" from mutual defense.[42] However, this is a murky area of public policy. Countries usually demand something in return for hosting the U.S. military, and this comes in the form of military aid and economic assistance.[43] The idea is simple— the United States needs land and, say, country X needs F-16s. The parties make a deal. James Blaker calls these deals "permission costs."[44]

The United States also expects its allies to participate in "responsibility sharing." The DoD produces an annual report detailing how much the allies contribute.[45] The countries are members of NATO and the Gulf Cooperation Council as well as wealthy Pacific allies (Australia, Japan, and South Korea). The U.S. goal is for each ally to contribute 50 percent of total nonpersonnel costs (i.e., stationing costs) associated with hosting U.S. forces. The DoD tracks, charts, and compares compliance against each nation's overall and per capita gross domestic product. For 2001 Oman topped the charts at funding 79 percent of stationing costs (but the total value is just $39 million). Japan came in a respectable second with funding 75 percent of stationing costs (the total value is an impressive $4.6 billion). South Korea and Italy contributed at a lesser level; they funded 39 percent ($805 million) and 34 percent ($324 million) respectively. All together, these allies contributed nearly $7.5 billion—not much compared against the over $400-billion defense budget of the United States. However, when compared to their gross domestic product (GDP), some nations spend over three times the U.S. rate. These numbers are important because much of the money "contributed" by the host nation either pays for the land the United States occupies or pays for construction and renovation of facilities. This also includes the costs of designing and constructing roads and buildings, providing utilities, and removing trash and lawn debris (which is in ample quantity given American's penchant for lush landscapes).

Realigning Imperial Power

In another Hollywood-quality production, with American flags (actual and virtual) behind and to his sides, President George W. Bush announced a major shift in the basing strategies of the U.S. military to an enthusiastic audience at the 105th Convention of the Veterans of Foreign Wars in August 2004. In a twenty-nine-minute speech, which the veterans interrupted thirty-four times with applause, the president spent less than three minutes outlining sweeping changes that had been in the works for several years. Interestingly, the biggest gap between the frequent applauses occurred when the president presented his realignment plan. This may be because the DoD had publicized elements of the plan already. The DoD did not wait for the president to make his speech at Cincinnati's cavernous Cinergy Center.[46] A year earlier, the undersecretary of defense for policy, Doug Feith, previewed part of the realignment strategy and said, "Everything is going to move everywhere. There is not going to be a place in the world where it's going to be the same as it used to be."[47] These are the musings of an "Ambitious Empire."

The most significant changes result from moving soldiers around in South Korea and Europe. A cynic may notice a pattern that ties the proportional contribution discussed above to locational decisions. In short, these recent realignment policies appear to leave U.S. forces unchanged in many countries that are paying more than the 50 percent target and reducing forces in countries that pay less. In a grand geopolitical irony, Japan pays more than the target and gets to keeps the U.S. troops; South Korea pays less than the target and loses some 12,500 troops (34 percent of them).[48] Of course, other issues are involved, from military strategy to political payback. In the end, land-use patterns and construction budgets flow from these decisions and are worth watching. In parts of the Middle East, U.S. forces have largely pulled out of Saudi Arabia. They have also started moving onto "temporary" bases in Eastern Europe and Central Asia, where some analysts suggest it is cheaper to station empire's police force due to less restrictive environmental rules than are typical in Western Europe.[49]

Overall, the plan may bring back to the United States as many as 70,000 soldiers (23 percent) and about 100,000 family members and civilian employees.[50] The pundits have been out in force questioning the wisdom of the plan. In South Korea, for example, the concern is that removing U.S. troops may increase the chances of war with North Korea. Many of the soldiers facing realignment are within artillery range of the Demilitarized Zone and act as a "tripwire," ensuring a swift and substantial retaliation if North Korea's Kim Jong-il makes any aggressive moves.[51]

Of course, some soldiers are not enthralled with that prospect and look forward to relocation. "I know a lot of the infantry there feel that they're just there to die in place," said Staff Sergeant Ralph Yates speaking from Camp Henry in Taegu, a safer location in the southern part of the country. Soldiers are keenly aware of the fact that the North Korean Army has "had 50 years to plot grids" to target its guns, he said. "So like I said, their mentality is, 'We're gonna be wiped out.' So spreading them out on the peninsula is good."[52] Relocation means safer locations and better housing, so it is hard to disagree with Sergeant Yates. Some South Koreans, however, are less enthusiastic. Don Kirk notes that "South Korean officials see the move as part of an elaborate American scheme in which the United States could then feel free to stage a preemptive strike on North Korean nuclear facilities without fear of North Korean artillery."[53]

The Congressional Budget Office (CBO) looked at numerous realignment options for Army outposts and produced a comprehensive report detailing the findings.[54] The CBO analyzed seven options for realigning Army functions stationed in South Korea and Germany. The options ranged from the minor change of making tours in Europe unaccompanied, which means soldiers could no longer bring their families to their European assignment ($825 million one-time cost) to completely removing all Army forces stationed overseas ($8.37 to $9.35 billion one-time cost). The CBO generated these costs using parametric cost estimates for construction, prepositioned equipment, and moving expenses.

The CBO estimated the cost of a new base in South Korea at $225 million; the cost of administrative buildings at $110,000 per person; the cost of barracks at $51,400 per person; and the cost of schools at almost $29,000 per student. The CBO also determined that the cost of new housing for soldiers and their families returning to the States would be $25,000 per year in DoD-owned housing, half the cost of barracks overseas, and $29,300 per year in leased housing. (The ramifications of paying more for leased or "free-market" family housing will resurface in chapter 5.) After extensive analysis, the CBO concluded that any major realignment will result in significant spending elsewhere and, in the most aggressive case, a greatly reduced U.S. presence overseas would produce an annual savings of $1 billion but require a substantial $7 billion upfront investment to relocate the troops and their families.

The CBO issued the report three months before the president outlined his proposal in Cincinnati, which did not address the report's findings. It is as if the White House placed the report in the dumpster. However, according to one Pentagon official, the realignment "was never about the money." Rather, the plans aligned with former secretary of defense Donald Rumsfeld's desires for "transformation" from a network of bases rooted in Cold War politics "to a more mobile force that is based closer to the likely sites of future conflicts—places such as Africa, the Middle East or the oil-rich Caspian Sea region of the former Soviet Union."[55]

Arguably, what was missing from the CBO study was the geopolitical reality regarding the location of these outposts. In South Korea, for instance, local officials acknowledge the importance of the bases to their national security. Moreover, polls regularly show most South Koreans want the U.S. outposts to remain. It was not surprising, then, that the South Korean media distorted the CBO findings. In an article in the *Korea Herald* on May 21, 2004, just after the CBO analysis went public, the reporter quoted the study as saying realignment "might increase the likelihood of war," then added, this time not in quotes, that the realignment "will not bring about the cost savings the Pentagon is seeking."[56] Nowhere in the report did the CBO discuss an increased likelihood of war resulting from the implementation of the analysis. The issue of U.S. outposts in South Korea is indeed quite sensitive, and imperial arrogance has two sides. On the one hand, continued basing of tens of thousands of U.S. soldiers in South Korea is in itself an imperial act. On the other hand, some may argue that a complete withdrawal is an action just as self-centered as a massive buildup. Walking away from the long-standing defense commitment could present serious challenges to the bilateral relationship. The United States has built up not only bases but also an expectation regarding its commitment to help defend the peninsula. South Korea's leadership has publicly opposed the realignment, fearing that it would raise tensions on the Korean peninsula, thereby increasing the chance of war.[57]

In their musings about the realignment proposals, editorial writers at the *New York Times* made an interesting cultural case for keeping soldiers overseas. They argued, "[T]he military will lose the advantage that comes with giving large numbers of its men and women experience of living in other cultures."[58] One would hope that these experiences could mitigate the effects of "cultural imperialism," which in the words of Dr. Zac Niringiye, African regional director of the Church Mission Society in Uganda, "can be considered the devaluation and consequent suppression of cultural expression of the receptor cultures." This suppression is in the service of a type of conversion experience—for some empires the goal was religious conversion; for the new American Empire, the goal is conversion of a nation's political and economic systems. Democratic elections and neoliberal policies are the hoped-for outcomes. The danger in exporting conversion is that the question becomes, "Who needs to be converted?" The imperial answer is, "Those people over there." Cultural imperialists assume conversion is a one-way street. However, "once you meet people who are different than you," argues Dr. Niringiye, "then you have a new definition of yourself—this only happens when you cross a boundary. In the encounter with the other, you have a fresh encounter with yourself. This does not happen in familiar space."[59] One of the dangers of the proposed realignment is that the U.S. military will retreat to this "familiar space"—either back in the United States or into increasingly isolated compounds. Avoidance, not interaction, is the new model. Under this scenario, the United States can avoid complications of knowing the "other." Cultural imperialism can proceed unfettered by entangling associations.

The Rub with Realignment

The realignment proposals are especially troubling to the affected U.S. allies. South Korea stands to lose up to 34 percent of its U.S. soldiers as a result of the proposals, which may shift most Americans away from the

Demilitarized Zone and out of heavily populated Seoul to areas south of Seoul under a proposal known as the Land Partnership Plan (LPP) (see chapter 7 for more details of the plan). According to one report, the LPP may eliminate up to eighteen U.S. bases and consolidate "all U.S. forces in South Korea onto Camp Humphreys and Osan Air Base. This option would put the forces outside of North Korean artillery range, make supporting dependents easier and thereby increase accompanied (family) tours from the current 10 percent to 25 percent."[60] Major General James Soligan, former U.S. Forces Korea deputy chief of staff, said the United States has a long-term vision that locates most of its soldiers in the Osan/Pyeongtaek area.[61] The CBO report estimates this vision will be quite expensive, with a price tag of up to $4.95 billion.[62]

While the South Korean leadership may be reticent toward realignment, some Japanese residents in Okinawa are disturbed that the U.S. presence there may not change. Richard Lawless, former deputy defense undersecretary for Asian and Pacific affairs, presented to Japanese officials at a meeting in San Francisco in the summer of 2004 several force realignment proposals that largely maintained the status quo. This would not be surprising since Japan pays a substantial portion of all the costs of the U.S. military there, including salaries for Japanese staff at U.S. bases, costs for most construction, and utility bills. In the fiscal 2004 budget, the Japanese government allocated ¥244 billion ($2.2 billion) to direct host-nation support of the U.S. forces.[63] Earlier in the spring of 2004, U.S. officials dropped hints that realignment might bypass Japan. The commander of the largest base in the region, Brig. Gen. Jeffrey Remington, indicated that the United States might need the base for fifty more years given its key strategic role in the Pacific. As a result, the *Japan Times* reported, "Instead of being scaled down, the base's operations have been bolstered, with an eye on the situation on the Korean Peninsula and relations between China and Taiwan."[64] This policy will translate into significant new construction for the base.

In Europe the realignments officially began in December of 2005 with U.S. secretary of state Condoleeza Rice signing a basing agreement with Romania. The United States will use Mihail Kogalnice Air Base in southeast Romania near the Black Sea, a strategic location given the growing importance of the region in the global oil distribution network.[65] While the United States will get access to an airfield unencumbered by many of the environmental and political constraints found in Western

European countries, the Romanian government is hoping the "facility" will bring diplomatic and economic gains to the former communist country. According to Romanian defense minister Teodor Atanasiu, "It is very important to us to have U.S. military bases on our territory... from the government's point of view, there is no reservation. From the parliament, it is OK. From the military's point of view, there is no reservation, and from the population, there are no major issues."[66] But given the experiences of the U.S. military elsewhere, it is only a matter of time before many Romanians grow weary of their imperial guests. The United States also hopes to "share" military facilities in Bulgaria and signed an agreement in late 2005 that allows for U.S. use of Manas Air Base in Kyrgyzstan.[67]

These outposts will be unlike those in Western Europe. They will be for unaccompanied tours—DoD terminology for assignments where soldiers cannot bring their families. Without families, the United States will not need to build family housing, schools, daycare centers, elaborate hospitals, or large shopping centers.[68] While the Bush administration and its supporters advertised this approach as a way to save money and improve the military's strategic position,[69] the CBO concluded that, in addition to costing $7 billion, the realignment offers little strategic advantage since the new installations are not significantly closer to potential areas of conflict.[70]

Some local leaders in Germany around Ramstein Air Base, the largest U.S. air base in Germany, expressed pleasure at the direction of the realignment. For example, Kaiserslautern lord mayor Bernhard Deubig said, "For Germany as a whole, the withdrawal of U.S. troops will mean a certain loss of stability and security and, naturally, will cause considerable economic problems in the affected areas. The city and county of Kaiserslautern therefore are all the more pleased to hear that this region will apparently not be affected." He also argued that the presence of American troops has had "an enormously positive effect on the local population's attitude and has encouraged a more open-minded approach to the challenges of globalization."[71] While many would argue with the mayor on the positive impact, it would be hard to discount the economic impact of the U.S. military on the local economy. Like the British Empire in India, the Americans have cultivated beneficial relationships with local political leaders largely through financial largess.

Some want the U.S. soldiers to stay; others want them to go. Some want U.S. money; others want their land back. Some want interaction; others want to be left alone. There is simply no black and white answer for an Entangled Empire. The British experience raises a relevant question: does realignment precede imperial decline? For the British it certainly did. There are hints that today's realignment is due in part to imperial overextension. Under the guise of transformation, the DoD is relocating troops from Asia and Western Europe to locations where they could be more immediately useful. In 2004, for example, the secretary of defense sent over 3,000 soldiers from South Korea to Iraq—marking the first time the United States pulled soldiers from the peninsula for duties elsewhere.[72]

Over the course of its brief history, the United States has exhibited a longing for empire in its unofficial and official policies. In just over two months, the United States established the foundations of global reach. The summer of 1898 was busy indeed—with new territories acquired from the Caribbean islands to the Philippines. This effort set the pattern for imperial annexations designed to spread the purported benefits of capitalism and democracy across the globe. But as was the case with Phuong in the *Quiet American,* Americans overseas have demonstrated an ability to ignore the presence of their "hosts" and keep on acting according to their own desires. In the new American Empire, with its preemptive wars and one-sided realignments, that attitude is evident in the spillover found around America's outposts.

CHAPTER THREE

Spillover: The U.S. Military's Sociospatial Impact

I was just starting to doze off after a day of meetings at Kunsan Air Base in southwest South Korea. A gentle breeze from the Yellow Sea, which was less than a half-mile from my fourth-floor hotel room, kept the small, sparsely decorated space cool. Then, without warning, a piercing alarm broke through the calm evening. After the noise subsided, a loud voice from outside my window took over and announced in a slow, drawn-out monotone, "ALARM YELLOW; ENEMY AIRCRAFT EN ROUTE; PROTECT VITAL RESOURCES."

My heart skipped several beats and I jumped out of bed wondering what was going on. The day's news reports were uneventful. North Korean leader Kim Jong-il had done nothing out of the ordinary. His army was reportedly surviving on the barest of rations and those few North Koreans unlucky enough not to be in the military were near starvation. Surely, they did not have the energy to mount a surprise attack on South Korea. Then, the voice from above echoed again through the previously peaceful village: "EXERCISE, EXERCISE, EXERCISE." With relief, I approached the window and noticed a loudspeaker mounted on a telephone pole just inside the base perimeter, which was less than 1,200 feet from my window.

After my pulse slowed and the adrenaline rush subsided, I tried to get some sleep. But the voice kept all of us informed as to the progress of the "war" whether we were on or off the base, whether we were military or civilian, whether we cared or not. Unfortunately, at least from my selfish perspective, the voice's reach did not stop at the base perimeter, which surely kept the locals awake as much as it kept me awake.

As I walked around the base the next morning, barbed wire and sandbag revetments were going up around nearly all the buildings. Soldiers lumbered around as best they could in the 90-degree heat even though chemical gear covered them from head to toe—thick, chemical-resistant pants and coats, steel helmets, black rubber gloves and boot covers, gas masks, and vinyl hoods. They were in MOPP 4, which is military-speak for the highest level of "Mission Oriented Protective Posture," during which they must wear all the gear.

For the next seventy-two hours, the base was much more like a prison. The soldiers had hunkered down in exercise mode, practicing for what could only be a worst-case scenario. After all, for North Korean warplanes to make it to Kunsan they would have to first get by Seoul's impressive defenses. Nevertheless, sentries at every door checked ID cards. American security police with grenade launchers and automatic weapons augmented the lightly armed South Korean guards at the main gate. Air Force personnel placed blackout boards on windows around the base. Throughout the exercise, the base's fighter jets kept a very busy schedule. Day and night, the eerie glow from their engines illuminated the sky and their din saturated the landscape.

This visual and audible spillover is not confined to exercise days. Neighbors living in the flight pattern of America's outposts must deal with the noise, the contamination, and the accidents that occur regularly because of military operations. Moreover, horrific crimes and the sociospatial impacts of prostitution routinely make headlines in the newspapers of the host nation. While the articles in these papers frequently show the bases in a regional context, the planning maps produced by the U.S. military rarely show anything beyond the fence line. For the Americans, the white space around their outposts is just that—it is nothing and it is nowhere.

During multiple visits to bases in South Korea, Japan, and Italy, the only documents I found that showed the outposts in their regional context were the aerial photos taken as a perfunctory part of the General Plan process. A checklist required an aerial photo. Check, one aerial photo is complete. Check, thinking about the context is complete. While they made for attractive posters on the walls of planning offices, and they were interesting graphics for the covers of planning documents, planners rarely referenced these photos and therefore they served little useful purpose. The widely used documents were facility maps and infrastructure plans that stopped at the border. The production of these maps reflects a deeply ingrained base-planning mind-set. Like the maps, the thinking about empire's impacts stops at the fencelines. However, the piercing sounds of an F-16 or the plumes from underground oil leaks do not stop when they reach the edge of the map. Before the United States made these maps, the land under each base was not an island of empire, floating in a sea of white space. Rather, the land belonged to a nation, a people, a family, and oftentimes to an individual farmer struggling to survive.

Legalizing Colonization: The Okinawan Example

The confiscation and consumption of land is clearly a form of spillover, but military leaders using the rhetoric of national security too quickly dismiss the cost. Military commanders justify their land needs with little consideration given to the sordid history of expropriation that preceded their tours of duty. Following the examples of earlier empires, the United States has adroitly practiced displacement and demolition. As a nation that governs itself by the rule of law, the United States justifies many of these actions through one-sided legal frameworks signed over fifty years ago in the name of freedom and democracy. A relevant example of this approach is the case of Okinawa, Japan. In Okinawa, as in so many other locations around the globe, for local residents in the way of American power, the "price of freedom" has been their own land. Masahide Ota, a former governor of the Prefecture of Okinawa, had this to say about the value of land in a 1996 hearing before the Supreme Court of Japan:

> As numerous records indicate, in Okinawa where the proclivities for ancestor worship are strong, land is not a mere plot of soil in which to grow crops. It is not a commodity, something that can be considered an object for buying and selling. If I may paraphrase further, land is an irreplaceable heritage graciously bequeathed to us by our ancestors or a spiritual string that ties us to them. My people's attachment to their land is firmly rooted, and their resistance against the forcible taking of their land is similarly strong.[1]

He was at the Supreme Court to justify his refusal to sign the leases of landowners who owned the land under U.S. outposts in Okinawa, a lush island that was part of the Ryukyu kingdom until forcibly annexed by Japan in 1879. The landowners refused to renew their agreements with the government of Japan and were an embarrassment for the prime minister. As the prefecture's governor, he had the right and the obligation to override the local landowners and sign the leases.

The controversy over U.S. land use in Okinawa is nothing new. It dates back to World War II, when the Americans engaged in a ferocious battle with Japanese forces dug in on the island. Left dead were 12,000 Americans, 75,000 Japanese soldiers, and over 150,000 Okinawans caught in the crossfire.[2] American forces killed many of the local residents, Japanese forces killed some, and a few killed themselves. The tropical island became a deathbed, nearly stripped of its people, its landscape, and its heritage. To be sure, the Okinawans first suffered under the Imperial Japanese Army. Land confiscations, rapes, and evictions turned much of the local population against the Imperial Army. After the Americans won the Battle of Okinawa, they moved onto the island in force and began converting it into a staging ground for a possible assault on the Japanese mainland. Many Okinawans remember a welcome period of relief beginning with the American arrival. The American soldiers studied Okinawan culture and dedicated 5,000 personnel to the work of meeting the needs of the civilian population. As Ota notes, "Had it not been for this American policy towards non-combatants, Okinawan civilians would have paid an immeasurably higher price during the battle."[3]

The welcome aspects of the American arrival did not last long, however. Although President Truman's decision to subject Hiroshima and Nagasaki to nuclear attack obviated the need for a staging location, the United States continued to build up its outposts on the island despite growing local resistance. Within one year, the United States took over 40,000 acres as an act of war, including 20 percent of all arable land on the island, and by 1955, justified by the Cold War, the United States displaced 250,000 people or nearly half of the island's entire population. The Americans even shipped 3,218 Okinawans to Bolivia in a largely failed bid at transcontinental displacement.[4] Across history, the hands of empire predictably travel past the same markers: displacements and demolitions are the norm.

A 1955 report by the U.S. House of Representatives criticized the inadequacy of the U.S. plan to occupy the island and the proposals to finally pay landowners.[5] However, the fallout from the war made identifying who owned the land quite complicated. According to Governor Ota,

> Since documents like family registers and ledgers were lost in the ravages of war, the confirmation of titles to privately-owned land was extremely difficult. One cannot deny that this situation made the arbitrary acquisition of land by the military easier. Moreover the acquisition was forced, the troops brandishing bayonets and bulldozers, as my people well remember.[6]

United States engineers kept those bulldozers busy converting small farms into air bases. The U.S. report noted that while a family of five could subsist on eight-tenths of an acre of arable land, the average size of a family's holdings before the war, the proposed U.S. compensation of less than $20 per year was inadequate. The United States based the payment level on a fixed rent at 6 percent of the land's assessed value. The Okinawans did not do the assessments, however. That was the task of the Army Corps of Engineers in 1952. The fact that the United States set both the land-use rules and land values was a clear conflict of interest.

The report claimed, however, that the rent did not account for the collateral value of the U.S. presence on the island:

> Okinawans [benefit by] the presence of U.S. forces, as for example the extensive employment of Okinawans by reason of the defense-construction activities of the United States forces, [and] the direct employment by the United States of Okinawans in other than defense construction. Permanent buildings on paved streets are replacing narrow dirt roads of Naha, the capital city, modern shopping centers are rising, theaters are being built, these latter being local, not United States activities.[7]

While some Okinawans did profit from the construction efforts and employment opportunities at the bases, many more had to find their own incomes and were unable to buy into the "benefits" of capitalism. Naha's shopping centers and the island's roads essentially belonged to the wealthy or the occupying force. The near total destruction of all pre-1945 buildings on the island facilitated the remaking of the island into a spatial setting more similar to Cold War suburbs in the United States than prewar villages in Okinawa. With a population density of 1,270 persons per square mile (23 times greater than that of the United States in 1955),[8] making room for shopping centers and wide boulevards forced even more Okinawans into the few crowded urban centers on the island. In a decade, the island went from being a largely self-sufficient agricultural economy to one heavily dependent on handouts from Tokyo and the United States. There were not enough jobs or arable land in the hands of Okinawans. Despite the economic impact of the U.S. military, Okinawa remains the poorest prefecture in Japan with an unemployment rate nearly twice the national average.[9] Given the persistent economic problems in Okinawa, one wonders whether the bases actually help, as their boosters say, or hurt the local economy by limiting other types of economic activity.

How did a nation that supposedly follows the rule of law come to control so much foreign land? Like empires past, the winner wrote the rules that justified its actions. Like the *Laws of the Indies* and the Cantonment Acts, the United States published regulations, official memos, and "joint" declarations giving it the right to occupy foreign land. And like its imperial predecessors, the United States relied on the complicity of the "governed." The displacements in Japan, for example, rest on a regularly updated series of "agreements" between the United States and Japan:

September 1947: The Emperor of Japan sent General Douglas MacArthur a memo welcoming the U.S. occupation of Okinawa under the auspices of a long-term lease.

June 1950: Not ready to limit U.S. forces to Okinawa, MacArthur issued an official memo stating, "The entire area of Japan must be regarded as a potential base for defensive maneuver with unrestricted freedom reserved to the United States. . . . Thus, by avoiding emphasis upon any specific points to be reserved as 'bases' for use of the security forces, not only will the reservation be realistically drawn to meet the requirements of modern defense but the distasteful connotation given the term 'bases,' as legitimate spoils of war, may be avoided."

September 1951: A two-page Security Treaty signed in San Francisco officially ended the war, and stated, "Japan grants, and the United States of America accepts, the right . . . to dispose of United States land, air and sea forces in and about Japan. Such forces may be utilized to contribute to the maintenance of international peace and security in the Far East and to the security of Japan against armed attack from without, including assistance given at the express request of the Japanese Government to put down large-scale internal riots and disturbances in Japan, caused through instigation or intervention by an outside power or powers."

December 1953: Major General David Ogden, Deputy Governor of the Ryukyu Islands, specified the physical manifestation of the treaty and issued a proclamation stating, "The right of the United States of America to the use and occupancy of the Military Areas heretofore taken by the Armed Forces of the United States under implied lease is hereby confirmed."

June 1957: President Dwight D. Eisenhower made explicit the link between imperialism and capitalism by declaring "the Secretary of Defense shall encourage the development of an effective and responsible Ryukyuan government, based on democratic principles and supported by a sound financial structure, [and] shall make every effort to improve the welfare and well-being of the inhabitants of the Ryukyu Islands."[10]

With the emperor's stamp of approval, the United States began its on-going occupation of Japan. The progression from occupier to patron took less than ten years. Regardless of what General MacArthur called them, the reservations that were "realistically drawn" were military outposts and no euphemism could conceal that basic fact. They were without question the "spoils of war." What else could they be? Did Japan have the option not to grant U.S. occupancy? Again, we see a government using language to conceal rather than reveal. Empires operate in a world where names often do not reflect reality.

Living under Imperial Wings

The fighter planes and fuel trucks that supported this imperial expansion ushered in new forms of spillover. These impacts fall into four broad categories: clamor, calamity, contamination, and crime. Each category reveals that sociocultural practices have spatial consequences. Noise travels across space regardless of the location of fencelines. Planes can come crashing down anytime or anywhere. Pollution moves along underground irrespective of property lines. U.S. soldiers commit crimes in every country they are "defending." The location of American outposts is disproportionate siting on multiple scales. Powerful nations pollute on their host nations, and outposts pollute on their neighboring cities.[11]

Clamor

Perhaps the most studied spillover concerns the noise generated from military operations. This applies primarily to outposts with significant flying missions—Naval and Marine Corps air stations, Army posts with flying operations, and Air Force bases. While public address systems and partygoers are noisy, jets and helicopters can be deafening. The noise, though, is not just a nuisance. It is a significant public health issue. In 1995 a study by Asahikawa Medical College in Okinawa found that 480,000 residents of Okinawa (38 percent) lived in areas with noise levels exceeding Japanese environmental noise standards.[12] In the fouryear study, researchers analyzed over 350,000 medical records, sent questionnaires to 1,580 school children and their parents, and surveyed 4,245 residents living on the island and concluded:

- Lower than average birth weights around the bases were due to aircraft noise.
- Children living around these bases had greater emotional and health problems than their peers on other parts of the island.
- Adults experienced higher stress levels that disturbed their work and sleep patterns.

In addition, retired schoolteacher Fujiko Nakasone claims that schoolchildren lose an average of two years during their twelve years of education due to the noise. They experience increased nervousness, hearing loss, and an inability to concentrate.[13] The U.S. military recognizes the detrimental effects of aircraft noise and has developed programs to monitor noise and limit construction in heavily affected areas it controls. The Air Force, for example, initiated the Air Installation Compatible Use Zone (AICUZ) program in the 1970s as a way of controlling development on its bases. Elaborate software plotted noise contours on maps using the flight patterns of aircraft stationed at each base. These are quite similar to topographic contours, only in the sky. The highest noise levels are along the flightline and follow aircraft as they take off and land; the farther away from the flightline, the less the impact. Air Force policymakers ban housing, schools, and daycare centers from the noisiest zones. While AICUZ contours extend far beyond the fenceline, planners overseas have little control over what occurs outside their base. This may be one reason why so many maps of military outposts do not show anything beyond an installation's borders except white space. These outposts might as well be islands. However, instead of water on all sides, increasingly dense development encroaches on many of America's outposts, exacerbating noise-related problems.

Since the United States has done little to mitigate the problem, many communities have taken the issue to court. In 2004 a South Korean court awarded 1,878 residents living near Kunsan Air Base payments totaling

$2.85 million following a class-action lawsuit. Resident Kim Joong-kon, who has lived near the base all his life, said vibrations from the fighter jets caused cracks in walls, distracted studying students, and made people quite irritable. According to Capt. Krista Carlos, the Kunsan Air Base spokesperson, Air Force pilots normally fly 175 "sorties" per week.[14] The judge, Son Yoon-ha, awarded the compensation to residents living in areas consistently exposed to more than 70 decibels, about as loud as a vacuum cleaner. This was the first time a South Korean court granted damages to residents living near a U.S. military base. In light of the lawsuit, the U.S. Air Force increased the use of special sound-insulating "hush houses" to conduct engine tests and limited the hours of jet-engine runs, but the award has been appealed. If the plaintiffs prevail, the Republic of Korea, not the United States, will make the payments.

Similar cases have made their way through the Japanese judicial system. In 1998 the Fukuoka High Court in Naha awarded $10.32 million as compensation to 867 residents living near Kadena Air Base in Okinawa who endured 75 decibels or more. In 1999 the Tokyo High Court awarded $1.5 million to residents living near the U.S. Atsugi Naval Air Facility. These cases have set a legal precedent in Japan and have resulted in several more lawsuits. Two recent cases are now in the legal system—200 residents living around Futenma Marine Corps Air Station have filed a suit against the base commander and the Japanese government seeking $2.56 million in damages and 6,000 residents living around Kadena Air Base have filed another suit. The second Kadena suit came after the government paid $814 million to install soundproofing in 59,000 homes near air bases in Okinawa. In Kadena-cho, one of three towns abutting Kadena Air Base, statistics show that aircraft noise exceeded 70 decibels 23,418 times between April 2001 and March 2002, a 21-percent increase over the previous period. Local residents blame increased flying on post–September 11 activity at the base.[15] As in South Korea, any payments made to the plaintiffs in cases in Japan come from the host nation, not from the United States, which does little to create an incentive for the United States to modify its behavior. This is one more imperial irony—making the very people who suffer from the spillover pay for their own compensation through the host nation's tax system.

Okinawa is not the only Japanese prefecture living with imperial clamor. In northern Japan's Aomori Prefecture, Misawa Air Base and its Ripsaw gunnery range occupy 7,649 acres.[16] The base was originally home to the Imperial Japanese Naval Air Force, but came under U.S. control in 1945. The U.S. Air Force and the U.S. Navy operate a variety of flying missions from the base. These missions have come in conflict with the daily lives of many Japanese who live in nearby Misawa City and the surrounding areas. One concern is noise from jet operations. For the Japanese, the acceptable level is up to 95 decibels, which is higher than Korea's standard of 70 decibels. However, even with this greater tolerance, which is like living with a jackhammer at work outside a bedroom window, the government of Japan has paid many residents to leave their homes near the base. In 2002 the Japanese government approved a plan to relocate 190 families who had been living in homes at the end of Misawa's runway.[17] This was after the government paid more than $2 billion in 1996 to relocate 1,617 people living under the wings of empire.

Additionally, in 2002, 95 families living near Misawa's Ripsaw range sought payment for relocation. The range's name is quite appropriate, given the ripsaw-like noise of the bombing and strafing practice that goes on at the 1,892-acre site. Typically, the Japanese government relocates homes to outlying farmland and pays for roads and utilities as well as compensation at fair market value (now calculated by the Japanese government) for the relocated families. But residents are nervous about building homes on ricefields and wonder if the proposed land is stable enough to support the roads, utilities, and homes of the families. This is a case of suburban sprawl in Japan, courtesy of the U.S. military.[18]

While the numbers tell one story, there is another perspective. Despite compensation, some residents remain emotionally attached to their land. Cash payments do not ease the pain of relocation. Mitsuko Conte, a local resident living near Misawa Air Base, said, "I've lived in this house for 40 years, why should I want to move now? It's too much trouble, and I have too many memories here."[19] Moreover, the noise of jets lifting off mixes with the sounds of sirens going off and rekindles painful emotions. In one training exercise, twenty-six residents living near Kadena Air Base complained of late-night sirens and announcements through the base's loudspeakers. Kadena's public affairs representative, Charles Steitz, said, "This training is conducted routinely at operational bases Air Force–wide to evaluate a [base's] ability to respond to contingencies." An official from Kadena-cho said, "Some senior residents were frightened by the noise because the sirens reminded them of air raids during World War II. They thought that Kadena Air Base was being attacked by terrorists."[20] In response, Air Force officials informed the mayor of Kadena-cho that the military did not authorize use of the sirens after midnight during the three-day exercise. Here, the military's mistakes mix with memories to create angst.

For many Okinawans who lived through World War II, these events do bring back painful memories. Kozo Hiramatsu, an expert in acoustic ecology and a professor at Mukogawa Women's University, studied the audio-emotional link by listening to the stories of Okinawans who lived through the war and the ensuing peace. Professor Hiramatsu argues:

> Certain sounds strongly attach to one's memory and life. . . . For instance, those who have grown up listening to sounds of summer festivals recall various events that happened at that time whenever they hear those sounds. For many senior citizens in Okinawa, the jet noise brings back dreadful memories of the Battles of Okinawa and Saipan.[21]

Given their strong emotional attachment to the land, Hiramatsu argues that Okinawans will not leave regardless of the impacts. Recognizing that the land has emotional value apart from its economic or use value is a difficult proposition at best for capitalist economies and their soldiers.

Calamity

While clamor can make life unbearable and even lead to health problems, more deadly examples of spillover have been the calamities surrounding the operation of American warplanes and fighting vehicles overseas. Airplanes and tanks crash. "I'm astonished," said Shigeyoshi Suzuki, mayor of Misawa, after one airplane crash that narrowly missed Japanese homes in 2001. "It would have been a disaster if this happened over a residential area."[22] Below is a listing of just a few of these dreadful events. Although it is not an all-inclusive list spread evenly across time, and it only accounts for aircraft, it is enough to establish a context for imperial spillover. When viewed as a whole the picture is one of continuous calamity.

> June 1959: An Air Force fighter jet crashes into Miyamori Elementary School in Okinawa, killing eleven children, six adults, and injuring 121; twenty-five homes burn to the ground.
> December 1962: A U.S. transport aircraft crashes on a private house in Kadena-cho, killing seven.
> June 1965: An eleven-year-old schoolgirl playing in her garden dies when equipment falls from a U.S. helicopter.

May 1968: An Air Force jet crashes at Kyushu University in Japan; the United States places the base on standby status.

November 1968: A B-52 crashes in Okinawa, killing sixteen civilians and damaging 365 homes.

April 1994: An F-15 crashes on Kadena Air Base after takeoff.

October 1995: An F-15 crashes sixty-five miles south of Okinawa.

August 1999: Two F-16s collide above Kunsan Air Base and two live bombs drop into the sea at the end of the runway.

November 2000: Two F-16s collide off the coast of Japan near Hokkaido.

June 2001: An F-16 crashes into a rice paddy near Kunsan Air Base, South Korea, killing pilot.

November 2001: An F-16 drops one unarmed missile and two fuel tanks with 500 gallons of jet fuel on a Misawa farm, contaminating 7,440 square yards and narrowly missing twenty-five homes and an elementary school.

April 2002: An F-16 crashes into Sea of Japan, eighty-two miles west of Misawa Air Base.

April 2002: An F-15 canopy blows off eighty miles southeast of Kadena Air Base.

April 2002: An F-15 accidentally drops its high-intensity magnesium flare over Kadena, Japan.

April 2002: A Marine helicopter drops its fuel tanks after takeoff.

August 2002: An F-15 crashes at sea off of the Okinawan coast.

August 2002: An Apache helicopter crashes on a hillside near Camp Page, South Korea, killing two crewmembers.

January 2003: A U-2 reconnaissance plane crashes near Osan Air Base, South Korea, injuring four and destroying one home and a repair shop.

May 2003: An F-16 crashes shortly after takeoff at Osan Air Base; falling debris injures one person.

August 2003: An Army C-12 crashes into a field seven miles from Camp Humphreys, South Korea.

September 2003: An F-16 crashes off of Korea's west coast.

November 2003: An F-16 crashes into the Pacific Ocean near Misawa Air Base due to catastrophic engine failure.

August 2004: A Marine helicopter crashes into Ginowan City, damaging an Okinawa International University administration building and leaving debris in a heavily developed residential area 370 yards from the crash site.

October 2004: Two F-15s collide over water near Okinawa but narrowly avoid populated areas in emergency landings.[23]

Planes crashing into schools, parts falling from the sky, and pilots ejecting into the ocean are not welcome news headlines for residents living around America's outposts. While there has not been an accident as catastrophic as the one in 1959 that killed eleven children, with dense development abutting almost every base the chances of a similar accident are high. The August 2004 helicopter crash in Japan barely missed being a major tragedy. The accidents and the ongoing environmental and human toll only further strain the relationship between nations. In a letter to the commander of Misawa Air Base following an F-16 crash in 2002, Misawa's Mayor Suzuki, who has been a vocal supporter of the base, stated, "I cannot help but think that you have an occupation forces mentality. [Your] outrageous behaviors and actions are tolerated by us. This is handling Japan like a U.S. colony."[24] When an ally of the United States becomes an enemy due to American spillover, imperial power is on the decline.

Contamination

While aircraft accidents make the headlines, largely unseen environmental contamination seeps into the soil of the nations housing U.S. forces. Fuel spills, chemical leaks, and illegal dumping continue to plague military bases. A few examples may suffice. In Japan, engineers at Misawa Air Base have attempted to clean up a plume of aviation fuel twenty-five feet deep that seeped into the ground and beyond the base's boundary following an explosion of a 420,000-gallon fuel tank in 1955. They have spent $1.5 million to clean up the spill since engineers discovered the plume in 1996. In January 2003, in South Korea, 2,000 gallons of diesel fuel leaked out of a fuel tank at Osan Air Base, and 700 gallons of jet fuel leaked out of a containment system following a spill at Kunsan Air Base. In Seoul, oil leaks around Yongsan garrison and at a religious retreat center near Mt. Namsan have saturated the ground, contaminating spring water in the process.[25]

While leaks occur on and off military bases wherever oil is present, a more egregious spill occurred in 2000 when a base worker intentionally dumped twenty gallons of formaldehyde into a drain that discharges into South Korea's Han River. Groups opposed to the military's presence called for the commander of all U.S. forces in South Korea to resign and suggested that they may send formaldehyde-filled bottles to the Mississippi River.[26] This would be a unique form of blowback. The controversy reached the U.S. ambassador, who said he personally regretted the spill, but this was five months after it occurred and was hardly an official apology.[27] U.S. officials unhelpfully noted that the chemical spilled into two million gallons of wastewater and passed through two purification systems before entering the scenic river. When formaldehyde goes into any river, the fine print is irrelevant from a political standpoint.

After the incident, the military tried to improve communication. "We can no longer afford to hide behind our fences and not talk to the Korean citizens," said Lt. Col. Dan Worth, director of public works at Yongsan. "We all live here, breathe the air, eat the food, and drink the water."[28] Part of the talk included a well-received announcement that the U.S. military would spend $100 million to replace fuel tanks on outposts around South Korea. Ongoing monitoring programs, frequent mitigation projects, and regular upgrade efforts, while helpful in that they minimize negative environmental and political effects, do come with a high price tag.

Another type of spillover that can lead to contamination is the disposal of trash. Okinawa, for example, is running out of landfill space and may have no room left for trash in the near future. At Kadena Air Base, it costs $2 million per year to dispose of 21,416 tons of trash. "We live on an island of limited land mass with a large number of people," said Richard Kuehn from Kadena. "We cannot indefinitely amass trash without running out of room and we're rapidly running out of room." Americans apparently have a difficult time managing the eighteen different categories of recycling used by the Japanese, so many of them just dump their trash illegally on the base. Base personnel then must relocate this garbage to a local landfill. Moreover, the American culture of consumption follows these families to their overseas assignments. Americans bring their big-screen televisions and their barrels of trash. In 2001 Americans generated about 2.5 times the daily household garbage per capita than their Japanese neighbors living on Okinawa. An American produces 1,500 pounds of trash a year. An Okinawan produces 590 pounds per year. But Americans in Okinawa are no different than their colleagues back home, who, it turns out, spend more on garbage bags than 90 of the world's 192 countries spend for everything. Imperial excess extends into the wastebasket.[29]

Crime

While formaldehyde flowing into the Han River draws out the protestors, and landfills reaching capacity are a worry for some, other heinous examples of spillover result from crimes committed by U.S. soldiers on foreign soil. Following World War II, the American occupation of Germany,

Italy, Japan, and Korea opened up these countries to the needs of capitalism while also exposing their residents to the occupation mentality and spatial demands of American soldiers. Oftentimes, this manifested itself in an arrogant attitude of superiority—an air of being above the law. After all, the United States wrote whatever laws justified its sociospatial needs. The predictable result was a crime spree around American outposts that other scholars have thoroughly detailed.[30] U.S. soldiers have been responsible for deadly traffic accidents, beatings, robberies, rapes, and murders. These acts can quickly become major international incidents involving presidents and prime ministers. While rapes have caused the most outrage, U.S. soldiers commit many other types of crimes. In addition to their human cost, these crimes have a direct financial cost. Between 1992 and 2003, for instance, the South Korean and U.S. governments paid $27.3 million in compensation for damages caused by American soldiers. In South Korea, between 1999 and 2001, Americans committed 1,246 criminal acts, from misdemeanors to felonies.[31]

Commanders, however, will unhelpfully explain that soldiers commit fewer crimes per capita than residents of the host nation. For instance, the Marine Corps' senior officer noted that in Okinawa, Americans made up 4 percent of the island's population but committed less than 1 percent of the crimes in 2000 (Americans were involved in 53 of 6,226 reported crimes).[32] However, other officers recognize that numbers do not matter; any crime committed by U.S. soldiers is automatically an international event rather than a domestic matter. Colonel Vic Warzinski, a former director of public affairs for U.S. Forces Japan, suggested that comparisons of crime statistics are not helpful. "After all we are guests in their country and are expected to conduct ourselves in an appropriate manner. The Japanese view this . . . as an additive thing. They don't look at it as a rate, crimes per thousand or crimes per 100,000. It's just one more crime on top of a long history of earlier misconduct."[33] The historical pattern adds up and can even turn longtime supporters like Misawa's Mayor Suzuki into opponents.

More telling from a sociospatial perspective is the variation in crime rates within the military community. In the same three-year period that South Korea experienced 1,246 criminal acts by U.S. soldiers, in Okinawa, Japan, soldiers committed 198 criminal acts.[34] The annualized per capita difference is quite instructive. In South Korea, there were 11.2 crimes per 1,000 soldiers. In Okinawa, there were 2.4 crimes per 1,000

U.S. soldiers. Why is the disparity so striking? I suggest that it is largely the result of policies related to housing and land use.

For the most part, the differences in the individual soldiers are minimal—in both countries they are generally men in their twenties and thirties, two-thirds with families. They rotate in and out of the United States, Japan, South Korea, and Europe. In Japan, 72 percent of the "tours" are accompanied, which means families can live with the "sponsor" or military member assigned to Japan. In South Korea, however, the ratio is nearly reversed; 90 percent of the "tours" are unaccompanied.[35] Thus, the U.S. military considers South Korea a "remote" or "hardship" assignment (as in remote from one's family) and unless a soldier has special permission, his or her family stays in the United States. Chalmers Johnson argues that these soldiers go to South Korea for a year of drunken debauchery. He claims that "the large numbers of troops based all over South Korea have had nothing to do since the armistice of 1953. They spend their days mostly dozing in their tanks and their evenings in the arms of prostitutes."[36]

While Johnson's generalizations about American soldiers are largely inaccurate—most soldiers work long hours and obviously not all soldiers frequent South Korean brothels—there is some merit to the fact that soldiers in South Korea behave differently than similar soldiers in Japan or any other country. Families can be a mellowing influence, not only for married soldiers but also for single soldiers who end up living around families. As Cynthia Enloe has shown, gendered dimensions exist when the military allows families in general, and wives in particular, to live on a base. Enloe argues, "The armed forces depend on their largely unpaid work to transform an overseas base into a 'community.'" The "community" that results when spouses move overseas may have less tolerance for sexual adventures. This presents a land use conundrum for base planners. Making room for families under the current model of imperial planning consumes vast quantities of land. As Enloe suggests, "Keeping soldiers happy on a foreign base requires keeping soldiers' wives happy."[37]

Without land and resources allocated for family functions, however, families stay away. Families require housing, schools, day care centers, parks, shopping centers, and expanded hospitals.[38] These spaces, though, do not determine behavior. Rather, the sociocultural practices either supported or inhibited by these environments shape behavior. The physicalist fallacy of architecture would assume that built environments (e.g. buildings, roads, and parks) determine behaviors. Sociologist Mark Gottdiener emphasizes that space is an important concept not because it promises some new form of life but because the built environment is critical to the transformation of everyday life.[39] Built form works like a stage on which people act out their lives. It can be transformative if it supports the needs of the people it serves. Or, like a prison, built form can be repressive if it attempts to control. What matters is less the type of stage than the fact that there is a stage at all. In South Korea, the stage for family life is missing; hence, families are missing and the behaviors of young soldiers with a steady income and easy access to alcohol and prostitutes are largely unconstrained by the norms of family life. Loneliness, alienation, and desire drive these young men into the bars and brothels found throughout South Korea. Crime is the predictable outcome.

For a variety of reasons, the United States decided to keep South Korea a remote assignment. One argument has been that the imminent "threat" posed by North Korea made the peninsula unsafe for families. As it is, the U.S. military issues gas masks and evacuation instructions to the few family members who do go to South Korea. Another argument has been that the outposts there do not have the land area to support all the facilities needed for spouses and children. Similarly, neither the United States nor the South Korean government has been willing to invest the billions of dollars required to build these facilities. Whatever the excuse, the fact remains that South Korea is a dangerous place for Koreans. While Kim Jong-il may have visions of a reunified peninsula under his command, some U.S. soldiers commit crimes against the people they are supposedly defending.

Leaving the statistical and land-use debates aside, some soldiers believe the media blows the crime issue out of proportion. While Airman Cory Chang acknowledges the majority of soldiers head off base "for one thing, which is women," some are just looking for somewhere to "relax and kick back and listen to music." But Ryan Sell, a Navy corpsman, has a different view, "When you're out on the street, you've got . . . people luring you into like bars and stuff. I was walking down the street just going a couple of blocks and—I call them drinky bars, I don't know what they're called—they grab you and freakin' pull you in."[40]

The convenient location and concentrated layout of the red-light districts facilitates this focus on drinking. Yet no visible or invisible force pulls soldiers into a bar against their will. They walk right in and place their order, which may be for far more than a bottle of beer. Many of the men walking in the bars know they have another purpose. The bars are the setting for a thriving sex trade. "Everything on Gate 2 Street (in Okinawa) is set up to make Americans look like sexist pigs and like the only thing they want is sex," argues Airman Dustin Wheeler. "Look [at] it. Every five feet you walk down the street is a buy-me-drinky girl."[41] Airman Wheeler may have a point but he fails to recognize that in capitalism's cruel balance of supply and demand, the morphology of Gate 2 Street is responding to the power and privilege of the regular paycheck.

Hooker Hill: Mapping Prostitution's Sociospatial Realities

Airmen Wheeler could have just as easily been referring to Itaewon, a rowdy bar and brothel district outside the Yongsan Army garrison in the heart of Seoul. Known informally as Hooker Hill, the place is a maze of shopping streets by day and a mass of dancing "hostesses" by night. Numerous scholars have added their voice to the growing debate surrounding these red-light districts, known as camptowns.[42] Their work has shown that the men in charge of these camptowns—the local bar owners, the wealthy landowners, and even national legislators—extend geopolitical domination into the back alleys of places like Itaewon and commodify women as products for rent. What is missing from these accounts, however, is the element of sociospatial practice. The people involved, their official policies, and their unofficial practices clearly dictate the course of events in these camptowns, but the dancing and drinking occur in real space given shape by seen and unseen forces. These camptowns consume space in response to the presence of the U.S. military. Although a century removed from the British cantonments, these places are the next chapter in the story of empire's sociospatial support for prostitution.

Itaewon's Red Lights

Itaewon is perhaps the best-known red-light district. It is a place where realities and fantasies collide. Its alleyways and police stations have been the setting for movies and novels that closely parallel real life.[43] Its main street has been the site of violent protests against the American presence in the heart of South Korea's capital city. Itaewon consists of multistory buildings snug to the sidewalks with shops and clubs on the lower floors and apartments and offices on the floors above. Glitzy storefront windows with waif-like fiberglass models display the latest fashion trends. Sleazy, smoke-filled bars fill the back alleys where American troops mingle with the dancers of a globalized world. Women from Korea, Thailand, the Philippines, Russia, and Uzbekistan entertain all night long.

Men from the U.S. military as well as from many of these same countries drink, fight, and then hook up with the women of the Hill, women like Lana. She arrived in South Korea in 2001 from the Kyrgyz Republic, where she worked in a shoe factory and was unable to afford an apartment. She responded to a newspaper add that wanted women to dance with U.S. soldiers in South Korea for $333 per month. When she arrived, the bar owner confiscated her passport and forced her to sell sex to the soldiers either in a nearby hotel or in a "VIP" room above the bar. Whether or not she knew that sex was going to be part of the job description, she became a sex slave. She usually worked every day from 5 P.M. until 1 A.M. Fearful of a corrupt South Korean police force around the base, she complied with the bar owner's demands and became one of hundreds of women forced into working around U.S. military bases in the country.[44] Without a passport and deeply in debt to the bar owner for her travel and living expenses (she lived in a small three-room apartment with nine other women which was monitored by a video-surveillance system), she had few options. Lana's experience anchors the U.S. military to the sad reality of Itaewon's dance clubs, VIP rooms, and short-term hotels.

Adjacent to Itaewon is the U.S. Army's Yongsan garrison, a sprawling 640-acre compound that consists mostly of single-story red-brick buildings and ample landscaping. Initially built by the Japanese in 1592, Yongsan has long been a military outpost for imperial powers stationed in the heart of Seoul. The U.S. Army occupied and built up Yongsan at the end of World War II, replacing the Imperial Japanese Army. From atop Seoul Tower, the mountains to the north and east, and the Army garrison to the south are the only features that interrupt the view of the unbroken density of Seoul. The fabric of buildings and streets that make up Seoul abruptly stops at the perimeter of the garrison and transforms into a lush, low-density enclave. Bungalows and baseball fields are typical. Once on the post, even locals, many of whom are used to walking around Seoul, find themselves at the mercy of the "buck-fifty" cabs to get around.

The Bars of Songtan

Hooker Hill is not an aberration. Around the outposts of empire, similar places with similar patrons are the norm. The common pattern is for camptowns to be right outside the gates, like Hooker Hill in Seoul or Songtan next to Osan Air Base, south of Seoul. These areas are a strange land where neither the United States nor South Korea exercises sole control. Inside each outpost, a Status of Forces Agreement gives the U.S. military legal jurisdiction. According to Senior Master Sergeant Andy Eskew, the superintendent of operations for the Security Police Squadron at Osan Air Base, "the Korean National Police allow up to a 10-mile radius around the base for us to patrol, which isn't necessary here since our activities are limited to a five or six block radius. We're here to keep the peace by preventing an assault or fight."[45] In the end, neither the Koreans nor the Americans are protecting the rights of the women working as prostitutes in these borderlands. This unique zoning in many ways puts the women out on their own, at the mercy of unscrupulous pimps, drunk and violent "customers," and demanding landlords.

Like Itaewon, the Songtan district patrolled by Sergeant Eskew is a regional draw, similar to an anchor store in a shopping mall. By day, it is a big outdoor market, filled with cheap tennis shoes, jackets of every National Football League team, and tailors ready to make a custom wool suit for $50. By night, it is a raucous bar district filled with women who can be bought as easily as a T-shirt and bartenders selling beer as fast as they can tap the kegs (Figure 3.1). The well-lit street fills to capacity. Street vendors sell fried, grilled, and baked foods of all kinds. Local kids dash in and out of the stores pointing their fingers at the machine guns of the military police patrolling the street. Despite the presence of these police patrols from the base charged with maintaining order, loud and ostentatious behavior goes on until the clearly posted curfew (Figure 3.2).

Songtan is home to ninety-two bars, all within 1,200 feet of the main gate, with most bars clustered along a pedestrian-only street. This gives a new dimension to this measure of walkability made popular by advocates of the "new urbanism."[46] The local government, with the support

Figure 3.1. Shinjang Mall. (a) By day, this street just outside Osan Air Base, South Korea, is a bustling pedestrian zone patrolled by U.S. military police. (b) At night, flashing neon lights and raucous music from dozens of cocktail bars and dance clubs fill the mall.

of the area's Chamber of Commerce, closed the street and converted it into the "Shinjang Shopping Mall," an attractive tree-lined promenade filled with comfortable wood and steel benches along its length. The pedestrian-only mall is the second-largest entertainment and shopping district for U.S. military in South Korea.[47] The well-maintained brick paving extends right to the bottom of glass storefronts that are only interrupted by a few side streets extending into the rest of the town. With approximately one bar every twenty-six feet, the astounding density of bars would put any college town in the United States to shame.

In the same area, twenty-one hotels have rooms that patrons can rent by the hour or by the month. Under the watchful eyes of the military police, on one short block, soldiers can buy a Big Mac at McDonalds or a Whopper at Burger King, grab an ice-cream cone at Baskin-Robbins or a Budweiser at 7–11, and play pool at the Club Eagle or meet their dream "date" at the Hustler Club. On the ground floor, fast-food joints compete with costume jewelry stores and luggage shops for the prime space.

Above and below are the nightclubs. The basements are where the most action is, with scantily clad dancers working the tables trying to sell drinks or a ticket for a "short time," which is a brief coupling in a

Figure 3.2. The curfew sign outside the main gate of Osan Air Base tells soldiers where they can go and when they need to be back. When curfew arrives, the line of soldiers waiting to get through security and return to base can be a block long.

private area of the bar. On the second floors, it is a bit tamer; pool tables and overstuffed sofas ring more dance floors, but the working women usually remain below. Steep, narrow staircases extend to the third and fourth floors (the average height along the street is 3.5 floors) where the cramped apartments for the dancers and bartenders vie for light and air. If the dancers make it out of the basement, they usually lean out the open casement windows of the second floors, waving down passersby and inviting them in for a "good time." The facades contrast transparency and uncertainty that keeps one guessing. Some consumables are on full display but others hide in the dark basements of desire. The layout of these narrow buildings inscribes capitalism's social divisions on the landscape.

Welcome to A-Town

By one count in South Korea alone, there are 180 "camptowns" around U.S. military bases.[48] About three miles east of Kunsan Air Base in southwest South Korea is a little patch of land officially called America Town, but known locally as "A-Town," "Silvertown," or "the Ville." With its neon signs inviting patrons into places like the Crystal Drinking Club, the Golden Butterfly, the Loading Zone, and the Club 69, A-Town is a prime attraction for many soldiers stationed at the nearby base. A flimsy metal sign welcoming customers to its bars and backrooms spans the main gate (Figure 3.3). Here, unfortunately, America is synonymous with a red-light district.

A-Town is a mix of bars, nightclubs, cafes, shops, and homes, set well back from the main highway and surrounded by rice paddies. Several shops and small apartments hide the bars from the highway. This works well to conceal both the soldiers mingling on the streets (there are no sidewalks) and the bright neon lights of the bar signs. The gateway to the five-acre compound opens onto a parking lot for a little strip mall that would fit right in outside a base in the United States—the first hint that this is not completely South Korea. Two narrow streets pass by small homes built for the women working the bars and lead into the heart of A-Town, with its ten restaurants and fourteen bars. With very few exceptions, the buildings at A-Town are one story—another sign that this is not actually Korea, since most of the buildings around the area have more than one story. A concrete and chain-link fence surrounds the entire site, nicely containing and controlling the actions of

Figure 3.3. America Town is more than a suburb: near Kunsan Air Base in South Korea it is also an officially sanctioned red-light district set aside for the private use of the U.S. military.

the soldiers and the "juicy girls." The rigid layout of the apartments contrasts sharply with the more organic layout of the village homes just outside the fence.

A-Town is perhaps best known for the dance clubs, where "juicy girls" will dance with patrons throughout the night. "Buy me juicy" is the request, and for $10 to $20, the soldiers can buy the woman a small juice drink and get her undivided attention until it is gone, which may be no more than five or ten minutes. The women get tickets for each glass of juice they buy from the bar and cash them at the end of a "pay period" for a small percentage of the actual sales price. For a little more money, soldiers may be able to buy a private table in a VIP room.

The history of Kunsan Air Base and A-Town is a remarkable study in land use, transportation, economics, and geopolitics. The Imperial Japanese Army first used the area as an airfield between 1938 and 1945. After World War II, the fledgling South Korean government took over the sod airstrip until the North Korea People's Army captured the area in a deadly surprise attack. U.S. forces recaptured the airfield in 1950 and have been using it ever since to support a variety of aircraft.

While the base proper was building up in the 1950s and 1960s, A-Town did not come into existence until 1969. The United States and South Korea supported the location and creation of A-Town for three primary reasons: apprehension over another North Korean attack, lack of control over U.S. soldiers, and fear of venereal disease. In January 1968 the North Korean military captured a U.S. warship—the first time in over 150 years that the Navy lost a ship this way. The USS *Pueblo* was on an intelligence mission off the coast of North Korea when North Korean naval vessels and fighter jets attacked the ship, killed one crewmember, then held the rest of the crew as prisoners for eleven months.[49] After the incident, U.S. military planners and the South Korean government were unsure of what the next attack might entail so they established three-mile exclusionary zones around existing bases in part to limit future development near U.S. military bases. After all, who would want to be close to a base when North Korean missiles came raining down? Of course, for economic reasons, any preexisting development was exempt, so places like Itaewon and Songtan were left alone.

In addition to the exclusionary zone, the ensuing political crisis resulted in a substantial buildup of Kunsan Air Base and brought in many more U.S. soldiers. Many of these soldiers wanted bars and brothels. Before

A-Town's construction, soldiers stationed at Kunsan Air Base patron-
ized the few bars in Kunsan City's red-light district that catered to Americans. If they missed the last bus back to the base they were stuck in the
city, effectively Absent Without Leave (AWOL), which was bad for the
soldier and reflected poorly on the commander. With a red-light district
near the base in an easily monitored area, the U.S. military could better
control its troops. In addition, commanders could easily recall their
soldiers since A-Town had an alarm connected to the base's warning
system.[50]

In an unfortunate imperial parallel, the official rates of sexually transmitted disease among U.S. soldiers in South Korea were as high as those
of the British a century earlier during their time in India. In 1895, when
the British were debating the morality of sponsoring prostitution, the
infection rate was 536 per 1,000 soldiers. In the early 1970s, the inci-
dence of gonorrhea among Army soldiers in Korea was 535.5 per 1,000
soldiers. That same year, active-duty Army personnel stationed in the
United States had an infection rate of just 34 per 1,000.[51] Given that the
U.S. military rotated most of its soldiers out of South Korea on an annual basis, these men were likely bringing the disease back to the United
States at an alarming level.

The influx of soldiers following the USS *Pueblo* incident, the need for
control over their after-hours activities, and the desire to reduce the incidents of sexually transmitted diseases all worked together to foster the
creation of A-Town. What was missing was land. Minimal development
existed near the base before the exclusionary zoning policy, just farmland
and a few small villages. Sensing an opportunity to turn low-yield farmland into high-yield real estate, a South Korean general and landowner
developed A-Town in 1969 specifically for this new market.[52] With the
exclusionary zoning, promoters could not build a new camptown adjacent to the base. The next best site was on rolling farmland just beyond
the three-mile limit. While it fell outside the exclusionary zone, the site
was still within the joint patrol zone that gave the U.S. military the right
to exercise police powers on Korean soil off the base. While many scholars have uncovered the connection between sprawl and the action of
the state and finance sectors in capitalist societies, A-Town is a novel
example of sprawl caused in part by the sexual hunger of imperial power.[53]

A-Town prospered through the Cold War and benefited from the
paychecks of the soldiers and the policies of the South Korean govern-

ment. When the Cold War ended in 1989, however, commercial establishments in A-Town started seeing a decline in revenue as Kunsan Air
Base slowly started to contract. While the United States assigned fewer
soldiers to the base, the military assigned those soldiers who remained
to new dormitories built on the base. Before this, A-Town had small
apartments that soldiers and their rented girlfriends lived in for the
duration of a typical tour. When the military required the soldiers to live
on-base, many of the buildings were torn down and the owners attempted to upgrade the appearance of A-Town: they paved over dirt
streets and covered open "binjo" ditches that served as sewer lines.[54]

Following the September 11, 2001, attacks, three major changes occurred
at Kunsan Air Base. First, ostensibly for security purposes, the base
leadership instituted a policy that placed off-limits most commercial
establishments outside the base, except for A-Town.[55] The U.S. military
also justified confining troops to A-Town on fire-safety grounds. While
the United States could monitor the buildings in A-Town and place off-
limits bars that looked dangerous, they did not have the same authority
in the city of Kunsan. This justification was especially relevant following
two tragic incidents in Kunsan City. In September 2000 five women
working as prostitutes in Kunsan's red-light district died because of a
fire in their apartment. Then in 2002, fourteen more women burned to
death in their cramped apartments.

The second change occurred when the United States and South Korea
decided to expand the base, which resulted in a major expansion in
planned construction (Figure 3.4). South Korean taxpayers funded almost $200 million.

Finally, the security presence was enhanced at camptowns and red-
light districts in Japan and Korea. Oftentimes, the military did this at
the request of local bar owners—not as a way to protect the areas from
al Qaeda but as a way to control the behavior of the soldiers.[56] To help
in this effort at A-Town, the Town Patrol mapped the area's buildings
and tracked the uses of every building through a numbered and color-
coded system (Figure 3.5). In addition to mapping the area, the Town
Patrol also occupied a small building as a security command post. From
the tallest two-level building in the area, they could have the best van-
tage point from which to monitor the activities at A-Town. Like Jeremy
Bentham's eighteenth-century panopticon, where a single eye of authority could watch over an entire prison, to see without being seen, the

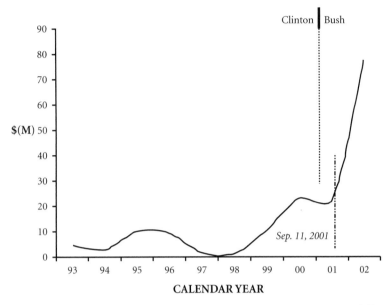

Figure 3.4. Construction at Kunsan Air Base. Numbers are in constant 2002 dollars.

Town Patrol's location gave them the ability to exercise unseen power. For Bentham, a substantial advantage of the panopticon was that it could supervise without staff. Prisoners could never know if the staff was watching them; their own doubt enforced the discipline.[57]

In A-Town, the "inmates" are women working as prostitutes. Many of these women entered into the business from Russia and Thailand because of a liberal visa program that allows "entertainers" into the country to fill the void created by a lack of willing South Korean women. According to one club owner and president of the Korean Special Tourism Association, a trade organization for clubs near the U.S. bases, "The Korean girls didn't want to work here anymore. The GIs aren't rich. The girls could get better tips working in clubs for Korean customers."[58]

At A-Town, the Town Patrols became a way to extend the disciplinary capacity of the U.S. military deep into the South Korean landscape. However, the very fact that a village surrounds A-Town reminded the military leadership at the base that soldiers there were vulnerable. The changing threat level kept A-Town on edge. Sometimes the base commander would place A-Town off-limits if he felt concerned about terrorist attacks. Other times, he would establish various curfews. The inconsistent operating schedule even brought a halt to the dueling public

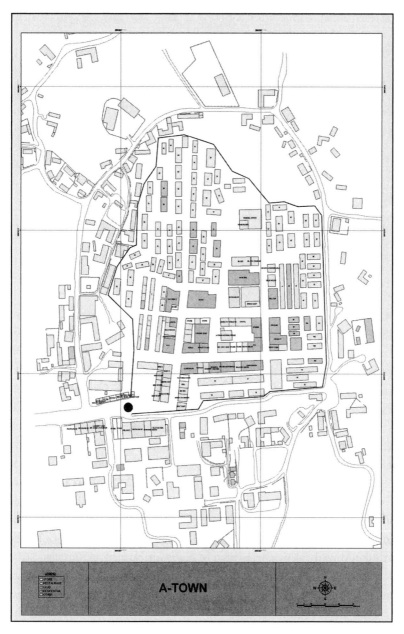

Figure 3.5. A-Town, with its small apartments, bars, and restaurants, is in the center, surrounded by a security fence. The circle at lower left marks A-Town's entry. Small homes and a few shops surround the camptown. Source: U.S. Air Force.

and private transportation systems serving the base and A-Town. In 2002 the city-operated bus service shut down and shortly afterwards a private bus service went out of business.[59] Now, for most soldiers, local taxis are the only way to get to A-Town since the U.S. military does not allow them to own private vehicles. As a result, a strange taxicab shuffle happens every night at the air base's main gate. Drunken soldiers must stumble out of the cabs that operate off-base, walk through the gate with their ID cards visible, and then catch another cab authorized by the U.S. military to drive on-base. Cab drivers eagerly line up on both sides of the gate waiting for their next fare; it will not be a long wait especially on the weekends.

The men who frequent the back rooms of A-Town get their thrills out of denigrating and using women as objects. The men who run the base are able to maintain some control over where their soldiers are and with whom they are consorting. The men who own the bars and land benefit from a steady income stream. But, like the women working as prostitutes in India (or anywhere), the women in A-Town are at the bottom of the social ladder. The sociospatial parallels between A-Town and cantonment chaklas are striking. Granted, A-Town is not on the base proper, but like the chaklas, it is in a location somewhat isolated from local men and easily controlled by the government. The location reinforces imperial prerogatives of control, access, and segregation. At A-Town, through 2001, the women had regular medical inspections, received identification cards, and worked according to the rhythms of the military. The military patrolled the narrow streets, watched for trouble, and, in a new tactic for imperial power, provided condoms if needed.[60] The money the women earn barely pays off their bills, and the United States does not even track their rate of disease; the official concern only relates to the health of the men. How many women the British in India and the Americans in Korea infected is a political and personal mystery. For imperial powers, mandatory examinations, segregated housing, and heavily patrolled pleasure playgrounds reserved for their exclusive use are the rule, not the exception.

In my four site visits to A-Town in 2002 and 2003, South Korean police officers never appeared. United States military police, though, were all over the place, keeping a careful watch over the rambunctious behavior of U.S. soldiers. In an understatement that discounts the real problems with places like A-Town, the man in charge of the A-Town Town Patrol

Figure 3.6. Homes in A-Town for the "juicy girls."

in the late 1990s, TSgt Gregg Wooten, reminded soldiers, "Whether you realize it or not, if you are an American in A-Town or Kunsan City, you are a reflection of the American people. What you do is remembered by the local people and, over time, dictates how all of us are treated and welcomed."[61] What escaped him was the fact that the mere presence of soldiers in A-Town reflects poorly on the U.S. military. Rules that ban cutoff shorts and open containers are trivial when compared to the practice of supporting a spatially segregated, heavily surveiled red-light district. Even in the twenty-first century, a boys-will-be-boys attitude is pervasive.

"A-town is popular because it's loaded with bars and dancers," according to Dan Edwards, a retired Air Force officer.

I was stationed at Kunsan in 1992 and 1993 and we had "squadron runs" where folks would go from bar to bar—some bars play different music—county, rock, disco, whatever so you could try it all out. The difference between Kunsan and other bases like Osan [south of Seoul] is that the Osan bar district is right outside the gate. At Kunsan, we had to take the bus, which was still in service, for 34 cents, to get to A-Town. That buffer had the effect of limiting and confining prostitution. A-Town sat like an island in the middle of a rice field.[62]

Figure 3.7. Except for neon bar signs, A-Town's "main street" is a dimly lit pedestrian-only zone that fills to capacity on weekends.

Like the base it supports, the analogy to an island is quite appropriate. Americans moved from one isolated encampment to another, from a place of production to a place of consumption. And like ferry boats, the government-run bus kept the flow going. Some passengers, though, had different motivations for their journeys to A-Town. According to Capt. James Wolfe, a social worker and former director of the Life Skills Center at Kunsan, A-Town attracts a specific type of soldier. "People who go to A-Town are typically shy, lacking social skills and they go there and feel an overwhelming sense of acceptance. Several have been married recently—one to a Russian woman."[63] It is a strange sign of this interconnected world that an American soldier can find a Russian wife on Korean soil. Sociopolitical forces at work in these three countries—countries that were not long ago engaged in various types of warfare with each other—now push and pull their men and women into each other's arms.

There is yet another perspective on A-Town. Captain Anne Wirth, an officer stationed at Kunsan who spent time at A-Town as part of an Air Force security patrol, presents a different picture:

The Security Forces' sole job is to patrol A-Town. I augmented them once and I wandered through the bars to make sure there were no altercations. If people were too drunk, we would escort them out and send them home. The juicy girls are just doing a job—you can see it on their faces. Girls had a juice quota of around $200 and that was their ticket. You can buy a ticket and they'll talk to you until you leave. She's not obligated to anything. You get a companion.[64]

Captain Wirth is correct in calling it a job, but she was unwilling to admit that prostitution still flourished. For the juicy girls, working at A-Town is an economic necessity, but bar owners enticed many of these women into the job with misleading and incomplete ads, and, like Lana, they must now work off their bills like an indentured servant. One soldier confessed to me that he felt "bad going there but I just want to hang out with my buddies but we were always getting bothered by Juicies and then I feel bad saying no."[65] Now that is an interesting twist. The man feels pressured by the women to buy drinks and possibly buy a "date." According to one observer, the sale of juice and even sex is secondary. The real goal may be to sell vast quantities of beer, and the juicy girls are the draw. On a weekend night, for example, the diminutive Stereo Club in A-Town might sell 400 bottles of beer, making a decent profit.[66] Since most of the soldiers cannot drive, they need not worry about citations for driving under the influence of alcohol (which can end a career in the military). Hence, few limits exist to the amount of alcohol that they can consume—drink up, then get ready for the taxi-cab shuffle.

Imperial Agents behind the Bar

The beneficiaries of camptowns are clearly men, but not just American men, whether shy or not. The bar owners benefit, too, and they are mostly men as well. They get the tax breaks, they get the profits, and they get the power. In South Korea, most of them belong to an association that lobbies for even more benefits. The A-Town Bar Owners Association, for example, "runs A-Town and they pay very little tax so they can sell a drink for $1.50 versus $5 in Kunsan City," according to Kim Yong-si, a sixty-one-year old Korean man and owner of a convenience store in Pyeongtaek.[67] The bar owners are also adept at public lobbying to get their way; in 2003, they joined other base supporters and held the first pro-U.S. rally ever held at Kunsan Air Base.[68] At Osan Air Base, 200 of the 500 bar owners and merchants in Songtan belong to a "special strike force" formed to counter anti-American protests outside the base.[69] By taking advantage of South Korea's Congregation and Demonstration Law, which forbids multiple groups from demonstrating in the same area, the merchants can block prime sites. When they hear about a planned protest, they "strike" first by getting their own permit to rally outside the main gate, thus depriving the anti-American protestors of their preferred site. This battle over land, even for its temporary occupancy, shows how resistance reveals different forms of power.[70] The merchants have a clear financial stake in the profitable existence of camptowns and will exercise whatever forms of power they need to maintain those benefits. At one point, however, the leader of one of the anti-military groups questioned the legality of the strike force. "Stopping anti-American protesters wouldn't be democratic," said Lee So-hui.

> If the rally is illegal, and if the rally should be stopped for some reason, it should be done by South Korean policemen, not by those people. . . . For them, it is [a] pretty natural reaction. It may be a matter of life and death as . . . most customers are coming from a U.S. base. They probably have mixed feelings toward U.S. troops. Even if they don't like them, they have to live with them to survive.[71]

The economic impact of losing the bases would be severe for them. Hence, they mount a stiff resistance against protests that may increase the chances of U.S. withdrawal. Otherwise, the price to pay would be their livelihoods. One example may suffice. At Osan, after September 11, the military went into a lockdown and kept everyone on-base for a month. The Songtan merchants lost an estimated $40,000 per day as a result. "We're businessmen," Casey Lee said. As the chair of the Songtan Chamber of Commerce, he knows the economic value of the U.S. military. "If there are protest demonstrations," he continued, ". . . the base gates are closed and we lose business. So, we keep protesters away."[72] These clashes over space highlight the contested nature of the U.S. presence in South Korea.

In addition to keeping other Koreans from protesting the presence of the U.S. military, the bar owners also keep other Koreans from mixing with the soldiers in bars around U.S. bases. Most bar owners work hard to keep their bars segregated with the help of conspicuous signs that read: "Korea Special Tourist Association: This facility is for foreigners, tourists, and U.S. soldiers stationed in Korea only." When citizens of a nation cannot access facilities on their own land, the idea of sovereignty comes into question. Friends and allies are looking out for more than the national security of the Korean peninsula. They are also looking out for their own pocketbooks and their own sexual desires.

The publicized experiences of women like Lana, which amount to human trafficking, have led to widespread calls for change. But the U.S. military defers to other government agencies when it comes to addressing the problem. A June 2002 State Department report found that trafficking in Korea is widespread and Korea is both a source of and destination for trafficked women.[73] "Does trafficking exist in Korea?" asked Maj. Gen. James Soligan, a former U.S. Forces Korea deputy chief of staff. "The State Department says so," was his curt answer to his own question. He claimed official policies restrict his actions—U.S. jurisdiction applies only to military members and questioning club workers would violate Korean sovereignty.[74] Thus, on the dance floor of one bar the rules of two countries apply.

While the United States remains in South Korea to defend its democracy, the women working as prostitutes around America's outposts are stuck in mini-totalitarian regimes that isolate them in "entertainment zones" and lock them in their rooms until the dance floors open. The U.S. military and its local supporters use space as an instrument of subjugation. At A-Town, bar owners hide the women behind fences, walls, and buildings in a borderland that is neither Korean nor American. At Songtan, bar owners relegate the women to the basements, concealed by the glittering display cases on the floors above. However, "out of sight" does not denote "out of mind." Rather, it denotes "out of options."

Spillover's Surprise: The Land-Use Connection

The spillover seeping out of America's outposts is profound. Some in the military call this "the price of freedom." But for the Okinawans shipped to Bolivia or the farmers left with nothing, freedom came with a steep price tag. For 4,000 Okinawan children fathered, then abandoned, by U.S. soldiers, the price is a childhood in orphanages and foster homes.[75] For the families living under the noisy flight paths and the falling parts, for the children who endure the constant "sound of freedom," and for the women coerced into satisfying the desires of the young men "defending" freedom, the homes and schools, and the basements and bars that frame their existence are far from free.

Admittedly, the United States is making some changes. It has changed its policies regarding prostitution and embarked on an educational campaign to make its soldiers aware of the sociocultural and personal impacts of exchanging money for sex. It has modified flight schedules and improved the reliability of its aircraft. It has even reduced the number of soldiers who can drive off its bases to minimize traffic accidents. However, apart from offering to give back largely rural land and vulnerable bases near the South Korean DMZ, the United States has done little to curb its appetite for valuable land. On the contrary, it has maintained planning policies and implemented new regulations that only drive up the demand for land around many of its outposts.

Can I offer some profound insight into the problems of spillover and their resolution? No. Given the spillover that results from the American presence, one could easily misread the concerns of those living with imperial "protectors." Moreover, given the scholarly focus on prostitution and all its ills, it would be justifiable to place this at the top of the list in terms of negative spillover. However, that would be premature. A survey of 1,200 South Koreans living near U.S. military bases tells a very different story—one that goes largely unreported in the United States because it would require new ways of thinking about empire's impact. Americans are more interested in the accounts of crashing planes and women forced to work against their will as prostitutes. In the survey, though, these were not the most pressing concerns. Rather, it was excessive use of land by the U.S. military. Land use, not clamor, crime, contamination, or even camptown prostitution, was the most pressing concern.

The survey, conducted by the Kyonggi Research Institute in the fall of 2001, revealed some startling attitudes. Not surprisingly, 30 percent of the 1,200 residents interviewed said that either they or their family members have suffered due to the presence of American military bases near their homes. They complained of traffic problems, theft, noise pollution, and violence. When asked to describe what they considered pressing concerns regarding U.S. troops, 56 percent pointed to environmental pollution and 62 percent noted crimes and undisciplined activ-

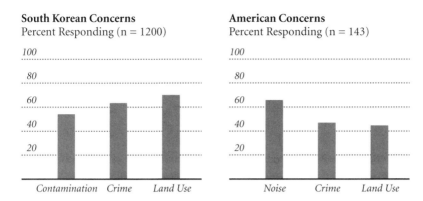

South Korean Concerns
Percent Responding (n = 1200)

American Concerns
Percent Responding (n = 143)

Figure 3.8. Comparing attitudes about spillover. Respondents could express more than one concern. Source: Author's survey, Kyonggi Research Institute.

ity. Most significantly, 68 percent cited the U.S. military's excessive use of Korean land as the burning issue.

In my similar survey of planners and architects working for the U.S. military, the result was quite different. Like the South Korean survey, more than one answer was acceptable. Those that responded had a very different view: 64 percent thought noise from military operations was the most pressing concern, 44 percent thought it was crime, and 43 percent thought it was land use. The results are nearly a mirror image of misunderstanding (Figure 3.8). Americans, used to living with ample land, fail to understand the importance residents of other nations place on land. By assuming noise is the key issue, they can be relieved of worrying about land use. They can then continue their confiscations with legal means.

"The real crime of the American bases," according to Linda Johnson, who has studied the situation in Okinawa, "consists of far more than the rapes and other ugly incidents committed by a few servicemen. The real crime is that these bases occupy one-fifth of the island, often polluting it with dangerous chemicals and preventing sensible urban planning."[76] Living under empire's wings means living with an occupying force justified through legal documents signed not among equals but among unequals, where the power disparity was and is profound. It means living with the din of fighter jets roaming the sky. It means living with the crime and contamination that comes with imperial arrogance. It means living with aircraft and their parts falling from the sky. Moreover, for South Koreans and residents of 142 other countries, it means living with a foreign power on their land. Sadly, the U.S. military largely refuses to acknowledge the impact of the spatial spillover resulting from its actions. In the next section, we will uncover how this one-sided attitude takes shape in built form.

PART II
Familiarity on the Frontlines

In the name of the imperial project, space is evaluated and overlain with desire: creating homely landscapes out of alien territories, drawing distant lands into the maps of empire, establishing ordered grids of occupation.

—Jane M. Jacobs, *Edge of Empire*

We bring you home
 —Slogan for the Armed Forces Radio and Television Network, 2004

CHAPTER FOUR

Homeward Bound:
Identity, Consumption, and Place

A few years ago, while sitting in a typical Burger King, with a view of the clogged drive-thru lane on one side and a mostly empty parking lot on the other, I had an enlightening conversation with a young woman. While her two children launched themselves into a big tub filled with colorful plastic balls, I asked her what she most liked about her neighborhood. Without hesitation, she said that the shopping mall, fast-food restaurants, and subdivisions felt like home. But she did not live in Colorado Springs or countless other stateside suburbias. She lived at Kadena Air Base in Japan. Her situation is by no means an exception. With their fast-food franchises, neighborhoods of split-level ranches, and the military equivalent of Wal-Mart, military personnel deployed overseas may not even notice they have left home unless they step outside their base's main gate, which, surprisingly, some never do.

America's outposts are similar to small towns, with offices, homes, shopping centers, schools, parks, fire stations, and industrial areas. Moreover, these outposts, whether controlled by the Air Force, Army, or Navy, look surprisingly alike. Underlying these familiar facades are familiar policies concerning design and construction that apply to outposts worldwide. These policies, in turn, reflect sociocultural norms exported across the globe by designers locked on a blueprint of their version of America. Wherever they go, America's soldiers are bound to arrive at the same familiar vision of "home."

While checking into the brand-new, $26-million hotel on Osan Air Base, Maj. Bernard Lightle said without irony, "It's nice to be back in

America."[1] The inside, with its soaring lobby, glittering tile floors, over-stuffed chairs, and free copies of *USA Today* on the Corian counter, could have passed for an American hotel. The exterior looked quite "American" as well. On one side of the hotel was a porte cochere large enough for two Greyhound buses and on the other side was a lush lawn with room enough for a game of baseball. But the welcome he received was unusual. "The rules," said the military desk clerk, "are no hookers, no parties, no drugs, and no open flames in your room." This was not exactly the Seoul Hilton. These kinds of rules reveal underlying problems—like a neighborhood with signs that say "Drug-Free Zone." Those signs rarely show up in places without drug problems; generally, authorities locate them in areas where drugs *are* a problem. This must have been the case at Osan—soldiers throwing flame-filled parties with free-flowing drugs and hookers brought in via fire escapes.

Despite sociocultural and political environments that are quite different from the context surrounding bases in the United States, these overseas outposts could easily be mistaken for stateside bases. Deployed soldiers are practicing what Ulrich Beck calls "place polygamy."[2] While at their homes overseas, they are paradoxically separated from but tied to their home in America. The U.S. government has dispersed its soldiers across the globe to protect the flows of empire. They are living a diaspora experience and are trying to define themselves by reference to their distant homeland, a common feature of diaspora communities.[3] They have multiple homes, but they are trying to reconcile difference through design. Wherever these soldiers go, they are homeward bound—bound to the same sprawling subdivisions, franchised restaurants, and vacuous shopping malls. In the march of empire, designers bring with them their settlement patterns and architectural styles. For today's empire, this connection to the homeland is fashioned in ways that raise questions about identity, power, culture, and place.

Defining Familiarity: Misawa Air Base, Japan

Fidgety children waited in line for their turn to scale the climbing wall, flail about in the "bounce" house, and zoom around the makeshift skateboard park. Rap music thumped in the background and the overly sweet smell of cotton candy filled the air. Motorcycle lovers paraded by on their polished Harley-Davidsons and spotless firetrucks lined Misawa's

Figure 4.1. The American Day festivities at Misawa Air Base, Japan. (a) A U.S. soldier watches over the events; (b) Japanese guests at the base.

main street. This was the setting for Misawa Air Base's annual American Day Festival, a popular event that brings citizens of Japan and America together in a celebration of cultures. Consumption is the order of the day, which in itself is a statement about American culture. Judging by the numbers, the event was a success. Over the course of the day, hundreds of people filled the parking lot on the American side and the blockaded streets on the Japanese side to get a taste of both countries.

Keeping a careful watch on the event were sharply dressed U.S. soldiers armed with their Mag lights and 9-mm pistols. A large stage covered an edge of the one-acre asphalt parking lot and around the perimeter were American flags and booths representing most of the states—Idaho was busy making French fries, Washington State was selling fried apples, and Pennsylvania doled out sugar-coated funnel cakes for $1 (the most popular food of the day). At each booth was a poster listing the historical details of the state: when the United States admitted it to statehood, what its motto is, and how many residents it has.

Americans were free to roam around, but Japanese visitors passed through the "American Day Immigration Gate and Passport Checkpoint" where they received a free "U.S. Passport" and a Statue of Liberty image stamped on their hands. One excited Japanese boy asked for two stamps and the "immigration agent" happily complied. The little red passports had a map of the festivities and more details on each state. It was a fun day for everyone.

Behind the "immigration gate," on the Japanese side, the party took on a more hybrid appearance. Japanese banners appeared between American flags. The dining options became less American, with sushi supplementing fried foods. While the advertised purpose of the event was to enhance understanding of each country's "culture," it also seems that Americans were creating an event about America to feel more American. The local residents eagerly joined in to learn more about America and sample its wide array of unhealthful foods.

American Day is just one of many festivals held on and around U.S. outposts. In Japan, Kadena's Americafest has drawn crowds of over 200,000 for an air show, American entertainment, and abundant food.[4] "Americafest is designed to build friendships between the people of Okinawa and the Americans," said Masao Doi, a Kadena representative. "You're going to find a lot of people from the mainland coming down just for the festival and to see Okinawa. American culture and American aircraft are very attractive to a wide range of people."[5] However, in 2004, following a nearby accident, the aircraft were not so popular. Mayors of the three towns surrounding Kadena Air Base requested that the Air Force's Thunderbirds not participate in the September 2004 air show, the first one scheduled since the September 11, 2001, attacks. Normally a big draw, the mayors thought the aerial acrobatics by the team of F-16s would be inappropriate following a Marine helicopter crash near the base on August 13, 2004. The Air Force complied and canceled the air portion of the festival. Instead of performing at Kadena in September 2004, the Thunderbirds made an appearance at Osan's Air Power Days festival in South Korea that same month. The military allowed thousands of Koreans on the base for the event.[6] Empire spells it out: "We own the air. And if we do not show it here, we will show it there."[7]

These popular events open up space normally closed to local residents and provide a glimpse into the American military's way of life. In 2003 Kunsan Air Base officials held an open house and festival to give South Koreans a closer look at the mission in hopes this opportunity would help make up for noise complaints. One visitor, Shin Dong-ho, a sixty-year-old angler from a nearby village who has filed noise complaints in the past claiming the jet noise frightened his children and shook his home, said, "It was my first time in my whole life visiting the Air Force Base. As a citizen of South Korea, I felt that we should know what they all do to defend this country, and their training must be inevitable in some sense. We might have to put up with their noises to a certain extent." A local farmer, Paik Jung-tu, added, "It was a pretty impressive experience. I didn't have any good feelings toward the air base before, but I feel like I have some kind of bond with them now." Kunsan Air Base is home to the USAF's Eighth Fighter Wing, which has averaged forty flying hours a day in the base's F-16s since 1981. The public-relations benefit of the event seemed to be working. Hosting an open house is a small price to pay for unfettered access to another nation's airspace.[8]

While many of these festivals make for good public relations, none of them do as thorough a job as the one at Misawa in highlighting cultural traditions of each nation in a 1,200-foot stretch of asphalt. The fact that America's public space for the event is a parking lot and Japan's is a street reveals more about each culture than the kinds of food sold. American Day joins a parking fest with a street fair in an entertaining display of identities. With little usable public space on the base, the best venue is in fact one of the hundreds of parking lots. Automobiles and their parking stalls dominate the landscape. Without even thinking about it, Americans have given their Japanese visitors a glimpse into American life that goes beyond popcorn and reveals the spatial priorities for a nation literally driven to consume.

Mapping Familiarity

Misawa also serves as a representative example of how the U.S. military has built a familiar, suburban setting in an unfamiliar land. Architects and planners use both settlement morphology and building typology to make "familiar" settings. Densities, setbacks, lot coverages, floor area ratios, average heights, and building footprints are all ingredients. Figure-ground drawings map these attributes and help in the analysis of urban form. These drawings, where built form is solid black and everything else is white, reveal the morphological structure of development and tell a story as convincing as the one revealed by the helicopter photo presented in the introduction.

The first example of a figure-ground drawing is for a portion of Misawa Air Base and Misawa City (Figure 4.2). By seeing just the relationships among buildings, the disparity between U.S. and Japanese settlement

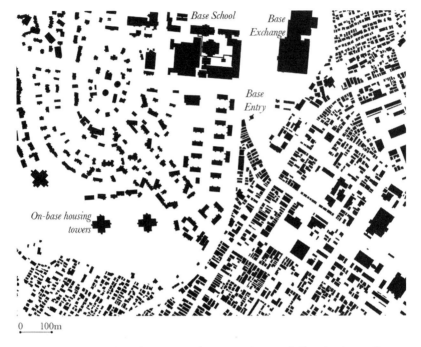

Figure 4.2. Ground plan of a portion of Misawa Air Base *(left)* and Misawa City *(right)* in northern Japan. The compact development patterns of the local area surround the low-density base and its widely spaced buildings. From author's fieldwork, 2003–4.

patterns becomes clear. There is really no need to draw the base's perimeter fence since the buildings do it quite nicely. The base's buildings (mostly in the center left and upper left of the drawing) are large and spread out; the city's buildings are smaller and more compact. The large black buildings near the top center of the image are the two-story base school *(left)* and the one-story base exchange or shopping center *(right)*. They have footprints five times larger than the largest building in Misawa City. The three cross-shaped buildings near the lower left are ten-story apartment towers on the base (approximately 95 feet tall). Most of the other buildings on the base side of the plan are two-story single-family homes and some two-story townhomes. The larger rectangles on the city's side, near the lower-right corner of the image, represent the footprints of commercial buildings. Other buildings are either two- and three-story homes or mixed-use buildings with retail shops on the ground and residences above.

Category	Base	City
Average building height (stories)	2	3
Residential density (dwelling units per acre)	5	15
Lot coverage (percent)	20	80
Floor Area Ratio	0.4	2.5
Parking (per dwelling unit)	2.0	0.8

Figure 4.3. Comparative urban form, Misawa, Japan. From author's fieldwork, 2003–4.

A few measures suffice to quantify the spatial difference (Figure 4.3). The floor area ratio is perhaps the most important measure in terms of density and reveals that Misawa City has over six times the floor space on the same ground area than the base. The density is not achieved by high-rise buildings, though, as shown by the average building height, which is just one story more off-base than on-base. Rather, density results from a more compact layout. One more measure that is important is parking. On-base, large parking lots line the streets, with two parking spaces per residence. Off-base, parking is behind or to the side of most buildings, with less than one space per residence. The sprawling base demands automobile use to get around and drivers, in turn, demand readily available parking lots.

Taken together, the image and the numerical indicators show a clear difference between development on and off the base. The morphology on the base is not very different from many suburbs and military bases in the United States, where densities are low, parking counts are high, and buildings are objects surrounded by asphalt and grass. In terms of built form, this defines "familiarity." These are "familiar"-looking places to the men and women of the armed forces. Moreover, "unfamiliar" urban development patterns surround the base. Densities are relatively high, parking ratios are low, and buildings are elements that give definition to public space (e.g., streets, parks, and plazas). Similar morphology helps ensure spatial familiarity. Exporting suburban morphologies exacerbates the negative effects of spillover and contributes to the excessive use of land so detested by America Town's neighbors.

Familiarity and Its Dilemmas

For American soldiers overseas, their familiar spatial world is a recognizable suburb, which is hardly surprising given the proliferation of low density, auto-oriented suburbs built across the United States. Over half of America lives in the suburbs.[9] Americans have a clear tendency to change the landscape into familiar forms despite differences in ecology, geology, and climate. In the United States and overseas, planners at military bases have wholeheartedly adopted the suburban ethos, with its focus on conformity and consumption. Hence, suburban morphology can help make the unfamiliar terrain of a foreign land familiar. Americans mold the environment to meet their preconceptions and shape their futures. Following this pattern, American military members overseas, who have left behind their existing suburban settlements, recreate them wherever they go. This is unsurprising since people are partial to areas that resemble places from which they came.[10]

Similarly, Amos Rapoport argues that familiar landscapes are desirable largely because they are supportive and provide symbols of identity. Rapoport's concept of "cultural landscapes" is relevant here. Landscapes, which encompass the built and natural environments, respond to cultural values and express societal rules governing spatial priorities and development practices.[11] If culture can be defined in part as the evolving and shared beliefs, attitudes, and practices of a group, then a form of American culture that travels with U.S. soldiers around the globe is a suburban pattern of development characterized by low net densities, isolated buildings, and auto dependency.

In addition to providing symbols of identity, familiar environments result from social values that privilege control. The U.S. soldiers and civilians working overseas produce their conception of an American culture, with a desire for consumption, certainty, and control.[12] American soldiers overseas live with demanding appetites. They may hunger for emotional, physical, or sexual fulfillment. Their garages are filled not so much with cars but with the unsightly leftovers of consumption, the stuff that keeps the American economy growing. This appetite calls for consumption of things and, for American capitalism, this leads to a process that demands big-box retail stores, isolated land uses, and acres of asphalt. The need for certainty requires making the unknown known. Single-family homes, generous lawns, and wide streets are attributes of the suburban "known." This certainty inevitably involves an aggressive application of a familiar spatiality. American soldiers overseas also strive for a sense of being in control, which for them requires dominance over the landscape. Status of Forces Agreements and security treaties legitimate this dominance. By publishing detailed regulations that dictate the shape of the built environment, the U.S. military can certify and control what a place will be and how it will function before the first shovel hits the dirt. What emerges, then, is a product of these forces not the result of a "natural" desire for sprawl.

These forces, the demands of the market, the quest for certainty, and the desire for control can present some dilemmas to soldiers abroad. Major Leslie Triano, an architect working for the Air Force in South Korea, said, "Sometimes it's nice to go back to the United States when you're in the middle of Korea. When you get here you inevitably feel like you're on an American base." Later, after thinking about the idea some more, she added, "Maybe that isn't a great thing, since you're in Korea, I think there is a need to know that somehow. Perhaps that would make going off-base less scary."[13]

This duality, the fact that Americans are at once abroad and at home, manifests itself in nonspatial ways as well. At Osan, many people can take Americana with them if they decide to go off-base. One evening at a popular country-western bar in Songtan, interior designer Elizabeth Brown, looking around the crowded bar and dance floor, observed, "Maybe that cowboy stuff—boots, hats, big belt buckles—makes the guys feel more at home." But this was not your average dance bar back in the United States. With LeAnn Rimes singing "Feels Like Home" blasting from the floor-to-ceiling speakers, young Korean women dressed in the miniest of mini skirts were making the rounds looking for business. It was not like home in the men's bathroom either. In the grungy, little room was a U.S. Town Patrol officer seemingly keeping an eye on the condom machine. Sex in the bathroom was not an option. Moreover, the steel bars on the bathroom's lone window made it impossible for any of the dancers to leave the club secretly. While several scholars have written about hybrid urbanism, soldiers in this bar were experiencing hybrid entertainment.[14]

"I like being immersed in different cultures," said Airman Ron Walker. "I've been here six months and I'm feeling a bit trapped, though. I was surprised at the way it's so American on base. I thought everything would be different but, you know, it's nice to have similar things—it helps you adjust." His friend, Airman Daniel Fallino, added, "There is a sense of you're home but you're not."[15]

In his 300-square-foot office at Kadena Air Base, Mike Kleeman talked about his experience at Kadena. This was his second assignment in Japan.

He was from South Dakota and had been working for several years at Ellsworth Air Force Base near Rapid City. Before his assignment in Japan, he had never worked overseas. As a civilian, he and his family can stay in Japan for a maximum of five years before they are required to return to the United States. After a friend of his volunteered for an assignment at Kadena and returned to South Dakota with some engaging stories, Kleeman and his family decided to make the move. "I pay $2,400 a month for a nice three-bedroom house and my housing allowance is $3,300 so I make a little bit of money on that. It has a side yard, four parking spaces, and is only fifteen minutes from the base [by car]." As one of the 1,909 U.S. civilians working on the base, he was not allowed to live on the base, so finding suitable housing was a priority when he arrived.[16] For the most part, only soldiers and their families can live on a military base. Kleeman had built his home in South Dakota, with a large yard and oversized garage, so he and his family were looking for something similar, and they were happy to find it so close to the base. Kleeman said:

> Coming to the base is like America—except you drive on the wrong side of the road. Both sides are nice though; if you want America come on-base for a taste of home, with Chili's, Dunkin' Donuts—you can really see that coming on-base. The buildings are spread out, green grass and all, but off-base buildings are bumper-to-bumper. I think we bring the American mindset with us.

The similarity is not limited to American bases in Asia. At Aviano Air Base in Italy, Lisa Prater lived with her husband in a private apartment they rented off-base. She explained her thoughts about living off the base in Italy:

> I do find that most U.S. bases have a similar look and feel everywhere I go . . . the base itself is pretty much just like any other base stateside. I personally don't find this important, but apparently, someone does. Perhaps it helps with morale or homesick issues. I'm someone who likes new and different cultures . . . to an extent. I love good old American things and miss them from time to time, but I love being surrounded by the Italian way of life. Living in the community is great, even if a little lonely sometimes. A lot of Americans don't take advantage of this even though they are within walking distance of great cultural experiences. They choose to live only in their own apartment complexes and not get out to see or do things in the local area. We chose to not live in an American community because we wanted as much "experience" as we could get. Only one person on our street speaks English. Our landlord

lives next door to us, but only speaks Italian and Spanish. Americans are everywhere in Aviano and most make an effort to blend in and take full advantage of the culture, but some never will, and for them, the services and support of the base is extremely important and helpful.[17]

Prater's story raises several important issues. While she personally does not think familiarity in the built environment is important, she can see that "someone else does." All it takes is a walk around the sprawling air base to see that. More important, she reinforces the dual desires of many Americans abroad. They like the conveniences of America but want to experience the cultures of their host nation. Prater called this an "experience" and was willing to live "on the economy." One of the biggest hurdles of living off-base seems to be the language barrier, as Prater pointed out. This not only applies to finding housing, but also to the production of space. When planners, architects, and builders speak different languages, the building process becomes even more complicated. For Prater, the language barrier did not stop her from venturing out of the protective enclave that is Aviano Air Base. Even though she liked the little American community at Aviano, she was not ready to go back to the United States. She wanted to move to Germany next.

Back in Japan, Capt. Katie Murrey was actively in search of an "authentic living experience." She could not live in housing on-base since she was single and she did not like the dormitories for officers on-base. When she arrived at Kadena Air Base, she wanted a Japanese-style apartment with tatami mats, shoji doors, and a tile roof. However, the housing agency she was working with could not show her any Japanese units because they did not have any on the "approved list." The policy is quite strict overseas; the military will only reimburse soldiers for their rental costs if they rent a home on the list. To get on the list, homes and apartments must meet a variety of U.S. military standards. Once on the list, local housing agencies rent the homes, which presents a problem for people like Captain Murrey:

> I tried to get an eighth-floor penthouse—it had huge windows over-looking the Pacific Ocean, but the housing office inspected it and required two exits so they would not allow it to be rented to Americans because it only had one exit. Off-base housing must meet our standards and our presence has been driving the market off-base. Appliances are bigger for Americans—many Japanese homes have small ovens but we need space big enough for American refrigerators, washers, and dryers. Wherever

you go off-base you must go to the off-base housing agency and they must certify that the home meets Air Force standards and criteria—one car space, two exits, etc.[18]

The penthouse she wanted off-base overlooked a lovely beach, was an easy walk to the base, and had unlimited ocean views. After dreaming about the penthouse, she ended up in an apartment that could just as easily be in a suburb in America: low ceilings, double-loaded corridors, and windows on one side with a lovely parking-lot view. But it did have two exits. Unfortunately, at least for Captain Murrey, the policies of the U.S. military and the practices of local developers building apartments to U.S. standards guaranteed her a familiar setting.

Dana Willis and her husband waited patiently in the dreary departure lobby of Tokyo's Narita International Airport. Stuff surrounded them—handbags, shopping bags, and bulging backpacks. Beside them were five giant suitcases. It looked like they were moving back to the United States with their booty from Japan, stuff by which to remember the Japan they never really experienced. Their extra luggage charge was going to be steep—the price of consumption no doubt. They lived at Yokota Air Base, an American outpost in Tokyo. Like Yongsan garrison in Seoul, the U.S. military has a major military presence in another Asian capital city. One could wonder what Americans would think of a Japanese or Korean outpost in Washington, D.C. "I don't go off-base much," Willis said. "Living here makes you appreciate what we have back home that's not here." When asked if she looked forward to moving back to the United States, she looked puzzled. "No," she said, "Why would we do that? We're moving to Europe."[19]

These Americans were living inside a dilemma. Their dual desires for the advantages of home and the experience of a foreign place, however, are lost on many of those responsible for planning the bases. The senior South Korean in the planning office of one U.S. base described how he was implementing plans to make the base look "more American," with more green space and more stucco. He said, "I would like American soldiers to feel at home on the base." Similarly, a planner at Kunsan Air Base said that living overseas makes it even more important to provide a "pleasant hometown feel for the folks here from home." For him, "hometown" meant greenspace and convenient shopping. He might be extrapolating from his own desires or from the desire of people like Kelly Portal, a kindergarten teacher at Yongsan garrison. "I don't like Korea," she said.

"I want my space—I'm from South Carolina. We rent an apartment in a high-rise about two miles from Yongsan. I like a yard with room for kids to run around." When asked to describe what she liked about Korea, she said, "We have Domino's, Dunkin' Donuts, and Kentucky Fried Chicken out the door."[20]

For Portal, franchised fast food a few steps away does not ameliorate the discomfort of high-rise living. But the attributes of the high-rise seemed to be the real problem with Korea, not the country itself. The dislike of high-rises has been a common theme on America's outposts. Even at Misawa, with its ten-story "towers," a housing manager on the base said they are the last choice for families.[21] Objections centered on the lack of yards, the long walk from the parking lot to one's front door, and the institutional "feel" of the towers. The base commander, an F-16 pilot with no planning or design background, received so many complaints from people living in the towers that he canceled the planned construction of even more of them and required new construction to be two-level townhomes.[22] At Misawa, the promise of modernism best drawn by Le Corbusier and his "towers in the park" gave way to "towers in the parking lot" (Figure 4.4). Disconnected from the ground and forced to share hallways with neighbors, many of the towers' residents found the experience dreadful. But abandoning the plan to build more towers came with a steep price. The new townhomes, while they gave all residents their own front door facing a large yard, consumed three times the land area per residence than the towers built twenty years earlier did.[23]

Victor Lee is an architect who has worked at military bases in the United States and Okinawa, Japan, and he had a different perspective on similar towers at Okinawa's Kadena Air Base. "Whether you have a yard is not really a big impact. People in our office lived in these towers and the fact that you did not have to live there made a big difference—you could hold out for a house, maybe it took a year and half but you were not forced to live where you did not want to live." The idea of choice is clearly important here but does not reconcile the different attitudes. One difference between Lee's experience and the experience of those interviewed in Misawa concerns family composition. Lee was at Kadena with his wife and no children. In Misawa, family members were unhappy in the towers precisely because of the difficulty in getting their kids to a playground. Parents were naturally unwilling to let their children play unsupervised ten floors down and across a parking lot. At Misawa, their

Figure 4.4. Housing at Misawa Air Base. To meet a growing demand for on-base housing, the United States augmented the unpopular residential towers *(left)* with low-slung townhomes *(right)*. The townhomes consume considerably more land per residence than the older towers.

complaints led to a more familiar suburban setting. When asked to share his thoughts on the concept of familiarity, Lee responded, "The need for it is minimal—if you could pick out what was good about American planning that may be fine. But to carte blanche say Americans need yards when land is not available is not appropriate. We are temporary guests. Why are we out watering and mowing huge lawns in an area with limited water? To me this isn't appropriate."[24]

Lee's attitude mirrored the results of my own survey of architects and planners working for the U.S. military (Figure 4.5). These results present a confusing picture. By an overwhelming margin, these professionals claimed that overseas bases do not need to look like stateside bases. Even more, by almost the same margin, they said that these same bases should reflect the planning and design traditions of the host nation. This is a classic example of "Do as I say, not as I do." Despite their stated desires, these designers continue to build familiar places and regularly ignore the host-nation development patterns.

As demonstrated in the next chapter, rigid policies and inflexible institutional procedures hamper their desires. These policies are largely written in Washington, D.C., by people like Marty Holland, the Air Force's former senior planner. According to Holland, trying to make overseas bases more like the local area would be "like asking Americans to behave like [them]. A base is like a little island of America in a far away land that's making Americans more comfortable in foreign areas." By conflat-

How important is it for overseas bases to look like stateside bases?
Percent responding (n = 127)

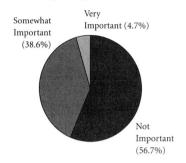

How important is it for oversease bases to reflect the planning and design traditions of the host nation?
Percent responding (n = 128)

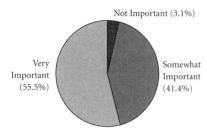

Figure 4.5. American attitudes about familiarity. From author's survey, 2004.

ing comfort with familiarity, the policymakers are more likely projecting their own ideas. "Yes," he added, "we are very land-inefficient compared to the Japanese or Koreans. It's a cultural difference." With that, he stopped commenting on this topic. He played the cultural trump card, which to some is unarguable. He was living in what Alfred Schutz defines as a "taken for granted" reality where experience is "not in need of further analysis."[25]

If the difference, in Holland's world, is cultural, then it is natural and in no need of explication, no need for thinking of these differences as political or ideological. His beliefs are an example of essentializing: attributing difference to a culture as if it were an unalterable fact. While the difference is partly cultural, policymakers have shaped and produced this culture by making assumptions based on habits, and making decisions based on either profit (the shopping malls built by the Army and Air Force Exchange Service), or fear (the military's planning responses to recent attacks on U.S. interests worldwide). The difference is scripted, not an intrinsic characteristic.

Inconspicuous Consumption

Outside of festival days, the United States lets few residents of host nations onto its outposts. What goes on inside the fence remains a mystery. This not only conceals the everyday activities of the U.S. military, but it also conceals a culture of consumption. In 1899, social critic Thorstein Veblen coined the term *conspicuous consumption*. Such consumption, for Veblen, visibly marked one's class. For U.S. soldiers overseas, such consumption also helps mark their cultural identity. "The American city," argues David Harvey, "is now designed to stimulate consumption." The result is a material and symbolic landscape of consumption. Like its suburban counterparts in the United States, the preeminent space of consumption on every outpost is the shopping mall. Familiarity extends overseas not only to the morphology of settlements but to the typology of buildings and supports a ravenous shopping culture.[26]

A Shopping Culture

Sociologist Sharon Zukin has asserted that by the end of the twentieth century, "marketing analysts and social critics agreed that the clearest product of modern times was a shopping culture." By 2004, for example, Americans had built double the number of shopping malls as high schools. They had also built over nineteen square feet of retail space per person, twice as much as any other country in the world.[27] This culture of consumption, stoked by an increasingly profit-driven mentality, drives development patterns at home and on outposts overseas while overriding both local planning concerns and the stated desires of many planners and architects working for the U.S. military.

Franchised shopping is the norm on America's outposts and the biggest franchise is the Army and Air Force Exchange Service (AAFES), which dictates development patterns on every outpost. Established in 1895, AAFES exists to meet the purchasing needs of 11.5 million "authorized" customers at military installations worldwide. They build shopping malls, called base or post exchanges (BX on an Air Force base or PX on an Army post) that are the military equivalent of Wal-Mart. They usually add to this big-box morphology a food court, often called "Main Street USA," and a shopping concourse that is a wide hallway with smaller franchised shops on one or both sides. Shoppers can buy everything from new tires to perfume. Through enabling legislation, the U.S. Congress has mandated that AAFES generate "reasonable earnings" in order to pay back the "customer" in a variety of ways with the profit. AAFES "returns" 67 percent of its net earnings to improve life on military bases, which may fund construction, operation, and maintenance of libraries, swimming pools, hobby shops, car-repair centers, and outdoor sports facilities. In the most recent ten-year period, AAFES returned $2.24 billion to the bases.

By any measure, AAFES gets a very good deal on these bases. First, when they build, they normally dictate where, when, and what is built. If the base does not like the siting or architectural plans, AAFES may threaten to walk away and leave the base without a bigger, newer, more profitable shopping mall. The threats usually work and AAFES usually gets the site it wants. Additionally, they pay no impact fees, are not required to do any traffic studies, and usually expect the bases to give them at no cost a site free of buildings and contamination. Wal-Mart would delight in such freedom. Second, they pay no income taxes. Third, they do not pay for utilities or transportation costs to ship most of the stuff overseas. American taxpayers pay those bills. Fourth, the military does not allow competition on the base. Target, for example, cannot set up a store across the street. Fifth, they know who their customers are and can call their customers' supervisors if there is a problem. Imagine Wal-Mart calling a customer's boss about a bounced check.

With these significant advantages, AAFES's return is one percent greater than Wal-Mart's return. In 2002 AAFES reported a return of 4.7 percent on sales of $7.04 billion. In the same period, Wal-Mart reported a return of 3.7 percent on sales of $218 billion, but also paid 2 percent ($4.5 billion) in taxes and must pay for their land.[28] Where does AAFES spend their money? Much of it goes to replacing its 3,150 retail facilities in more than thirty-five countries with ever bigger boxes—the bigger the box, the more the sales, the higher the return, the greater the fund for building even bigger boxes—a circle of consumption that is rarely broken.

In yet another example of obfuscating the truth through language, the AAFES shopping malls are usually in areas labeled on planning maps as the "Community Center." The actual center is the massive parking lot, around which are the AAFES stores and other retail facilities. The "community" must linger in the privatized space of the mall and its food court, which of course is not new for Americans anywhere and has been the subject of many other studies.[29] The AAFES manager at one outpost presented a gripping example of this landscape of consumption.

> We have a 38,000 square foot sales area and will soon expand 17,000 square feet into the grassy area by the car sales lot. Pizza Hut is coming and Subway is going [to be here] as well. In the wintertime, everyone hangs out at the Community Center—they shop at the commissary,

Figure 4.6. The twenty-acre Kadena Air Base "Community Center."

put groceries in [their] cars, then have a Cinnabon roll, shop at the
Base Exchange, and then have lunch at the food court.[30]

It sounds like quite a Saturday. She is also planning a new 30,000- to
40,000-square-foot gas station and convenience store with eight pumps,
another fast-food franchise, and a car repair area. This would be twice
as large as any gas station in the local area with a population almost ten
times larger than the base.[31] This is a "supersized empire."

At Kadena Air Base, AAFES has the highest grossing BX in the world—
$6 million per month.[32] However, their planners in Dallas have deter-
mined the building needs to be bigger to accommodate more "product."
To expand, they told Capt. Katie Murrey to find them a 350,000-square-
foot site. "The AAFES guy told me he wanted virgin land—one big open
space and he didn't care where it was since he had a captive audience.
He wasn't concerned about locating it in an appropriate area. He just
has a big-box mentality."[33] Their current location is in the Kadena "Community Center," which includes the base exchange, the base grocery store,
and abundant parking. Blank walls and a dearth of sidewalks confront
pedestrians. This base's main shopping area contrasts sharply with the
main shopping street of Okinawa-chi, less than a ten-minute walk away.
On this narrow street, a covered arcade protects pedestrians, traffic-
calming strategies slow cars, and glazed storefronts line the wide sidewalks.

Captain Murrey, an architect educated at the University of Notre Dame,

Figure 4.7. Okinawa-chi's main shopping street, less than one mile from Kadena's community center. A tree-lined street and covered walkway protect pedestrians from inclement weather. Hundreds of Americans frequent the ground-level retail shops every weekend, and some rent the apartments on the floors above.

balked at AAFES's request for more land. She knew the base did not have an extra 350,000 square feet open for construction. She asked if they would consider building two levels on a 200,000-square-foot site. She made the case that Hickam Air Force Base in Hawaii has a two-story shopping center, and Yokota Air Base in Tokyo has a two-story facility. Even Target has built some two-story retail stores in the United States with escalators for shopping carts. However, Target must pay for their land. AAFES gets free land.

After the local AAFES manager called his headquarters in Dallas, he told Captain Murrey that they would not build it if the base only provided a 200,000-square-foot site. Moreover, he said the corporate board would not approve a two-story facility. The Kadena AAFES manager later complained that Captain Murrey really wanted a pedestrian mall. "Look," he said as he pointed across a mostly empty parking lot to his already massive facility, "AAFES doesn't build pedestrian malls, we build boxes."[34] He was clearly telling the truth. Captain Murrey had mentioned the idea of a pedestrian mall to him. She said that many soldiers preferred to shop along Okinawa-chi's tree-lined main street. The multistory, mixed-use buildings clearly define a pedestrian realm and the continuous arcade protects shoppers from the harsh tropical sun and frequent rains. But she knew that convincing AAFES to model even a small part of Okinawa-chi's main street would be an impossible task. She was more concerned about the footprint of the BX and at one story she could not find a large enough site on the base.

Kadena is not an exception when it comes to dealing with the pur-veyors of stuff. Across the military, AAFES engineers demand more land for their bigger stores and oversized parking lots. This gives new mean-ing to the phrase "military-industrial complex." No longer does this just refer to the large corporations making the weapons, but it also refers to the industrial scale of retail consumption and the unyielding agenda of AAFES planners and policymakers. For them, profit-and-loss statements override planning concerns of the "host" base.

These landscapes of consumption have led to an additional form of spillover. Black marketeers have been attracted to all that stuff—shipped over courtesy of the U.S. taxpayer, then bought tax-free on America's outposts, creating what some analysts have labeled the PX economy. South Korean historian Lee Suk-bok sets today's events in a historical context that begins with the arrival of American forces in 1945:

> The effect of the Post Exchange (PX) economy had both positive and negative aspects. PX goods were leaked into Korean society by U.S. soldiers for the purpose of earning money for their entertainment expenses in the early years. Later on, blackmarketeers collaborated with PX employees and mass leakings occurred. These leakings from the PX were referred to as the "PX economy." When the PX economy prevailed, about 60 percent of total sales was believed to flow into Korean society. Since a U.S.-ROK (Republic of Korea) Status of Forces Agreement was concluded in 1966, ROK and U.S. joint efforts have combined to prevent the leaking of PX goods. Nevertheless, the PX economy still hides under-ground, even though it has diminished.[35]

This black-market system is efficient. Authorized customers (military members or their families) buy more than they need, then sell the extra on the black market. Hampering their efforts is the fact that the U.S. military keeps a database of the buying habits of all individuals who shop at all DoD facilities in South Korea. In the checkout lane, the little scanner sends the data to the cash register and to a central database that officials use to run customer profiles to see who bought what, where, and when. In one case, the military accused a family member of buying VCRs in excess of "need." The person bought six in a two-day period. When military police apprehended the suspect, she had already sold three VCRs to Koreans who were not authorized duty-free goods. The PX economy is certainly contributing to what Benjamin Barber calls a "homogenized McWorld—common markets demand a common language and produce common behaviors." In addition to producing criminal and consumptive behaviors, "corporate globalization" also demands specific spatial behaviors.[36] The governments and corporations that make the demands seem to prefer the spaces of suburbia. They are easy to move goods through, support the ever-expanding footprints of increasingly fewer retailers, and breed consumption. And overseas, these super-sized stores must also be oversized as the supplies exceed the needs of honest and qualified shoppers.

An Eating Culture

Joe Bing, a character in *The Ugly American,* described commissaries that "stocked wholesome American food for Americans stationed all over the world." These commissaries were not mere fiction; they existed all over Vietnam during the 1950s and 1960s. In addition, he claimed, "You can buy the same food in Asia that you can in Peoria. Even, say, in Saigon they stock American ice cream, bread, cake, and, well, anything you want. We look out for our people. When you live overseas it's still on the high American standard."[37]

This highly unhealthy American standard is still available tax free at the grocery stores/commissaries on every outpost. Bing could just as easily be a character in a new edition of the book referring to the work of the Defense Commissary Agency (DECA). In addition to AAFES, base planners must accommodate DECA, the owner of commissaries. Headquartered in Fort Lee, Virginia, DECA had sales in 2000 of $5 billion at 284 commissaries around the globe.[38] They sell their products for cost plus a 5 percent surcharge used to build and renovate their stores. In 2000 the surcharge gave them $250 million for construction projects. Even with the surcharge, they claim that customers save 30 percent on their grocery bill, which results in a family of four saving $2,700 a year when compared to shopping at a regular grocery store.[39] This is a bit of an overstatement. By military custom, shoppers tip the baggers, a position usually staffed overseas by local nationals. They work for tips alone, making only $7 to $9 per hour.[40]

Even if savings are less than $2,700, that is only one benefit of having subsidized shopping malls and grocery stores on America's outposts.

According to DECA's deputy director, Patrick Nixon, commissaries serve other functions as well. "People see each other every day. They meet at church, they meet at schools, and they meet at the commissary, too. It serves as a focal point."[41] Soldiers have an unimpressive choice of public spaces—they can meet at the food court or the grocery store. Like AAFES, DECA has money to spend on new facilities. At Kunsan Air Base, South Korea, for instance, the Shinsaegye Construction Company recently built a new $4.56-million commissary that is twice as large as the old store and accommodates 1,000 new items on top of the 5,000 items they stocked previously.[42] At Yokota Air Base, Japan, DECA built a new 37,000-square-foot store in 2001, modeled after upscale supermarkets in the United States, with a deli, café, and pastry shop. The store is twice as large as the old commissary and pleases many customers. Dian Zentner, living at nearby Camp Zama, said, "I've seen how this place has grown . . . and I appreciate it. I remember once I had to wait three months for vinegar to come back in stock and a month for clothing soap."[43] Now the super-sized store can stock at least 400 more items and plenty of soap. Yokota's commissary is in an $84-million, two-story facility shared with the new base exchange. The planners at Dallas approved two levels at Yokota but were not about to do the same at Kadena.

In addition to grocery stores and food courts, some U.S. bases have gone slightly upscale when it comes to dining choices. At Kadena Air Base in Japan, for example, Chili's has built a 6,100-square-foot sit-down restaurant. "It's really bringing a piece of America to the island," said Don Whalen, manager of the Kadena Noncommissioned Officer Club.[44] Like most franchise restaurants, the Chili's on Kadena looks no different from the Chili's at Osan Air Base in South Korea or any Chili's in America. Opening day sales at Kadena in October 2003 set a record for Chili's worldwide.[45] Like familiar places, familiar food is in high demand on America's outposts.

Leisure World

On America's outposts, the culture of consumption has an aggressive spatial appetite. Consumption requires space to produce, transport, store, sell, and use stuff. While the area required for a base exchange and its paving is part of the equation when it comes to determining land use, another component is the space required to use some of the stuff bought at the BX. Basketballs, bowling bags, and golf clubs require adequate ground area. When it comes to the pursuit of leisure on America's outposts, golf courses consume the most land. In 2002 the USAF owned sixty-eight golf courses. The ratio of course to consumer was 1 : 8,842. The United States had 15,827 golf courses in the same period. The ratio was 1 : 18,323. The Air Force, then, has more than double the number of golf courses per capita than the United States as a whole. This gluttony of golf comes with a spatial price since an eighteen-hole golf course consumes approximately 120 acres. But these places are mostly off-limits when it comes to development. Preserving this land is a high priority at most outposts, even if it translates into annexing additional land. The planner at Osan complained that he had a real space problem. However, looking out the window of the base headquarters building toward the gently rolling hills and lavishly landscaped valleys of the "Lakes at Osan Golf Course," one could only wonder what the problem was. The base had plenty of green space. Those in charge of development just did not want to build on it (Figure 4.8).

Americans are not the only ones going out for a round of golf. In 2004, residents of South Korea who have access to the base used the course constantly, despite the fact that South Korean guests must pay up to $65 for a round while U.S. military members pay only $8 to $11

Figure 4.8. The Lakes at Osan Golf Course, a highly profitable golfing paradise.

per round. For the locals, this is still a good deal. If they work on a U.S. outpost, they pay reduced green fees (to $20) if they join the Korean Employee Golf Association. Many local residents do just that since the fees are substantially less than at public golf courses in South Korea and the U.S. courses are easier to get to since they are in the center of many cities.[46] The close-in locations of America's golf courses let South Koreans spend more time golfing and less time driving. The chief of construction at Osan Air Base said, "The biggest thing locals want is access to the golf course."[47] He should know since his office was involved in the realignment of several holes due to construction on the base.

This demand makes the Lakes at Osan the most profitable and most heavily used golf course in the Air Force, bringing in approximately $2 million in profit in 2004.[48] Growth pressures have reshaped but not reduced the number of holes at Osan. Two dormitories built on the course in 2003 led to a realignment of several holes. Since the course is a moneymaker for the base, reducing the number of holes would hurt the funding stream that goes into "Quality of Life Programs" at the base. The profit pays for a variety of activities, from base-wide picnics to after-school programs. The course also draws in distinguished visitors from around the South Korean peninsula and is a location for informal meetings of all kinds. It is a place to play, a profit-center, and a source of pride for the base. At Kunsan Air Base, planners are hoping to fill in part of the Yellow Sea so that they can expand a small nine-hole course to eighteen holes. This will be one of the few courses in the world where one can putt under the protection of Patriot missiles (Figure 4.9).

Farther south, in Taegu, South Korea, the U.S. military recently completed a $4-million renovation of the nine-hole course at Camp Walker. The course supports 100,000 rounds of golf a year and produces $600,000 in annual profits.[49] Like the PX economy, the golf course economy is causing international tension. In 2001 more than a dozen South Korean cities asked for over $15 million in replacement revenue from the national government. They determined that South Koreans were spending $153 million a year at U.S.-controlled golf courses and gambling halls, resulting in lost tax revenue to the municipalities.[50]

Like other aspects of the empire, providing places for the pursuit of leisure is nothing new. Golf courses have replaced polo fields as the land-intensive play fields for the privileged classes. In Britain's India, this

Figure 4.9. Golf at Kunsan Air Base: (a) the Yellow Sea, site of a proposed eighteen-hole golf course on the base; (b) a Patriot missile battery defending empire and its golfers.

willingness to commit resources to recreation was not simply about making soldiers happy. It was also about keeping them healthy. Given the staggeringly high rates of venereal disease among British soldiers, recreation became an alternative to fornication. Similar motivations may be at work today. "This place [Songtan's bar district] is like Disneyland," said Lt. Col. Gerald Hillyard at Osan Air Base. "It's the entertainment center for Osan—troops have too much fun riding the rides—if you're on them too long you're bound to get sick."[51] Equating the bars and the poor women working as prostitutes with "rides" turns them into consumable products, which is the ugly privilege of empire.

In addition to realigning their golf course to make room for construction, Osan has recently built a new fitness center and more baseball fields. If we can consider airfield and industrial areas on a base as spaces for production, making space for consumption takes over half of a typical base's land area (Figure 4.10).

These places also have a political value that can smooth the building process. Victor Lee, who has worked as a planner at Kadena Air Base, describes a story of a construction change order where a golf course was quite helpful:

> We were finishing construction of a new operations building at Kadena with one-foot thick bomb-proof walls but the new commander wanted the building enlarged. We went to a million meetings with the Japanese construction managers before we built it, but then they never want to see a change. To change it shows you screwed up. Do not change it during

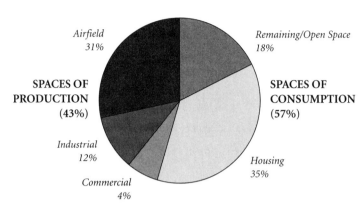

Airfield
31%

Remaining/Open Space
18%

SPACES OF
PRODUCTION
(43%)

SPACES OF
CONSUMPTION
(57%)

Industrial
12%

Commercial
4%

Housing
35%

Figure 4.10. Making room for consumption: land-use patterns at Kadena Air Base.

construction was their motto. But the commander called my boss and wanted his office bigger. My boss called me and I talked with our planner who called the building contractor and asked if he would make the change. He told the planner, "If you hold a golf tournament we will change it." To golf on the base cost $100 for local nationals unless you hold a tournament; then it was about $40. We set up [the] tournament, the wall got moved, and we all went to play golf.[52]

Golf courses, fitness centers, and baseball fields are not the only types of recreation spaces built for the U.S. military and their guests. Again, following the British model of using north Indian towns like Darjeeling and Simla as rest and recreation (R&R) sites, the United States has established major R&R sites in Germany and South Korea, complete with poolside spas and lavish hotels. "Have you seen the lobby?" asked Hildegard Stetler, a receptionist at a private hotel in Garmisch, Germany. "It goes up and up. There is nothing else like it here. Plus, there is a big indoor pool and an outdoor one, too. It is a very nice place."[53] She was referring to the posh new resort and its spacious lobby built in Garmisch for exclusive use by the U.S. military, one of four major resorts operated by the Armed Forces Recreation Center. The resorts, designed to support affordable vacations, are self-supporting and funded by revenues generated internally from operations, not by U.S. taxpayer funds. The military uses the profits to build, renovate, and maintain these resorts.[54] In October 2004, the U.S. military opened the $80 million Edelweiss Lodge and Resort in Garmisch and paid for the project using a thirty-year commercial loan, a first for the military.[55] Apparently, the lender thinks it will be a profitable venture. The 330-room, four-star resort, reserved for the exclusive use of the U.S. military, is set against the dramatic backdrop of the 10,000-foot Zugspitze. Inside, guests can relax by the massive stone fireplace in the lobby or they can enjoy spa treatments, massages, an indoor pool, and meals from several restaurants. Outside, they can play golf at the military's nine-hole Alpine Course, go skiing at Garmisch, home of the 1936 Winter Olympics, or soak in a heated outdoor pool on the resort grounds (Figure 4.11).

Edelweiss replaced the 113-room General Patton Hotel and several smaller recreation areas in Germany. From base exchanges to luxury resorts, the trend is to build bigger buildings requiring more land. Unlike other hotels in the area, which are set closely to the street, Edelweiss is set back several hundred feet from the public street and surrounded by an impressive stone wall. Armed guards control the entry and an American flag welcomes vacationing soldiers and their families. For some nearby hotels, the lodge has even helped their business. The U.S. Army has contracted with several area hotels to accommodate the overflow of soldiers wanting a little R&R in Garmisch.[56]

The demand extends beyond rooms to parking lots as well. On one winter day in 2004, the only SUVs parked within a twenty-minute walk of the American resort were the dozens of Chevy Suburbans and Ford

Figure 4.11. Edelweiss Resort, Garmisch, Germany: (a) lobby; (b) soaking pool. This luxury resort caters to the recreation needs of American soldiers and their families.

Explorers in the Edelweiss parking lot. Americans not only bring their building culture but they also bring their driving culture, which is made easier by the availability of subsidized gasoline for American soldiers—in some cases reducing the cost by more than half. But, for the host-nation civilians working on a sprawling base, gas prices are an important concern. "We don't even think about gas," said Dale Sherman, the housing manager at Aviano Air Base, in Italy. "For me $2 a gallon is not a big deal, but at $5 a gallon it is a big deal and a financial crunch for the locals."[57]

In Seoul, even more SUVs filled in the lots of the Dragon Hill lodge. The military built the 299-room lodge at Yongsan garrison in 1990. Like Edelweiss, it is a luxury resort with restaurants, a gym, an indoor pool, and even an indoor shopping mall called "Market Square." Dragon Hill Lodge is an odd fit with Yongsan garrison. Most buildings on the outpost in central Seoul are one or two stories, but the lodge is ten stories crowned with a hipped roof. The brick exterior stands in sharp contrast against the gray skies of Seoul and is noticeable for miles since there are no buildings anywhere around it blocking the views. Inside, the views into Seoul are only equaled from atop Mt. Namsan. Dragon Hill is one of the few examples of conspicuous consumption, readily visible every day by millions of South Koreans.

In addition to these major resorts, the DoD manages numerous minor recreation centers tucked away in remote parts of foreign countries and reserved for the exclusive use of U.S. soldiers. Many such places are run-down beach resorts that contrast with resort development in the local area. At Camp Darby, near Pisa, Italy, 50,000 military guests visit its resort-like beach during the summer. The outpost even has a marketing director. To fix the decaying resort, in 2002 the military spent $500,000 upgrading the infrastructure.[58] On July 4, Italians in the area are treated to fireworks, a unique type of celebratory spillover.

The military also manages the Okuma resort on Okinawa. To get to the popular but rundown resort, soldiers must first drive through the impressive Japan Airline (JAL) Private Resort, with colorful cottages designed according to the Okinawa Convention and Visitors Bureau in an "American west-coast" style, with low-slung hip roofs, small stoops, and double-hung windows.[59] A narrow, two-lane street, bordered on one side by JAL cottages and shops and the other by an outdoor pool and JAL's excellent beachfront grill, is the only access to Okuma. Soldiers driving by in their second-hand cars do not make an attractive backdrop for guests swimming at JAL's heated pool or dining on prawns and steak at their open-air grill. A chain-link fence divides JAL's beach from Okuma's, effectively keeping Americans out of the JAL resort and Japanese out of the American resort. The former director of Okuma, Captain Rob Hurst, described the attributes of the place:

> If you've been here, you know we offer every water activity you can imagine, like banana boats, water skiing, wake boarding, Jet Skis, paddleboats, water beetles, kayaks, glassbottom boats, diving, and more. If sunning on the beach is what you're all about, Okuma has two of the biggest sandy beaches on Okinawa. You don't have to stay in the water or on the beach, because there is a lot to do on shore, like buggy bikes, tandem bikes, tennis, volleyball, basketball, walking trails, and our new 19 hole mini golf, to name a few things to keep you busy.[60]

This is an impressive collection of leisure options. At Okuma, the U.S. military has plans to upgrade the nine-hole golf course, replace the log cabins, spruce up the campground, and rebuild the cottages to reflect Okinawan architectural traditions. The disparity in size of the clashing resorts (the sixty-nine-unit Okuma resort is 135 acres and the 184-unit JAL resort is only 2.4 acres) attests to the disparity in power between Okinawans and their imperial "guests."[61] The JAL resort supports seventy-six guest rooms per acre and the U.S. resort supports 0.51 guest rooms per acre. Part of the reason Okuma's infrastructure has been in a state of decay was that the Japanese government would not fund construction at the beach resort since they wanted the land back. The United States had other priorities for its money, so Okuma's built environment languished in an international political standoff. Any extra money from Kadena Air Base, which had responsibility for Okuma, went to upgrade the Kadena Marina, another private beach adjacent to the base. Nevertheless, Okuma clearly has much to offer the leisure class. Perhaps the profits from Garmisch will be used to upgrade Okuma's worn-out infrastructure and awkward log cabins. Alternatively, perhaps the government of Japan will buy it out to eliminate the hassle of dealing with soldiers driving through JAL's luxury resort. The government of Japan has expressed interest in getting this prime beachfront property. The United States did offer to give the land back, provided the government of Japan provided a suitable replacement, which, of course, was not likely since Okuma is perhaps the most beautiful and least-used beachfront on Okinawa (Figure 4.12).[62]

Figure 4.12. Okuma Beach Resort, Okinawa, Japan. This spacious resort is reserved for exclusive use by the guardians of empire.

The spatial hunger of the American Empire is a source of tension not only in a remote corner of Japan but also in the heart of the capital city. In the fall of 1999, the governor of Tokyo, Shintaro Ishihara, visited the Tama Hills Recreation Center, another U.S. military playground. Just forty-five minutes from Tokyo, the carefully secluded and serene mountainside resort occupies 300 acres of land with an eighteen-hole golf course, horse and bike trails, a paintball course, and a wide variety of overnight accommodations. After touring the center, Ishihara said, "[They] have this extravagant place in the capital of a nation like Japan, and they use it as a matter of course." He then called for the return of the land to Japan. According to USAF officials, however, the site is already open to Japanese guests, who accounted for 32 percent or 16,886 of the 52,725 visitors to the area in 1998. Ishihara was unmoved by the statistics and added, "They say they're sharing the facility with many Japanese, but I say the Japanese can use all this, and share it with U.S. military personnel."[63] Even accounting for the military's statistics, Ishihara and the Japanese visitors to Tama Hills are in the minority in their country. Very few of the 130 million residents of Japan get to see how the U.S. military consumes their land. The Japanese that do visit America's outposts leave with valid concerns. "Japanese visitors would see Kadena," said Victor Lee, "and see the sprawl versus what they had and they would give us a bad time. They would come over to our house and say, 'Victor-san, you have a very big place and lots of land.' They would then complain about how little space they had in comparison."[64] Here is one way hybridity develops. Perceptions and expectations change based on encounters with "the other."

After his visit to Tama Hills, Governor Ishihara was one of the "complainers." He called the U.S. outposts "a ball and chain" to the development of Tokyo. U.S. forces, he added, "are not fully utilizing the site. It's almost vacant land and is a good example of extravagance."[65] Despite these protests, the United States would not return the land, which in one advertisement in a military publication is described as follows:

> Tama Hills is one of those places that comforts you, calls you, and lets you get away from it all. It's a place where you can golf, ride horseback, camp or soak in a hot tub. All of its 300+ acres exist to let you escape the daily grind. The rolling hills, lush greens, nice rooms and wide-open spaces are all a part of Yokota Services and it can be a part of your life too.[66]

This would be similar to the Japanese bragging about owning San Francisco's 1,013-acre Golden Gate Park for its exclusive use. The land consumed to support the military's leisure worlds is an example of an "extravagant empire." The military's need for wide-open spaces under exclusive control hints at the new imperial model of avoidance. Underpinning this extravagant approach is a specific script for development that reinforces the link between consumption, identity, and place.

Scripting Suburban Identities

On America's outposts, symbols of an American culture include not only flags and uniforms, but also familiar patterns and practices of building.[67] In the construction of these outposts, policymakers and designers use memories of past places and practices to frame their current thinking. They build what they know. Built form, in and of itself, however, does not "have" an identity. A wide street is no more American than it is French. Rather, it is the meaning attached to built form that establishes an identity. What may appear dense to someone from Rapid City, South Dakota, may appear spacious to someone from Manhattan. Since suburban settlement patterns respond to cultural norms about consumption, certainty, and control, Americans abroad who share those norms use similar patterns in their own developments. For these Americans, the suburban ensemble becomes an identifiable cultural landscape, with its specific land use, transportation, and architecture.

The concept of identity has received widespread scholarly consideration. One perspective sees identity defined primarily by difference. For imperial powers, that difference has largely been about racialized constructs.[68] This view has merit, especially when considered within the context of American outposts in Asia where racial differences between the occupiers and the occupied are quite clear. Suburban development, so at odds with adjoining local building practices, could be one more symbol of an American identity used to define difference. It is as if imperial designers are saying to their hosts, "We look, eat, dress, and live differently. We are Americans and you're not." But this does not fully explain the Italian case, discussed in detail in chapter 6, where racial differences between occupied and occupier are now minimal but spatial practices are still quite different. Other markers of identity are at work.

In conceptualizing cultural identity, a key issue concerns the origins of identity. Is identity fixed, based on essential aspects of a culture, or is it fluid, based on continuous representations of a culture? An essentialist view of American identity would argue that there is one fixed identity based on shared attributes like race and ethnicity. Given the multiplicity of ethnicities in a country like America, such a definition would be impossible to defend. Who we are does not depend on essential elements like ethnicity or class, but results from specific practices. Practices are no more an inherent aspect of a group than class. Essentialized definitions that rely on uncovering specific truths, a predetermined, shared history, or common practices, ignore the performative aspects of identity. A nonessentialist view of identity argues that identities form through representations of difference. Stuart Hall has explained at length how cultural identity is a matter of becoming rather than a statement of fact. He claims that identity is marked through differences that are not fixed but that are fluid and under construction.[69] Looking at common aspects of these views of identity may help break the dichotomy. Both views share the idea that cultural identity is a production. For the essentialists, the production is over. For nonessentialists, the production never ends.

The idea of a production is most relevant here.[70] On America's overseas outposts and in its stateside suburbs, identities have evolved in part as a response to the call of marketers for a culture of consumption. More-over, those with political and economic power have vested interests in maintaining a culture based on certainty and control. "If identity is a performance," according to Neil Leach, "then the location of that per-formance matters."[71] The location is the built environment, which, fol-lowing the analogy, can act as a stage set for the performance of identities. For Americans, there is no limit to the number of stages, just as there is no limit to the number of identities. On America's outposts, policymak-ers and planners have chosen to build their set based on one interpreta-tion of an American cultural identity.

A Suburban Production

The script for the production is suburban. Policymakers, planners, and even Hollywood producers use it in their daily practice. The suburban culture, with its focus on consumption and control, has even been the backdrop for numerous thought-provoking movies. In *The Truman Show* (1998), filmed in Seaside, Florida, suburbia (albeit a slightly more compact version) is the stage set for a reality television show in which all the residents except one are actors and the stage is largely an advertise-ment. Truman Burbank, played by Jim Carrey, is the only one unaware of the script. The audience tracks Truman's life and his slow realization that all is not as it appears. The developer planned Seaside as a "new urbanist" town, with higher densities, walkable streets, and a town center with apartments and offices above small shops.[72] The models for Sea-side were the many charming nineteenth-century small towns of the Southeast rather than the relentless strips of condominium towers that now mark much of the Florida coastline. But these older towns also concealed rigid class, race, and gender divisions that go unmentioned in Seaside's promotional material and in the movie. *Pleasantville* (1998) is a film based in a "perfect" 1950s suburb where white-picket fences and perfectly clipped lawns serve as the black-and-white backdrop for per-fectly scripted, entirely safe, flawlessly ordered, and color-free lives. Two teenagers, transported from their 1990s lives to Pleasantville by a TV technician, uncover the fiction of the setting and help shatter suburbia's myth. Their actions slowly reveal a world in color, which offends many of the townsfolk who rally against the "coloreds" in an ill-fated attempt at preserving their segregated suburb. These movies reveal a culture of consumption, certainty, and control that underpins suburban settings and suburban lives. In both films, suburbia was a stage set for dominance: whites over blacks, men over women, rich over poor. On America's outposts, the same equation applies linking conformity and control in a suburban production.

Planners of America's outposts are at work producing their own interpretation of America's suburban culture. At least they are being patriotic: suburbia has an American heritage.[73] Suburbia and its ills have been discussed elsewhere and need not be recounted in detail here. Suffice it to say, America's infatuation with suburban sprawl comes with a steep price. Many scholars argue that sprawl consumes valuable agricultural land, forces automobile use, isolates the young and elderly, pollutes air and water, and increases the cost of infrastructure.[74] What is more relevant for this study, though, is to recognize that America's outposts are simulacrums of suburbia, copies based on a specific script meant to tie the homeland and its territories. Historically, suburbs relied on linkages to a central city. America Towns, however, rely not on a nearby city but on a link to the distant homeland itself as a city.[75]

So, what is the script these military planners are using? In many ways, a script for a performance is like a checklist for a flight. Both define what to do, what to say, and where to go. The military regularly operates on a checklist mentality. Fighter pilots attach checklists to their flightsuits. Military engineers carry laminated checklists in their pockets. Inspection teams walk around with their clipboards and checklists making sure every base conforms to military standards. Planners keep a checklist at the ready as they create General Plans. Checklists ensure certainty through overarching control. In keeping with this checklist mentality, listed below are seven key attributes of a suburban script that policymakers and planners have exported to build America's outposts.

1. *Auto Focused.* Americans living in suburbs primarily get around in their cars. They take only 5 percent of their trips on foot; Europeans and Japanese take up to 50 percent of their trips on foot.[76] Parking lots rather than sidewalks are the priority for planners. And when possible, drive-thrus are the preferred architectural typology. To get around on America's sprawling outposts, most soldiers overseas can have one vehicle shipped at U.S. taxpayer expense.[77] Of course, many of them buy second- or third-hand cars that some soldiers charitably called "junkers" so that their family members can get around while they are at work. Their temporary owners usually pay more attention to the paint jobs than the

mechanical systems, which would fail a stateside emissions test. You can hear these cars coming, and you can certainly smell them going. Using a car to get around is common practice on overseas outposts, as this report shows, but it requires considerable acreage not only for the roads but also for the parking:

> For Americans, "running" errands often involves using a car. But since there are thousands of others with similar ambitions at U.S. military bases across Europe, strapping on some good shoes might be a better choice. Because there's that small matter of trying to find a place to park. "It requires an innovative approach within the land constraints," said Air Force Captain Chaz Williamson of the 100th Civil Engineer Squadron at RAF Mildenhall in England.[78]

Captain Williamson could have been referring to any outpost overseas. The constraints he talks about are on paper and not on the land. On most bases, the land is there, but the policies and practices used by the exporters of a suburban culture dictate inefficient, auto-oriented patterns of use. Auto dependency is, of course, one of the primary features of suburbs worldwide. Douglas Adams perhaps best captures this infatuation with the car in *The Hitchhiker's Guide to the Galaxy*. In the novel, Ford Prefect is a visiting alien who barely saves the main character from death as Vogons (galactic demolition experts) demolish earth to make room for an interstellar bypass. Ford names himself after what he initially considered our planet's dominant life-form—the car.[79]

2. *Abundantly Paved.* "Suburbia," says architect Douglas Kelbaugh, "may be paved with good intentions, but mainly it is paved."[80] Roads and parking lots respond to a tradition of mobility memorialized in songs, novels, and poetry:

> Highway I travel! O public road! Do you say to me, Do not leave me?
> Do you say, Venture not? If you leave me, you are lost?
> Public road! I say back, I am not afraid to leave you . . . yet I love you;
> You express me better than I can express myself[81]

Walt Whitman foreshadows America's century-long infatuation with the open road. This love affair with asphalt, and its deleterious aftermath, is perhaps best captured in the lyrics of Joni Mitchell's 1970 song, "Big Yellow Taxi":

> They took all the trees
> And put them in a tree museum

And they charged the people
A dollar and a half just to see 'em
Don't it always seem to go,
That you don't know what you've got
'Til it's gone
They paved paradise
And put up a parking lot

Americans, whether stateside or overseas, place a high priority on their parking lots even if, as is the case at Kadena Air Base, less than 50 percent of them fill up on a normal weekday. "[Parking] is near and dear to their hearts," according to Robert Graves, a senior leader at an American outpost in Germany.[82] *Stars and Stripes,* an independent newspaper distributed on America's outposts, confirmed the importance of parking when, in 2003, it devoted a 3,365-word article to the subject titled "Parking Problems on Bases across Europe." In my three-year study of articles in the newspaper dealing with the built environment, the next longest article was 1,569 words and the average length of an article was only 780 words. For Americans overseas, parking consumes an inordinate amount of space on the ground and in print. The figure-ground drawing (see Figure 4.13) shows roads and parking in black and demonstrates how that obsession is imprinted on a portion of Kadena Air Base, Japan. In this eighty-six-acre area, 40 percent of the land (34 acres) is paved. Howard Nicchols, the supervisor of Osan's environmental office, said with a grin, "We have one planning rule here, 'thou shalt not build anything without a parking lot.'"[83] The difference in paving between America Towns and their neighbors is striking. Japanese, Koreans, and Italians, for example, own and drive cars but do not let them dominate their landscapes. Cars are tucked into parking courts, screened from view by buildings.

3. *Widely Spaced.* The helicopter photo of Kadena Air Base (Figure I.1) and the figure-ground image of Misawa Air Base (Figure 4.2) both show how widely spaced buildings are on overseas outposts. This applies to commercial as well as residential buildings. One way to measure this is by calculating the number of dwelling units per acre. Typical residential densities in many contemporary American suburbs range from six to eight units per acre.[84] The Air Force is in line with this measure. Its 2004 *Family Housing Guide* specifies residential densities for its bases. In suburban areas, for senior officers, single-family homes occupy three to

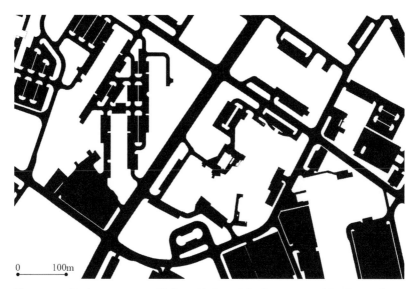

Figure 4.13. Paving patterns at Kadena Air Base. Mostly empty parking lots and copiously wide streets attest to the American fondness for paving.

four units per acre. For junior officers and enlisted soldiers, the density will be four to six units per acre.[85] Filling in the gap is paving and grass, which is typical for suburbs in America. In single-family residential areas on America's outposts, homes also need to be set back from the curb enough to accommodate one or two cars in the driveway. Rear yards on most outposts are anywhere from 50 to 150 feet deep. In other areas, most buildings need to be at least 82 feet from any street or sidewalk, a distance based on fear of terror addressed in more detail in chapter 5. All of this adds up to an environment with widely spaced buildings, which contributes to the need for even more paving to connect these buildings (Figure 4.13).

4. *Extensively Lawned.* Something must fill the increasing gap between buildings and, if it is not paving, it is usually grass. "We have too much grass here," complained Hugh MacBride, a housing manager at Misawa Air Base. "We have 9.6 acres of grass in the dorm area that takes my crew three days to mow."[86] This translates into 440 square feet of lawn per occupant, but it is largely unusable, devoid of benches, sidewalks, or easy access points from buildings. "Our lawns exist to unite us," argues Michael Pollan, "and so across a continent of almost unimaginable geographic variety... we have rolled out a single emerald carpet of lawn."[87] In most cases, however, lawns serve less to unite people than to unite a

Figure 4.14. Kadena Air Base is similar to all other American outposts. Buildings are so widely spaced one would think that the land is free—which it is, since the United States pays no rent to the nations hosting its military forces.

disparate array of buildings. This residential lawnscape can trace its roots back to the early nineteenth century and the work of Andrew Jackson Downing.[88] In Kenneth Jackson's language, they are "crabgrass frontiers" built by and for a capitalist class in and out of government.[89] This unrelenting devotion to grass creates a monoculture that the military maintains with chemicals and watering (Figure 4.15).

5. *Increasingly Franchised.* In suburbs, chain stores proliferate. They provide the certainty that some Americans crave. A Whopper is the same in Italy as it is in South Korea. And the building where it is made is the same as well. You can count on copyrighted consistency.[90] On overseas outposts, the retail experience is also a franchised experience. Burger King, Baskin Robbins, Chili's, and Taco Bell have the franchises to sell food fast. In addition to owning the shopping malls on base, AAFES owns the gas stations, carwashes, and bowling alleys. They also run one of the oddest ironies, "Mainstreet USA," which is essentially a food court inside a strip mall. However, there is never a real street. Even Walt Disney wanted a street at Disneyland. Rather, AAFES's places are usually poorly designed strip malls or food courts with Popeye's Chicken and Biscuits, Robin Hood sandwich shops, and perhaps a Chinese takeout. Not only is the street missing, but good design is missing as well. According to architect and author Craig Whitaker, actual Main Streets were places where communities put forward their best architectural efforts.[91] The military's simulated "Main Streets" are usually in underscaled and inadequately maintained buildings (Figure 4.16).

Figure 4.15. Heavily watered and effectively fertilized grass fills the broad gap between paving and building at Aviano Air Base, Italy.

Like food and shopping, play areas are increasingly franchised overseas. These are not playgrounds or parks. Rather, they are controlled places for supervised, indoor play. Burger King and McDonald's have mastered the playland as parental lure and Burger King has built many playlands on American outposts. "Playlands bring in children, who bring in parents, who bring in money," explains a manufacturer of play equipment.[92] On military bases, parks, plazas, and playgrounds have no funding classification or "category code." Hence getting dedicated money for these public spaces is difficult. "The Air Force has a five-foot mentality," said Ivan Louden. "Anything outside this line is not part of the project. This starts with the development of the 1391 [the official programming document used to get funding for a project] and the idea of the primary facility inside the five-foot line with supporting infrastructure being anything outside the five-foot line."[93] While parks and parking lots both fall outside the line, the funding priority goes to places for cars. At best, there may be recreation centers, with ballfields and a running track, but these are playlands for adults. The military franchises, structures, and controls play. Like any franchise, the military seeks uniformity and control to offer the same spatial experience at its bases worldwide.

Figure 4.16. "Mainstreet USA" at Kunsan Air Base in South Korea—little more than a franchised food court.

6. *Clearly Segregated.* Suburbs are not simply residential enclaves. They include segregated space for all the functions of life: sleeping, working, shopping, and recreating to name just four.[94] Outposts are similar. They must have color-coded land-use plans that segregate compatible land uses like offices and retail shops. Military installations, for example, must usually show the following zones on their land-use maps: airfield, airfield operations, industrial, administrative, family housing, unaccompanied housing (dorms), temporary housing, commercial, medical, recreation, and green space. Oscar Perman said,

> I could take you to any base in the Air Force and show you the gradation of land use—runway, hangars, maintenance shops, storage, administration, community center. Just take a look at any base and you'll see the same land use pattern, it really doesn't change that much. When you look at land use planning it's pretty much fixed.[95]

Perman, a landscape architect by education, was the Air Force's director of installation planning, one of the planners who made land-use planning "fixed." The "category code" of a building automatically sends it to a specific zone. Variances are rarely possible and, if needed, usually require a hearing before the installation commander in a meeting of the Facilities Utilization Board. Do not expect any kind of mixed-use on an outpost, though, as one planner lamented, "there is not an approved color for such a zone."[96] Getting the right color on a map is apparently a difficult exercise. "In 1981 everyone was doing their own thing and Air Staff (senior leadership) was looking at maps and they were not consistent so we all sat down and fought it out," said Marty Holland, the Air Force's former senior planner. "We had one big discussion on what color runways should be—white or gray—some said they should look like pavement—no that's industrial others would argue. We ended up with white."[97]

Color matters not only on paper but also on people as well. In addition to spatial segregation, there is also a form of racial segregation in the military. This is most evident in the distribution of housing. Officers, mostly white and generally well paid, live in one area of an outpost at lower densities. Enlisted soldiers, 23 percent African American, 8 percent Hispanic, and not well paid, live elsewhere at higher densities. The disparity is perhaps greatest in the Air Force where African Americans make up 6.5 percent of the officer corps and 18.6 percent of the enlisted corps. The idea of giving officers better housing is not novel. The British mastered the concept of spatial segregation at its cantonments in India by giving officers large plots of land and housing the rank-and-file soldiers in regimental barracks.[98]

Housing is not the only area where segregation is at work. Officers usually have their own clubs. Senior enlisted soldiers have their own clubs. And junior enlisted soldiers have their own clubs and dining halls. The justification for all of this is to avoid fraternization, which could undermine the military's chain of command. How, if they are good neighbors and share the same club, could a second lieutenant (an officer) order an enlisted soldier, who may be similar in age, to his or her possible death in a security patrol? Of course, they can shop, dine, and bowl in the same place if AAFES owns the franchise.

7. *Haphazardly Ordered.* At Osan Air Base, one officer said, "This base looks haphazard and needs to be reorganized from a human factors standpoint." As a pilot, he was aware that designers base the layout of F-16 cockpits on the physical needs of pilots. Designers measure, weigh, survey, and test pilots to determine optimal cockpit configurations. This ushered in the new field of ergonomic design. The Air Force calls this human factors engineering. However, designers do not plan the built environment that way—the needs of cars and franchises take precedence over people. Looking at base maps, it appears the process employed is more like "train-wreck" planning. Think of the scattering of train cars after a derailing. Nevertheless, there is an underlying order. Every building and road is "planned" in the sense that someone thinks about the siting. Is the site in the right land-use zone? Does it have room for parking and setbacks? If the answer is yes to these two questions, then the

wreck begins. Military planners refer to this as "vacant-lot" planning.[99] If there is an open plot of land, toss a building on it and that is planning. Since there is no desire to frame the public realm with buildings to enhance pedestrian comfort and safety, planners often site buildings at arbitrary angles to the streets. The result is a focus on buildings as objects, which according to architect Dan Solomon, is at the root of modern architecture that favors "the making of *things* as opposed to *places* and . . . disengagement of those things from what is around them."[100] This is yet another manifestation of avoidance where individual buildings avoid engaging with their context.

Suburban morphologies do not happen by accident or by "natural" forces. Planners and architects design them following a specific script or checklist that has many of the above elements. While not all-inclusive, if designers follow this seven-point list, they can build a reasonable reproduction of suburbia overseas.

Hybridized Suburbs

This reproduction, however, is not a mirror of stateside suburbs. On America's outposts, planners intermix multiple models in a process of hybrid suburbanism. At a simplistic level, they combine the sprawling and segregated patterns of suburbs, the social control so prevalent in nineteenth-century company towns, and the fear-driven enclosure of twentieth-century gated communities.[101] Hybridity has many dimensions. One of the valuable lessons from postcolonial scholarship is the recognition of the hybridity of all cultures.[102] Architectural historian Nezar AlSayyad anchors this notion of hybridity to spatial practices in his discussions of hybrid urbanism. Hybridity, he argues, emerges "from a space where elements encounter and transform each other."[103] As I will show in part 3 of this study, this transformation is at work in Italy, South Korea, and Japan. Thus, when considered in spatial terms, hybrid places do not simply combine attributes from multiple sources; rather, they alter the very models they emulate and produce new forms of spatial practice. Hybridity is not new to empire. Earlier imperial powers did not simply transplant their buildings, nor did the "host nation's" settlement patterns remain unchanged. Rather, urban forms merged through a process similar to cross-fertilization, where elements of each led to new but related forms.[104]

On America's outposts, soldiers live outside their "homeland," but they bring with them spatial ideas from their own homes, including experiences from previous assignments around the globe. But the local context is also an influence. As we saw with the development of A-Town in South Korea and even with Captain Murrey's search for housing in Japan, the American presence is changing more than the environments inside the fencelines of imperial outposts. Just outside these outposts, local developers and governments modify their settlement patterns to fit what they perceive to be the needs of empire. Local developers, eager to profit from the housing allowances and incomes of the military, build places they hope will be in demand. They may follow U.S. standards or they may follow local preconceptions. Likewise, inside these outposts, hybridity is at work. For instance, construction standards may follow local precedent due to climatic demands. For example, at Kadena Air Base in Okinawa, the Chili's restaurant was built completely in cast-in-place concrete. This is not the franchise standard. Even the gutters and "awnings," which are normally plastic in the United States, are cast concrete. Typhoons have no respect for plastic. Similarly, architectural compatibility standards may call for local design flourishes. Kadena's base hospital has a partial "Okinawan" clay tile roof and two cast stone shishi dogs—traditional lion-dogs ready to greet the ambulances out front. Bus stops at Kunsan Air Base have elaborate "Korean" roofs. And some "smoking shelters" for the tobacco-worshipping crowd at Misawa Air Base resemble small pagodas. These are, however, veneers of compatibility, a topic addressed in chapter 5.

Jane M. Jacobs argues, "Hybridity is not just a mixing together but a dynamic where the colonized appropriate and transform dominant cultures."[105] This is occurring at Misawa Air Base, Japan. Valerie Jansen, a city planner by training, lived at Misawa Air Base with her husband, Scott Jansen, who was the community planner for the base. She was involved in a few local planning issues in Misawa City. She described one project that, if built, would substantially alter the character of a local shopping street known as White Pole Street.

> The Misawa Chamber of Commerce wanted to create a strip mall and call it American Village—they felt that White Pole Street looks run down and they're losing business—it's [now] a main street for festivals. They wanted a common area to encourage more interaction between the

Japanese and Americans . . . they felt this would expose them to Japanese culture. A lady on base was connected with the Chamber pursuing anyone's opinion—so I submitted my thoughts. I put a plan together that borrowed elements from Japanese architecture but they hated it. What I presented was too Japanese—rooflines, architectural style and layout with parking on the street and in back and buildings on the setback (next to the sidewalk).[106]

Her ideas did not go over very well:

They [the Chamber of Commerce members] wanted something that re-flected American culture. But they're misled in thinking American style design would attract people from the base—if they want little America they could just go to the [base shopping center]. Scott [her husband] met with the government officials who brought in a plan with setback buildings and parking in front—just like a strip mall. The Chamber wants to buy the land but the Japanese government does not have emi-nent domain for this. They view White Pole Street as a dilapidated eyesore.

There are several interesting twists in this story. Here we have an American planner trying to work within the local design language to develop a shopping center for Japanese clients interested in attracting American consumers. The multiple readings of cultures are intriguing. Japanese developers associate strip malls with American culture and they are perfectly willing to demolish their own main street to provide for this culture of consumption. Rather than repair White Pole Street's sidewalks, curbs, and metal arcade, they would prefer to demolish part of it to attract more American consumers. The existing street is a nar-row, one-lane road lined with two- and three-story mixed-use buildings abutting the sidewalk. There are no setbacks. Shops and restaurants are on the ground floor and apartments and offices are above. A metal arcade covers the wide sidewalks on both sides of the street and runs the length of the street. What the developers found attractive on-base were the more open spaces, and they felt that the cramped nature of White Pole Street did not appeal to U.S. consumers. For their model, they used a street on the base with its row of street trees, easily accessible off-street parking lots, and prohibition of on-street parking (Figure 4.17).

It is revealing that Scott Jansen actually met with the Japanese officials. This was partly due to his capacity as the base planner but it was also due to his gender. The Misawa Chamber of Commerce is mostly male, and the developers are mostly male as well.[107] In the end,

Figure 4.17. (a) Covered walkways lined both sides of narrow White Pole Street in Misawa City until Japanese developers decided to make way for an American-style street, replete with a strip mall and even a few street trees. (b) Birch Street on Misawa Air Base was the model local Japanese boosters emulated in their reconstruction plans for White Pole Street.

the developer's spatial reading of American culture deferred to parking requirements. With Valerie Jansen's plan rejected, the Chamber could proceed with their original idea. "It was laid out by an American firm," she said, "with that American flair—big boxes and a big parking lot." As is the case in the United States, real estate development, argues Zukin, "implies the hidden hand of local place-based elites."[108] The developers at Misawa hope to reshape the environment into one more conducive to American consumption and more profitable to Japanese investors.

For Jansen, the encounters revealed confused assumptions and, in her opinion, careless planning. As an empire entangled with its host nation in economic, legal, political, and spatial relationships, the United States does not have a completely free hand as it extends its imperial reach. In many cases, when the host nation has a spatial request, the United States will try to respond. Dan Edwards, a retired Air Force officer who lived at Kunsan Air Base in South Korea in the 1990s, recounts a case study in hybridity at that base.[109] Accountants at Korean Air Lines (KAL) and civic boosters for Kunsan City determined that a new air route into and out of Kunsan would be profitable. National destinations like the resort island of Chejudo and the capital city of Seoul would be big draws. The military traffic would undoubtedly add to the bottom line since the turnover was so high at the base. However, the government and KAL did not want to fund the exorbitant costs associated with building an airport from scratch. Rather, they wanted to use the Air Force's runway and just build a passenger terminal. "The interface was obviously going to be a big issue," said Edwards. "We decided we would need a massive sliding gate built to U.S. criteria to cordon off the airfield from the terminal. Even the taxiway lighting to the terminal would have to meet U.S. criteria." The whole episode was also a matter of politics. "The governor of the prefecture was in a political battle with his opponent and needed to show his constituents something was happening," added Edwards (Figure 4.18).

In the end, the USAF and the South Korean government agreed to the plan. Now, when a KAL flight lands, the hefty steel gate slides out of the way and the planes taxi quickly to the terminal. For departures, once the U.S. military air-traffic controllers give KAL clearance, the gate again moves out of the way and the aircraft proceeds to the runway. In both cases, passengers can get a full view of the sprawling air base, from the flightline to the fitness center. Taking one of these flights reveals an eerie contrast. Planes full of South Koreans, ready for their tropical vacations or business meetings, wait for the gate to slide out of the way. When it does, the planes taxi past rows of neatly aligned F-16s waiting for war. The shared runway has worked well since it was implemented in the late 1990s and may become a model for other nations. For example, in Yamaguchi Prefecture, Japan, local officials have been working to open the runway at Iwakuni Marine Corps Air Station for commercial use. In their negotiations, they cited examples of other airfields as a precedent. Officials from the prefecture have estimated that the shared airfield will add about $74 million (8 billion yen) to the local economy by 2010.[110]

Bound to Sprawl

At America's outposts, built form joins social practice in the production and performance of identity. Base planners have chosen a simulacrum of suburbia in their search for identity. In terms of design, the regular ranks of dwelling units, the strict hierarchy of architectural forms, and the standardized building styles represent order and control. The military cannot tolerate deviations. Military authorities even monitor lawn care and award "prizes" to the lawn that best conforms to the military's standards. To some politicians, America's infatuation with the suburbs actually served a military purpose during the Cold War. Apparently, the Soviets were missing out on suburbia. Knowing that their economic system could not produce it, their only apparent choice, as can be seen from the interview below, was to surrender to the culture of consumption. In an interview with Chris Wallace shortly after Ronald Reagan

Figure 4.18. The rolling taxiway gate at Kunsan Air Base, South Korea, secures the military's airfield from the adjacent civilian airport. The gate rolls out of the way when "civilian" aircraft need to access the shared runway.

died, former secretary of state Colin Powell described how American suburbs contributed to the end of the Cold War:

> CHRIS WALLACE: What did you learn from Ronald Reagan, as a politician, as a statesman, a world leader, and as a man?
> COLIN POWELL: Have a vision, but it's not enough to have a vision, you have to communicate that vision to others. . . . When we talked about Gorbachev coming to the United States: What do we show him? And Reagan always had a simple answer to that: Let's show him our subdivisions. Let's show him our shopping centers. I want to show him America. No missile fields, no submarines. I want to show him the American people and the American system, and to show him what he's missing. . . . It reflected the American people, reflected American values.[111]

While Reagan was most impressed with the political economy that could produce suburbia, he also understood that built form has representational power. The use of space is an attribute of imperial power. Suburban space meets the demands of capital and the desires of a diaspora community longing for the familiarity of shopping centers and subdivisions. But these desires add up to an insatiable demand for land, resulting in sprawling landscapes of consumption. While some scholars suggest that these sprawling patterns of development have given Americans enhanced mobility, choice, and privacy, others argue that such land-scapes damage the environment, consume an inordinate amount of fiscal resources, and contribute to a segregated social structure. While both arguments may have some merit, the reality is that privacy and mobility come with land-use costs that cannot be easily dismissed. Empire's guardians are indeed homeward bound; wherever they go, they make familiar places; places made to look like home. How these places are built in spite of their destructive consumption of land requires an understanding of the modes of practice employed on America's outposts.

CHAPTER FIVE

Ruling the World:
Exporting Bureaucracy, Privatization, and Fear

> The consideration of cultural landscapes consists essentially of the discussion of the underlying ordering schemata, ideals, preferences and purposes of different groups, and how these are given physical expression through the various rule systems guiding systematic choices.
>
> —Amos Rapoport, *On Cultural Landscapes*

Thousands of pages of rules govern planning and architectural practice on America's outposts. These rules cover everything from the placement of signs to the length of runways. They dictate what is seen and what is unseen. While buildings, streets, and parking lots are the most visible manifestations, numerous policies place an imaginary architecture on, over, and under the landscape. Invisible lines that dictate building setbacks, height limits, and land-use zones structure the visible environment. These lines lead to familiar landscapes in unfamiliar lands.

In this chapter, I examine some of the rules and practices that form the ordering schemata used by empire's designers. The military operates within its own world of rules that requires making simplistic maps rather than planning comprehensively. Although language barriers, staff turnover, and active involvement by frequently changing senior leaders who are uneducated in planning practice may make planning challenging at America's outposts, an increasing reliance on private contractors and ever more detailed policies driven by fear minimize the role of military planners. In the U.S. military, planning results from numerous sources of inputs, changing rules, and even conflicting actions of a variety of players.

The World of Rules

Regulating imperial planning is nothing new. As shown in chapter 1, empires used regulations like the *Laws of the Indies* and the Cantonment Acts to direct sociospatial practice. These rules governed the processes of displacement and demolition. Planners followed them to bring imperial "order" to native "disorder." Policymakers relied on them to bring certainty and control to their dominions across the globe. Some scholars refer to this as a social ontology, or the ways in which everyday life is constituted by people whose activities are coordinated and controlled.[1] The work of planners and architects is shaped by the very rules that they help produce. These rules or "texts" coordinate their actions regardless of location. Rules embedded in policy statements, planning documents, and official regulations lead to a familiar suburban "style." Planners and their processes are at once part of the problem and part of the solution.

In Benedict Anderson's concept of imagined communities, print media served as the primary avenue for coordinating the formation of a geographically separated nation-state. For the military, detailed regulations, whether available on paper or on the Internet, coordinate not only their actions but also their conception of a "corporate body," a connected group of people with an institutional heritage and common mission. The rules lead to consistency. "The capacity to rule," argue Marie Campbell and Frances Gregor, "depends on carrying messages across sites, coordinating someone's action here with someone else's there." For the U.S. military, the Web-based system of regulations, the downloadable design guides, and the interconnected network of secure computers link far-flung organizations. The result is familiarity. "Repetitious spaces," argues Henri Lefebvre, "are the outcome of repetitive gestures (those of the workers) associated with instruments which are both duplicatable and designed to duplicate." Lefebvre contrasts settlement patterns designed by a professional elite with those that are built outside of the influence of such a controlling hierarchy in a more spontaneous fashion. "The result," he argues, "is an extraordinary spatial duality (that) creates the strong impression that there exists a duality of political power." Around America's outposts, the duality is not merely an impression, it is a fact.[2]

The rules themselves are also part of these instruments of repetition. But as military designers use these instruments and struggle to meet the needs of one group, they may be jeopardizing the needs of another group. By siting buildings according to one set of value-driven, text-based rules, they may be contributing to the spillover that, in part, led to other rules. For example, at Osan Air Base, new rules called for larger apartments for U.S. soldiers, which generated a demand for new housing developments. But "standoff" distances dictated by military police limited locations for siting those new buildings. Rather than reconsider either set of rules, the default position was to annex land adjacent to the base, displace South Korean families in the way of the development, and to demolish their village. The spillover involved angry protests and a commensurate loss of respect for the U.S. military and could eventually lead to damaging "blowback," which would then be used to justify even more draconian land-use measures. This could be a never-ending cycle. These rules also blind planners to the ample open land found on all of America's outposts, offering further "justification" for their annexation mentality. Abetting this process are imperial maps that inscribe these rules on the landscape. In the following sections, I concentrate on rules that govern design and planning using case studies from the Air Force, but it is important to note that the other branches of the U.S. military have very similar rules, even if they have different titles and numbering systems.

Imperial Mapping

For the U.S. military, mapping their domain is an essential task. In Korea, for example, the U.S. maintains a warehouse with nine million maps of the peninsula.[3] Mapping is not a new task for empires. Imperial powers have long used maps to document, project, and justify their territorial ambitions. They mapped boundaries and plotted trade routes. Maps have also played a role in the solidification of Anderson's imagined communities. He shows that maps, rather than representing a historical condition, prefigured imperial action:

> A map anticipated spatial reality, not vice versa. In other words, a map was a model for, rather than a model of, what it purported to represent. . . . It had become a real instrument to concretize projections on the earth's surface. A map was now necessary for the new administrative mechanisms and for the troops to back up their claims.[4]

Once those in power map space, they can then assign ownership and control. This mapping is clearly not an apolitical act. One should not underestimate the role of the mapmaker. Geographer Isaiah Bowman recounts that in making his empire, President Woodrow Wilson recognized that maps displayed not just facts but also "the subtle and else invisible forces that lurk in the events and in the minds of men."[5] Mapmaking is a political act. And what is not shown reveals as much about imperial power as what is shown.

At the bases analyzed in this study, every planner complained about the lack of land and the impacts this had on their master planning efforts. They would list all the "constraints" on their maps and point to the white space on their maps when they discussed annexation plans. Never did they acknowledge that these "constraints" were self-imposed or that the white spaces were not necessarily the implied tabula rasa. In my own survey of military planners and architects, over 90 percent (115 out of 123 who responded to the question) said land availability was a key concern. Across the military, designers think there is not enough land (Figures 5.1 to 5.4). The reality on the ground, however, shows that the space exists. What, then, constrains the use of the ample land the military controls? For these planners, it is the imperial map, now part of a General Plan. Planners produce these General Plans following a rigid

Figure 5.1. Misawa Air Base, Japan. Quotation from base planner: "Look at our base. It seems we have a lot of land but we don't, because facilities are hard to site."

Figure 5.2. Kadena Air Base, Japan. Base planner: "It's amazing that we have so much space between buildings but such a hard time siting facilities."

set of rules that direct planning and design efforts worldwide. The Air Force has euphemistically called these types of governing rules "instructions" and has placed them in thirty-eight "publication series" that correspond to major career fields, like public affairs, law, flying operations, and health services. Compliance with each instruction is mandatory. For our purposes, Series 32, *Civil Engineering,* holds the rules that shape development at bases worldwide.

The organizational structure of the military is similar to the structure of various levels of government. As with many hierarchical organizations, the rules follow a top-down process similar to the ways laws are handed down from Washington, D.C. (Figure 5.5). Policymakers at the Pentagon develop rules, with some input from various agencies "in the field," then distribute them across the Air Force. At the Headquarters Air Force level (at the Pentagon), 118 *Series 32 Air Force Instructions* (AFIs) set policy across the service. In addition, below the Pentagon, regional headquarters, called major commands, and the individual bases these commands oversee issue more "instructions." Two Air Force regional commands are overseas: Pacific Air Forces Command (PACAF) and United States Air Forces Europe (USAFE). In the United States, the commands are based on function and supervise "outer" space (Space Command), military transportation (Air Mobility Command), warfighting (Air

Figure 5.3. Osan Air Base, South Korea. Base planner: "The whole issue at Osan is one word—space. We don't have any."

Figure 5.4. Kunsan Air Base, South Korea. Base planner: "We have no space for growth here, so we're working to fill in part of the Yellow Sea."

Combat Command), reserve operations (Air Force Reserve Command), education (Air Education and Training Command), search and rescue (Air Force Special Operations Command), and weapon system procurement (Air Force Materiel Command). Senior generals run each major command and are similar to governors responsible for setting command-wide policies, managing budgets, and interfacing with other

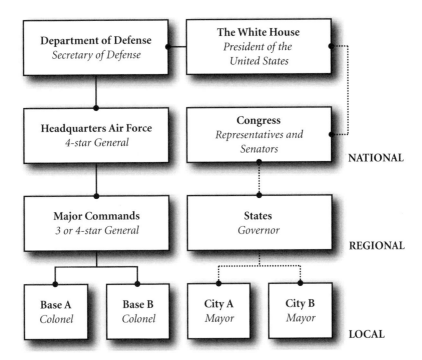

Figure 5.5. Comparing "organizational" structures.

agencies. Each command oversees numerous bases led mostly by colonels, frequently referred to as "the mayor." Their role is to implement policies, not make them.

For planning, *AFI 32–7062—Air Force Comprehensive Planning* (AFI 32–7062) is the primary "instruction." Published in 1994, revised in 1997, and revised again in 2001, this "instruction" applies the requirements of the 1969 National Environmental Policy Act (NEPA) to the Air Force. One intention of the 1969 act was to improve coordination in the planning process and to use both the physical and social sciences in planning and decision making.[6] Planning, in NEPA terms, is not about aesthetics, nor is it about quantifying traffic demands. Rather, it is about a process that is both qualitative and quantitative. One of the primary requirements of AFI 32–7062 is that all bases produce a General Plan following a process that identifies goals and objectives and carefully evaluates alternatives. The concept is for this plan to guide decision making. The General Plan includes four component plans: constraints and opportunities; infrastructure; land use and transportation planning; and the capital improvements program. The constraints plan integrates natural and cultural information, environmental issues, airspace restrictions, and other safety requirements. Composite constraints plans show existing buildings and required "clear zones" around the airfield, which correspond to historical locations for aircraft accidents.[7] They also show required setbacks around bomb storage bunkers, known as quantity-distance safety arcs, or "Q-D arcs" for short. The distance from the bunker is a factor of the explosive capacity of the bomb being stored. In some cases, the plans also show areas controlled by the host-nation military. When base planners look at these maps and all the constraints, they immediately think they have no room for development. "We're very constrained in a number of ways," said the chief of plans and programs at one U.S. outpost, "airfield clear zones, a river to the north, city to the south and east, and Q-D to the west."[8] This is one justification for a planned annexation of over 400 acres at his base.

Since most maps show no context beyond the base, one could easily mistake the base for an actual island. The real situation is, however, quite different. Dense urban development surrounds most overseas bases on several sides and the base's "constraints," including most of the Q-D arcs and airfield clear zones, extend well into the local community. This is invisible spillover. For instance, if a bomb accidentally explodes in a bunker, it may take with it dozens of local homes built within the Q-D arc. In some cases these homes preceded the arcs, in other cases they came after the arcs, and in yet other cases existing arcs changed when the bombs stored inside changed, thus placing previously "safe" homes in danger. This encroachment occurs because the United States has very little control over what is built beyond its borders. These densely developed neighborhoods within the Q-D arcs and clear zones are largely invisible to the mapmakers and decision makers. There is no need to show any development off-base, however, since it is an optional feature of "planning." The "instruction" has a checklist of features required to be mapped, including wetlands and flood plains, Q-D arcs, and airfield clear zones, but almost anything outside the fence is optional, including off-base development, land use, and zoning. This further exacerbates an avoidance mentality. It is easy to ignore or avoid development that mapmakers do not even show on the map. Deciding what to include and what to exclude on these maps is an exercise in imperial power.

Even though maps proliferate, some planners admit that effective mapping and effective planning are not the same. "We have identified

[as] a mission essential task that all installations must be effectively planned," said Mike Ramirez, the planner for a command that oversees numerous bases around the world.[9] He added, "We need to develop performance measures." When asked how he was going to measure planning effectiveness, he replied that he would require all of "his" bases to have a regularly updated General Plan. He would "score" compliance with a color-coded "stop-light" system: red signifies no plan or an outdated plan; yellow indicates plan under revision; green means recently updated plan on file. Of course, his boss, a general, wants all the lights to be green. In the future, Ramirez's bases will have current plans. But does that make them effective? To this question he replied,

> We plan for missions and the installation commander says here is where he wants a building and what he wants it to be, so to gauge how well he is planning we need to see how well he answered the questions. We can see lists of projects in his capital improvements program and the map of circles where he is going to build. So I can examine his records: minutes of meetings, etc.

But what good would this do given the immense effort it would require of every base to go back through their hundreds of pages of meeting minutes to track down who said what and when? "Here is how it will help," he replied. "Has he implemented the plan through a focus on siting approvals? Do the sites connect to what he said in the plan?"

Just because a building is sited where an arrow on a map pointed still does not make for effective planning. The arrow could have pointed to a South Korean village in the way of development. Is demolishing the village for a new housing tower, for example, effective planning? Mike was caught in a place, in the words of Henri Lefebvre, "where a pure culture of the quantitative reigns supreme."[10] Count, measure, and map; then planning by this definition must be effective. Numbers are important, but so are sociocultural needs. Herein lies the first problem. Numbers are easy to measure. More nebulous concepts like "social factors" are more difficult to measure. Mike referred to his commanders as men. Since over 80 percent of Air Force officers are male, he is speaking from his perspective as a planner for a male-dominated career field. This in itself is a topic for future research, to explore how a more gender-balanced planning staff might affect base planning.[11]

At some bases, General Plans—however well or poorly done—are ineffective because they are not being used. "Though our base's General

Plans have been updated [regularly] since 1995, the current revision was halted at 35 percent [in 2003] due to funding withdrawal," said one planner at an overseas base. She added, "This and prior versions sit on a shelf in a cabinet and are not referenced for near-future planning. At no time in [the base's] history has an installation commander succeeded—assuming there were attempts—in bringing order to the arrangement through a vision that was translated into a General Plan."[12] Creating an expensive binder that just sits on a shelf was clearly not the intent of AFI 32–7062. The Air Force's senior planner described the justification for these plans:

> In 1981, we did not have real plans just maps called master plans—that [proposed] building box fit at that place on the ground. We knew airfield and explosive safety were driving criteria primarily to keep things like a childcare center out of [a] Q-D arc. In the 1990s, the Civil Engineer [the officer in charge of all engineering and architecture at the time] sent me a handwritten note saying don't do this—pointing to inconsistent plans across the Air Force. The note read, "I'm getting sick and tired of opening comprehensive plans and seeing no consistency—it should be a corporate document."[13]

After receiving the note, planners held meetings, commissioned studies, and rewrote policies. The result was eventually AFI 32–7062 with its rules to make General Plans look consistent. The comment about the "building box" is especially revealing. Planners would place a square that represented a future building on an open site on the map and that would lock in the site and, more often than not, the design. This reduced planning to a technical exercise of finding an open site with the least constraints. But in most cases, even these boxes are missing, and these plans are usually no more than a report card identifying the condition of the base with maps of current infrastructure, a list of future projects, and a color-coded land-use map showing functional zones. Some bases may even place a number on a future land-use map representing a location for a particular project. Very few actually have maps that show details of future development such as possible roads, parking, or building outlines. According to Victor Lee, an architect who has worked as a planner at Kadena Air Base, the General Plan at Kadena was "rarely used—it was never up-to-date." He continues,

> The Community Planner was in our office so we would chat on a case-by-case basis. When people asked for a building I would walk over to his

office and we would find a site. Most stuff was fairly logically located—
we grouped dorms, placed the operations buildings near [the] flightline,
and put maintenance buildings in maintenance areas. The General Plan
just was not too helpful.[14]

This is a common complaint among military planners. When asked
why he thought the plans were unhelpful, Lee replied, "The Air Force
doesn't hire innovative enough people to do them—they're just rubber-
stamped from another base with preconceived patterns where stuff
should go—the Air Force just doesn't listen." Here, Lee was referring to
a contentious personnel issue. According to the rules, every base is
required to have a planner who is the staff member responsible for producing the General Plan and other planning documents. In the past,
that planner was also required to have a planning degree, like a master's
in city planning.[15] But the Air Force changed the rules and considers
practically anyone with a college degree a planner now. Marty Holland,
the Air Force's former senior planner laments the change:

> The Air Force's planning talent is going away—corporate knowledge is
> leaving; some are going to work for consultants—25 percent of the people
> in the planning career field have over 30 years of service; 25 percent have
> less than 5 years, the other 50 percent are not really planners. There are
> 150 planning positions in the Air Force and less than 80 are filled with
> planners.[16]

When asked how this happened, he replied,

> When people left, the base held planning positions [unfilled] for a pos-
> sible RIF [future layoff or Reduction in Force]. At many bases, rather
> than fill the position with a civilian, the commanders just stuck a new
> second lieutenant in the job as planner.

While a few of these young officers might be architects, as well as being
inexperienced, most are civil engineers and have little knowledge of planning. Moreover, they may even have little interest in planning, as Holland describes:

> After sending emails out to all Air Force planners one year, I got an email
> back from a Second Lieutenant Riley who said, "I'm not the planner here,
> Lieutenant Sollow is." So, I sent Sollow the email and he sent an email in
> reply, "I'm not interested." I sent back an email, "But aren't you the base
> planner," I asked. "Yes," he replied. "Why aren't you interested?" I asked.
> He said, "We don't do that here anymore."[17]

Although Holland was quite upset that a base would staff its planning position with someone who thought planning was not needed and would even say so, perhaps Lieutenant Sollow was referring to the fact that the Air Force has privatized its planning functions. Private Architecture-Engineering (A-E) firms do most planning at America's outposts and military staffers manage the contract. According to Holland, this was not supposed to happen:

> The whole idea of the General Plan was to do it in-house; we dummied it so all you had to do was fill in the blanks. You give them all the tools to make it happen and now commanders say we can't let base planners do it because it will not be right so we need consultants. Their plans are cookie cutter though. Look at who is doing the planning... retired civil engineers; a lot of people doing military planning are not even planners. They got the jobs because they could speak military jargon; one guy was a retired helicopter pilot.[18]

In a fit of efficiency, the Air Force "dummied down" planning and produced a Microsoft Word template that any base planner could use to write their own General Plan. The template came with detailed instructions and a checklist to ensure completeness. With the template, even inexperienced young officers could, theoretically, make a plan. Despite the investment in this template, few bases make their own plans, and instead rely on planning firms, many staffed by retired military engineers or reservists. As Holland realized, their connections and their understanding of the military language clearly help them in their marketing efforts. Hiring military retirees, however, is normal practice for defense contractors.[19]

Most of the planning work goes to firms like URS, GRW, Black & Veatch, CH2M Hill, 3DI, and Parsons. In a study of U.S. architects and engineers working overseas, Jeffrey Cody shows how Parsons was one of the main firms that carried out master planning efforts in the Western Pacific after World War II.[20] The firm has stayed active in preparing plans for the military in Asia. Parsons, for example, acquired Harland Bartholomew and Associates and has prepared General Plans at Misawa, Kadena, Kunsan, and Osan. To prepare Kadena's General Plan update in the late 1990s, Parsons engineers visited the base four times, usually for just a few days. "The biggest pain," according to Capt. Troy Halpin, "was that they were in the States."[21] As one of the planners at the base, Captain Halpin was aware of the limitations of preparing master plans from afar. These plans provided little guidance for future development other than lists of potential projects and a land-use map. These uninspired documents are, however, in keeping with Harland Bartholomew's 1915 doctrine that "[c]ity planning is neither extravagant nor grandiose; it is nothing more than practicality, avoidance of needless future expense by exercise of wise forethought."[22] This attitude does not make at least one base planner very happy. Jamal Stevenson laments that "after the end of the Cold War community planners at bases stopped being visionary and got lost in the details—air quality, asbestos, underground tanks."[23] Planning became reactive rather than proactive.

Another firm, GRW Engineers, has also prepared plans for Air Force bases worldwide. In 2004, on their Web site, they advertised master planning capabilities for state and local governments, but they clearly focused on military work—80 of the 120 projects listed were for military bases. Other work they highlighted included airports and prisons. Their focus was on technical competence. Web site visitors could even download a sewer rehabilitation brochure from their Web site, but not a planning brochure.

The short-term nature of visits by these consultants, dictated in part by the cost of travel and per diem, gives them little time to study the local culture. Victor Lee complained,

> Because the designers don't stay here long enough, they don't have time to think outside the box, which for us is outside the gate. We had a consulting team here that redid all of our housing, 1,400 units, but they didn't have the attitude of trying to follow local building patterns, they just imported American ideas—cul-de-sacs, big yards, and parking lots instead of streets.[24]

Despite Lee's valid complaints, this plan won an Air Force Design Award in 2000 in part because the designers employed a "survey" of 800 housing residents. A closer look, however, reveals that the survey itself was flawed and the consulting planners blatantly disregarded its few valid findings.[25]

Imperial Design

Rules govern not only the production of the General Plan, but also the design and construction of individual buildings. While the Army and Air Force Exchange Service and the Defense Commissary Agency have their own sets of rules that dictate the design of shopping centers and grocery stores, hundreds of guides and "instructions" dictate the design of most other buildings. Once programmers identify a need for a new building, the first "instruction" usually referenced is *AFI 32–1084, Facility Requirements.* This 283-page regulation sets sizes or "space allowances" for nearly 200 types of buildings, from aircraft hangars to vehicle maintenance facilities. The sizes correspond to the total population served, which at times may be the number of soldiers at a base and other times may include families and civilians. Commanders rarely authorize variances. Over 100 additional design guides, for everything from bowling centers to fire stations, supplement this regulation. In some cases, designers can download entire plan sets as PDFs or AutoCAD files. The content of these guides normally emerges out of a process that includes Headquarters Air Force and Major Command representatives. Once they determine the policy, the Air Force typically hires private design firms to prepare the actual guides.

Housing is perhaps the most heavily regulated area. The *Air Force Family Housing Guide* is the main reference. The guide has been regularly revised with the latest edition published in 2004. For site planning, the focus was on regulating densities (Figure 5.6). Allowable densities differed by rank: the higher the rank, the lower the density. Unlike the 1995 edition, though, the 2004 version recognized the need for greater densities overseas and allowed for up to forty units per acre in high-rise developments outside the United States. If designers wanted to build townhomes overseas, however, they could only do so at seven to fifteen units per acre. There was no middle ground. In addition to regulating densities, the guide encouraged the extensive use of cul-de-sacs and clustered development, regardless of location. The requirements initially came from the Department of Housing and Urban Development's (HUD) Section 202 Program, which began in 1959 as a way to finance low-income housing in the United States. "Someone took the HUD 202 manual and turned it into (an) Air Force regulation for housing," said Marty Holland, the Air Force's former senior planner. "We called it Military Family Housing but they were looking at the 202 program in the mid-1980s."[26]

The 1995 guidelines were also quite similar to Federal Housing Administration (FHA) recommended subdivision layouts published in the 1930s. The FHA designers considered a grid layout "bad" and a cul-de-sac system "good."[27] The 1995 edition of the housing guide stated that

Rank	Low density (suburban and rural areas)	Medium density (urban areas)	High density (most overseas locations)
Majors and above	3–4	5–6	7–8
Captains and below	4–6	7–10	11–15

Figure 5.6. Authorized housing densities (units per acre). From *Air Force Family Housing Guide,* 2004.

"homes of identical design set in a monotonous, 90 degree street grid pattern with very little physical definition between public and private spaces, create an unattractive, 'cookie cutter' appearance to the neighborhood."[28] This is quite different from the example set by the Romans 2000 years earlier in their gridded outposts. Perhaps learning from the work of "new urbanists," the 2004 Air Force guidelines removed the ban on grids. But the guide's authors still favored clustering "neighborhoods" around a cul-de-sac network:

> In either designing or improving an Air Force neighborhood, it is essential to understand the "planning unit" concept—the relationship of each dwelling unit to a cluster of units, a neighborhood, and the installation as a whole. This is an important planning concept since the monotony often found in large tract-housing neighborhoods makes it difficult for families to develop a sense of identity, ownership, and belonging within their home, street, and neighborhood. People relate more easily to small groups or clusters of homes than to a large undifferentiated housing tract. Therefore, it is imperative that means be found to strengthen peoples' sense of belonging to their own local street or cluster.[29]

The guide then advises designers to "plan the site so that housing units are clustered into mini- or sub-neighborhoods organized around a central element, such as a cul-de-sac or common area."[30] The claims made in this policy are specious at best. The erroneous assumption is that identical homes, which the military leadership seems to prefer, built in a cul-de-sac arrangement would not be monotonous or "cookie-cutter."

Like the FHA recommendations, the Air Force guide also addressed street widths. The discussion concerns street nomenclature—plans are to show major arterials, collector streets (36 feet wide with parking on both sides), and local streets (preferably cul-de-sacs, 32 feet wide with parking on both sides). The end result, whether based on the 1995 or 2004 guide, was a clustered form of sprawl (Figure 5.7). At one base, the military even assigned soldiers to act as "cluster chiefs" to keep track of

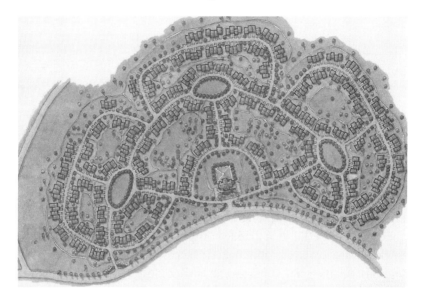

Figure 5.7. Clustering sprawl: the site planning standards recommended by the Air Force call for clusters of houses surrounded by what is arguably unnecessary open space that few people want to maintain. The front is given over to the car, and the back is a shared "natural" area. One predictable result is that no one gets much privacy. From *Air Force Family Housing Guide*, 2004.

the residents of each "cluster." At the same base, when residents asked to put up wood fences in their backyards to screen them from the "collector" and "arterial" streets, the housing manager rejected the request, stating that such a move would limit her ability to monitor what goes on in the backyards of each cluster.[31]

The result for each family was no privacy—the front yards are like parking lots and the backyards are like aquariums. Suburban developments like this, with their identifiable clusters, wide streets, and low densities, allow the military to extend surveillance into the neighborhood. The housing guides, however, did not dwell on any potential drawbacks of developing at such low densities and in a way that gives residents so little privacy. The military instructed designers to follow the guide, which is one reason why consulting firms rarely stray from its recommendations. Any deviations would take time to justify and, since they normally design using a fixed fee, anything that can reduce the time investment in the design process can increase their profit margin.

One interesting difference between the 1995 and 2004 guides was the addition of extensive discussions on "sustainability" in the latter edition. The 2004 guide even required the use of "sustainable" planning and development principles for family housing. But the principles addressed in the guide primarily focused on individual buildings and called for more efficient materials, use of recycled products, and better lighting. While these goals are laudable, the guide did not address the quite unsustainable practice of creating housing tracts that force automobile use and consume an inordinate amount of land for low-density development. When the difficult-to-define concept of sustainability is reduced to better light bulbs, the whole concept is undermined.

Since the FHA published its planning and design guidance, the Air Force has progressed from propeller-driven aircraft to the B-2 bomber, but it remains committed to seventy-year old planning strategies that drive up the demand for land in countries that have the least amount of land to spare. What the Air Force does change on a regular basis is the authorized size of units. Over the last fifty years, homes in the Air Force have more than doubled in size. This is in keeping with the trend in the United States, where, since 1950, the average house has grown from 983 square feet to 2,329 square feet.[32]

In addition to regulating family housing, the Air Force has additional rules that cover dormitories, which the military builds for soldiers without families. The seventy-nine-page *Facility Design Guide for Enlisted Dormitories* provides definitive site plans, building plans, and room plans. Similar to family housing sizes, the guidance for dormitories has changed considerably over the years.

- 1950s: Open bay barracks with centralized bathrooms.
- 1983: 2+2 standard implemented that authorized shared rooms for two occupants; each two room suite shared a bathroom; 90 square feet per occupant.
- 1995: 1+1 standard announced that provided private bedroom with a shared bathroom and shared kitchen in a two-room suite; 118 square feet per occupant.
- 2001: Quad standard approved that provided private bathroom and bedroom in a four-room suite, where four soldiers share a kitchen and social space; 129 square feet per occupant.[33]

These changing rules have significant consequences on the ground since programmers use the revised rules to justify new construction. With every rule change, the buildings expanded in size to accommodate rooms that are more private. Between 1996 and 2003, the Air Force

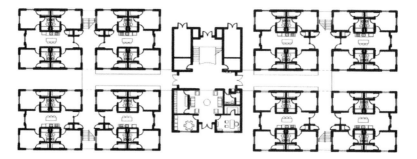

Figure 5.8. The preferred Air Force dormitory layout, which requires five stairs, excessive walkways, and plentiful land. From *Enlisted Dormitory Design Guide*, U.S. Air Force.

spent more than $1 billion building 1+1 dorms and plans to spend nearly $900 million to meet the quad standard.[34]

The buildings that these quads create are quite inefficient. They require up to five staircases and allot twice the area to corridors than in the older 2+2 plan. Nevertheless, the architect prepared this design, and the military approved it, despite a random survey in 2002 of nearly 90,000 soldiers (with a response rate of 45 percent) in which half the enlisted soldiers living in dorms stated that they were dissatisfied with their living conditions mainly because the rooms were too small and lacked storage.[35] They did not clamor for their own bathroom or a shared "social space." No matter, the Air Force implemented the idea worldwide, without any postoccupancy evaluation to see how well the quad plan actually works (Figure 5.8).

The rooms in the quad standard are quite spacious compared to earlier empires and even the rooms given to some allies today. The minimum net area allowed for each U.S. soldier is 129 square feet. This is more than double the 64 square feet the British Army gave their enlisted soldiers in India a century ago.[36] More important, it is more than three times the area the South Korean Army gives its soldiers today. They get just 36 square feet.[37] To fit all these quads on the landscape requires Americans to occupy more acreage—land that their South Korean counterparts, stuck in cramped quarters, are helping defend. Empires map their power and prerogative onto the landscape in every conceivable way.

In my own interviews of twenty dormitory residents at Misawa Air Base, none was thrilled about the idea of sharing a kitchen with three other soldiers. Unsurprisingly, their clear preference was for their own private suite. At least one senior officer recognizes the value of privacy. Colonel Edward Piekarczyk, a former commander of the Civil Engineering squadron at Osan Air Base, said, "When you get older you just need more space and privacy."[38] While he was referring to the benefits of moving out of the shared-room concept, his observation applies to the shared spaces in the quad concept as well. One young soldier said he was not happy with the dorm standard. "Back home I had my own apartment and it was nice—two bedrooms. Now I live in a dorm and the bed takes up half my space."[39] With the new policy, he gets ten more square feet (mainly in his bathroom), not much of an improvement. But in the words of Colonel James Holland, the Air Force housing chief, "We think it's a win-win [situation] . . . the new plan takes us further in the continuous journey of enhancing quality of life for our airmen."[40] This is an expensive journey. For instance, at Osan Air Base in South Korea, the consulting firm hired by the military to determine all the service's future dormitory requirements identified $135 million of construction, just at one base, resulting in a demand for up to seventeen new buildings.[41]

The Air Force hired the same architectural firm that developed the quad plan to go to every base and prepare a Dormitory Master Plan showing how its inventory of older dorms could be either upgraded or replaced to meet this new standard. The architects went armed with the freshly published design guide and planted the same building type across the Air Force. According to the planner at one overseas base, instead of interviewing the occupants and maintenance staff, instead of spending time analyzing the site, the architects used aerial photos and base maps to "plop down" building footprints. The planner at Misawa adds,

> This Dormitory Master Plan process is taking the top down approach— same old dog new trick type stuff. The A-E's short-range plan is not viable; tearing down dorms with 20+ years of life remaining is not viable. The government of Japan standard is to replace [buildings] at forty-seven years. Proposing 1+1s, 2+2s, or quads in a poor neighborhood layout should not be acceptable. We must move away from the institutional campus concept toward something that is a real neighborhood. Otherwise the dorms remain stigmatized as places where young airmen have to live and want to leave.[42]

Exporting suburban development patterns, tearing down perfectly serviceable buildings, and creating places young soldiers want to abandon quickly does not happen by chance. Grasping this new dormitory policy is fundamental to understanding the increasing demand for space at America's outposts. With the new standard, all old dormitories become obsolete, even if they are structurally sound. The military can then justify replacement buildings that are bigger, thus requiring more land. But as can be seen from the history of dormitory design, the policy constantly changes. The policy will inevitably change again when senior leaders realize that their soldiers want privacy more than they want a shared social space. This is an inefficient cycle of consumptive construction.

Veneers of Compatibility

Like all other on-base buildings, designers will cloak the dormitories built to the quad standard in veneers of compatibility. This happens because the Air Force requires all its installations to develop Architectural Compatibility Plans to ensure some visual consistency on the base and across the service. To understand architectural compatibility and how it affects the Air Force, an understanding of how the Air Force defines the term is helpful:

> Compatible is generally defined as capable of existing together in harmony, or to be consistent. Architectural compatibility would therefore be concerned not only with the physical appearance of buildings, but interfacing with planning, landscape development and interior design goals and objectives.[43]

From this definition, one may think the Air Force has a broad approach to compatibility. But the reality is otherwise. Repeating the template-driven nature of imperial mapping and design, architects working at America's outposts can download a Microsoft Word template to create their own compatibility plan. They can also download a PowerPoint briefing template and a compatibility guide. The recommendations, however, tilt to superficial elements of design. The guide directs bases to establish "themes" that combine materials, textures, colors, form, details, and type of construction. "A theme," according to the guide, "may be based on historical, cultural, technological, and other standards. Examples include Spanish, Western, Korean, modern, colonial and high-tech."[44] The guide notes that designers should not select themes arbitrarily; rather, they should reflect the region. So, a nation's architectural traditions are collapsed into a visual theme. Osan Air Base's guide, written by a South Korean, has this to say about the theme:

The Republic of Korea's built environment is rich in styles, both new and old. But high turnover rate of people at Osan is likely to foster different interpretations of architectural compatibility and creates an eclectic overall base appearance. Consideration should include Korean cultural and historical constraints and environmental constraints. The "Korean" architectural features such as roof tile treatments, gatehouses, arches, and garden design and landscaping should be repeated on projects such as picnic shelters, bus stops, identification signage, gateways etc.[45]

This is yet another case of local residents working with imperial power. In this statement, a "Korean" theme is a defense against the turnover rate among U.S. military designers, who stay at Osan for usually no more than one or two years. The author of the Osan guide has joined his American employers and reduced Korean architecture to a representational appliqué. This simplifies its applicability to counter personal whim. Moreover, it applies this theme to minor elements in the built environment: picnic shelters, bus stops, and church bells. Larger projects, like the 170,000-square-foot shopping mall built at Osan in 2004, are exempt. Another South Korean architect working at Osan had a different perspective. He argued, "Nothing will change. I'm amused at the talk of architectural compatibility—they're all brown buildings with metal roofs!"[46] Korean tile roofs, reproduced in metal facsimiles, and elaborate bus stops contribute to what Sharon Zukin would call an imaginary visual landscape that offers "a retreat from the real world of power."[47] The real world, the world that annexes prime farmland, demolishes existing villages, and exports America Towns, follows rules that supersede the architectural compatibility standards at bases like Osan.

The application of local styles is not a new imperial exercise.[48] Edward Said has offered an explanation for this effort: "[A]ll cultures tend to make representations of foreign cultures, the better to master or in some way control them."[49] Local architecture plays a subservient role to empire, just like all other things local. This is most evident at Osan where the diminutive "local" bus stop faces the supersized "American" shopping mall.

Osan's forty-page compatibility guide is representative of how architects use the template (Figure 5.10). The guide devotes seventeen pages to a primer on compatibility copied directly from the Air Force template; it covers interior design issues (type of carpet allowed, paint color, and so on) in seventeen pages, addresses building design in five pages, and

Figure 5.9. Achieving "compatibility" at Osan Air Base, South Korea: (a) the golf course starter's pavilion; (b) the base chapel's bell cover.

devotes less than one page to site planning. Compatibility in terms of morphology is an afterthought at best. By devoting such a small amount of attention to site design issues, the authors of the guide implicitly condone the sprawling morphology exported from the United States. Compatibility is seen as wallpaper, wrapping low-density, widely spaced, auto-focused design in a veneer. But even the color of the veneer is regulated. The bulk of the exterior design section regulates the exterior color scheme; which is the standard light brown and dark brown seen across the Air Force. Colonel Neil Kanno, a senior officer at the base, explains how these colors came to be the Air Force standard.

> Have you ever wondered why all Air Force buildings are painted a light or dark shade of brown? Do you think it's a plot by Air Force civil engineers to save operations and maintenance funds by having to stock only two colors of paint? Creech Brown, familiar shades of brown some of us old-timers have come to know and love, was the brainchild of General William Creech, former Tactical Air Command (TAC) commander. Why did TAC do it? According to the general, leaders engender pride and convey a pervasive sense of excellence so people feel good about themselves and perform their mission accordingly.[50]

General Creech thought a consistent paint scheme was one way to "engender pride" in his subordinates. The idea that the Air Force could paint

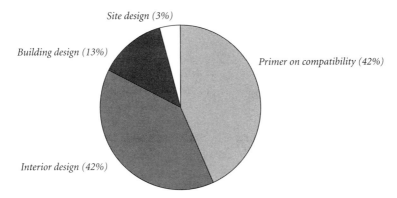

Figure 5.10. Prioritizing compatibility. From Osan Air Base Architectural Compatibility Guide.

its 84,712 buildings light brown with dark brown trim to enhance performance is nothing more than a fatuous hope. General Creech was in part reacting to the "supergraphics" of the 1970s and early 1980s and wanted consistency across his bases, and what better, cheaper way to do it than through paint? But exporting a consistent color is not a new exercise for imperial powers. The French, for instance, exported ochre-colored dirt used in making paint from the Vaucluse region to southeast Asia, Africa, and the Caribbean to make their colonies feel more like home.[51] In addition to consistent colors, the architectural compatibility guide also recommends that bases use the standards to "control design expression." Frank Gehry, the architect of the Walt Disney Concert Hall in Los Angeles and Bilbao's Guggenheim museum, need not apply.

Suburbia by Default?

All of these rules require isolated land-use zones neatly represented on base maps. They require low-density development that ensures equivalency across America's outposts. They require wide roads and deep setbacks for efficiency and safety. But these ingrained patterns also happen due to institutional reasons. Language barriers, frequent staff changes, and ongoing intervention by senior officers make the consideration of alternatives difficult at best. Rather than try alternatives, planners default to what has been done before, to what is familiar. Jonathan Barnett offers this explanation for spatial familiarity:

> The decision is made by the book, by a government official who knows
> that good performance is not laying oneself open to criticism. If a building

looks precisely like one that was built five years ago, any construction cost increase must be the result of inflation. If the building looks different, even if it might cost less than repeating the same building, the official is open to criticism.[52]

Babel

Making decisions "by the book" obviates the need for developing a better understanding of the host nation's building culture, which would require a better understanding of their language as well. Since the U.S. military assigns most of its soldiers to overseas locations for one- or two-year periods, few have the time to learn the language of their host country. "The language barrier is hard when we talk about technical issues," said Capt. Chris Rodgers, chief of construction at Osan Air Base. Referring to his communication with local national employees at the base, of course speaking in English, again the prerogative of empire, he added, "It seems like we need to talk at a second-grade level. And if they don't understand they just say 'yeh, yeh' when it should be no, no."[53] If the local nationals were to speak in Korean, few Americans could even understand at a kindergarten level. Major Leslie Triano adds, "It is very hard for them to speak a second language. Once they've tried to explain their ideas perhaps four times, the Americans they're talking to think they don't know what they're talking about."[54]

The language barrier also compounds the problems associated with the organizational hierarchy at a base. In almost all cases, the supervisors are Americans. Local nationals, many with years of experience on the base, end up working under an American with little experience. Since the Air Force fills many of the supervisory positions overseas with junior officers, the reality may be twenty-one-year-old Americans supervising several local nationals who may be twice their age. This oftentimes results in a culture clash where South Korean employees must answer to someone vastly less experienced and much younger.

Oftentimes, the language barrier creates more work for everyone. The local national employee will go back and try to figure out how to either communicate more clearly or just follow along. Major Triano added that it is Korean culture on the base to follow the U.S. lead. She explained the estimating process for one small project at Osan: "Mr. Yu did a detailed estimate for a project over several days and came in at $310,000. But I told him our rules said it had to be under $300,000. So he came back in ten minutes with an estimate of $295,000." Rather than try to bridge the communication gap, Americans may just go do the work themselves. "Our biggest challenge is [that the] Civil Engineering [squadron] has 400 people, just like Luke Air Force Base in Arizona, but here half are locals," said Carl Bristol, the director of Osan's housing program. "At Luke, we could task the civilians to do Staff Summary Sheets [official government reports] but not here since English is a second language. So the U.S. guys work like mad."[55] This problem is not a new experience for imperial power. For earlier empires, learning the language of the conquered nation was not a priority. As a result, imperial powers, like Britain in India, were dependent on the local clerks who had bothered to learn the language of the occupying power.[56] The constraints posed by this aspect of avoidance, the avoidance of learning the language, clearly present challenges. This was a topic in *The Ugly American:*

> Americans . . . who cannot speak the language, can have no more than an academic understanding of a country's customs, beliefs, religion, and humor. Restricted to communication with only that special, small, and usually well-to-do segment of the native population fluent in English, they receive a limited and often misleading picture of the nation.[57]

A Climate of Change

Lieutenant Colonel Jorge Cuellar, the former base civil engineer at Kunsan, stressed the importance of long-range planning and its link to staff turnover. Sitting in his well-appointed office, with pictures of his six kids covering his desk, numerous award certificates on a large wood credenza, and polished military plaques adorning the walls, he said, "We need a long-range vision since there is quick turnover here. We need to make Kunsan an assignment of choice. We lose so many people when they get assigned to Korea but when they get here they really do love it. Is there room for family housing?"[58] Without family housing and other support facilities, Korea is not a choice assignment for today's married military. Many of them leave the service rather than accept an assignment to Korea. The ones that do accept are only required to stay for one or two years. So, because of its inability to provide adequate space for families, either the Air Force loses experienced soldiers or they accept rapid turnover and the attendant management problems. Planners at Osan are also trying to determine if the base can accept more families, which could lower the turnover rate. While looking for a plan prepared by a consulting firm that supposedly showed how more housing could be built at Osan, Jamal Stevenson, the base's planner, said, "People come and people go, and that's why the base is planned like this. I've had five military supervisors in two years."[59] After searching through an endless maze of office cubicles, he never did find the plan, most likely since a previous planner completed the plan more that two years earlier and filed it somewhere unknown to the new staff.

Today's computer technology combines with these frequent staff changes to hamper continuity. "There is just constant turnover here," said Capt. Chris Rodgers at Osan. "In my office, eight Korean engineers work for two officers who don't have all the history. Email is also a challenge. In the old days we had project folders with memos but now the continuity file is the Outlook .pst folder."[60] Recreating a project's history through Microsoft Outlook, though, can be difficult. Hard drives crash, personal folders expire, or the volume of saved emails makes reading them all but impossible. At Kunsan Air Base, almost the entire military staff had changed between 2002 and 2003. In 2002 the staff helped develop a plan that won an award from the American Planning Association's Federal Planning Division. But by 2003, according to the former planner, Capt. Anne Wirth, "The focus at Kunsan had shifted, none of the new leaders knew the plan, they needed to make their mark in the short time they were there."[61] The new planner at Kunsan Air Base, Captain Nicole Davidson, said that the base operates on a one-year planning cycle:

> Military serving at Kunsan Air Base schedule dates for their midtours [when they can return for a vacation to the U.S.]. They do not plan for ten years from now. A lot can change with ten changes of command. All of the planning issues/lack of planning relate back to the changing face of [the base]. I could list all of the issues we are currently dealing with—nine new dorms, a new community center, new [hotel], an Army beddown, replacing infrastructure, [and] fifty-year-old airfield pavement. We're building new buildings to house the activities of the [base] but we could do so much more if we plan for more than the next 364 days.[62]

Captain Davidson raises a very relevant point. Change occurs across the base—in the planning office and in the commanders' offices. By "ten changes of command" she was referring to the various agencies on the base that see new leadership every year as a result of the military's assignment policies. Because the United States staffs planning and design offices at America's outposts with a mix of host nation employees, U.S. military, and DoD civilian employees, they need to work together.

One of the impacts of frequent change is an inability for the American and South Korean staff to develop trusting relationships. As Richard Sennett argues, "Basic social bonds like trust, loyalty and obligation are not instantly formed; they require a long time to develop; they require continuity rather than rupture."[63] The rupture is visible on the ground in a fragmented pattern of development. The local engineers also recognize this staffing problem. Mr. Kim, a South Korean architect working in the planning section at an American air base in his country, said, "The main problem here is military rotation—so no continuity. When the commander changes, our direction changes."[64]

The change also affects the way the local engineers work. Mr. Han, an engineer responsible for developing building programs at another American air base in South Korea, said,

> I know what needs to be done and I do it. If I have a good boss, it works well. But if not, I just do the work. A few years ago, I had a very bad captain so I just ignored her. A long-range plan is good but one commander says put it here and another says no, put it here. Plans are constantly changing, it makes our work very difficult.[65]

The staffing pattern at these bases is like a sandwich. At the top are American officers, in charge of the overall base as well as offices that govern planning and design. In the middle, local national civilians work as the architects, engineers, and planners that do the bulk of the work. They manage the construction projects, prepare in-house designs, and fill out the necessary government forms. At the bottom are American enlisted soldiers who staff the drafting sections. They plot out the maps, make the reproductions, and prepare as-built surveys and drawings. Language barriers and continuous turnover limit the effectiveness of what could otherwise be arguably a healthy mix of local nationals and U.S. personnel.

Intervention from Above

"I'm generally not interested in a five-year plan. I'm interested in a five-minute plan."[66] For someone working for the officer who said this—Gen. Robert Foglesong, former commander of U.S. Air Forces in Europe—planning anything that would take longer than five minutes may

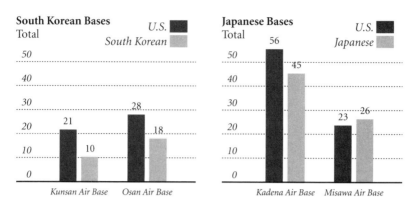

Figure 5.11. Professional engineering and design staff. From author's fieldwork, 2003–4.

not be that person's highest priority. On military bases, the leaders set the tone. But the involvement of high-ranking officials is not a new concept in the world of planning. Napoléon III, for example, drew out the new roads he wanted in Paris and color-coded them based on their priority.[67] On military bases, though, in addition to knowing little about planning and design, these leaders do not stay long; they move on average every two years. Changing leadership leads to changing plans. Commanders have abandoned completed master plans and they have re-sited fully designed facilities.

In my survey of planners and architects working for the U.S. military, 80 percent (102) cited changing leadership as one of their most important concerns. Below are excerpts from some comments that reveal a frustration not only with the rate of leadership change but also with the planning qualifications of the leaders:

It seems that many leaders become "designers" when they achieve the rank of colonel. Then they challenge base standards and simply make changes without heeding the plans that we pay lots of money to establish.

The General Plan can change as often as the Wing Commander changes.

When effective planning is accomplished, it is too often overruled by senior leadership without the background to make planning decisions.

What concerns . . . me is that we follow . . . the "whim" of commanders who change every two years.

Every commander is a planner and wants to show accomplishment during their tour, even if it doesn't fit long-term development.

We are subjected to each incoming commander's whims and grand visions, when in reality they are going to be there only for a short period of time. All they are looking for [is] a high visibility legacy project to say, "I made that happen!"

The seemingly arbitrary decisions clearly frustrate these planners. When it takes up to two years to produce a General Plan, those making the plan will likely have to deal with at least two commanders who may have very different ideas. The Air Force lets pilots site buildings but does not let architects design aircraft. Nor does the Air Force give a Wing Commander the option of relocating the wings on a B-1 bomber. But the Air Force has given these pilots (most commanders are former pilots) authority over base planning in order to have someone with clear authority ultimately responsible for the plan. This may be appropriate since many bases have second lieutenants in the planning jobs who are neither planners nor architects. At military bases in the United States and overseas, numerous commanders have said that they wanted to be architects. They finally have a chance. When senior officers retire or depart a base, they can leave their legacy in built form. At many "going-away" and retirement ceremonies, the accomplishments highlighted are not the number of tickets issued by military police on their watch, the quantity of jet fuel consumed, or the number of patients served in the base hospital. Rather, the emcees frequently highlight the number of buildings built and the dollar value of construction completed under the departing leader's command.

To some in the DoD, however, planning was not supposed to happen this way. Jimmy Dishner, the former deputy assistant secretary of the Air Force (Installations) and one of the senior civilians at the Pentagon responsible for planning, design, and construction at Air Force bases, has said, "Wing Commanders should worry about flying, not the General Plan."[68] But they do worry about the plans, and they make changes frequently. The regulation that governs installation planning dictates the level of involvement of a base's leadership. Although a planner wrote AFI 32–7062, it gives responsibility for the plan to the installation commander, not the base's planners or architects. According to Marty Holland, the Air Force's senior planner, "When we were writing the General Plan [regulation] the question came up about who was in charge, and we decided the installation commander was. The Command and the installation commander are responsible for the plan. It should be about how base planners support the vision of the installation commander."[69] Since the commanders have to sign the plans, they are naturally curious about what they are signing. The regulation only requires that the base planner brief the commander on the plan and review it annually. Holland recounted this story:

> I was in a meeting with a base planner recently and I made the comment that the General Plan should be succinct and short. But she told me, "I cannot get all my stuff in 40 pages." But I said, "It's not your plan." She replied, "But it is my plan." I said, "It is not your plan . . . the plan belongs to the installation commander."[70]

Engineers Stanley Hart and Alvin Spivak argue that, "Urban planners do not plan. They follow along behind the parade of those who do— the land developers. The role of professional planners is to sweep up the dung."[71] On military bases, commanders have taken on the role of land developers. The rules devalue the role of base planners. Jamal Stevenson, a former planner at Osan, said:

> The Community Planner becomes a dummy of the Colonels' office since the Colonels do all the planning. The AAFES guy has some power since he plays golf with the general and they're in the money business. He has the ears of the general who tells Jamal to be quiet since it's all worked out. The general says, "Good idea, Jamal, but . . ." [and] you know what's coming and it's not good. The only thing the base leadership knows about Civil Engineering [the organization tasked with preparing the General Plan] is that they can fix the air conditioning, not that they can do comprehensive planning.[72]

Stevenson said this over lunch at Osan's officers club. He sat at a small table in one corner of the cavernous ballroom/lunchroom; across the room was a large table filled with high-ranking American and South Korean officers. A three-star general was presenting the latest planning ideas to this distinguished group, but no one from the office that "prepared" the plan was at the table. Stevenson had not even been notified of this important planning meeting.

In his writings on identity, Paul Gilroy argues that soldiers appear as interchangeable cogs in a machine that attempts to dissolve their individuality and limit their individual agency.[73] This is certainly the case for planners working for the U.S. military. The military's rules work to stamp out individuality and enforce certainty and control. However, designers cannot abrogate completely the responsibility.[74] By accepting and/or defaulting to the suburban known, designers at America's outposts are accomplices in empire's increasing demand for land.

Housing Privatization

One contributing factor to the demand for more land is the demand for bigger homes. But the military thinks it cannot afford to build them, so it has gone to the private sector for help. The firms the military has contracted with are some of the biggest builders in the United States, including the Hunt Building Corporation (the ninth-largest multifamily homebuilder in the United States), Clark Realty (the fifth-largest multifamily homebuilder in the United States), and Forest City (developers of 10 million square feet of shopping centers and 35,000 multifamily units). These firms have done well in American suburbs and are sharing their expertise with the military. Some of the firms have completed projects both in the United States and overseas. As discussed in chapter 2, the Congressional Budget Office (CBO) determined that the cost of new housing for soldiers and their families returning to the States would be $25,000 per year in DoD-owned housing and $29,300 per year in leased housing. The leased housing the CBO refers to is what the military calls "privatized" housing, where private developers, using their own money, build the houses on land given to them by the military. The military then rents the houses for a specified period. The traditional method has been for the military to build housing using congressional appropriations.

According to Jimmy Dishner, the military is interested in privatization for two reasons, even if it is more expensive. First, he has argued, the military's biggest asset is its land. Second, Congress is not providing the money to replace all the housing on military bases.[75] Since Congress does not offer its money, the military offers its land and rent payments in exchange for privatized housing. Despite this possible 17 percent premium, the DoD has moved quickly to privatize its housing stock both on-base and off-base. Contracts for on-base projects are let for up to fifty years, and the land may be given or leased to the developer. Off-base housing occurs when a private company buys its own land in the civilian community and builds the houses.[76]

Unfortunately, the military has not completed postoccupancy evaluations of the units its soldiers have occupied to determine if they indeed are better than DoD-owned housing. Similar leased housing built in the 1990s on at least one Air Force base had substantial failure; in one case, the military vacated many units shortly after construction. Lawyers quickly joined the fray. After the Air Force unsuccessfully tried to resolve the conflict, the Department of Justice took over the case.

The Air Force was trying to meet a serious housing shortfall at the base and developed the concept of "build-lease" where a builder is given land and, through a Request for Proposals (RFP), is told to follow basic requirements in terms of floor area, number of bedrooms, and distribution of units. The developer designs and builds the units and then leases them to the U.S. military. Rather than paying the up-front cost of the units from a congressional appropriation, the military can use each soldier's monthly housing allowance to make the lease payments.

The accountants blessed this concept because without the housing, the allowance would have been spent anyway, so why not spend it on housing that meets minimum military criteria? All of a sudden, a DoD-wide housing deficit could disappear as quickly as the government could contract with developers to build the units. For the developers, this was a sweet deal, too. They had a guaranteed revenue stream that made their projected budgets like gold. They could take these financial projections to a lending institution and usually get attractive financing packages. Banks were loaning money to developers to build housing for the military on the military's land. Developers repaid the banks using the military's monthly housing stipend. The flaw in this scenario? Banks charge interest.

As a result, at the end of a typical lease period, the houses may actually cost substantially more than they would have if the military could have convinced Congress to appropriate the money over a regular period. Another big problem—the military does not own the homes and will need to renegotiate a lease to continue using them. Unlike a home loan, where the occupant eventually pays off the principle, in a lease the lessee never pays principle. But there is a benefit: the base did get the houses more quickly than it would have if it had waited on Congress and, perhaps more important, congressional appropriations could be used for other things, say part of a B-2 bomber. But Congress is paying more over time for the houses it could have built had it just appropriated enough money on a regular basis, as it had done since the founding of the U.S. Army. "Fiscally conservative" Republican politicians now use privatized housing to project costs into the future, repaid later at a higher cost when they may not even be in office. This pattern of shifting expenses to future generations did not seem to bother the Bush administration, which transformed the federal budget from a massive surplus into a record deficit. In addition to the government paying more for the same house, perhaps the developer cut a few corners in construction to get the homes built even faster. Now, repeated below are the published details of a case involving a contractor, a military base, and privatized housing:

> The nation's largest builder of military family housing has agreed to pay the U.S. government $8 million over a five-year period to settle a fraud claim brought by the Justice Department. Hunt Building Corp. also agreed to make repairs to an allegedly faultily designed and constructed 828-unit family housing project at Ellsworth AFB, S.D. "This settlement will ensure that our servicemen and -women will be able to live in habitable housing on Ellsworth AFB and that the United States recovers rents that were paid in the past for uninhabitable housing units," said U.S. Attorney Karen E. Schreier of Sioux Falls, S.D. The project, known as Centennial Estates, was built between 1989 and 1991. Alleged structural and design defects included violations of fire-safety requirements, flaws that caused the units to twist and break apart in the fierce winds of the high plains, and pipes simply inserted into the ground to make it appear as if they were mandatory sewer clean-outs. The Air Force had declared 500 of these units uninhabitable.[77]

Imagine building 828 homes and only 328 are inhabitable after just a few short years. This is a remarkable story of the dangers of wanting too much too quickly. Privatization is not a panacea. But the ability to defer costs for housing leases rather than raise taxes for housing construction makes this scheme attractive to politicians charged with oversight of the DoD. Hence, the military has moved into privatization with gusto. In his 2003 testimony to Congress, Deputy Undersecretary of Defense Raymond DuBois said, "The Department's longstanding policy is to rely primarily on the private sector for its housing needs. Currently, two-thirds of military families reside in private sector housing, and that number will increase as we privatize the existing inventory of housing units owned by the Military Departments."[78]

Jimmy Dishner had this to say before Congress:

> Using the private sector to revitalize or replace over 15,700 housing units will be a great success for the Air Force in addressing critical quality of life concerns. This translates into upgrading 25 percent of our substandard

housing. We firmly believe that through privatization, we can provide improved housing to more airmen in less time than using the standard military construction process.[79]

While the timing claim is certainly accurate, this is also a cover for fiscal inefficiencies. In any case, the Air Force hopes to privatize approximately 31,389 residential units at a cost of approximately $2 billion.[80]

Relying on private contractors is nothing new for the military. As Ann Markusen has shown, the military's strategy of outsourcing arms production led to the rise of the Sunbelt states as a "gunbelt."[81] From fighter jets to suburban homes, the Air Force has led the way in outsourcing and privatization. The Army, historically reluctant to outsource, has also joined the effort. They hope to privatize 85,000 homes on forty-five installations. This represents 92 percent of all their homes.[82] Now armsmakers and homebuilders can join together, lobbying for their own interests. The military-industrial complex has gained a new member.

One way to make the privatization program even more attractive is to make the lease payments higher. Officials have noted that a greater cash flow will attract more contractors to the program.[83] The only way to do that is to increase the maximum monthly housing allowance for soldiers, which the military then gives to the residential developer. This is just what happened in 2000, when the DoD approved one of the largest rate increases in history.[84]

Started in 1996, the privatization program initially focused on bases in the United States, but the military quickly transferred the idea to America's overseas outposts. The first location was Aviano Air Base in northern Italy, where officials considered the base too dense, so housing privatization became the "only" option.[85] Private developers have built over 500 homes there in an innovative program that required the developers to provide the land and the homes (see chapter 6 for more details on this program). A similar program has been on hold at a base in England because the Air Force wants to build houses that are bigger and have more rooms than is the standard in the area.[86] The British are resisting sprawl and have the influence to say no, so far. Now the idea is moving to South Korea, where officials hope to build several thousand homes using a variant of the program. The exchange below, from a 2000 hearing before a subcommittee of the House Armed Services Committee, shows how hybrid policies are formed.[87] Politicians visit a site and view its successes, and then they return to their offices and consider how to apply those policies in the United States:

CONGRESSMAN JOEL HEFLEY (R-Colorado), Chairman, Military Instal-lations and Facilities Subcommittee, U.S. House of Representatives: As you know, this committee has been the spear point of the whole privatization effort. We came up with it, along with Secretary Pirie. We have pushed it, we have believed in it. I'm glad to hear you believe in it still. I was out at Aviano a week or two ago, and looked at the build and lease housing that they have out there. And they are begin-ning to cut in, and they are doing it scattered within a 30-mile range of the air field—or a 30-minute range of the air field, so that you don't develop American military ghettos. They kind of blend into the community. Wonderful housing, and maybe not the cheapest way to do it in the world, but you get wonderful housing on a 10-year lease, and so forth. Have you thought much about pursuing privatization from that kind of a standpoint more in the continental United States?

MR. RUBY DEMESME, Assistant Secretary of the Air Force for Manpower, Reserve Affairs, Installations and Environment: We've thought about it, sir. We're trying real hard to attract the kind of people who would be interested in offering us those kinds of opportunities. So every chance we get, we're out there meeting with groups who have expressed an interest in helping us to move toward the kind of situation where we don't have to put the money up first. As you know, it varies based on location what the capability is in the different communities.

MR. HEFLEY: I think from looking at Aviano, I think that that's some-thing that we shouldn't preclude, the idea of building and lease—and maybe the numbers won't work, but it sure looked like it was working nice out there.

MR. DEMESME: I wish it were possible that we could do that here in the States but, as you know, we can't use the same guidelines here that we use overseas. Now the way that we score our projects here prohibits us from using that concept.

MR. HEFLEY: Would it help if we put in legislation to broaden your ability to use innovative approaches?

MR. DEMESME: If we had the ability, we would certainly do our best to make it work.

There are several noteworthy aspects of this exchange. First, Hefley wants to make it clear that a Republican Congress came up with the idea of privatization showing the link between land use and politics. Second, Hefley admits that privatization is more expensive but the concept clearly appeals to Republicans who can spend more (in the future) without appearing to spend more (in the present). Third, he wants the scattered-site Aviano model imported to the United States, which will require some rule changes. The Pentagon's representative, DeMesme, informs the committee that current laws stand in the way of the model but, if given the chance, he would do his "best" to make it work in the United States. Note that Hefley likes the fact that the Aviano housing "blends into the community" because the rest of the base certainly does not. He likely toured a carefully selected sample of Aviano's housing. Of the eight sites visited for this study, only two looked remotely like anything built in the local community.

What we are witnessing is a transfer of power, from government planning to privatized planning. We saw this earlier with places of consumption, the base exchanges and commissaries at America's outposts. Now we are seeing it with housing. As Dolores Hayden notes, the physical realization of stateside suburbia is "in the hands of developers trying to turn a profit through suburban growth."[88] Since construction generates higher than average profits,[89] it is no wonder that we see the conservative advocates of a "free market" pushing government land-use policy in the direction of private development. Kenneth Jackson shows us how this marriage between public and private interests built suburban America, and now we are seeing it build suburbs in foreign lands.[90]

Whether in the United States or overseas, an asymmetry of power favoring the private sector is the result.[91] Ivan Louden, a planner who has worked at bases in the United States and overseas, recounts this story of AAFES looking for a gas-station site at an Air Force base in the United States:

> We asked AAFES, how much room do you need? They told us one-fifth of an acre. But that was only for the building! It didn't account for all the parking and roads they wanted. So, I found a three-acre site they would actually fill. My boss saw both site plans, the AAFES one-fifth of an acre diagram and my three-acre site plan and asked why they looked different. Why, I told her, was because they operate in a world of unconstrained thinking.

By unconstrained thinking, Ivan meant that AAFES could get away with siting a building wherever they wanted and would adjust down the initially proposed size of the building to fit the site they wanted. Then, when the base approved the site, AAFES would come back and ask for more land in the same area in which to expand. Louden continued, "The biggest problem is how to represent counter rationale—will a General Plan help? No, anything that's not set in stone is up for grabs."[92]

The AAFES approach clearly frustrated Louden. This has occurred at other bases as well. AAFES planners ask for a small site to get approval from the base, then come back later with a plan that requires several times the area initially approved. At this point, AAFES refuses to change sites since they have already invested design funds and any change would be a "lost effort." With the General Plan useless, the siting decisions are left up to the whims of engineers at AAFES headquarters in Dallas. Louden added, "AAFES folks are like big time trial lawyers coming to Mayberry. 'I've been in touch with Dallas,' they say. How can the base compete?"[93]

For the most part, the base cannot compete. AAFES usually gets their way. And now, private housing developers will get their way as well, even if it is more expensive and may be blown over by strong winds. While privatization in all its forms is one significant trend influencing planning at today's outposts, an even more aggressive policy from a spatial consumption perspective deals with the U.S. military's increasing fear of terrorism.

Policies of Fear

On October 14, 2004, two men hand-carried small bombs in their backpacks into the Iraqi Green Zone in Baghdad, a heavily protected compound where the American leadership has lived and worked. After having tea in the popular Green Zone Café, one man left but the other stayed behind. A few minutes later, a bomb exploded in a nearby open-air street market, and then the man at the café detonated his bomb. Seven people died, including the suicide bombers.[94] The U.S. military controls security for the Green Zone and, following the incident, increased air surveillance over Baghdad, added armed patrols in and around the Green Zone, and strengthened checkpoint security. The zone, however, is not strictly a government or military compound; hundreds of Americans and approximately 10,000 Iraqis live in the four-square-mile area.[95] Two months after the attack in the Green Zone, a suicide bomber attacked a military dining hall in northern Iraq killing 21 U.S. and Iraqi personnel and injuring sixty.[96] The attacker made it onto the heavily guarded base, walked into the dining hall, then detonated his explosive devices.

This is the evolving face of terror confronting the new American Empire. Military planners, though, are not facing this new threat. They are responding to car bombs, not backpack bombs. They hope to create a new type of *cordon sanitaire,* a new barrier to quell their fears. Rather than draw a line against floating miasmas, they are drawing a line against driving terrorists. In both cases, the prescriptions are ill conceived. However, they are also understandable given the deadly history of explosions at American targets:[97]

> October 1983: A truck drives past unarmed guards and explodes under a
>   U.S. Marine barracks in Beirut, killing 241.
> February 1993: A truck drives into the unguarded underground parking
>   garage of the World Trade Center in New York City and explodes,
>   killing six and injuring more than 1,000.
> April 1995: A truck parks next to the Murrah Building in Oklahoma City
>   and explodes, killing 168 and injuring more than 200.
> June 1996: A tanker truck filled with 5,000 pounds of explosives parks
>   next to a U.S. Air Force compound in Saudi Arabia and explodes,
>   killing 19 and wounding 372.
> August 1998: Two cars park next to U.S. embassies in Tanzania and
>   Kenya and explode, killing over 200 and wounding thousands.

This is, of course, an abbreviated list. Trucks and cars link these five events. The simple-minded solution is to keep trucks and cars away from buildings. The military commissioned studies. Then they wrote sweeping rules that have influenced the use of land in unprecedented ways. As is so often the case in the use of space, the U.S. military is following examples from the past made futile by the changing tactics of terror.

As European empires extended their reach into India and Africa in the nineteenth and early twentieth centuries, they justified their spatial policies on fear, not of local residents with car bombs, but of unclean environments. British soldiers in India did die at an alarming rate. In addition to an astonishing rate of venereal disease, malaria also took its toll on the British Army. The combined death rate was over three times the death rate in England, and this does not account for war-related deaths. Moreover, life expectancy dropped by twenty-two years for soldiers spending time in India. While one solution was to regulate prostitution (see chapter 1), another was to separate the soldiers from the other vectors. One of the solutions to the problem of disease was to surround the cantonment with a defensive wall and a clear zone of up to two miles, undisturbed by agricultural use.[98] The British separated native towns, like Calcutta, with their "foul" smells, filth, and dirty air, from the cantonments and forts. In Calcutta, the 1,250-acre, two-mile long Esplanade could contain a crowd of a million people, under the watchful eye and deadly cannons of Britain's Fort William.[99] The Esplanade was an impressive open field of fire. Even within the cantonments, the apparently chaotic and dirty quarters of camp followers, prostitutes, and sepoys confronted the "orderliness" of the British areas.[100]

While the cost of defensive perimeters led nineteenth-century imperial powers to focus on compact cantonments both within their colonial cities and at the edges, the fear of an atomic explosion led twentieth-century empires to focus on dispersing development. Suburban development patterns were actually promoted as a defensive measure. Numerous scholars have revealed how policymakers and politicians justified American suburbs as a response to the fear induced by the Soviet threat.[101] What better way to avoid the fallout of an atomic bomb than spreading out development across the landscape? But in hindsight, one could argue that even the lowest density development

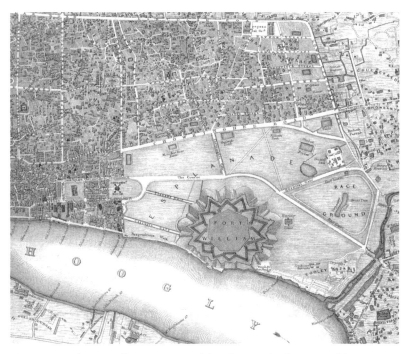

Figure 5.12. Calcutta, India, 1842. Recognizing the security threat posed by a restless populace, the British Empire employed wide esplanades to separate their forts from the locals. From Melville Branch, *An Atlas of Rare City Maps.*

would do little to ameliorate the effects of a nuclear detonation. Dispersal is, in fact, a common military tactic and the dispersion (read sprawl) of suburban life was seen as one way of dealing with Cold War threats. This rationale resurfaced following the September 11, 2001, attacks with office users dispersing into the suburbs from major metropolitan areas for security reasons.[102] Post–September 11, the military has implemented dispersal on multiple scales. At the macro scale, the military has planned to relocate out of some congested and vulnerable urban centers overseas. At the micro scale, the military has implemented sweeping measures aimed at dispersing its buildings on each installation to a greater extent than even imagined during the Cold War. Ironically, this dispersal has occurred at the same time the military has discounted the value of its own defensive perimeters.

The End of the Wall

In one of the few breaks from past imperial powers, the new American Empire has abandoned the wall as an effective defensive measure. To be sure, walls are not all powerful. Hitler went around France's Maginot Line. But discounting their ability to keep twenty-first-century terrorists at bay comes with a spatial price. The problem with this is that the U.S. military does not consider limited land availability an impediment to its antiterrorism planning philosophy. U.S. military planners are dealing with the fear of terrorism in several ways. They are consolidating missions and trying to reduce the number of installations overseas. They are relocating bases from urban areas like Seoul to more remote areas. They are making these bases even more self-contained in an attempt to minimize the need for soldiers to go off-base. As a result, the United States has built new hotels, homes, and shopping malls on many of its overseas outposts. In addition, military planners have implemented detailed antiterrorism planning requirements. However, these rules reveal a continued desire to develop at extremely low densities, which only complicates consolidation efforts.

While fears of locals protesting against the presence of expansive military facilities is driving down the number of overseas bases, the fear of terrorism is driving up the size of bases that remain. In a classic example of what seems to be fighting the previous war, these new planning directives applicable to all bases worldwide focus on providing "stand-

Figure 5.13. Palmanova, Italy, 1593–1623. Built by the Venetians, Palmanova exemplified the principle of perimeter stand-off. Today's military commanders have reversed the model and have largely given up on the secured perimeter. They have implemented wide setbacks within their outposts, separating buildings, streets, and parking lots in a costly effort to protect people from car bombs. If Palmanova had twenty-five-meter setbacks between all the buildings and all the internal roads, it would have required immensely more land and would have created a perimeter that would have been difficult to defend. From Pubbli Aer Foto.

off" distance of twenty-five meters from most buildings and perceived threats. Military police define standoff as the distance between an asset (i.e., building) and a threat (i.e., car bomb). Standoff distances are not new in military planning: Palmanova, in Italy, for example, built in the late sixteenth century, had considerable standoff distance (Figure 5.13). The difference now is that the U.S. military wants standoff distances between buildings on-base in addition to a cordon sanitaire between the base and adjacent development.

This policy is not in response to September 11, 2001, but to the 1996 Khobar Towers bombing. Where did the twenty-five meters come from? A group of structural engineers working at the Pentagon determined it was an appropriate distance given the type of construction normally found on military bases and the explosive potential of a typical car bomb.

It was also roughly the distance separating a tanker truck and its 5,000 pounds of plastic explosives from the most heavily damaged dormitory at Khobar Towers. But applying this distance to every building inside a base is a misreading of the Khobar Towers incident. The tanker truck could not get inside the perimeter fence; drivers parked it off the base in a lot that the military knew was a potential problem site.

The political repercussions following this incident are worth noting because they illuminate ways in which policies that increase land consumption become the norm. According to former secretary of defense William Cohen, even the installation commander at the time, Brig. Gen. Terryl Schwalier, understood that a "truck bomb parked at the perimeter of the Khobar Towers compound, where many of his forces were housed, represented one of the most serious threats facing his command." In assigning blame for the incident, Secretary Cohen noted that Schwalier did not "take adequate account of the implications of this threat or develop an effective plan for how his command should respond to it." Although the general did fail to effectively raise the issue with his superiors and his Saudi counterparts, planners working for him tried repeatedly to close the parking lot adjacent to the base, but Saudi officials ignored their requests. For General Schwalier's failure of "leadership," Secretary Cohen publicly "recommended to the President that his name be removed from the list of those to be promoted to [the] grade" of major general.[103] In the military, this is tantamount to being fired. Schwalier retired a month later. In addition, three days before Secretary Cohen's public announcement, the highest-ranking officer in the Air Force effectively resigned under the euphemism of an "early retirement" over the matter. General Ronald Fogleman stated:

> [I] simply lost respect and confidence in the leadership that I was supposed to be following [and] watched the way the United States Air Force as an institution was treated, for purely political reasons, and the way an individual was treated and came to the conclusion that it was fundamentally wrong. I just could not begin to imagine facing the Air Force after Secretary Cohen made the decision to cancel General Schwalier's promotion.[104]

The shock waves echoed through the entire U.S. military. The resignation of a chief of staff, even if couched in terms of an "early retirement," was profound. While the Secretary of Defense and even President Clinton may have been looking for someone to blame for the event, the vulnerability on the ground, from a land-planning perspective, was well known before the event. No other commander wanted to be the next one forced to retire. Force protection was the hot topic, and no one wanted to jeopardize the safety of American soldiers. Planners, military police, and senior leaders were looking for easy solutions. The eventual adoption of the twenty-five-meter standoff distance was the easiest solution.

Military police have created this standoff distance as part of a set of far-reaching planning regulations that affect every new project built on every U.S. military installation. Planners have ceded their domain to police. As Nan Ellin argues, "form follows fear."[105] Two policy documents direct this new response to fear. In 1997, the Air Force published the *Installation Force Protection Guide*. The guide introduced the concept of "Anti-Terrorism/Force-Protection," known in the military as AT/FP. The anonymous authors recognized that there are no universal solutions to terrorist attacks but proceeded to privilege standoff distance as the preferred solution. At the time, the "recommendations" applied to buildings with over 300 personnel. The guide recommends that buildings be arranged into "complexes with strongly delineated boundaries" and that they be oriented to enhance "surveillance opportunities" and "defensible space," which can be "protected more efficiently than scattered buildings."[106] The language borrows the title and ideas from Oscar Newman's book, and its use of surveillance is similar to Jane Jacobs's concept of "eyes-on-the-street."[107] The guide even recommended fewer windows and also specified the use of earth-tone-colored buildings to diminish their prominence. The guide, however, did not regulate the exact standoff distance. That came after September 11, 2001, at the height of imperial fear. In 2002 the DoD published its *Minimum Antiterrorism Standards for Buildings*. Oscar Perman, the Air Force's director of installation planning at the time, expressed mixed feelings about the standards:

> I have some feeling that the distances are arbitrary. What difference does it make if I'm one side of the line or the other. A lot has to do with the amount of explosive in a vehicle. The fact is standards exist until someone says they're ridiculous.[108]

Amazingly, Perman confirms that planners had no input on the policy documents:

> We [Air Force planners] had no role in it—it was solely from explosive things you had to deal with. They're just like Q-D arcs—based on damage based on amount of explosives. At least with munitions facilities we control the net explosive weights [size of bombs;] with a car it could be anywhere.

When asked if this meant planners had handed over planning to the military police, he replied: "Planning is not being dictated by police, we just have to follow criteria—I put it in the palette I use. It's just part of it. Those are the rules you play by. We don't have choices."[109] This is a contradictory statement. If rules do not dictate action, what good are they? The rules reflect the will of those in charge, in this case the security police.

American military planners did not participate in creating the rules. They did not object, knowing the vast amount of real estate the policies would require. They did not challenge the flawed assumption that the next bomb would always be from a car or truck. The requirements are just one more set of "criteria" to meet. There is no choice. However, planners had a choice and they decided, for whatever reasons, to have no role in shaping the standards. Perhaps no one invited them to the meetings at the "Force Protection Battlelab" to discuss these changes. Or perhaps they felt, like Oscar Perman, that planners just follow rules written by someone else. Interestingly, Marty Holland, the Air Force's former senior planner, had another perspective, "AT/FP is an impossible constraint—no waivers, it's like we're force protection monkeys—a sergeant from security police is in charge of planning the base now."[110] This seems to be the more realistic view.

While planners have turned planning over to the police, the police have largely given up on the defended perimeter, which at most bases is flimsy chainlink fencing topped by a few strands of barbed wire. There is some merit to their concern. In South Korea, for example, the United States has investigated allegations that almost anyone can gain access by bribing with as little as $10 the South Korean soldiers who guard the gates of America's outposts.[111] Without the protection of a wall or effective gate, the defensive perimeter moves into the base, around every building. The space required to implement the policy is immense. Buildings with occupancies of fifty or more people must be twenty-five meters (82 feet) away from any road, parking lot, or dumpster. Inhabited buildings have occupancies between eleven and forty-nine and they need to

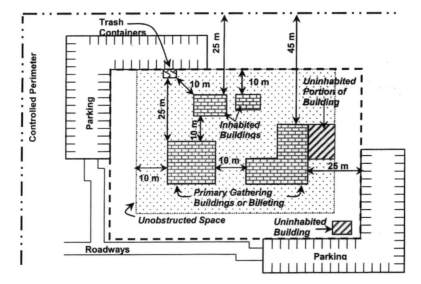

Figure 5.14. The required stand-off distances and building separations for all U.S. military installations. The net effect is increasingly sprawled-out bases with ever-longer perimeters. Every "primary gathering building" on an installation (buildings with occupant loads of fifty or more) must have a ten-meter clear zone (grass only) and a twenty-five-meter setback (or stand-off) between all roads and parking lots. From Department of Defense, Unified Facilities Criteria 4–010–01.

be ten meters (33 feet) away from any road, parking lot, or dumpster. All buildings need to have a minimum separation of ten meters and must have an unobstructed space (i.e., no landscaping other than grass) of ten meters as well.

Some exceptions provide interesting contradictions. For instance, military family housing buildings with twelve units or less are exempt. Suppose each family has four people: that means forty-eight people could live in one building, exempt from the standards. But dormitories with eleven or more occupants must have a twenty-five-meter standoff. So one base could build a dormitory with eleven occupants with a required twenty-five-meter standoff next to a family housing building with forty-eight occupants and no standoff. In addition to exempting family housing with twelve units or less, shopping centers and fast-food franchises are also exempt since "their operation require[s] parking in close proximity."[112] These are just two of the inconsistencies in the policy. When the military fully implements the AT/FP policies, the only certain conclusion will be increasingly sprawled-out compounds with longer perimeters that will only be more difficult to defend. Or worse, these polices are driving designers to build fewer larger buildings, thereby concentrating personnel, which makes these buildings much more attractive targets. Enforcing twenty-five-meter setbacks that require designers to site one twelve-story building rather than four three-story buildings puts the entire occupancy of the building at risk if a backpack bomber walks through the doors. As one planner struggling with the requirements recounted, "the rules are making me put all my eggs in one basket. But as soon as you say something the response is 9/11 and the subject is closed. The setbacks just spread everything out—they're killing us." By killing he meant he could not find sites for new buildings that had twenty-five-meter setbacks from roads or parking.[113] Another planner had this to say:

> My largest concern is in regard to antiterrorism, force protection setback requirements. It is undisputed that the first and most important aspect of base security is perimeter security. Therefore, gates should be improved, fences and perimeter surveillance improved, etc. Instead, our setback requirements are driving less dense bases that require more vehicle traffic and consume land indiscriminately.[114]

These planners struggle to make the rules work but recognize their flaws. As bases get less dense, they will need to expand. Just one twenty-meter-wide building with a road in front and parking to the rear requires seventy meters of space—that is bigger than a Portland, Oregon, city block. These policies contradict current thinking as articulated by advocates of crime prevention through environmental design and may jeopardize the ability of bases to accommodate new or relocated missions, which is an essential element in the strategy currently underway that aims to reduce bases by consolidating missions on select bases.[115]

With all the required setbacks, planners argue there is little room for these missions on existing bases. For example, as part of the joint Korea–U.S. Land Partnership Plan, the United States intends to give up leases on 30,000 acres in exchange for 3,000 additional acres on which to relocate the affected troops.[116] At Osan Air Base, the U.S. military needed additional acreage to build a new housing complex that met the antiterrorism setback requirements. So, at the request of the U.S. military and to make room for the $36-million housing complex, the South Korean government relocated several South Korean families from their small collection of homes standing in the way of the project.

The paranoia that swept the military, post–September 11, filtered into a policy document that is drastically changing the spatiality of every U.S. military base around the world. However, the prescriptions are a misreading of the events. The twenty-five-meter standoff distance is a knee-jerk reaction to the Khobar Towers bombing. Of course, twenty-five meters is meaningless against an airplane or missile attack. In Beirut and New York City, the trucks drove past lightly guarded or unguarded gates. In Oklahoma City, Khobar, and Africa, the trucks and cars were on uncontrolled public streets. The lesson from these events should not be that a car will freely drive onto a base, park next to an office building, and detonate a trunkload of explosives. Rather, the lesson should be that the military should protect the gate and the perimeter as a first step.

The British thought bad air caused malaria and promulgated policies to clean the air. The U.S. military plans as if bomb-filled vehicles are the only culprits and is promoting policies to clear the roads. In India, the vector was the lowly mosquito. Today the vector is an angry person who may use a vehicle, plane, missile, or backpack. Clearly, it is faulty to focus on protecting from only one mode of attack. But military police have little control over what happens outside the gates of a base; so, they are now exercising new control over the building process inside the gates and advocating bases that will be even more like prisons.

Imperial powers have adopted regimes of control to exercise overriding power and to address their own fears. The cordon sanitaire was one such system. It accommodated imperial power and assuaged imperial fear. Now, standoff distance is another system. Military police have parlayed September 11 into a vast expansion of their power. Not only do they get better automatic weapons, but they can now veto master plans. No planner is prepared to challenge a well-armed military police officer. At every base post–September 11, a force protection officer will take out a scale and verify that the plan has the required twenty-five-meter setbacks. If it does not, the officer will send it back rejected. But it is not the nine-millimeter pistol that is intimidating; rather it is the backing of these policies by those with the power to hire and fire that can intimidate. Military police are in the fear business. The more fear, the more business they get; including the power to approve or reject development plans.

Many U.S. soldiers stationed overseas have a more balanced view. "The military is really solidified in the community; the locals seem happy that we're here," said Col. Wayne Kennedy, the former commander for all Army outposts in South Korea's southern half. "I actually like it better overseas, I feel safer and it's a tighter community."[117] His feelings are justifiable. With surveillance cameras, controlled entries, perimeter fences (as flimsy as they may be), and armed security patrols, bases are gated enclaves. Background checks on residents screen out convicted felons, fingerprints of most residents remain on file, and one's neighbors are likely to be experts with automatic weapons. "For an American over here, it's as safe or safer to live here than any urban area in the United States," said Col. John Ley, an attorney for U.S. Forces Korea at Yongsan garrison in Seoul.[118]

Conclusion: Conflicting Rules

The fragmented practice of architecture and planning on America's outposts results from a plethora of oftentimes contradictory rules. These rules combine with unqualified planners, unable to control the process. In many cases, planning is done by second lieutenants just out of college who either do not understand or do not care about it, installation commanders who can fly an F-16 but know little about planning, and military police who know how to wield a ruler or automatic weapon but are oblivious to the larger impacts of their standoff rules. All this adds up to massive land use and a failure, in the end, to increase either safety or sustainability.

On America's outposts, architects and planners are literally foot soldiers, dealing with a world of rules partly of their making that link disparate sites together into a global military corporation. Their suburban development plans may seem explainable in a foreign land for they are an indicator of power relationships with minimal negotiation. Suburban spaces can be easily controlled and monitored. Their wide streets, low densities, and easily surveiled landscapes simplify certainty and control. Designers write compatibility guides that call for more contextual design that contradict painting rules calling for light brown buildings everywhere. They publish transportation rules that limit who can drive on-base that conflict with rules creating sprawling bases that force driving. They create force protection rules that require extensive standoff, resulting in extremely low densities, at odds with the U.S. military's requirement that all construction be "sustainable," as measured by mandatory compliance with the U.S. Green Building Council's Leadership in Energy and Environmental Design (LEED) criteria. This is one

Floor Area Ratio

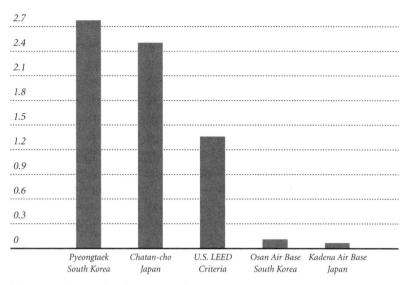

Figure 5.15. Comparing floor area ratios.

conflict worthy of elaboration. The LEED criteria calls for "sustainable sites" with a preference for densities of 60,000 square feet per acre, which translates into an overall Floor Area Ratio (FAR) of 1.38.[119] Not including the area devoted to the airfield and its functions, Osan Air Base, for instance, has 3,960 square feet of building per acre (FAR 0.09) and Kadena Air Base in Japan has just 1,689 square feet of building per acre (FAR 0.04). Sustainability on these bases defaults to recycled carpet and more efficient light bulbs (Figure 5.15).

As Christine Boyer notes, "against the chaos of the city with its simultaneity of land uses, jumble of vehicles, multitudes of people, corrupt politicians, and labor unrest, there stood an idea: the city as a perfectly disciplined spatial order."[120] Suburbia offers up this spatial order. To make these places, planners have an abridged role. Rather than plan, they map. Rather than design, they download AutoCAD templates. The result, however, is not suburbia by default. While designers complain about language barriers, staff changes, and intervention from above, privatization and policies of fear largely dictate the design of today's outposts. While the military has modified some policies over the years, the underlying desire for sprawling compounds has changed little in five decades. While the Cold War threat used to justify suburban sprawl was a Soviet SS-18 Intercontinental Ballistic Missile, the latest threat is a car bomb. Ironically, policies that call for even bigger homes and dormitories, substantial security buffers around every building, and larger shopping malls only increase the demand for land. When coupled with a new desire to build increasingly self-contained bases in more remote areas of "host" nations, the new model of avoidance requires even more of someone else's land.

Michel Foucault's description of the panopticon raises disturbing questions in this era of American hegemony. "At the periphery," he writes, "an annular building; at the center a tower.... All that is needed, then, is to place a supervisor in a central tower and to shut up in each cell a madman, a patient, a condemned man, a worker or a schoolboy."[121] Where are today's cells? The windowless buildings built under an architecture of fear? The locked-down bases developed for an expanding military-commercial complex? Or the unlucky nation-states that find themselves under the disciplinary gaze of the "new" American Empire? The space of America's outposts allows us to see with alarming clarity relationships of hegemony and subordination. In the next section, we will see examples of how the U.S. military has inscribed these relationships on specific landscapes in Italy, South Korea, and Japan.

PART III
Outposts under Construction

We owe the clearest cultural map of structural change not to novelists or literary critics, but to architects and designers. Their products, their social roles as cultural producers, and the organization of consumption in which they intervene create shifting landscapes in the most material sense.

—Sharon Zukin, *Landscapes of Power*

CHAPTER SIX

Reinforcing the Southern Flank: Aviano 2000

On January 17, 1966, near Palomares, Spain, a USAF B-52 bomber collided at 30,500 feet with a KC-135 tanker aircraft during routine high-altitude refueling. The B-52 accidentally dropped four nuclear bombs; three landed near the town of Palomares and one landed in the ocean. High-explosive material blew up and spread radioactive debris over 588 acres of farmland. Both planes crashed near the Spanish town, killing seven of the eleven crewmembers. It took eighty days to recover the nuclear bombs, which did not detonate. The United States also removed 1,400 tons of contaminated soil and vegetation from the site.[1]

On February 3, 1998, Marine captain Richard Ashby's EA-6B Grumman Prowler jet sliced two gondola cables near Aviano, Italy. The gondola fell over 300 feet to the ground, killing twenty. The U.S. military charged the pilot with twenty counts of involuntary manslaughter. During opening arguments, prosecutors told jurors that Ashby performed an unauthorized corkscrew roll and was flying more than 1,600 feet below the 2,000-foot limit. The event prompted calls to close Aviano Air Base in Italy. A U.S. military court-martial acquitted the pilot. Controversy erupted over the use of maps: although Italian maps provided to the United States showed the cable, U.S. maps used by the pilot did not. Of course, had he not been flying too low the maps would not have been necessary. The U.S. Congress paid $20 million to rebuild the cables, the U.S. maps did not change, and the base remains open.[2]

Geopolitics, Calamity, and Place

These two tragic events tie Italy, Spain, and the United States in an imperial triangle that exposes the link between geopolitics and land-use planning. Following the nuclear accident at Palomares, Spain's U.S.-supported dictator Gen. Francisco Franco quickly suppressed anti-American protests and brushed off the calamity. After his death in 1975, Spanish politicians used the unforgettable event to justify Amendment 6 of the 1976 treaty between the United States and Spain. The amendment prohibited the United States from storing nuclear weapons in Spain, despite $1.22 billion in economic aid from the U.S. military. The U.S. Air Force's Torrejón Air Base was an especially controversial site since it was on the outskirts of Madrid and its F-16s were capable of carrying nuclear missiles.

Opposition to the U.S. presence in Spain grew until finally in January 1988 the two countries decided on a withdrawal of most U.S. forces from Spain. The United States agreed to remove its seventy-two F-16s from Torrejón Air Base by 1992. However, the United States was reluctant to vacate NATO's southern flank, so the Reagan and (first) Bush administrations sought out other locations in the region. The Italian government offered up land outside of Crotone, in a remote portion of southern Italy. The only restriction was that the United States could not equip aircraft at a new air base in Crotone with nuclear armaments. Since the United States and Italy had already agreed that Aviano Air Base in northern Italy would be made available for the forward deployment of U.S. nuclear-capable aircraft, the United States accepted the restriction at Crotone and the two governments agreed that this would be an acceptable replacement for Torrejón.[3] The U.S. military then engaged a U.S. planning and engineering firm to prepare a master plan for the site (Figure 6.1).

In addition to the consulting team, the Air Force assigned Oscar Perman, at the time a landscape architect and planner working in the United States, to assist with the effort. Perman describes how the Crotone plan came about: "It pretty much mirrored everything we had already. Our bases look like major farm areas to locals. They can see land use there but they don't understand what part of that deals with requirements of explosives, and airfield lateral clearances." When asked if he made it to Crotone, Perman replied, "I never made it to the site. They already had it picked out—the challenge was how do I take land I have and put facilities in place."[4]

Map 6.1. The U.S. Air Force in Italy: Aviano Air Base is north of Venice and the proposed Crotone Air Base site is on the southern coastline.

Here a team of designers had an opportunity to create an entire base from scratch, and they just "mirrored everything" else. The team supposedly designed the plan with "an overriding concern for human-scale pedestrian experiences" and attempted to evoke attributes "of the local cultural setting."[5] This was supposed to occur even though some on the planning team never made it to the site. Despite the rhetoric, the plan was neither "human-scaled" nor reflective of any local planning patterns.

Figure 6.1. A suburban production in Italy: the proposed master plan for Crotone Air Base. The plan for the neatly segregated but quite sprawling base sited the airfield on the left side, the commercial area in the center, and the housing on the right. From U.S. Air Force.

Another Air Force planner involved with the Crotone plan was Jack Lundy. He said one of the planning objectives was to "[p]rovide the most efficient, maintainable, and cost effective use of base resources to support the mission and provide a high quality of life for base personnel and their families." One can question whether the sprawling plan is actually efficient or contributes to quality of life. In any case, Lundy also highlights one key problem with the site. It was "on the path of one of three major migratory bird routes in Europe. Since the site was near the Mediterranean Sea, the birds stopped there before crossing the water. The F-16 is very vulnerable to bird strikes."[6] This is an understatement since one bird, if sucked into the jet intake, can bring down the $35-million fighter. And if the migratory birds were not enough of a problem, the site given to the United States was adjacent to a landfill and its population of birds.

Despite the bird hazards, the team prepared the master plan, which in the end could be for a base anywhere. The master planners acted as if they had a tabula rasa. But there is no such thing as a tabula rasa or blank site. Every place has layers of history, cultural meaning, and environmental constraints. In spite of these layers, the team proposed an American suburb. Recalling the checklist for a suburban production presented in chapter 4, this plan meets all the criteria. It is auto focused, abundantly paved, widely spaced, extensively lawned, franchised, and clearly segregated (Figure 6.2). To be fair, the planners did lay out a "pedestrian mall" in the heart of the "community center" that made for an attractive rendering when the artist cropped out the twenty-three acres of asphalt surrounding the center (Figure 6.3). The area is hardly different from a suburban U.S. shopping mall, though. The Crotone mall is an island in a sea of parking. Reinforcing the franchised nature of the place, anchoring one end is the base exchange, in the middle is the commissary, and at the other end is a hotel.

In 1990, as part of its annual design awards program, the Air Force

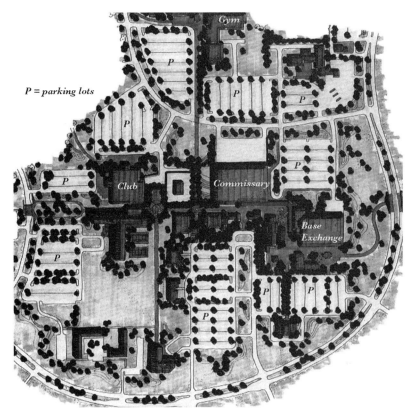

Figure 6.2. Site plan of Crotone Community Center. The plan called for an open-air shopping mall at the heart of the base surrounded by acres of asphalt. From U.S. Air Force.

Figure 6.3. Pedestrian mall of Crotone Community Center. From U.S. Air Force.

gave the planning firm a Merit Award for the plan. The five-member jury consisted of two planners, a landscape architect, an architect, and an engineer, all from private consulting firms. The landscape architect worked for the Rouse Company, developer of the "New Town" of Columbia, Maryland. The Crotone plan shares many attributes with Columbia, from the central importance of a village center/shopping mall to the use of superblocks bisected by meandering bike paths. The engineer was a retired military officer serving as chief of the Military Family Housing Branch of the National Association of Homebuilders. He authored the Army's *Family Housing Guide,* which was similar to the Air Force's housing guide. As an employee of a lobbying group for low-density housing in the United States, this engineer clearly was supportive of exporting the same development patterns overseas.

The award was not the only Crotone-related event in 1990. That same year, Rep. Patricia Schroeder, a Democrat from Colorado, introduced House Resolution 498 with twenty-seven cosponsors. The bill's longwinded title was also its purpose: "To prohibit the construction of facilities for the purpose of relocating functions of the DoD located at Torrejón Air Base, Madrid, Spain, to Crotone, Italy, or any other location outside the United States."[7] The congressional Democrats did not look too kindly on building a new base in Italy. The political opposition both in the United States and in Italy, the substantial price tag, the bird problem, and the waning of the Cold War convinced the DoD to drop its support for the plan, and Congress then voted not to fund construction of the new air base.[8]

Spain, however, would not rescind its withdrawal demands for the F-16s. So the homeless jets relocated temporarily to the little used airfield at Aviano Air Base in northern Italy in 1992, near the Italian town of Aviano, north of Venice. The 1,207-acre base (population 8,500) and the Italian town of Aviano (population 8,000) are located at the base of the Alps at the edge of the Po Valley, a rich agricultural plain.[9] The town has supported a military airfield since 1911. Aviano Air Base's history goes back to the early days of Italian military aviation and shares the distinction with two other bases as the "Cradle of the Italian Air Force." Italy started a flight training school in 1912. During World War I, Italy used the airfield in missions against the Austro-German armies. Between the world wars, Aviano served as a training and operational base that housed both fighter and bomber squadrons.

During World War II, both the Italian Air Force and the German Luftwaffe flew missions from Aviano. In the later stages of the war, the base received severe damage from Allied bombings and required significant repairs. The British captured the base in 1945 and conducted air operations until 1947. Then, in 1954, the U.S. and Italian governments signed an agreement that converted Aviano into a North Atlantic Treaty Organization (NATO) base. The threat was the Soviet Union and the goal was to stop a first strike by the Red Army. The primary NATO bases were in Germany, guarding the Fulda Gap, which military strategists assumed would be the site of the first clash between NATO and the Red Army. As a result, NATO and U.S. funds for buildings flowed to Germany, not Italy. Throughout the Cold War and up to the first Gulf War in 1992, the base was primarily a staging and logistics storage location with no permanently assigned aircraft. Many soldiers even called the base "Sleepy Hollow." When the Cold War ended in the late 1980s, changes came to Europe. With the Soviet threat gone, the United States cut its military presence in Europe from 350,000 to roughly 85,000 and closed numerous bases in both Germany and England. The U.S. Air Force, for instance, eliminated ten of sixteen major bases in Europe.[10]

Aviano had a different future. Torrejón's F-16s changed the role of the base. In 1992 the United States made permanent the fighter wing's move from Torrejón to Aviano Air Base. Even though the F-16s had a new home, the hope was that they would remain unused. The political climate focused on the promise of a "New World Order," with peace and prosperity replacing the Cold War's fears and warfare economies. However, the peace imagined by politicians never materialized. Regional conflicts across the globe led to military responses by the United States, NATO, and the United Nations. Aviano's location made it a central player in all the conflicts. Aviano was the closest NATO base to the former Yugoslavia and was only one of the few permanent joint U.S./NATO bases near the Mediterranean capable of sustaining operations in the Middle East. This strategic location transferred the center of gravity for NATO military operations from Germany to Italy.

Since the F-16s moved from Torrejón, Aviano has supported flying operations for numerous regional conflicts: the Persian Gulf War, Bosnia, Kosovo, Afghanistan, and the Iraq War. Throughout the 1990s, the base supported more than 200 aircraft on an airfield designed for seventy-five. With these airplanes came a host of personnel—from fighter pilots to dental technicians. The base's military population went from 1,600 to 3,500 practically overnight. Soldiers were sleeping in tents or renting rooms ninety minutes away, resulting in traffic jams in Aviano and nearby towns. Local citizens and politicians complained bitterly about the spill-over. "It was a nightmare," said Col. Gary LaGassey, the lead construction manager at Aviano. The Air Force picked LaGassey, a career officer fluent in Italian, to oversee all construction at the base. He added, "Housing prices skyrocketed. We had people living in substandard homes, even barns." President Clinton highlighted Aviano's problems, including the inadequacies of the built environment, during his remarks at the base in the summer of 1999. "I know this has been difficult for many of you," he said. "To sleep ten to a tent, work twelve-hour shifts, six days a week." Change was on its way.[11]

Aviano 2000

The change came under a program dubbed "Aviano 2000." After Clinton's visit, the base experienced an unprecedented building boom. One could call this an "ambitious empire." The goal was to get people out of the barns and tents and into permanent buildings. LaGassey, who retired in 2005 after serving for nearly six years as the head of Aviano 2000, was the driving force in executing the grand plan. When looking back on his time at Aviano, he said, "It's a part of my soul."[12] He spent more than twenty years on a variety of assignments in Italy and even met his wife, Luciana, while in Italy. The fact that the base is not contained in one area complicated an already complex project for LaGassey. Unlike most other American outposts, Aviano has separate areas for the shopping center, engineering complex, dormitories, administrative offices, and flightline. These areas are scattered around and in the town of Aviano.

Thanks to money from the Clinton administration and NATO, construction cranes became commonplace in the picturesque Po Valley. The work pleased many people at the base, including Brig. Gen. Mike Worden, the installation commander. In 2004 he said, "I have the best job in the Air Force. I get to cut ribbons and not turn out lights and shut down buildings. It's really heartwarming to be part of growth and not stagnate." Aviano is a place, he added, where "you see cranes and buildings popping up like daisies."[13] While General Worden may have liked the view, many Italians were not as pleased. Mario Puiatti, a Green Party regional representative from nearby Pordenone, said the growth at Aviano will only further turn the base into a "fortress." "The Americans live among themselves," said Puiatti. "Now more than ever it's a very closed environment."[14]

This is a well-appointed fortress. The players (NATO, the United States, and the Italian Air Force) have built new housing, new airfield facilities, a new school, and numerous new support facilities on and around the base. With nearly 300 construction projects and a total cost of $565 million, this development was one of the largest single DoD construction programs in the world. The U.S. military has built a new town surrounded by farmland and graced with unparalleled views. However, the United States did not even pay half the bill—NATO funded $352 million. Moreover, to make room for the development, the base claimed they did not have enough land. As a result, the United States acquired a prime open space to support even more sprawling, low-density construction. In May 1996 the Italian government ceded to the United States an additional 210 acres of land adjacent to the base for use in the Aviano 2000 project. Hence, the taxpayers of Italy, through their NATO contributions, are partly paying for American sprawl in their backyard.[15]

The controversy over this annexation and accompanying growth was severe and resulted in demands by some locals for the base to close. Opponents formed a vocal group, the Unified Committee Against Aviano

2000, to coordinate the opposition. They sponsored conferences, published position papers, and demonstrated against the presence of the American base. Despite the opposition, the plans proceeded. Below are just a few examples of the ambitious construction program:

Movie theater, library, youth center, baseball fields, and control tower
Six 100-person dormitories
21,000-square-foot minimall with furniture, uniform, and convenience stores
$6.1-million runway upgrade
$1.2-million entry gate
$6.3-million, 100-suite hotel
$20-million, 150,000-square-foot base exchange and commissary
$4.1-million, 31,000-square-foot fitness center
$3.5-million kindergarten
$5.5-million club
$8-million daycare center
$22-million hospital
$3.4-million, 30,000-square-foot fire station
$34-million, 250,000-square-foot combined school for grades 1–12.[16]

In addition to the raw numbers, it is also helpful to make a few comparisons. The supersizing of suburbia so prevalent in the United States has hit Aviano. The shopping center and minimall are three times larger than the old buildings. The hotel's suites are nearly 50 percent bigger than the Air Force standard (420 square feet versus 280 square feet). In the old areas of the base, the United States is demolishing many of the existing buildings and replacing them with parking lots. This is a clear sign of support for America's auto-dominated habits.

Managing the construction effort was quite a challenge. Initially, uncontrolled changes to the construction work led to expensive cost overruns. Not helping matters, a fire destroyed all drawings of the existing buildings and utilities at Aviano. Without accurate drawings, contractors "were hitting [underground] stuff all the time," according to the U.S. Navy's Cdr. Dave Kelly. He added that in the beginning, "There were no change controls, deadlines were missed, there were not enough people, and there was no communication."[17] This is a recipe for disaster when it comes to managing a half-billion-dollar project. Recognizing the problem, in 1999 the Air Force hired a Virginia Beach, Virginia, con-

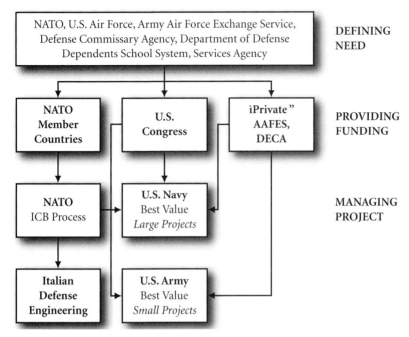

Figure 6.4. Implementing Aviano 2000. The complex bureaucratic structure led to numerous problems.

sulting firm to develop a master schedule and work with a newly established Aviano 2000 program office to minimize conflicts, changes, and delays.

Part of the problem was structural, however, and could not be resolved using a computer program. Under an agreement reached in 1947 to appease the U.S. Army Corps of Engineers and the U.S. Navy Facilities Engineering Command, the Air Force had agreed that it would not act as a construction agent on most projects. This meant that the Air Force would literally hire either the Army or Navy to manage the programming, design, and construction of its projects. At Aviano the Air Force turned most construction over to the U.S. Navy, but they also hired the Army for several small projects. NATO and the Italian Air Force managed projects as well. This added extra layers of management to an already bureaucratic process. According to Mike Bellamy, a Navy construction manager who worked at Aviano, "The melding of U.S. and Italian building codes along with contractors becoming more familiar with the U.S. Navy's contracting and administration methods has been our most significant challenge." All NATO projects, for example, had to conform to the International Competitive Bidding (ICB) rules requiring fixed-priced bids. Recognizing the complexity of the process, Lt. Col. Ken Polasek, the deputy program manager for Aviano 2000 said, "We face many challenges . . . bid preparation to native language, differences with regard to contract specifications, and other cultural differences. With many international players, the project and funding approval processes are heavily weighed in bureaucracy" (Figure 6.4).[18]

While NATO preferred the ICB process, the U.S. Navy preferred to select contractors using a "best value" approach that included the fee proposal, past experience, team member qualifications, and other factors. The result at Aviano: very different building cultures came into conflict. Moreover, NATO's involvement complicated an already complex process. John Kosowatz, a writer from *Engineering News Record,* explains:

> NATO lacked standards for buildings such as hospitals, dormitories, child-care facilities, and some utilities. As the program progressed, NATO's contract review operation in Brussels fell behind as the number of contracts increased and the number of reviewers fell. Eventually, only one screener was available to approve documents. The process further jammed because design and construction contracts had to be advertised, most of them separately, through the embassies of 19 NATO member countries.[19]

In addition, any NATO country could hold up a project for any reason. Spain, for example, effectively delayed eight projects between 2003 and 2005 because it wanted to "study" them in more detail. This was clearly in response to the U.S. refusal to allow NATO funding of several projects in Spain.[20]

Regardless of who hired them or what country they came from, once awarded construction contracts, contractors had difficulty in finding labor. "Construction shortages of manpower in Italy's Northeastern region have become a way of life," said Jim Weslowski. "Current Italian demographics show zero growth rates, a move away from labor due to higher levels of education and increased labor costs."[21] The project that likely suffered the most from the rules and labor shortages was the eighty-seven-classroom school. Following NATO rules, the United States accepted the low bid of $22.1 million in 1998, despite the fact that the average low bid was $26 million and the lowest bid was 15 percent under the government estimate.[22] A bid gap like this usually means the contractor is either trying to lowball the bid and make up the difference on change orders, or else missed elements in the estimating process. Either way, it was not a good sign.

Nevertheless, the United States hired the Italian contractor who immediately had difficulty finding workers. Work progressed slowly for two years, with about half the project completed in the time allotted for the entire scope of work. Unhappy with the pace of work, the United States fired the contractor in 2000. "It was pretty well expected," said John Mueller, the principal of Aviano elementary school. "Let's say, having watched the construction going on for a year, I was not surprised that more hadn't been accomplished. The level of progress was consistent. It was consistently slow."[23] As one might expect, the second bids came in at a substantially higher price than the original bids. After all, few contractors relish the thought of cleaning up a mess left by their failed competitors. In the end, rather than save money, relying on the low bid actually cost an extra $12 million and delayed the project two full years.

When the 1,400-student school finally opened, the reviews were generally positive. "Visually, it's very pleasing to the eye. The teachers and students are very excited to get into it," said Doug McEnery, the high school principal. "We have a world-class theater, top-of-the-line fiber optic Internet connections, lockers for all the students and wider hallways for everyone to get around."[24] Sue Maloney, an English and French teacher, echoed the principal's comments, "This is the best facility. We have huge classrooms. Lots of storage."[25] These two educators reveal that this is a school for a "supersized empire" (Figure 6.5).

With over $500 million to spend on construction at Aviano, local politics naturally played a role in the process. Some of the players included U.S., Italian, and NATO defense officials, regional and provincial administrators, and a group of mayors whose communities live with the presence of the American base. "To fully appreciate the complexity of their interests," Mike Bellamy argues, "one must know that Italy currently has more than 20 political parties at the national level, and each is represented at regional, provincial and local levels."[26]

One of the most interested local politicians was Aviano mayor Gianluigi Rellini, who said that the program will have a positive impact by reducing traffic congestion in the town of Aviano and by reducing demand for housing, which would lead to a drop in the high rents in the

Figure 6.5. Dozens of charter buses haul the 1,400 children of Aviano Air Base from their homes in the region to and from the school with its pseudo–bell tower (in the background). Buses crowd the narrow, winding streets of the local towns where most of the Americans live.

area. "We will all gain from it," the mayor said, "and that can only be good."[27] General Luciano Alberici Da Barbiano, the senior Italian army officer in the region, said that many Italians are enthusiastic about the project but humorously quelled any fears that they may take over the posh base. "No, no, no. We don't need such a facility. We have our own

schools. Our own homes. This base is built up for the United States culture."[28] The culture General Da Berbiano referred to is one based on the
consumption of space and the certainty of familiarity.

The Zappala Plan

In order to find room for all the planned construction, the United States
created a plan for the Zappala site that called for approximately twenty
acres of parking, twenty acres of buildings, thirty acres of recreation
fields, and ninety acres of open space. Since most of the open space
filled the gaps between widely spaced buildings, it served little useful
purpose. While land use allocations like this may be the norm in new
suburban developments in the United States, the result in Aviano was
the decanting of existing areas of the base and the consumption of prime
land in the heart of the Po Valley. The face of American development
was unrestrained sprawl and yet another example of imperial arrogance.
Planners, however, tried to cloak the sprawl in a veneer of compatibility.
For Zappala, the planning team looked to the local environment for
compatibility cues:

> There are many features in the surrounding Italian architecture that
> can provide fine references to enhance architectural compatibility in
> Zappala. . . . The roofs in this area of Italy are almost exclusively red clay
> tile, either hip or gabled, with a medium slope. The tile roofs are elegant
> and architecturally compatible, but more importantly are very durable
> and "low maintenance.". . . The exterior finishes of the surrounding
> architecture can easily be reflected in Zappala with a stucco finish.[29]

The team reduced compatibility to roof and wall materials. The twelve-
person planning team had three members trained in city planning and
three architects. With this professional balance, one would have expected
a more careful analysis of the planning attributes of the local area and
possibly an expansion of the concept of compatibility to include more
than veneers. Instead, the planners focused on vehicular circulation and
provided excessive parking for the buildings sized and placed on the
site plan by the architects. One area where the planners exerted some
influence concerned the connections between buildings. In their view,
"Local architecture makes extensive use of loggias, which are colonnaded
walkways along the streets, recessed under the building's second story
(Figure 6.6). This theme is well suited to the Zappala Community Service Center Mall, where loggias can tie . . . the facilities together."[30]

Figure 6.6. Arcade, Italian style: covered walkways line the main street of
Pordenone, Italy. Apartments and offices fill the floors above the street-level shops.

One difference, though, between local architecture and what this team
proposed was the relationship between buildings and public space. In
the local area, connected three- and four-story buildings clearly define
streets and piazzas and the loggias, or arcades, cover the public sidewalks.
Pedestrians generally walk under the arcades, *parallel* to the building
walls, and parking, if available, is on the street adjacent to the sidewalks,
behind the buildings or in parking courts within buildings. In nearby
Pordenone, for example, the half-mile-long main street has building
entries every twenty-five feet on average, and cars wait in a large parking
lot at the perimeter of the town center. At the base, the plan called for a
large parking lot in the center of a shopping area around which would
be the various buildings. The loggias attached to the face of these one-
story buildings and pedestrian movement would be *perpendicular* to
the loggia, from the parking lot to the limited building entries. The arcade

Figure 6.7. Arcade, American style: the covered walkway attached to the Aviano Base Exchange reduces compatibility to an appliqué, but the row of squat bollards "protects" it from terrorists who might find a way onto the base.

attached to the "community center" has entries every 130 feet, largely eliminating the functional benefit of the loggia. The result mimics a typical strip shopping center in the United States: big-box retail stores with an applied arcade of little value. Moreover, the attached arcade does not connect to any other building and is primarily a cosmetic enhancement rather than a functional amenity (Figure 6.7).

Behind the arcades, the differences are even more profound and result in part from property lines and retailing strategies. Pordenone's closely spaced entries are the result of narrow buildings shaped largely by closely spaced property lines. Small shops line the arcades and the global imprint of corporate capitalism is largely missing. Aviano's paucity of entries results in part from the shear footprint dictated by AAFES's big-box retail mindset. At best, a large base exchange may have two or three entries along a mostly blank façade. The scale of consumption of the

American Empire requires vast tracts of land, enormous areas of uninterrupted sales floor, and few doors to simplify control.

Given the functional irrelevance of such an arcade, it is no surprise that programmers largely eliminated arcades from the final plans for other buildings on the base. The "community center" is also the site of a controversial quasi-bell tower. One young architect working for the Air Force at the time, Capt. Jason Pell, spent considerable time looking at towers in the surrounding communities and convinced Dallas (as we said, where all the decisions regarding shopping centers are made) to pay for the tower.[31] But these types of towers in the towns surrounding the base are reserved for cathedrals of God, not cathedrals of commerce. And towers in nearby towns are usually the tallest structures in the landscape (Figure 6.8). At Aviano, surrounding buildings dwarf the tower. The Americans used a tower to celebrate consumption in an area euphemistically labeled the "community center" (Figure 6.9). But unlike nearby towns, where the "community center" is just that—a place for communities to gather in significant public spaces, in generous civic buildings, and in grand churches, on base it is a jazzed-up strip-mall—a place for consumers to gather in oversized parking lots, in windowless shops, and in franchised food courts.

U.S. planners wanted the 210 additional acres to build their "new town" with its absurdly low densities because they could not envision any other development scenarios. Aviano designers, however, did their best to emulate their reading of the architectural style of the local area. But tile roofs, arched arcades, bell towers, and rusticated bases are superficial elements meant to connect with the built-form traditions of the area. With its expansive roadways, ballfields, parking lots, and building setbacks, Aviano's underlying morphological patterns are in direct contrast to the dense, mixed-use character of Italian towns in the region.

Colonel Michael Dredla, a senior commander at the base, said, "It's not like we're sticking a Luke Air Force Base [Arizona] into the middle of Italy. The base blends right into the local area."[32] This is simply not true. The only element missing at Luke is the belltower celebrating the landscape of consumption. Luke has sloped roofs, stucco walls, widely spaced buildings, isolated land uses, superblocks, and acres of asphalt. Back in Italy, Aviano most decidedly does not blend in. Giuseppe Fallino, a resident of the area, has a more accurate perspective of Aviano's

Figure 6.8. Bell tower, Italian style: The bell tower of San Foca Cathedral is a landmark visible across town.

development: "The base is a piece of America in a strategic location that can hold under its control Eastern Europe."[33]

In a rare moment of introspection, Aviano's designers recognized the error of their ways. As part of the base's *Architectural Compatibility Guide*, planners reevaluated the Zappala area in 2004, while it was still under construction, and concluded the "roadway network" was "flawed" and the pedestrian network lacked "coordination." They continue:

Five years ago, the Zappala Area consisted primarily of a golf course, extensive open space populated with jackrabbits, and a row of vacant aircraft shelters. The area has since been transformed into a vibrant district characterized by wide spacing of buildings and broad boulevards. While the facilities themselves generally comply with base design standards and are compatible with one another, the wide spacing of the facilities and dominating roadway network tends to discourage walking

Figure 6.9. Bell tower, American style: attached to Aviano's shopping mall, the tower is dwarfed by the three-story dormitories built across the mall's mostly vacant parking lot.

and cycling as a mode of transport. Broad expanses of asphalt parking lots are a predominant feature.[34]

The base's design standards call for replicating a historicizing aesthetic that largely fails to make the area compatible with local building contexts, despite all the verbiage by American designers claiming compatibility. In a discussion among three architects working on the base, Andrea Nicolleta, an Italian architect working for the United States at Aviano, took umbrage with the American fixation on a historicizing compatibility. Gill Sanchez, an architect from the Major Command headquarters, challenged the contextual references. Patricia Yates, the base architect, reminded the others that it was the local mayor who asked for the "style."

ANDREA NICOLLETA: The whole architectural language of the base is wrong. The Americans try to mimic something that does not belong. The BX tower and the arcades come from a time long ago. Why not link it to modern Italian architecture?

PATRICIA YATES: But I look around modern architecture in Italy and it is not that great. The local mayor wanted a Mediterranean look, not an American look.

GILL SANCHEZ: But you could drop this style anywhere—in Florida, California, and it would be "American."

ANDREA NICOLLETA: The mayor was saying it would not be nice to have an American-looking installation but it is American-looking. In Italy, we do not have this luxury to have buildings so spread out. In my opinion, it is too spread out and all the land was entirely used. Americans used it all—and when they need more they just expropriate it.[35]

This conversation exposed the dilemmas of compatibility and hybridity. Here, the American Empire deferred to a local mayor on matters of architectural style. But it would not defer on matters of urban planning. Adding arcades is relatively simple; abandoning or even modifying a lifestyle of consumption would be exceedingly difficult. "Bases are a sign of power," argues Danilo Columbrano, a member of the Unified Committee Against Aviano 2000.[36] Underlying the facades is the power to wage war, annex land, and export the controlling patterns of suburbia.

Privatization: The Italian Hybrid

In addition to the ongoing work at Zappala, the U.S. military has subsidized a homebuilding binge in the Italian countryside. While some Italian contractors are busy building an admittedly flawed America Town, others are profiting from privatization, America-style. The United States has leased over 500 homes built to its specifications in an effort to address some of the most pressing housing needs in the military. One of the American architects involved in developing the housing describes how it happened. "The idea was to bypass contracting rules and let private developers propose solutions. This is a real estate action so we could avoid contracting altogether."[37] This is indeed a creative solution. Unlike most privatized housing in the United States, the Air Force neither owned the land nor paid for the construction. Instead, U.S. officials just told Italian developers they would lease the new homes for ten years if they met minimum criteria. The mechanism was a real estate transaction, not a construction contract, and as such very different rules apply.

The military was not interested in developing one large housing tract. Unlike privatized housing in the United States, where large contractors build large tracts (e.g., 828 homes by the Hunt Corporation at Ellsworth Air Force Base, S.D.), the Aviano idea was for multiple contractors to build homes on smaller sites that accommodated twenty-five to seventy-five units. According to Capt. Jason Pell, "The worst thing we could do would be to make isolated enclaves. A developer from California wanted a U.S. type subdivision for all [the homes] but he could not find a site—this is Italy; you can't take a vineyard and turn it into a subdivision."[38]

He had a good point. Since the Air Force was simply planning to rent the units, the actual construction had to abide by all local planning and zoning rules. Building one 500+ unit subdivision would have been a difficult task given land-use restrictions in Italy aimed at preserving farmland. In terms of their location, the Air Force wanted all the homes within a thirty-five-minute drive of the base. In the end, the largest development ended up with just fifty-eight homes. "You don't get 100, 200, or 300 units in one location, where it becomes a big American community," said Duncan Gilpin, Aviano's housing director.[39] The results clearly pleased Gilpin.

To get these homes, the U.S. military issued a Request for Proposals (RFP) in 1997 which specified the selection criteria.[40] Although the military did not stipulate minimum sizes, the composition of what the RFP called "estates" had to conform to the military's standard of 15 percent two-bedroom, 55 percent three-bedroom, and 30 percent four-bedroom units. On top of this constraint, the proposals had to meet criteria in four other areas: unit and estate design, maintenance and repair schedule, termination liability, and proximity and commute time. Fifteen developers submitted proposals, but several challenged the "termination liability." The United States wanted homes that developers could easily rent in the local market if needed, which would reduce the risk for both the United States and the developer. If the developers could not rent the homes once the United States ended the lease, then they would charge substantially more to accept the risk. Essentially, the United States would absorb the total cost of the development in its ten-year lease rather than spread out the cost over the life of the buildings.

To grade the risk of termination, U.S. evaluators analyzed potential risks that could undermine the project and looked for proposals that minimized risk. They called these "natural and contractual minimizers." "Natural" attributes that minimized risk included smaller "estate" sizes, proximity to shopping and recreation areas, and architectural styles that were "compatible" with the local area, although they did not define compatibility. With these attributes, the assumption was that the developers could easily rent the units on the Italian market once the United States vacated them. Hence, the United States would not be liable for paying the full bill for construction during its ten-year lease. The developers could spread the bill out over many years and many renters, similar to a mortgage. "Contractual" minimizers that reduced risk included the elimination of penalties if the Air Force terminated the leases early and preapproval from the local municipality for construction, which added certainty to the project. But the U.S. requirement for large homes was one of the biggest risks of all, and it was a risk that the military was unwilling to minimize.

The United States wanted homes that would satisfy both the American and Italian market and felt that this would reduce the contractors' risk and the military's liability if, for example, it terminated the leases early. However, the criteria for each home were not a hybrid. Rather, the size, number of bedrooms, number of bathrooms, and number of off-street parking spaces reflected what the military considered American preferences. Most developers who responded to the RFP noted that the units would not be standard for Italy and the United States could realize substantial cost savings if it allowed modifications to the criteria. The most onerous burden was the insistence on 85 percent of the units having three and four bedrooms with multiple bathrooms. Also, units could be no higher than two levels, which was atypical for the Italian market. Most rental units in the region are two-bedroom, one-bath units, in buildings up to four levels high.[41] The result was an American-"style" home in Italy.

Exporting American housing preferences came with a steep price. The annual rent indicated in the proposals averaged $21,549 in 2003 dollars. However, the military did not give that much in rent subsidies to its soldiers. The U.S. military's Overseas Housing Allowance (OHA) for the target housing residents (enlisted and junior officers) was only $15,372 in 2003. Moreover, the average market rent for a similar distribution of homes in the area was just $11,500. However calculated, the difference was significant. The annual difference, for example, between the average proposal rent and the average market rent was $5.2 million. American-"style" homes, with their separate laundry rooms, ample yards, extra bathrooms, and extra bedrooms came with a steep premium.

Much of the leased housing follows the same sprawl-inducing pattern as suburban development in the United States, built on the outskirts of a developed area on agricultural or other minimally developed land. This was primarily due to land prices in the area. The most desirable residential sites are in the heart of Pordenone, a classic Italian city a

Figure 6.10. American tract homes spread across Italy's Po Valley: the privatized housing neighborhoods of (a) Sedrano and (b) San Foca.

short drive from the base. Pordenone has many of the features that attract U.S. architecture students to Italy for summer studies: a rich history, elegantly detailed buildings, well-proportioned piazzas, and a mixture of uses in three- and four-story buildings, with residences above cafes and shops. Connecting all these buildings are generous arcades that protect pedestrians from sun and rain. Land in Pordenone at the time was selling for $18.50 per square foot. Developers could purchase land in the outlying areas, however, for as little as $3.50 per square foot.[42] To get the desired financial returns, the land had to be cheap, so most of the developers proposed building in the outlying areas. In the end, the private developers built 530 homes at seventeen locations. Most of the developments look little different from attached multifamily housing in the United States, where punched windows and pastel colors are the norm. One difference, however, is that carports replace garages, making the front yards little more than parking areas (Figure 6.10).

There are two notable exceptions where multilevel attached townhomes cluster around common greens and parking is underground, beneath the residences. The San Quirino Housing area received a USAF Merit Award in 2001 (Figure 6.11). Its townhomes are above an underground parking garage and they share a landscaped courtyard that covers the garage. The simple lines of these townhomes contrast with the historicism advocated by the base for projects in the Zappala area. In San Quirino, Italian designers did not add false arches and belltowers. Another project that won a design award is the Vallenoncello housing development. The fifty-one-unit development is near the city of Pordenone and wraps around an existing housing area. Members of the local community initially opposed the project on aesthetic grounds. According to

Figure 6.11. In an award-winning departure from the norm, the San Quirino privatized housing project, designed by Italian architects for American residents, places the parking underneath an interior courtyard. Small yards, rather than parking lots, address the street.

the Italian designers, the concept generated considerable political opposition in the area. Representatives of the local municipality and residents of the area feared the United States would build an "alien island" in the core of an existing residential area.

In response, Italian architect Roberto Drigo attempted to blend significant features of the local architectural style, including the reinterpretation of design elements found in nearby historical buildings, with the requirements of the Air Force. The 2.57-acre site has a density of sixteen units per acre and parking is underground. The end result is similar to recently built homes in the area in several respects: (1) morphologically, in terms of lot coverage and density as measured by the Floor Area Ratio; (2) typologically, in terms of unit layout and massing; and (3) materially through the use of stucco, tile roofs, and working shutters. The local architect's contextual approach at Vallenoncello placated the opposition and its Italian neighbors, U.S. residents, and the local politicians view the project as a success (Figures 6.12 and 6.13).[43]

Getting the support of politicians was especially important. According to Dale Sherman, Aviano's housing manager, "The mayors oversee everything we do in their communities and they do not want us building junk. We had twelve mayors to work with in this project and they helped us lead town meetings. When you congregate Americans in small communities, it is a big deal." It is quite remarkable that the local residents were concerned about American architecture invading their neighborhoods, not Americans living next door. Local landowners were even more accommodating to the Americans. Sherman recounted this story: "When I arrived here I went to look for a home to rent but I needed a garage for my Corvette. One property owner opened his garage and showed me his sports car, a five-year-old Ferrari that he bought after selling his land to a developer for one of the housing projects."[44] Converting farmland in Italy to housing developments for Americans can be a profitable venture and mirrors similar forces at work advancing the sprawling agendas in the United States.

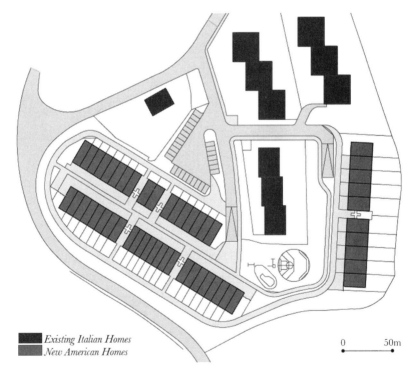

Existing Italian Homes
New American Homes

0   50m

Figure 6.12. Like San Quirino, local architects designed the award-winning Vallenoncello privatized housing project near Pordenone, Italy. The rowhouses built for Americans surround existing private homes occupied by Italian families. Parking is underground.

Figure 6.13. Designers were inspired by local customs for Vallenoncello's compact layouts, working shutters, local colors, and simple shapes.

According to one official who works in Aviano Air Base's housing office, most residents enjoy living in the community and interacting with their Italian neighbors.[45] Like Dale Sherman, they prefer to live off-base. Lisa Prater is an Air Force spouse who favors living in the local area. "We have grocery stores, meat markets, dry cleaners, everything you can imagine one block away in our little Italian town. The military does a pretty good job of building their housing communities within the Italian communities." When asked about living off-base after September 11, she replied: "I don't worry about . . . attacks. We do have protests and demonstrations, but they are usually announced well in advance and we know to stay away from the base or the area designated to avoid any confrontations. Living in Italy, it is common practice to keep as low a profile as you can."[46]

While she was keeping a low profile, the U.S. military was doing the opposite. The low-density development patterns used on-base require a high profile use of land. Despite widespread calls for the base's closure following the deadly accident in 1998, not only has the base remained open, but it also has grown substantially. The Italian government gave the United States the Zappala area so the military could build at even lower densities. The United States then demolished buildings in existing areas to make room for more parking lots and sent families to live in subdivisions up to thirty-five minutes away from the base, contributing to suburban sprawl in Italy. Granted, Europeans build their own version of sprawling suburbs on the outskirts of their historic cities.[47] However, when another nation's military imports suburbia and its ills, local residents of the "host" nation have a right to be disturbed.

But living off-base in locally designed and built housing may be a relic of the pre–September 11 era. Now, leaders at many overseas bases are building more housing on-base in order to reduce vulnerability to terrorist attacks. For a look at this latest trend and the impacts of a worldwide realignment of the U.S. military, we will turn our focus to Asia and look at current planning and construction at U.S. outposts in South Korea.

CHAPTER SEVEN

Rewarding Realignment:
South Korea's Land Partnership Plan

On June 13, 2002, near Yangju, South Korea, Army Sergeant Mark Walker crushed two thirteen-year-old South Korean schoolgirls under his fifty-ton armored vehicle while driving near the 38th parallel. Shim Mi-son and Shin Hyo-sun were walking to a birthday party on the side of a narrow country road when a U.S. convoy came rumbling by. Sergeant Walker claimed he could not see the girls or hear warnings in his headset due to radio interference. Army Specialist Joshua Ray blamed senior officers for requiring the convoy to use the narrow road rather than the nearby Munsan Bypass. "On those small roads where farmers, children, and other pedestrians frequently walk, they had our unit as well as others moving quickly, not thinking about pedestrians." Massive public rallies across the country called for a withdrawal of U.S. troops and South Koreans elected Roh Moo-hyun, an opponent of the U.S. presence, as the nation's new president. Although the U.S. ambassador to South Korea apologized, a U.S. military court-martial acquitted the driver and his assistant.[1]

Residents of the Korean peninsula have lived with imperial powers long before this deadly accident. The Chinese Empire occupied Korea from 1637 to 1895. Then, after a brief period of freedom, the Imperial Japanese Army moved in to occupy the country from 1905 until the end of the Second World War. Following the surrender of Japan, Joseph Stalin, Winston Churchill, and Franklin Roosevelt agreed to a partition of the Korean peninsula in an exercise that underscores the importance of mapping. Around midnight on August 10, 1945, the assistant secretary of war

China

NORTH KOREA

● Pyongyang

Sea of Japan

DMZ

38th parallel

● Seoul

● Osan Air Base

SOUTH KOREA

Yellow Sea

● Kunsan Air Base

0   100km

Cheju

Japan

Map 7.1. The Korean peninsula.

at the Pentagon gave Col. Charles Bonesteel and Maj. Dean Rusk thirty minutes to define zones of occupation for the American and Soviet forces. The only map in their Pentagon office was a small map of the region. Colonel Bonesteel observed that the 38th parallel divided the peninsula into roughly equal parts and was north of Seoul, a city the United States wanted under its influence. They presented the idea to their superiors and in short order the United States divided the peninsula at this imaginary line. The Soviet Army occupied the area to the north and helped establish the Democratic People's Republic of Korea, a quite undemocratic nation. The U.S. Army occupied the south and helped establish the Republic of Korea, a nation that has also struggled with dictatorial leadership.

Unsatisfied with a divided peninsula, on June 25, 1950, the North Korean People's Army crossed the 38th parallel and invaded South Korea. The well-equipped army (courtesy of the Soviet Union) quickly captured almost all of its poorly defended neighbor. South Korean and U.S. forces retreated to a small area near Pusan at the southeast end of the peninsula. Then in September 1950, operating under the approval of the United Nations, Gen. Douglas MacArthur led a fifteen-nation force in an assault on Inchon, near Seoul. By August, MacArthur's forces recaptured much of South Korea. Ignoring threats from China not to cross the imaginary line of the 38th parallel, MacArthur went ahead and by November the allied army reached the Yalu River at the border between China and North Korea. Fearing MacArthur would invade their country as well, the Chinese launched a surprise attack on the allied army, forcing them back south of Seoul. Both capital cities, Seoul and Pyongyang, changed hands twice in the war. By 1951, the conflict bogged down near the 38th parallel. In 1953 the warring parties signed an armistice treaty, slightly readjusted the dividing line, and established the Demilitarized Zone (DMZ). The final human toll: 3 million Koreans dead, wounded, or missing, 103,284 Americans injured, and 54,246 American deaths.[2]

After the tragedy of war comes the occupation of land. In language that is strikingly similar to that used in Japan's surrender, Article 4 of the Mutual Defense Treaty signed in 1953 by the United States and South Korea reads, "The Republic of Korea grants, and the United States of America accepts, the right to dispose United States land, air, and sea forces in and about the territory of the Republic of Korea as determined by mutual agreement."[3] On the surface, it would appear South Korea led this effort. But given that the country was in no position to haggle with its larger ally, Article 4 was written under the imbalance of power that follows imperial powers and set the stage for a build-up of U.S. outposts across South Korea.

In South Korea, as of fiscal year 2006, the U.S. Department of Defense spread 57,052 military and civilian personnel across ninety-five sites and 59,907 acres.[4] Because of the spillover from American operations, numerous protest groups have formed over the years and demanded either a reduction of U.S. forces or a complete withdrawal. Pro-U.S. groups have also formed and have held competing demonstrations throughout the country. In March 2003, for example, 100,000 pro-U.S. South Koreans held a rally in front of Seoul City Hall. Nevertheless, there has been a growing anti-American attitude in the country, especially among members of the postwar generation that has little connection to the Korean War and does not see North Korea as the greatest threat.[5] In a Korean Gallup poll in 2002, 53.7 percent of South Koreans held an "unfavorable" or "somewhat unfavorable" view of U.S. forces in their country.[6] "Anti-American sentiment is rather abstract," said Auh Taik-suo, a mass communications professor at Korea University, "resulting in an affective, emotional and passive dislike of America and things American."[7]

Perhaps exacerbated by the U.S. approach in the Middle East, some protestors consider the United States selfish, arrogant, and indifferent to public opinion. This partly explains why, in 2003, South Koreans elected an antibase politician as their new president. After he took office, however, President Roh Moo-hyun publicly declared his support for the U.S. presence and urged President Bush to keep American forces in his country, especially near the DMZ. The new president may have realized the economic advantage of the U.S. presence. According to South Korean military officials, to "fill the vacuum of war-waging capability that [would] be created by the pullout of U.S. forces," South Korea would have to double defense expenditures to approximately $26 billion, or 5 percent of the South Korean gross domestic product. The reversal was in line with former president Kim Dae-jung's policies, who has said protestors do not want a full withdrawal of U.S. forces. The United States does want to remove its forces from at least part of the country. Pentagon officials have said that the "tripwire" function of American troops stationed near the DMZ is of very little military value. Rather, these officials believe the troops may be a tempting target for the North Korean Army and want to clear out of the vulnerable area.[8]

The Land Partnership Plan

In light of this turbulent sociopolitical context, South Korean and U.S. officials agreed to a phased withdrawal of 12,500 soldiers from the peninsula, a return of 32,000 acres of land worth $1.3 billion used by the United States, and a reduction in the number of main operating locations from 41 to 23.[9] The South Korean National Assembly ratified the land component of the plan on October 30, 2002, four months after the accident that killed the two schoolgirls. If completed, this will reduce the U.S. "footprint" by 53 percent. The two governments called the land-use agreement the Land Partnership Plan (LPP). According to Gen. Leon J. LaPorte, former commander-in-chief, U.S. Forces Korea (USFK), the ten-year plan, which military officials have compared to the Base Realignment and Closure process in the United States, has many benefits:

> LPP will greatly benefit the Republic of Korea economy because there is a significant amount of land being returned that can potentially be used for commercial development. The consolidation of our installations will also result in less congestion, pollution and traffic in many communities throughout Korea, and should also reduce the chances of military vehicles being involved in traffic accidents.[10]

The last point is perhaps the most relevant. As Nam Chang-hee, a researcher at the Korea Institute for Defense Analysis, noted, "[D]espite official denials by the U.S. government that the realignment plan has anything to do with rising anti-U.S. sentiments in the wake of the accidental deaths of two middle school girls caused by a U.S. armored vehicle, it is likely that complaints related to U.S. bases and growing anti-U.S. resistance play some role."[11] Given General LaPorte's statement, the connection between land-use decisions and the accident is clear. As was the case with Torrejón, Crotone, and Aviano, it appears the United States only makes dramatic land-use changes in the aftermath of deadly accidents, a pattern that will be explored further when looking at bases in Japan in the next chapter. The U.S. Army also sees benefits for U.S. forces because of the plan:

> The plan improves the quality of life of our service members and their families while optimizing military readiness of the U.S. Forces Korea.

The LPP will make Korea an assignment of choice by improving the quality and quantity of our family housing. Both new construction and renovation of facilities to bring them up to standard will improve the living and working conditions of our people to a level commensurate with those in Germany and Japan.[12]

The realignment then is a reaction to local events (accidents and congestion), national events (an upsurge in anti-Americanism and changing demographics that favor less U.S. involvement in South Korea), and international politics (relying on U.S. forces in other locations where they are better supported financially by the host nation [Japan] and shifting others to actual war zones [Middle East]).

The crux of the plan calls for relocating U.S. soldiers away from the DMZ and out of Seoul into less "urbanized" areas in the central and southern part of the country. As South Korea has urbanized, development has encroached on military bases, which has led to conflicts in land use and ever more deadly spillover. According to Army Colonel Robert E. Durbin, the chief U.S. negotiator for the LPP, "With the urbanization and urban sprawl over the years, we find those camps or stations either almost in the center, or within the city, [that] creates a problem for force protection and standoff."[13] South Korean urban sprawl, however, is very different from American sprawl. Instead of building single-family homes on one-acre sites, in Seoul they build eighteen-story apartment buildings on half-acre sites. Given its mountainous terrain, South Korea's 47 million people live on just 15 percent of the land, making for some of the most densely populated cities in the world. South Korea, with a population density of 1,272 people per square mile, has the fourth-highest population density in the world. It supports over fifteen times the number of people per square mile than the United States, which has a population density of just eighty-two people per square mile.

But the Americans are not the only ones heading south. In August 2004, five days before George W. Bush announced his realignment plan that will reduce U.S. forces in South Korea by one-third, the South Korean government announced it would move its capital to the Yeongi-Kongju area in central South Korea. The government promoted this $45 billion move as a way to ease congestion in Seoul.[14] But looking at it from a military perspective, the new capital city would be behind the largest USAF base in the country rather than between the base and North Korea. In any case, it is a striking coincidence that the political leadership of South Korea and the military leadership of the United States are retreating from Seoul into the same general area at the same time.

As noted in chapter 2, any U.S. relocation will be expensive with limited strategic benefits. Moreover, the United States expects the South Koreans to pay for relocating soldiers out of Seoul to areas farther south. To sell the plan to the South Koreans, the U.S. Army initially determined that it could be "self-financing" and even turn a modest profit of $230 million if the South Korean government sold the returned land. But this is a risky math exercise. To get this profit, in 2004, the Army assumed a $2.3-billion cost for the construction and relocation costs; other sources, though, have estimated the cost to be $3 billion or more. By 2006 the projected cost had grown to $6.8 billion, wiping out any presumed profit. The Army also assumed the United States would continue to fund construction at the current rate of $1.2 billion over the projected ten-year period. While the United States was unwilling to increase its spending to build in Korea, it was more than willing to spend ten times that amount on new weapons systems to reward the South Korean government for going along with the realignment. The United States planned to spend $11 billion by 2007 to improve South Korean defenses. But rather than be used to pay South Korean contractors to build homes and hangars, this money will be used to pay U.S. defense contractors to build tanks and fighter jets. Moreover, the economics assumed the South Korean government will sell off all of Yongsan. This may be impossible since part of the garrison has already been designated a no-build "green zone" by city planning law in Seoul.[15]

While the plan called for reducing U.S. land use in some areas, it also called for additional land in other areas, including two Air Force "hubs": Kunsan Air Base and Osan Air Base.[16] It also called for expanding Camp Humphreys, an Army helicopter base near Osan. The biggest demand for land comes with the relocation of the 640-acre Yongsan Garrison out of the heart of Seoul to an area near Osan. However, even with the move, the United States planned to leave 1,000 of the 3,200 soldiers in Yongsan.[17] At one point in the LPP negotiations, the United States threatened to expand the troop cuts if it could not keep some land in Seoul. "The U.S. side pressed us, saying that additional troop reductions would be inevitable if the amount of land were reduced, so the atmosphere of the talks was cool at one stage," said Ahn Kwang-chan, the chief South Korean delegate. "But we succeeded in getting a compromise after raising the worsening of public sentiment following the (South Korean) government's decision to send [3,000] additional troops to Iraq."[18] Since the Bush administration transferred its own soldiers from South Korea to Iraq, the thought of South Korea pulling out of Iraq would be an embarrassment and would likely require additional U.S. soldiers to replace the South Koreans. Here, land use, imperial realignment, and the Iraq War intersected in unsettling ways.

During the initial round of negotiations over the plan in 2001 and 2002, the United States indicated it would need approximately 600 acres to house the troops relocated from closed bases.[19] But by the fall of 2004, the "need" had inexplicably increased to 3,000 acres. The South Korean government agreed to meet the need and provide large tracts of public and private land in the Pyeongtaek area to accommodate growth at Osan Air Base and Camp Humphreys. As with most military land-use decisions, this one has its supporters and opponents. Many businesses and local landowners in the Pyeongtaek area welcome the potential new business, but other landowners have balked "at giving up or selling their land."[20] One reason some landowners opposed the move is that the South Korean government has not compensated other owners of private land occupied by the United States.[21] This is very different from the case in Japan, where the government of Japan compensates landowners it forces to lease land to the U.S. military.

North Korea, through the Korea Central News Agency, also weighed in on the plan. In characteristically dramatic language, the North Korean government called it a "hypocritical farce" and a "dangerous plot . . . by U.S. imperialists . . . to grab new land for increasing the capability to attack the north in return for giving back useless land."[22] Green Korea United, an anti-U.S. environmental group, has also weighed in on the plan in a public statement:

> It looks like the United States gives a big piece of the pie back to the Korean people—they return 40 million pyong [32,000 acres] of land to the Korean people! Actually, no! They do not. Of the proposed 40 million pyong of land to be returned, about 39 million pyong [31,200 acres] covers training facilities, which have almost been abandoned by U.S. troops. Until now the USFK has just been holding that land to prohibit the Korean people's access. South Korea does not know how much money we need for the restoration of the polluted area.[23]

The United States did not dispute the report and even published it in its press pack summarizing the LPP. This raises the troubling question of land value, not in an economic sense but from an emotional point of view. Some South Koreans may view giving back largely rural and possibly polluted land that the United States has not used regularly in exchange for land in heavily urbanized areas as a less-than-optimal deal. If the United States only returned 800 acres of regularly used land in exchange for 3,000 acres of new land in the urbanized areas like Pyeongtaek, it would appear that the purported benefits to the Korean people were somewhat overestimated. Some in the United States even questioned the plan. The 2003 analysis of the LPP by the U.S. General Accountability Office (GAO) recommended that it be reconsidered as part of a broader master planning effort for the U.S. military's presence in the entire country in light of the Bush administration's realignment proposals.

Building Planned Communities

With several billion dollars to spend on new facilities through the LPP, architects and planners may wonder just what the United States will build. According to Army Colonel Russell A. Bucy, who was a senior commander in South Korea in 2002, the Army will be "planning our communities in Korea to better serve the servicemember[s]. We're going from a kind of 'Let's fix what we've got'... to an end state of planned communities."[24]

The pressure to build these communities, with homes, hospitals, schools, and other facilities that support family life, responds to two issues. First, as discussed in chapter 3, where U.S. soldiers live with their families overseas, the crime rate drops dramatically. The needs of family life occupy off-duty hours. Second, the price of staffing South Korea has become especially high in a "married army." Providing homes allows the military to increase the length of stay at an overseas outpost, thereby reducing the cost of frequent moves. Homes are also a motivator to stay in the service. Two-thirds of the soldiers assigned to South Korea are married, but fewer than 10 percent of them can bring their families since there are few facilities that support family life.[25] This is one of the main reasons why South Korea is, according to one commander, the country soldiers most hate to live in.[26] One U.S. military study made public in 2002 found that in one three-year period, half of the 60,000 soldiers given orders to Korea refused, opting to leave the military instead of leave their families in the United States. This is in stark contrast to the situation in Japan and countries in Europe, where 72 percent of U.S. soldiers in Japan and 74 percent in Germany live with their families. Of all U.S. soldiers living apart from their families on permanent assignments, 85 percent are in South Korea.[27] The military cannot afford to lose so many highly trained soldiers in a time when it is calling the Guards and Reserves for extended periods of active duty to serve across the globe.

But even for the few soldiers who can bring their spouses to South Korea, the conditions are less than ideal. "When we first walked in[to our apartment], it was like a prison," said Candy Glerup, who is married to a Navy petty officer. She arrived in 1999 with her two children and on her first day told her husband, "This is our punishment for coming to Korea." Putrid brown water bubbled up from her bathroom drain whenever she did laundry; a small air conditioner covered one of the few windows in her apartment and rarely worked, leaving the place hot, dark, and depressing. "I was just stunned. I cried for days."[28] The GAO has noted that South Korea is the worst assignment location in the DoD.[29]

To address the concerns of families already in South Korea, and families who want to join their spouses there, the United States is turning to construction. It hopes to build its way out of the problem. By 2010, the military plans to have enough homes and support facilities to allow 25 percent of the soldiers to bring their families. The goal is 50 percent by 2020. Many senior officers compare the situation to Europe. "There's no command sponsorship in Europe," according to Brig. Gen. William Holland, Osan's commander in 2002. He was referring to the policy in South Korea that requires anyone bringing a family to be sponsored, or approved, by the command headquarters as a way of limiting families in Korea. "People serve normal tours there [Europe]. Maybe we eventually can consider Osan a place for normal overseas tours. Our people may be able to come here for a longer period, bring their families and live a good quality of life." Colonel Bob Durbin, former assistant deputy chief of staff for U.S. Forces Korea, explains, "To improve the quality of life of our servicemembers here means you've got to build things." The plans call for building many "things," including 3,799 apartments in ten years.[30]

One significant drawback to the ambitious plans is money. The United States has not wanted to spend additional money on new housing. So, taking a lesson from Aviano, the military hopes to convince private contractors to build most of the homes in the South Korean version of privatization. According to Gen. Leon J. LaPorte, former commander-in-chief, U.S. Forces Korea, the goal is to add 1,500 units, a shopping center, and recreation facilities at Camp Humphreys in the Pyeongtaek area.[31] Colonel Daniel Wilson, a former U.S. Forces Korea command engineer, said, "Basically we're saying 'build us a city, and we'll lease it. The Koreans go out and build cities all the time. Let's leverage their expertise." According to Colonel Wilson, the idea stirred considerable interest among Korean firms. He added that it would cost about $600 million for the United States to build, but only $50 million a year to lease.[32] At Camp Humphreys, the growth will be substantial—the outpost has six family housing units and will grow to 1,500. It will also get a $22-million 30,000-square-foot commissary to replace a 5,400-square-foot building. And it will get a $25-million dormitory/dining-hall complex, a $3.2-million sixteen-lane bowling alley, and tree-lined streets.[33]

Sohn Hak-gyu, the governor of the Gyeonggi Province in 2003, welcomed the news of construction in his jurisdiction. He announced plans to build the innocuous-sounding "international peace city" on 4,000 acres in Pyeongtaek for soldiers relocated from Seoul. The $3.3-billion new town will accommodate up to 200,000 residents. The name of the development is like names of many subdivisions in the United States where developers name places after what they or their customers are wistfully hoping for (e.g., "Pleasant Creek" when the only creek on the site has been placed in a culvert, or "Oak Hill Estates" when the oaks have all been cut down and the hill leveled for tract homes). That a place for tens of thousands of U.S. soldiers could be a "peace" city stretches the meaning of peace. Just as General MacArthur called American bases in Japan "reservations" to make them more palatable to the occupier and the occupied, so too are South Korean politicians using language to conceal rather than reveal.

Despite its name, many local residents came out in opposition to the plan. The governor, however, remained focused on what he called the "brightest side—that the U.S. base will contribute greatly to regional development." He added, "The international peace city will be self-sufficient, with residential areas for the families of U.S. soldiers and regular citizens. There will also be a golf course and commercial facilities."[34] The circle of consumption has arrived at Pyeongtaek. Seven years earlier, in the mid-1990s, private developers in Pyeongtaek put in a proposal for similar leased housing for Osan Air Base, but the United States rejected it.[35] In 2006, with the pressure on from the tragic accident in Yangju, the global war on terror stretching U.S. soldiers to the limit, and a desire to build away from Seoul in increasingly self-contained compounds, building "planned communities," with better housing and more shopping centers paid for by the South Koreans was a fashionable idea.

While most of the land the United States planned to give back under the Land Partnership Plan was rural land, the 3,000 acres it wanted was mostly valuable urban land. The urban area most impacted will be the Pyeongtaek area around Osan Air Base and Camp Humphreys. In Pyeongtaek the South Korean government has already acquired 408 acres and has transferred most of the land to Osan Air Base in line with the recommendations of the LPP.[36] In listening to the advocates of the plan, one could be thinking that the relocated soldiers are moving into an undeveloped area. This is not the case. Pyeongtaek is heavily developed; it is just not the capital city. The planned expansion of the base and neighboring Camp Humphreys has stirred emotions on all sides:

> *Opposed:* "Unacceptable," said Kim Yong-hwan, who is leading the movement opposing the USFK (U.S. Forces Korea) base expansion in the Osan-Pyeongtaek area. "I will lie in front of the bulldozers when the day comes."
>
> *Neutral if compensated:* "I am not particularly for or against more U.S. soldiers coming here," said an elderly man from a nearby farming village. "Many of my neighbors could accept the deal if we get the proper compensation for our homes and land and maybe buy apartments somewhere else."
>
> *Supportive:* "It's more than about economics," said Choi Chung-hyup, a Pyeongtaek representative in the (Gyeonggi) Provincial Assembly. "We realize the USFK's significance on the peninsula and want to contribute to their mission by hosting the USFK headquarters."[37]

For landowners who get to sell their holdings, the new development could prove to be lucrative since just the announcement of the move sparked a 10 percent rise in real estate values in the area between January and April of 2003. But for the opponents, economics do not justify the expansion. On March 17, 2006, for instance, hundreds of local farmers and their supporters rallied against the plan that called for the eviction of the 1,000 residents of Daechuri village. The residents have resisted two eviction attempts and have claimed that "the compensation offered will not be enough to buy equivalent land elsewhere and their livelihoods are at stake." As part of the LPP, in 2004, the South Korean government approved the transfer of 2,851 acres to the U.S. Army's Camp Humphreys. Then, in December 2005 the South Korean government used its authority to take the land, which outlawed the occupation of the land by its previous owners.[38] This is yet another chapter in the process of displacement and demolition.

In a unique form of protest, the Korea Confederation of Trade Unions coordinated the efforts of 600 citizens under a "buy one *pyong* movement" to acquire land just outside Osan Air Base as a symbolic foothold against its growth.[39] One pyong is about 35.5 square feet. Like the Japanese *tsubo* (which is also roughly 35.5 square feet), this measure is a telling example of the value of land. American planners typically measure land in terms of acres. One acre is 43,560 square feet. While land has been plentiful in America, the units of measure in South Korea and Japan reveal that land is a precious resource. After all, banks do not measure gold by the ton but by the ounce.

The Osan Expansion

Osan Air Base, at one time an out-of-the-way location that generated little controversy, has attracted all manner of protests because of the LPP. The base is located about forty miles south of Seoul, near the west coast of the Korean Peninsula. Located just six minutes by air from the DMZ, Osan claims it is "the tip of the spear" defending the Republic of Korea. Osan is near Pyeongtaek, the densely populated business and service center for the agricultural region surrounding the base. The base and its ammunition storage annex cover 2,391 acres. As of 2006, the United States employed 5,416 soldiers, 159 U.S. civilians, and 1,215 Korean nationals.[40] About 4,000 dependents also called Osan home. In 2004 Osan had an impressive development program, with projects totaling over $2 billion either programmed, in design, or under construction.[41] In 2001 its construction budget was one-third of the entire Air Force's military construction program.[42]

Before the American presence, the area consisted of several small villages. The only remnant of the previous settlement is a large 700-year-old ginkgo tree that was in the square of one of the villages but now sits prominently on Osan's golf course. Construction progressed rapidly during the Korean War, starting in 1952 and quickly engulfing a fifth village.

The area changed hands several times during the war with some of the most intense fighting occurring on "Hill 180," which is now the location of the headquarters building.[43] It has commanding views of the entire area, including the lovely eighteen-hole Lakes at Osan golf course. The base has supported a variety of aircraft, from bombers to fighters and now hosts F-16s, A-10s, and reconnaissance aircraft.[44]

The difference between the base and the local area in terms of built form is striking. The base is a low-density fortified enclave embedded within the high-density fabric of the Songtan area of Pyeongtaek. The base is a network of parking lots; the town is a network of streets. Figure-ground plans, taken at the base border, show the difference. Both areas developed simultaneously, starting in 1952 with the construction of the base. The South Korean side shows a preference for buildings and the American side shows a preference for paving. This may be one reason why car ownership on-base is 67 percent greater than off-base. As the base spreads out, walking becomes more difficult, cars become more prevalent, and parking becomes more important (Figure 7.1).

One of the biggest complaints from the Osan planning staff is that there is simply no room for any construction. The figure-ground plans show otherwise. There is no room for rethinking the rules that dictate sprawling and inefficient development. As a result, the base is on an annexation binge, asking for another 411 acres to support its building needs.[45] When the base real-estate officer, Carl Bristol, was giving a tour of the annexation areas, half-jokingly he told the driver, "Keep your engines running and the van in gear in case protestors come by." Just the week before the tour, a mixed group of students, retirees, and farmers was out in force protesting the annexation. Carl could not understand their actions, though. "Landowners," he said, "think the U.S. is taking land but it is really the ROK [Republic of Korea]. The base does not take the property away—the U.S. identifies a need to ROK and they're supposed to buy the land." When asked if he was aware of the compensation package given to landowners, he replied, "That's not our business." He was, of course, technically correct. Perhaps, however, the United States should make an effort to better understand the ramifications of its appetite for space. The protests were wearing on him. "We had a better relationship in 1990–1991 since the ROKAF [Republic of Korea Air Force] property manager, Mr. Yoon, would jump in an official car with siren blaring and lights flashing and tell the encroachers to

Building Figure Ground Plan: Osan Air Base (left); Songtan, South Korea (right)

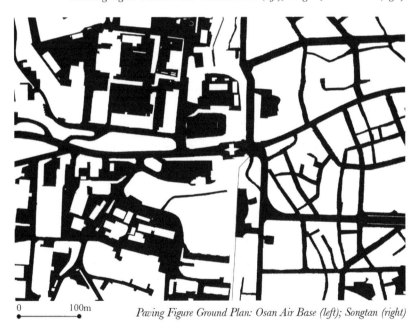

0   100m

Paving Figure Ground Plan: Osan Air Base (left); Songtan (right)

Figure 7.1. Ground plans for Osan Air Base and Songtan, South Korea.

Category	Osan Air Base	Songtan
Average building height (floors)	1.5	3.5
Residential density (units per acre)	8	40
Lot coverage (percent)	10	92
Floor Area Ratio (FAR)	0.1	3.2
Parking (per dwelling unit)	1	0.1

Figure 7.2. Comparing urban form. From author's fieldwork, 2003–4.

leave. But now he has retired."[46] With Mr. Yoon and his intimidating car gone, the United States must see, even if for a short time, the human dimension of expansion.

Osan's aggressive design and construction program includes operational facilities (supply buildings, logistics buildings, and a control tower), housing for single soldiers and families, and commercial facilities (base exchange, "community center," franchised restaurant). To see how bases have responded to the demand for more housing, Osan is a good case study.

Building in Mustang Valley Village

To support additional housing at Osan Air Base, planners sited one of several new housing towers in an area labeled Mustang Valley Village Plus. The new apartments would help the base meet the housing needs of 255 families relocated from Sochong Air Force Village, off-base leased housing, following the September 11 attacks. Built by the Korean National Housing Corporation (KNHC) and leased to the military, the apartments in Air Force Village are about a twenty-minute walk from the base and are located in a residential area of Pyeongtaek City. The ten-acre site consists of three-story buildings with stacked flats, red sloped roofs, and surface parking. At the time the Air Force occupied the site, the density was twenty-five units per acre (Figure 7.4).[47]

Even before September 11, in November 1997, the DoD conducted a "vulnerability assessment" and stated, "Surrounded by urban environment and limited physical security measures . . . Air Force Village provides the number one terrorist-vulnerable target at Osan Air Base."[48] Subsequently, the engineers at Pacific Command Headquarters in Honolulu, the command that oversees all Air Force installations in the Pacific, designated Air Force Village as the number one vulnerable location throughout the entire Pacific.

Figure 7.3. Songtan and Osan Air Base, South Korea. The compact development patterns of Songtan (foreground) border the low-density base (background) and make for a remarkable study in land-use differences between cultures.

Even though there had never been a terrorist incident at Air Force Village in its eleven-year history, with this kind of attention, the "village" was ripe for closure. Nevertheless, the Air Force was slow to vacate the development. September 11 spurred action. Shortly after the attacks in New York City and Washington, D.C., the Air Force terminated the lease with the KNHC.[49] In yet another imperial irony, the KNHC sold the property to private developers, who then renovated the units for sale as high-end condominiums. The 641-square-foot, two-bedroom units are larger than neighboring apartments. The South Korean real-estate agent representing the property said that the demand was very high for the renovated units. "They are bigger than other apartments in the area and the land is much more open, with more parking and big trees. Korean apartments are much closer together and don't have many big trees." When asked if anyone cared that they were former Air Force housing units, he replied, "Of course most buyers know the Air Force was here but that doesn't matter to them. After all, it was built for them with bigger units and more yards. We even kept the name Sochong Village."[50] They were, though, quick to drop the "Air Force" portion. While

Koreans were moving into Sochong Village to get larger units, U.S. personnel were moving out in part because the units were too small.

In preparing plans for the new requirement of on-base apartments, the military analyzed a hillside off the base and adjacent to an on-base housing area called Mustang Valley Village. Given the maximum densities allowed by Air Force standards, the planning team determined that the 8.8-acre hillside site could support the required housing at a density of 14.4 units per acre—just under the maximum allowable of sixteen units per acre. For comparison, the vacated Air Force Village had densities of twenty-five units per acre. The flaw in this measure, however, is that the hillside is just that—a steeply sloping hill. On paper, the 8.8 acres looks big enough. But on the ground it is clear that the site is largely unbuildable. The site's official name—Mustang Valley Village Plus—obfuscates the fact that the site is a hill, not a valley. If the goal of limiting densities is to allow ample open space, the very nature of the rules developed in Washington undermined this goal.

The planners did look at a few other sites, including the base commissary area and the base golf course. While the former was unrealistic, given that there was no foreseeable funding to replace the 101,000-square-foot commissary, the latter was politically unpopular since Osan's golf course is the most profitable one in the Air Force.[51] At fourteen acres, the development would have eliminated up to two holes. The team noted that to preserve as many holes as possible, the layout would dictate smaller buildings spread around the course, which was seen as a benefit in terms of antiterrorism planning. "In other words," according to the housing plan, "personnel would be dispersed among multiple building sites, thus reducing population density."[52] Another benefit of the golf course site in terms of antiterrorism planning was its location in the middle of the base, which was optimal from a security standpoint.

Of the options discussed here, Mustang Valley Village Plus was the most expensive, with an estimated cost at $54.3 million. The commissary site came in at $51 million, not including replacement costs for the commissary itself. And the golf course site was the least expensive, with an estimated cost of $49.5 million. So, given that the golf course site would have (1) saved an estimated $5 million, (2) required no land acquisition, (3) be easy to build on given its minimal elevation changes, and (4) be safer in terms of antiterrorism planning, which site did the United States select for construction of its new housing?

Figure 7.4. Air Force Village, Pyeongtaek, South Korea. The United States abandoned this off-base apartment complex shortly after the September 11 attacks. Although surrounded by concertina wire and protected by several entry control gates, military commanders considered the three-level stacked flats vulnerable to a terrorist strike and returned the development to the Korean National Housing Corporation. With its ample parking, generous landscaping, and spacious units, the apartments have since been converted to high-end housing for the local market.

Unwilling to sacrifice a portion of the golf course and unable to fund a replacement for the commissary, the United States picked the hillside site—the only off-base site (thus necessitating annexation) and the only site that presented substantial constructability and security issues. Although the South Korean government had to move numerous families to make room for the project and the relocated fenceline, the South Korean government did benefit from a land exchange. The United States returned to the South Korean government a nineteen-acre site on the other side of the base that the military could not use due to force protection concerns. It was a hill surrounded by public roads. The local government planned to turn that area into a city park. In selecting the steeply sloped site, the engineers at Osan changed the definition of a buildable hillside set by their counterparts in Okinawa where designers claimed they could not build on slopes greater than 15 percent. The Osan team built on a much steeper slope (Figures 7.5 and 7.6).[53]

Hyunjin Ville Apartments: A Lesson in Local Design

While the military paid for construction of Mustang Valley Village Plus, other projects on the books have called for private developers to construct the housing and lease it to the United States. This desire builds on

Figure 7.5. Qwhang Ku Chi Village, South Korea.

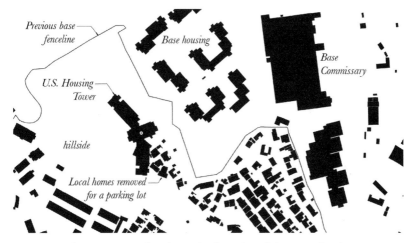

Previous base fenceline

Base housing

Base Commissary

U.S. Housing Tower

hillside

Local homes removed for a parking lot

Figure 7.6. This composite plan shows the footprint of the 112-unit, nine-story housing tower built by the United States, along with some of the homes in Qwhang Ku Chi Village that were later demolished to make way for a U.S. parking lot.

the "success" of the military's privatized housing at Aviano, Italy. Given this trend and my own interest in seeing how local developers design and build housing, I explored the Pyeongtaek area and found several notable examples. After asking local real-estate agents to identify good examples of local housing design, two of them directed me to a private development in Pyeongtaek known as Hyunjin Ville. As was the case at Aviano, the local market and the American market are worlds apart. This development, built in 2003 as market-rate apartments for South Koreans, is also quite different from other projects built in Pyeongtaek in the last twenty years. South Korean developers typically built ten- to twenty-story towers in a rather rigid alignment with parking between and under the towers and a few small playgrounds. Like many American apartments, including Mustang Valley Village Plus, these older buildings have apartments along both sides of a double-loaded corridor.

Hyunjin Ville was different, though. Tucked into a two-acre parcel and hidden from the bustling main avenue by several fifteen-story apartment buildings, Hyunjin is a new residential development with sixty units evenly distributed in six reinforced concrete frame buildings. Each building has five floors with just two units per floor and, in what the military housing staff would not tolerate, the buildings have no elevators (but neither do the existing apartment buildings at Osan) and only one parking space per unit. The layout of each apartment feels

Figure 7.7. Hyunjin Ville apartments, Pyeongtaek, South Korea. This local market-rate housing was built at the same time the United States was annexing Qwhang Ku Chi Village and building its own nine-story tower.

spacious, with large windows, minimal hallway space, and a balcony the width of the unit facing the parking court (Figure 7.7). With the design of each building, every unit has windows on at least two sides—a remarkable achievement and one that offers environmental and psychological benefits. After all, who would not want to have ample natural light and an ability to open windows to get a cooling cross breeze? The sad answer is that apparently designers for new military housing at Osan think the soldiers and their families do not want such a basic amenity. Unfortunately, the new apartments built on-base typically have windows on only one side and sacrifice valuable floor area to long double-loaded corridors.

It is instructive to compare the apartments built on-base with those built at Hyunjin Ville (Figure 7.8). The similarities between off-base and

balcony

Osan Air Base (Mustang Valley Village Plus) Apartment Plan

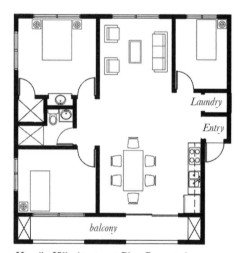

Storage   Laundry   Entry   Laundry   Entry   balcony

Hyunjin Ville Apartment Plan, Pyeongtaek

0   3m

Figure 7.8. Comparing apartment plans. Osan Air Base's Mustang Valley Village Plus apartments replaced in part the units lost when the military vacated the off-base Air Force Village. The newer three-bedroom units were 40 percent larger than the older models. In Hyunjin Ville, South Korean designers created a three-bedroom design in about half the area.

on-base apartments end with the number of bedrooms. The comparison shows how Americans' need for space manifests itself in the design of individual apartments, which necessitates significantly bigger buildings on a per-occupant basis. While the American apartment was 90 percent larger than the South Korean version, it was also 415 percent more expensive to build. Culturally, perhaps, American families in South Korea "expect" double the space of their South Korean counterparts. But at nine floors, the American building was more like private apartments built in Pyeongtaek in the 1980s. Each floor has about thirteen apartments strung along a double-loaded corridor. In buildings like this, apartments typically have windows on just one wall since the side walls separate adjacent apartments, and the other wall is along the corridor. This results in no natural cross-ventilation and poor light distribution. In addition to the double-loaded corridors, elevators make the American building much less efficient than the Hyunjin model. Each Hyunjin building has just two apartments per floor and no elevator. With fewer common hallways, stairs, and lobbies, the Hyunjin building's ratio of rentable area to gross area is substantially higher than the Osan model. Rentable area is one way developers measure efficiency.

From an occupant's perspective, while the Hyunjin units are small, they have ample windows, which improve natural ventilation and lighting. Recall Candy Glerup's complaint: not that her off-base apartment was small (which it was), but that it was "hot, dark, and depressing." Windows make the difference, and double-loaded corridors preclude effective window placement. Although advertised as "high-end housing with authentic western style" the Hyunjin design was more typical of newer Korean apartments than American ones in terms of overall efficiency, size, and access to natural light.[54] The apartment layout was also quite different from the American model. Rather than string rooms along a hallway within the apartment, at Hyunjin Ville the rooms are organized around a main hall that functions as a living room, dining area, circulation area, and greeting space. This is a common pattern for Korean homes.[55]

As U.S. military planners search for more land to build their bigger apartment buildings, they should evaluate the costs and benefits of their demands. However, the default position seems to be bigger units placed in inefficient "towers" spread across mostly useless open space. Captain Chris Rodgers, the former chief of construction at Osan, said,

Category	Osan Air Base	Hyunjin Ville
Bedrooms	3	3
Bathrooms	2	1.5
Storage Room (sf)	84	0
Gross Area (sf)	1673	884
Balcony Area (sf)	72	112
Corridor Area (sf)	104	0
Windows	5	7
Cross ventilation	No	Yes
Unit Cost	$313,000	$70,000

Figure 7.9. Comparative analysis of two apartments. From author's fieldwork, 2003–4.

"We're trying to get more command sponsored positions [families], so we'll need towers. We want to get to 20 to 25 percent command sponsored to improve the quality of life here and make it a base of choice."[56] As an engineer, he is used to solving problems—housing is like an equation: $f + lc = t$. Families (f) plus land constraints (lc) equals towers (t). But the example of Misawa, Japan, where the commander refused to build more towers because families did not like living in them, is a lesson lost on the military's designers at Osan. The military does not have a middle ground—it is either towers or townhomes.

In building at Mustang Valley Village, the military's designers inserted American-sized apartments into a twenty-year-old Korean building typology. If they were truly interested in learning from the private sector, they only needed to walk outside the gate and look to new developments like Hyunjin Ville to see how apartments could be built that are more efficient and more cost effective. From a land-use perspective, developments like Hyunjin Ville show how buildings no taller than five floors can be built at nearly double the densities of America's nine-floor housing "towers" (30 dwellings per acre vs. 14.4). Moreover, the off-base developments show how, at even greater densities, each apartment can have substantially better access to light and air.

Franchised Community

For the military, housing is only one aspect of building "planned communities." In another conversation with Captain Rodgers, he said, in addition to new housing, "We're building a new BX and renovating the commissary."[57] The purveyors of stuff have been busy building new "community centers" in the Pyeongtaek area to complete these "planned communities." The prospect of more military families in the area has generated widespread interest among the franchised interests. In 2004, for example, AAFES built the largest shopping mall on any U.S. outpost in South Korea. Designed by a U.S. firm, built by a South Korean contractor, and paid for out of AAFES profits, the $24-million, 170,000-square-foot, one-story mall at Osan will have a base exchange three times bigger than the original building.[58] Its food court has locations for Cinnabon, Seattle's Best Coffee, Taco Bell, and Baskin Robbins. It has a U.S. post office and a franchised bank.

With all the complaints about the lack of land, which led to the annexation of the 8.8-acre Mustang Valley Village Plus site in 2002, it is amazingly inconsistent that the base built a 170,000-square-foot one-story building. In urban areas in the United States, architects place multiple levels of housing on top of large retail stores in a model that recalls an old pattern of housing above shops. Jamal Stevenson, Osan's beleaguered planner, lobbied for a multifloor facility with the BX below housing.[59] At Osan, they could have easily built the apartments on two levels over the shopping center, obviating the need for annexation. But that would require mixing AAFES funding with housing funding and that is just too complicated for the U.S. DoD. In the end, Dallas overruled Stevenson, claiming Americans would not shop in a multistory facility. Ironically, in South Korea, leading retailer E-Mart builds multistory centers that are a major attraction for U.S. military members. The Saturday buses from Kunsan Air Base to the E-Mart in Kunsan City are usually full. Apparently, these soldiers have figured out how to push a shopping cart up an inclined moving walkway.

In addition to the AAFES projects, Osan recently celebrated the grand opening of its ninth sit-down restaurant, a Chili's franchise. The Air Force bought the franchise and hired a management team with Chili's experience to run the profitable restaurant. The managers anticipate up to $400,000 per year in profit.[60] It is located directly across the street from the new base exchange on a site next to the humble Base Chapel, a 1950s-era "temporary" building. An astute observer would wonder why, if the base is so short of land, would they continue building all these one-story facilities? It seems that policymakers and designers default to modes of practice that dictate familiarity in all its forms regardless of the costs.

The Taegu Connection

I ordered what was by now my standard entrée choice in a Korean restaurant—grilled beef bulgogi with a side of steamed rice and bean curd with garlic. The elderly Korean woman serving us gently placed six small dishes of kimchi on the worn-out wood-grain Formica tabletop. The busy restaurant looked like countless other Korean restaurants around most U.S. military bases. Koreans in coats, ties, slacks, and dresses. Americans in their distinctive Battle Dress Uniforms (BDUs) that conveniently camouflage any spilled sauces and the mess that can occur due to dropped chopsticks. Colonel Wayne Kennedy, in crisply pressed BDUs, and Mr. Dean Jackson, in a custom-tailored Korean suit, had agreed to join me for lunch to discuss the LPP.[61] As the commander of Area IV, which encompasses all the Army outposts in the lower half of the Republic of Korea, Colonel Kennedy was quite familiar with the LPP and its impacts. Like the Osan–Camp Humphreys area, the United States has defined the Taegu area and its outposts as an enduring hub, which means the U.S. presence will grow substantially. As a civilian at one of those outposts, Jackson was also dealing with the ramifications of the realignment. Colonel Kennedy, who has spent most of his career at various overseas outposts, including two assignments in South Korea, was more than willing to talk about the realignment proposals.

> We're developing a master plan for our bases around Taegu. Camp George will be a family housing area, Camp Henry will be an administrative area, and Camp Walker will have housing, the Post Exchange [shopping center] and the commissary [grocery store]. At Walker, we're planning for five ten-story towers with six units per floor. Our goal is to get these 300 units as a build-lease program with Korean developers building them for us to lease. Here, buildings go up not out and we don't have any room on Walker. But this will really change the atmosphere of the base, which is pretty flat—mostly two-story buildings. When you fly into Taegu it's sure easy to pick out the American bases; they're literally the only greenspace around. But these towers will make it look more like Taegu. We don't have much choice though . . . no way in hell we're going to build on the golf course, it's a real money-maker; the locals use it all the time during the week and the Americans use it on the weekend.

All over the peninsula, the defenders of democracy are also defending their golf courses. Colonel Kennedy is sounding the same themes: consumption, privatization, and golf. And like his counterparts at Osan, the default position is housing towers. At this point, Jackson jumped into the conversation. The Army assigned him to South Korea three times, and he even met his South Korean wife there. He started describing the elaborate plans for the 681-acre Camp Carroll:

> We're working on a twelve-lane bowling alley and club and have just finished a fifty-room visiting quarters [hotel]. The big thing now is family housing, that's my number one planning issue—we need 420 units but we don't have any right now. I wanted to build six ten-story towers but I don't think we have the room so we may end up with four twelve-story towers but we also need a school and more shopping. But we can't seem to get U.S. funding for this so we're seeing if developers can build the schools and shopping as part of the housing project and lease the space to us along with the units.

Colonel Kennedy stressed that this last piece was critical:

> We can't open the new housing if we can't open the schools and shopping centers. If I can't get the Post Exchange, commissary, and school by lease then we would have to go to Congress and if they paid for it, it would take us five years [until the project would be completed] just because the process is so long. And we can't wait that long.

Camp Carroll has many needs and the Army is not very patient. As it exists, the place is primarily a big warehouse; many of its 245 buildings store materials for some future war. But it is an attractive candidate for growth since it has ample land. After our main courses arrived, the conversation continued between bites of kimchi:

> COLONEL KENNEDY: Going downtown is a scary proposition for many troops here. It seems most guys are here for one tour or more than two. They either love it or hate it. For those guys who haven't experienced it here—it's hard; you know, hard to get around even with a map. And it's different down south. When we lived in Seoul, it was easy to use the subway since the maps were clear and the stops were obvious. But around Taegu you're not in control and as a Westerner you stand out. You look different.
>
> JACKSON: It's really a shock for most guys coming here from, say, Texas, it's a culture shock. You stand out. You can't speak the language or even understand the street signs. That's one reason why we have a high alcoholism rate on-post—some people are afraid to go off-post so they just stay in their rooms and drink.
>
> COLONEL KENNEDY: I have two boys and we've been overseas nearly all their life—16 years. When we're at a new post, my wife will ask them, "Boys, how ya' doing here?" Their reply is almost always the same,

"It's home mom, we're OK." These places look and feel like home. I think it's important to some folks for the place to look familiar. Most Americans are more comfortable with what looks, tastes, and smells like the U.S.

At America's outposts, with places like Chili's pumping out its exhaust in one area and Burger King belching its tallow-scented smoke down the street, the place certainly does smell like America. I was struck by how both men referred to the idea of Westerners, as people, standing out, but were not too concerned about the bases standing out, as they do when someone flies over them or walks by them and peers in the chain link fence. When I mentioned this, Jackson said, "But sometimes we build with a local influence." Colonel Kennedy reacted strongly to this suggestion, stating forcefully, "But it's absolutely just a façade—the inside is still American." Here is a senior Army officer, trained as a logistician, who sees through the veneers of compatibility. Whether in Italy, Japan, or South Korea, planning that stops with sloped tile roofs and stucco walls does not make a place compatible. But the American style seems to be spreading to the local area. Jackson commented that he has noticed more Western-style housing going up: single-family homes with big yards and two-car garages. It seems local residents are learning from the planning patterns of the military.

Jackson was looking a bit anxious, then told his boss they had best be going. Their next meeting started in about ten minutes. We wrapped up our conversation, paid the bill, and then quickly headed to Colonel Kennedy's car. The parking lot overflowed with vehicles, and we had difficulty getting through the thick traffic to the main gate of the Army post. While stuck at a long traffic light, both men raised questions about a recent policy limiting who in the U.S. military can drive in South Korea. The Army based the Korea-wide policy on rank—lower-ranking soldiers cannot have a privately owned vehicle (POV) anymore. And they instituted it shortly after the accident that killed the two young schoolgirls. Jackson claimed that even though it helps with traffic on the base and opens up parking spaces, it was really an automatic reaction based on some "studies" proving that these younger soldiers are the culprits in most accidents. "But it probably won't last long," said Colonel Kennedy. "It sends a mixed message—on the one hand we want families to come over here but on the other we won't let you drive." There is some irony here, as Jackson noted, "They can't drive POVs but they can drive Humvees."

But the Humvees, tanks, and armored personnel carriers are the problem, not the Hyundais.

As we were driving away, I noticed the ubiquitous Burger King on a corner. Then a Virginia Highway Patrol car speeding by caught my attention. We were not at a U.S. outpost in South Korea; we were in Alexandria, Virginia, adjacent to the Army's Fort Belvoir. Borders are indeed blurry in this transnational age. The Army had sent the two men to Virginia for a management course and I was there as guest speaker discussing the planning of overseas outposts. They had been in Alexandria two weeks and already found five Korean restaurants around the base. This is hybridity in action.

Realignments "Rewards"

In 2003 the senior U.S. military officer in South Korea, Gen. Leon J. La-Porte, introduced a "Good Neighbor" program designed to improve relations with the citizens of South Korea.[62] One tangible example, according to LaPorte, is moving most U.S. soldiers out of the Yongsan garrison and out of Seoul, because, he said, that was what the South Korean people want. He had direct hotlines installed with Korean-speaking operators and eventually had the U.S. Forces Korea website translated into Korean.

This commendable plan, however, did not filter down to some officers responsible for land-use decisions. A year after General LaPorte introduced the Good Neighbor plan, an officer at Osan Air Base said there is still a philosophy among senior U.S. officers in South Korea that "land is cheap."[63] On the one hand, this is technically correct. From an economic standpoint, the land is not cheap, it is free. The United States pays no rent. On the other hand, that idea is narrow-minded. From a sociopolitical perspective, land is very expensive. For the hundreds of South Korean families relocated from their villages so that the United States could build the Mustang Valley Village Plus tower or expand Camp Humphreys, the U.S. demand was not cheap. For the communities burdened with accommodating a realigned empire, the demand for more land is not cheap. If the United States intends to be a "good neighbor," it should also consider the sociospatial consequences of its actions.

The "rewards" for South Korea acquiescing to the realignment plans of the Bush administration are minimal. While the United States returned some land (mostly remote sites near the DMZ), it demanded replacement acreage in densely developed cities outside the existing capital of Seoul. Moreover, while the United States agreed to "give" the South Korean government $11 billion in military aid (used to buy U.S. manufactured weapons), it demanded replacement facilities funded by the South Korean taxpayer. In the age of American Empire, an aggressive administration can place high demands on its allies. Like Britain's Lt. Gen. Robert Napier in nineteenth-century India, emissaries of the American Empire justify expropriation, demolition, and displacement using the language of national security. With its new land, the United States can build bigger, more self-contained bases filled with generously sized apartments, expansive shopping centers, immaculate golf courses, and ample parking. Much has been written about America's arrogant attitude. This is just one more chapter.

CHAPTER EIGHT

Reacting to Rape:
Japan's Special Action Committee Okinawa

On September 4, 1995, in Okinawa, Japan, three U.S. Marines raped a twelve-year-old Japanese girl. In the trial's first session in November 1995, the victim's father said he wished he could kill the three Americans himself. The event brought U.S. and Japan relations to a post–World War II low—85,000 Okinawans rallied and demanded a U.S. withdrawal from Okinawa. Admiral Richard Macke publicly commented that the soldiers could have "had" a girl for the price of their rental car. A three-judge panel in Japanese court convicted all three Marines and sentenced them to seven years in Japanese prison; the U.S. military "retired" Admiral Macke.[1]

This tragic example of spillover shows that rape is not only a personal issue. It also involves issues of interpersonal and international power. The rally adopted by acclamation a resolution condemning the United States for an "occupation mentality."[2] Given that the United States occupies 20 percent of the land on the island of Okinawa, this claim is understandable. Exacerbating the situation was an F-15 crash over water just days before the rally, further highlighting the dangers of living under empire's accident-prone wings. "These incidents cause great fear," said the mayor of Naha, Okinawa. "The root of the trouble is the presence of military bases. We demand the reduction and eventual removal of military bases on Okinawa."[3]

Justifying Okinawa's America Towns

But the military is unlikely to leave Japan, let alone Okinawa. The United States has a substantial investment in Japan, where 65,717 DoD personnel

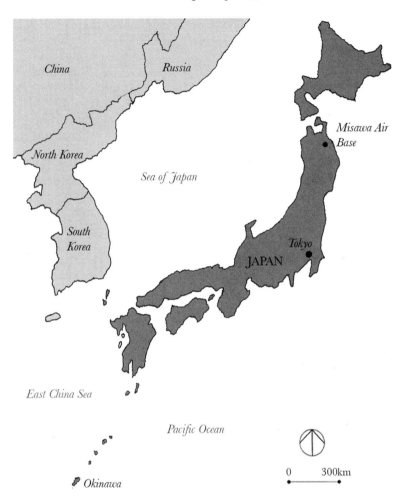

Map 8.1. Japan.

operate out of 97 locations on 127,810 acres. Okinawa's strategic value increased dramatically in June 1991 when Mt. Pinatubo erupted in the Philippines.[4] Volcanic ash covered Clark Air Base, the largest American outpost in the world. Although the Philippine Senate had earlier refused to renew the base lease agreement at Clark, it took several feet of ash to finally get the U.S. military off the island. The United States abandoned the base and began to rely more on Okinawa's Kadena Air Base as its main "platform" in East Asia. In 1996 Kurt Campbell, former deputy assistant secretary of defense for East Asia and Pacific affairs, explained why the U.S. government thinks Kadena Air Base is so important:

Kadena will be a base—a platform for our forward deployment in Asia for a significant period of time. . . . One of the functions of Kadena Air Base, obviously, is to be ready to respond to a contingency. And as we look at the Korean Peninsula, obviously, you can't help but want to make sure that our capabilities, with regard to Kadena, are kept viable.[5]

Campbell reveals the interconnected relationship between America's outposts and regional security issues. He links Kadena to the Korean peninsula and uses the North Korean threat as a justification for Kadena Air Base's continued presence.[6]

Perhaps the most telling rationalization came in the 1998 report by the Government Accountability Office (GAO). The GAO highlighted the importance of Okinawa in the U.S. force structure and offered explanations as to why the United States would not accept relocating these forces:

Relocating these forces outside the region would increase political risk by appearing to decrease commitment to regional security and treaty obligations and undercut deterrence. Furthermore, relocating U. S. forces outside of Japan could adversely affect military operations by increasing transit times to areas where crises are occurring. Finally, the cost of the U.S. presence in Japan is shared by the government of Japan, which also provides bases and other infrastructure used by U.S. forces on Okinawa.[7]

The "crisis" areas are China and North Korea. These are places easily reached by America's phalanx of warplanes on Kadena's 1,194-acre airfield. The report's final point is perhaps the most germane. Japan is a generous host. As discussed in chapter 2, levels of host-nation funding correlate with recent realignment policies. The more a host nation funded stationing costs, the less inclined the United States was to leave that country. The United States desires an empire paid for by others, even establishing a "burden sharing" target of 50 percent. Japan exceeds this funding target, providing $4.3 billion in host-nation support, representing 75 percent of the cost of stationing U.S. soldiers in Japan. The United States deprives the citizens of Japan of the use of their land and requires that they pay handsomely for the "privilege" of having U.S. troops stationed in their country.

In 2000, participants in the Quadrennial Defense Review (QDR) process reaffirmed Kadena's importance in the face of possible threats by China: "The air base at Kadena is vital to U.S. security because it is the only U.S. air base within tactical fighter range of Taiwan. Without access to Kadena, the United States would be forced to rely primarily on carrier-based aviation to support the defense of Taiwan in the event of a Chinese attack."[8] Less than three weeks after the September 11 attacks, the DoD published the results of the QDR, which called for "maintaining regionally tailored forces forward stationed."[9] Referring to this as "deter forward," the essence of the concept was to keep soldiers overseas. This marked an end to the drawdown of U.S. forces worldwide. Three years later, in 2004, the Bush administration's global realignment policy bypassed Japan, implicitly reaffirming once again the importance of Kadena as a major hub while recognizing the importance of Japan's financial contributions.

Shin Kanemaru, a former director of Japan's Defense Agency, referred to the practice of funding U.S. operations as the *omoiyari yosan* or sympathy budget.[10] Under President Carter, U.S. funding of overseas outposts dropped and the government of Japan decided to step in and pay the salaries of Japanese employees, including architects and engineers, working at American outposts in Japan. The sympathy budget in 1978 was approximately $56.27 million ($159 million in 2003 dollars).[11] But by 2003, the sympathy budget totaled $4.3 billion, 28 times greater after adjusting for inflation, paying for most construction as well the salaries of 23,000 Japanese employees working on U.S. outposts. In light of Japan's economic decline in the 1990s, one Japanese official said, "This time, Japan needs America's sympathy."[12]

Such sympathy was not forthcoming. The United States has asked for increases to the sympathy budget almost every year. Former U.S. ambassador to Japan Thomas Foley said Japan's contributions are "an important element of Japan's strategic contributions."[13] And former secretary of defense William Cohen stressed that host-nation support was not a "sympathy budget," but rather an integral part of Japan's security budget and an important contribution to regional stability.[14] While at first glance, "sympathy" may seem a strange term, a look at its definition reveals that at least in one respect it is appropriate: "Sympathy (n). A relationship or affinity between persons or things in which whatever affects one correspondingly affects the other."[15]

What the United States does in Japan affects the Japanese. The spillover and spending patterns are part of this "relationship." The sympathy budget has funded construction at U.S. military locations throughout Japan, including 10,021 homes, 20,950 dormitory rooms, 117 headquarters and operations buildings, 31 medical and dental clinics, 61 schools and child-care centers, 80 aircraft shelters, 130 warehouses, 110 maintenance shops, and much more.[16] In one controversial project, the program even paid for a new $84-million shopping center at Yokota Air Base in the suburbs of Tokyo.[17] The U.S. military is proud of this monument to America's shopping culture, courtesy of the Japanese taxpayer. In yet another example of building for a "supersized empire," this building doubled the size of the commissary and increased the size of the base exchange by 25 percent. Its "plaza" is an oversized sidewalk and designers placed its "Japanese Garden" next to a bank of fire stairs. With its "expansive" food court, the project also uncovers the nature of the "franchised empire." Soldiers can now order the same fast food in U.S. military food courts at nearly all of America's far-flung outposts. The military described the building, which opened in 2001, this way:

> This new three-story, 250,000-square-foot facility houses the newest and best Army and Air Force Exchange Service, commissary, and food court in mainland Japan. The 80,000-square-foot commissary is double the size of its predecessor. The new 80,000-square-foot exchange has 20,000 more square feet than in our previous exchange facilities. The expansive food court includes Robin Hood Deli Sandwiches, Anthony's Pizza, Taco Bell, Baskin Robbins, Charlie's Steakery, A&W, and Cinnabon (with a Seattle's Best Coffee store). And all of this is conveniently located under one roof.[18]

The unique aspect is the "one roof" concept. This building does not follow the typology of most "community centers," in itself a telling title for the place, where "community" is a euphemism for "consumption." This large shopping mall is an excellent example of twenty-first-century "hybrid urbanism." It follows the multifloor, rooftop-parking model established by E-mart in South Korea.[19] E-mart designers use multifloor stores incorporating sales departments that sell everything from hair spray to high-definition televisions. These departments are accessible through internal escalators designed to accommodate customers and their overloaded shopping carts. Many E-marts even have an open central atrium reinforcing the integrated nature of the store. But at Yokota, the commissary, the base exchange, and offices are all on separate levels, reflecting the separated organizations of the two primary tenants: AAFES and DECA. At many bases in the United States, these two functions are side by side. At Yokota, they are stacked. While the rooftop parking was

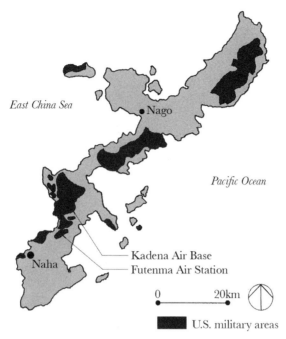

East China Sea

• Nago

Pacific Ocean

Kadena Air Base
Futenma Air Station

• Naha

0   20km

U.S. military areas

Map 8.2. Okinawa, Japan. The land area on Okinawa under control of the
U.S. military accounts for 20 percent of the main island.

an innovation for the normally conservative military building establishment, it has presented security challenges in the wake of September 11.
On "high-threat" days, military police cordon off the roof and parking
spillover permeates the entire area. While these barricades provide little
defense against a backpack bomb, a vehicle with a bomb in its trunk
could do serious damage if it detonated on the shopping mall's roof.

Special Action Committee Okinawa

While Yokota was building its massive "community center" using funds
from Japan's sympathy budget, planners at Kadena Air Base were eagerly
anticipating the inflow of funds coming from the Special Action Committee Okinawa (SACO). Two months after the 1995 rape and accompanying protests, the governments of Japan and the United States established SACO to "reduce the burden on the people of Okinawa."[20] The
burden is a heavy one. The United States occupies 57,793 acres (20 percent) of the main island of Okinawa and 10 percent of the land in the
entire Okinawa prefecture (Map 8.2).[21]

This burden affects Okinawa much more than any other prefecture in Japan. The prefecture accounts for 0.67 percent of Japan's total land area but provides 72 percent of the land used by all U.S. military forces in Japan, which gives a new meaning to "out of sight, out of mind." For most Japanese, the American presence is tucked away on a remote island where they will likely never see or experience the spillover. But for the 1.3 million Okinawans, the impacts are severe. This is a case of internal imperialism.[22] The discrepancy in land allocated to the U.S. military across Japan is a continuation of the sacrificial treatment of Okinawa by the government of Japan. Former Okinawan prefectural governor Ota adds to the complex story: "What must be pointed out in this connection is that the military bases on the mainland of Japan sit on land that is 87 percent state-owned, while more than 30 percent of the land used by the bases in Okinawa is privately owned."[23]

Conflicts between the landowners, the United States, and the government of Japan over land use are common. Under Japanese land-use law known as the "Special Measures for Law and Land Required by the U.S. Military Bases," landowners must lease their land to the government of Japan, which then subleases it to the U.S. military for no charge.[24] The Japanese Diet passed the law in 1972 when the United States returned Okinawa to the government of Japan and secretly agreed to pay $4 million for outstanding claims against land appropriated for U.S. bases.[25] Known as "reversion," this turnover led to an awkward land-use situation. With the United States no longer legally in control of the island, the landowners wanted their land back, land that the United States had expropriated for its use during and after World War II. To avoid a situation whereby local landowners could impede the functioning of the U.S. military, Japan used its Land Acquisition Law to maintain control of the parcels. But unlike eminent domain laws in the United States that require one-time compensation for the forced sale of private land for public use, the Japanese law allowed for continued private ownership but forced lease.

With the legal basis for the forced leases in place, the government of Japan could use the new Special Measures law to sublease the land to the U.S. military. To make the arrangement more palatable, the government of Japan provided landowners with rental payments up to five times market rate.[26] Because of this largesse, many landowners forced into the arrangement are content to collect annual rent payments from their government. Some Japanese politicians have actively supported the program as well. Muneo Suzuki, a former minister of the Okinawa Development Bureau, went a bit too far in his support. He used the rent payments as political payoff. In 1997, he accepted donations from "The Landowner's Association of U.S. Military Bases" in exchange for securing bigger land-lease payments. Since the government of Japan's Defense Facilities Administration had to receive Suzuki's approval in setting land rental fees, he could demand higher payments in exchange for kickbacks from the beneficiaries. Under his watch, in one year, the lease payments increased 3.5 percent (roughly $20 million).[27]

Of the approximately 32,000 landowners, roughly 3,000 are opposed to the leases.[28] In light of their protests, the United States made some concessions. The United States does, for example, give access to a few Okinawan farmers. They can farm a total of 110 acres of their land on the base. Also, on May 14, 1996, after extensive negotiations, the U.S. military allowed one landowner, Soichi Chibana, to return to his ancestral land on the base for a two-hour visit. He brought his family to his small plot for a picnic and to "feel the spirit of his ancestors."[29] Chibana's plight is a reminder of the land's emotional value. His attitude counters the apparent U.S. position that land is strictly a commodity, useful at various times for military and/or economic purposes.

Despite the concessions, some opponents have refused to lease their land, including some plots located under Kadena's runway.[30] Similar to what is occurring in South Korea, one group formed the "Committee of Hitotsubo Landowners" to protest the forced leases.[31] About 2,800 Japanese residents each own one *tsubo* of land, which then requires the government of Japan to negotiate with each of them for its lease. One tsubo is about 35.5 square feet and was the traditional unit of measure of land in Okinawa.

Following the 1995 rape, Okinawa governor Masahide Ota supported the oppositional landowners' call and refused to extend their leases to the U.S. military. Clearly, the governments of Japan and the United States could not tolerate Ota's actions. After he refused to enforce the leases, the matter went to the Supreme Court of Japan and the judges summarily dismissed the case. The court allowed the national government to override Ota's policy decision. But he was not ready to give up. On September 8, 1996, he sponsored a referendum on Okinawa Island on the issue of U.S. military bases. Even though 89 percent (480,000) of those that voted favored downsizing, Governor Ota felt that with only 45 percent of all eligible voters either abstaining or voting no, he could not continue his legal battle. The hope was for a two-thirds majority. While a vote in which nearly 90 percent of the ballots cast favored one position would constitute a landslide in the United States, Governor Ota considered abstentions nonsupport. After the referendum, the governor retreated from his position and agreed to get the oppositional landowners to abandon their protests.[32]

These patterns of voter abstention tie land use to political support. The 28,000 members of the All Okinawa Landowners Association abstained, military base workers formed a union and abstained, and the All Okinawa Housing Rental Association's 3,000 members abstained.[33] All three of these groups benefit from the U.S. presence. Toshi Hayashi, an Okinawan resident who is paradoxically both an opponent and a supporter, said, "Those bases aren't protecting anyone any more. The Cold War is over we all know that. We want the bases off of Okinawa. They're just taking up all our best land. On the other hand, I make several thousand dollars a month teaching on the base. I need the money."[34] The irony is that even with the economic impact of these bases, Okinawa has the highest unemployment and lowest per capita income rates in Japan, leading one to ask just what are the benefits of imperial power?[35]

Another fact that highlights disparities, this time between the United States and the three towns adjacent to Kadena Air Base, is the difference in population densities, as measured in people per square kilometer (Figure 8.1). U.S. soldiers and their families live in sprawling compounds while Okinawans live at much higher densities in three adjacent areas: Okinawa-chi, Chatan-cho, and Kadena-cho.[36] Kadena is indeed a familiar place when it comes to population densities. It has almost the same density as Walnut Creek, a suburb in California's Bay Area. This contrasts with the towns adjacent to Kadena that have densities four times greater.

Although "density" is a geographical measurement, "crowding" is a perception. For some people, Walnut Creek or Kadena would feel crowded. For others, these places would seem spacious. What makes densities tolerable, though, is not space. Rather, it is the ability to regulate privacy, to control one's space.[37] If one can exercise control, then it is easier to deal with density. A small but private backyard may feel less crowded than a shared common area that numerous homes overlook. American

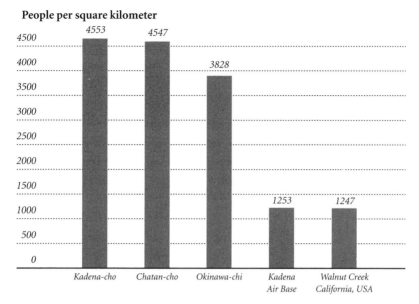

Figure 8.1. Density disparities. Data from Census of Japan (2000) and U.S. Census (2000).

designers working at Kadena Air Base failed to grasp this concept, as we will see shortly.

As is typical of America's outposts, Kadena Air Base is a low-density enclave surrounded by relatively dense urban development. As measured by the FAR, Okinawa-chi is eight times "denser" than Kadena. But the difference is not due to high-rise construction; rather, it is due to layouts that are more compact. Comparing street morphologies also highlights important differences. Okinawa-chi uses a "gridiron" layout and Kadena Air Base uses what Michael Southworth calls a "loops and lollipops" street layout.[38] On the base, street patterns reinforce a low-density, auto-oriented character of development. Off the base, in Okinawa-chi, the gridiron supports a much finer grain of development that allows for improved pedestrian accessibility and distributes vehicular traffic more evenly across the network. Street networks are also an important indicator of infrastructure costs. More streets cost more money to build and maintain. In this case, a relevant measure of infrastructure cost is the total area of street per floor area. From a purely economic standpoint, Okinawa-chi supports eight times the floor area with roughly double the paving area as Kadena, making the Japanese model four times more efficient on a paving per floor area basis (Figures 8.2 and 8.3).

In my survey of planners and architects working for the U.S. military, 67 percent of the respondents indicated funding for construction was a very important concern, and 65 percent considered infrastructure condition a very important concern. These were the two leading concerns regarding base planning. But by following a low-density model of development, these planners and policymakers divert funding for buildings to streets and parking lots. If they followed a different model of development, they could free up a substantial amount of money for more construction. Perhaps even worse, the limited resources dedicated to infrastructure maintenance dissolve across a profligate network with utility lines and paving inefficiently stretched to meet up with widely spaced and haphazardly ordered buildings. It is inaccurate to argue, as many in the military do, that these bases do not have enough land. The land is there; the policies and practices that dictate low-density development, from antiterrorism standoff distances to family-housing density limits, are the problem. Likewise, it is erroneous to assume that these bases do not have enough money for construction and maintenance. Those in charge of base development have elected to build in a wasteful manner. One young student living in Kadena-cho cleverly sums up the situation, "If you compare Kadena (cho) to a steak, the U.S. military is the meat and we are the fat around the edge."[39]

SACO's Snails' Pace

The Special Action Committee Okinawa (SACO) process was supposed to address the disparities in land use among Okinawa, the rest of Japan, and the U.S. military. The intent was to reduce the U.S. presence, give land back to its original owners, and use vacated municipal land for economic development. Negotiations lasted over a year and concluded in the *SACO Final Report* on December 2, 1996. As part of the process, the United States agreed to return 21 percent of the land that it used (12,361 acres), adjust training procedures, and implement noise-reduction measures.[40] Even with this reduction, Okinawa's share of the total area used by the U.S. military in Japan will only drop from 75 percent to 70.2 percent.[41]

After the parties finalized the report, former secretary of defense William Perry stated, "Perhaps some good has come out of the tragedy—

Building Figure-Ground Plan: Okinawa-chi, Japan

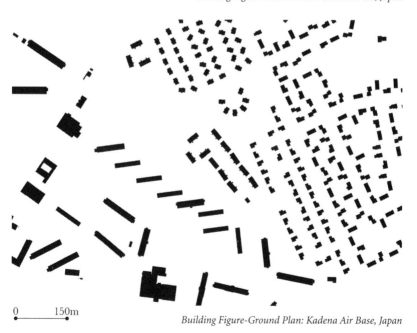

0   150m

Building Figure-Ground Plan: Kadena Air Base, Japan

Figure 8.2. Compact development versus sprawl: drawn at the same scale, these building figure-ground plans of nearby areas show the development patterns in representative portions of Okinawa-chi *(top)* and the adjacent Kadena Air Base *(bottom)*.

Paving Figure-Ground Plan: Okinawa-chi, Japan

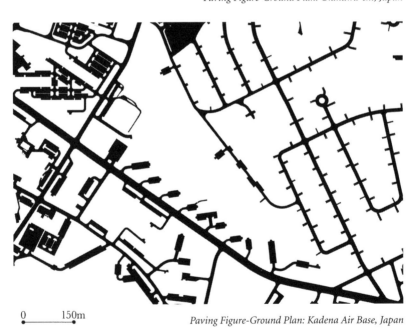

0   150m

Paving Figure-Ground Plan: Kadena Air Base, Japan

Figure 8.3. Streets versus parking lots. These paving figure-ground plans (drawn at the same scale) for the same areas in Okinawa-chi and Kadena reveal the American preference for parking lots over streets.

	Kadena Air Base	Okinawa-chi
Buildings		
Average building height (floors)	2	3
Residential density (units/acre)	2.5	20
Lot coverage (percent)	15	80
Floor Area Ratio	0.3	2.4
Streets		
Intersections	34	217
Access Points	26	63
Loops and cul-de-sacs	17	4
Blocks	16	140

Figure 8.4. Comparative analysis of urban form. From author's fieldwork, 2002–3.

the rape. It was a wake up call."[42] He added, "We were able to work out and finalize negotiations with the Japanese Government to lighten the burden of the Okinawan people this month, the fifty-year anniversary of when I went to Okinawa as a young engineer in the Army to construct bases."[43] Even with Secretary Perry's stated willingness to close bases he may have helped build, the United States has been slow to act. As John Purves, who has analyzed the U.S. military's role in Okinawa, argues, "After the 1995 rape incident Washington and Tokyo needed to show that they were taking the base situation in Okinawa seriously. Ten years on, however, and nothing of substance has resulted from this committee's activities. In terms of bringing about change in the military base struc-ture on Okinawa, SACO has done nothing constructive whatsoever."[44]

The land area in Japan occupied by the U.S. military has remained essentially unchanged.[45] The U.S. rationale is that the United States will relocate once the government of Japan finds the land and builds suit-able replacement facilities, from golf courses to hospitals. But the gov-ernment of Japan is not inclined to build some of these facilities. For example, an agreement to return the 116-acre Awase Meadows golf course in Okinawa collapsed when the Japanese government refused to build the U.S. military a replacement course at the Kadena Ammunition Stor-age Dump. The mayor of Okinawa-chi opposed the plan, and it could not move forward without his approval.[46] In Okinawa, the three mayors whose towns overlap with Kadena Air Base have near veto power over almost all construction, not just golf courses.[47] The U.S. military seeks their approval on relocating aircraft parking ramps, building operational facilities, and installing noise walls.[48] In World War II Okinawa was a sacrificial battleground. Now it is both a military encampment and a pleasure ground, with bars, dance halls, golf courses, and private beaches reserved for the use of the U.S. military. But the guest does not want to pay for these pleasures.

SACO and the Growth of Kadena

Kadena Air Base, the largest overseas air base with a population exceeding 25,000 people, is a significant beneficiary of SACO and the sympathy budget.[49] The two countries designated Kadena as a place to relocate equipment and people from other installations on Okinawa that will eventually close. This relocation will cost the Japanese taxpayers several billion dollars. Whether one calls it a sympathy budget or host-nation support, the result is the same. While other countries, like Germany and South Korea, provide their own form of support, according to the U.S. Army Corps of Engineers, Japan's program is by far the largest, providing $800 million annually for construction projects. The Corps manages the money through its Japan Engineer District, which employs 300 engineers and technicians, about half of whom are Japanese.[50]

While the host-nation money typically pays for construction and some design, the U.S. Congress has also provided $16 to $18 million annually, primarily for planning and preliminary design, which is mostly done by U.S. architectural and engineering firms under contract to the Army Corps of Engineers. These designers produce a "criteria package" that may include conceptual site plans, floor plans, and schematic elevations.[51] The United States then gives the package to the government of Japan for final design and construction purposes. This work then goes to Japanese architects, engineers, and contracting companies.

The spending difference on construction between the United States and Japan is substantial. Between 2000 and 2004, planners at Kadena projected that the Japanese taxpayer would pay for nearly $300 million in nonhousing construction projects, while the United States would pay less than $40 million. Approximately 75 percent of the U.S. funding would come from "Non-Appropriated Funds" (NAF). As the title suggests, Congress does not appropriate this money; rather, it comes from profit-generating places like base golf courses, beaches, and marinas. While the government of Japan funds most construction on bases in Japan, they will not fund certain projects. These include revenue-generating buildings like a BX or commissary (except at Yokota), buildings that support offensive military capabilities like certain aircraft facilities, and community buildings like chapels or youth centers. Not including NAF projects, Kadena's planners projected that the U.S. taxpayer would fund less than 10 percent of the construction at the base.

Two of the primary SACO proposals were to (1) close Futenma Marine Corps Air Station, and (2) relocate functions from that installation to a new "sea-based facility" and to Kadena. While Futenma has not closed, construction has proceeded at Kadena. In 1999, the United States approved a fifteen-phase, $95-million program to improve 560 multifamily homes on Kadena in what the military called the Post Acquisition Improvement Program. The project also increased parking to 2.5 spaces per unit, a very high number for multifamily housing, but reflective of Americans' ongoing infatuation with the car.

This was the first time the U.S. government agreed to spend such a substantial sum at Kadena. Since the government of Japan does not pay for renovations, Congress had to pay this bill. But this program was minor compared to what the government of Japan agreed to fund. "SACO housing is a $2 billion program," said Ryan Martini, a planner at Kadena Air Base.[52] In 1996, as part of the SACO process, the two governments agreed to replace 1,473 homes at Kadena Air Base and 1,777 units at nearby Camp Foster at densities of at least ten units per acre.[53] So what started out as a response to a rape ended up being a major housing construction program, providing new homes at no cost to the new American Empire and its representatives. The rape catalyzed action from those Japanese residents who had likely been unhappy with the military's presence in Okinawa for some time. But, in a case of imperial backfire, the residents of Japan were stuck with the bases and a major construction bill. Overall, Kadena's planners projected that the Japanese taxpayer would fund nearly 95 percent of the construction at the base and neighboring U.S. outposts.

Skewed Surveys/Suburban Solutions

Given that the housing program was the largest piece of the SACO budget, the United States was eager to determine its housing need and move forward with construction, even if Futenma stayed open. To do this, the military hired a U.S. consulting firm to produce a *Housing Requirements and Market Analysis,* which is a "a detailed study to determine

Figure 8.5. The "undersized" housing at Kadena Air Base is scheduled to be replaced as part of the SACO process. While the neighborhood layouts are hardly "compatible" with local patterns, the "Okinawan" clay tile roofs are the base's nod to regional architecture.

Military Family Housing (MFH) assets the U.S. government must provide to ensure that all families... have access to acceptable housing."[54] The military defines "acceptable" housing as "affordable, within a reasonable commute, of good quality, and with the proper number of bedrooms for each family."[55] To design this acceptable housing, the military then hired a U.S. engineering firm to survey the residents of Kadena's housing area and prepare a master plan. Before beginning design, they sent out 800 questionnaires, received 400 back, and made the following conclusions. Respondents placed a high value on "single units," and when given an option, preferred "less dense housing." For instance, duplexes with yards were more popular than townhomes without yards. Townhomes were more popular than towers. Only 17 percent of the respondents said they would be either interested or very interested in living in towers. Only 25 percent said they would be interested in living in quadplexes. They wanted their homes to be distinguished from other homes. They placed larger units at the top of their priority when it came to interior layout, followed by more storage. Regarding their own lot, they cited visual privacy as the highest priority, followed by parking adjacent to the unit. In addition to the findings, the consultants made design recommendations based on the results of the survey:[56]

> Create housing areas that are quiet, with low traffic and spacious
>   yards . . . an open feeling, but with a sense of yard privacy.
> Emphasize convenience to schools, parks, and work.
> People value a single unit, therefore create individual unit identity—
>   take every step to avoid the feeling of congest(ed), crowded, and
>   "cookie cutter" design.

These recommendations had little in common with the survey findings. Respondents did not express a desire for "spacious yards" or an "open feeling"; they wanted visual privacy and easily accessible parking. They did not indicate a dislike for "congested" areas; they wanted single homes rather than towers. The survey itself was hardly gender balanced. Of the total number of respondents, 90 percent were married. Additionally, 72 percent were male and 28 percent were female. The team was getting a male-dominated perspective on neighborhood and home design. This was largely because they sent the surveys primarily to workplaces, and given that the majority of soldiers are men, it should have been clear that this imbalance would occur. There was no discussion of the ramifications of this potential flaw in their analysis. Apparently, the input of spouses was of little interest to the surveyors, even though appealing to families is a stated goal of military planners.

The base got a "survey" to tout, and the designers had "data" to reference during the design. Following the survey, the designers prepared a master plan for 1,473 new homes at Kadena. And what did they provide? They ignored their own survey results and even some of their own recommendations. In a clear distortion of the results, the design team, referring to the survey, stated, "Two of the key findings from the survey were that residents had a strong preference for dense housing with extra yards versus high-rise housing and that 84 percent of the residents desired pedestrian pathways."[57] The residents did prefer housing with yards to high-rises when given only those choices. However, the residents clearly preferred single-family homes, not anything else. They also wanted yards, but there was no discussion of "extra yards" or even of the total size of the yards. Yes, they disliked towers, but they also disliked quadplexes (71 percent disliked towers and 56 percent disliked townhomes). What the designers were referring to was an evaluation of four neighborhood types conducted as part of the survey: towers, townhomes with community playgrounds, townhomes with private yards, and duplexes with private yards. Respondents gave their highest ratings to townhomes and duplexes with private yards. The design/survey team, however, did not give the respondents the option to evaluate single-family homes against the other typologies. This was likely the result of an agreement between the government of Japan and the United States that required densities to be ten units per acre rather than the existing three units per acre. Since the Japanese were going to pay for the project through funds dedicated for SACO, they did have some influence and wanted the Americans to be a little more judicious when it comes to land use.

In creating several development scenarios, the team struggled with the "challenge of maximizing housing unit density to the goal."[58] Some of the self-imposed challenges included limiting development to areas with slopes less than 15 percent, calling for front-yard setbacks of twenty-five feet, backyards of at least twenty-six feet, and mid-block pedestrian areas at least thirty-two feet wide. While most people responded favorably to the idea of pedestrian pathways (who wouldn't?), this was not the respondents' priority. When asked to state their first priority within their neighborhoods, they responded as follows: visual privacy (36 percent); parking adjacent to unit (27 percent); plants in yard (13 percent); less traffic on street (12 percent); bike/jogging trails (12 percent). While 84 percent did desire bike/jogging trails (which the designers called "pedestrian pathways"), they were a low priority. But the designers gave them these trails at the expense of the top two priorities: privacy and adjacent parking.

The designers assumed that an arrangement of single-family homes was impossible at the approved density standards. Hence, there was no need to give the residents a single-family option to evaluate, since they would not get it anyway. The designers misread the survey recommendations in order to justify an odd combination of attached homes and sprawling blocks. They created a plan with mostly quadplexes and six-plexes, the second-least-favored configuration after towers. And these units shared large common back yards. Unfortunately, the plan provided for little visual privacy.

Regarding traffic, the designers replaced streets in front of units with drive-through parking lots. But given the average front-yard setback of thirty-six feet, these parking spaces were not adjacent to the unit. They also called for twenty-four-foot-wide, two-lane roads, which makes for an individual lane of twelve feet, about as wide as a lane on a U.S. interstate and one reason why so many drivers ignore the fifteen mile-per-hour signs posted in base housing areas. Wide lanes encourage higher speeds.

Even worse, the team used Institute of Transportation Engineers (ITE) Trip Generation Standards to predict the number of vehicle trips per day from each new home. They assumed "that the number for Kadena will range closer to the high-end generation rate of [9.55 daily trips] due to the number of vehicles and convenience of driving on . . . base."[59] They then concluded that traffic congestion would increase in the area, justifying their excessively wide roads. The 9.55 rate is for detached single-family homes in the United States, not multifamily homes. The team also ignored the residents' stated desire to be close to schools and shopping areas and located most of the housing in areas that necessitated driving.

As part of the planning process at Kadena, the installation commander offered up his thoughts on how the base should develop:

> As we take the opportunity of redeveloping over 40 percent of our housing due to the Special Action Committee on Okinawa Agreement, we need to maximize green space and ensure future expansion is there for schools, parks and fields. Driving anywhere on Okinawa is a problem and traffic gets worse every year. We all need more accessibility in our vehicle-oriented base. This means providing for pedestrian access corridors and enhancing parks and playgrounds.[60]

The consulting team clearly listened to the Wing Commander rather than the residents. The layout of their plan maximized green space and provided places for several new parks at a ratio of 6.8 parks per 1,000 households. For comparison, the city of Berkeley, California, supports 1.1 parks per 1,000 households.[61] Overall, Berkeley has two acres of city parks and open space per 1,000 residents. Not including its eighteen-hole golf course, Kadena has twenty-six acres of parks and open space per 1,000 residents. We could call this the "overparked empire." Respondents to the survey did not indicate a desire for more parks. Kadena already had numerous parks scattered around the base. The designers misread the desire of the 13 percent who wanted plants in their yard. This morphed into large yards and abundant parks. Moreover, the team's auto-dependent plan will only increase traffic problems on base. Their segregation of uses and separation of workplaces and shopping areas from homes means most residents will resort to driving. The proposed loops of pedestrian paths go nowhere, thus doing little to increase non-automobile accessibility. The commander continued, "And with all that we do on Okinawa, we need to remind ourselves that we are only guests on this wonderful island. Impacts to their cultural sites, their farming, their livelihoods and their environment need to be minimized as best as we can."[62]

As guests, one would think the United States would do all it could to minimize the impacts of its land-use patterns on their host. While preserving cultural sites is laudable, the disregard for valuable land is embedded in the military's development mentality. Making more green space comes at the expense of either returning more land to the local governments and landowners or developing more facilities for operational requirements. Exporting auto-dependent development patterns only exacerbates what some at Kadena consider a traffic problem. Why did the designers ignore the priorities of the residents? They were operating within familiar modes of practice that favor what the installation commander wanted—green space, parks, and parking. Nor could they see outside their own bias for big yards and repeatable floor plans.

Not surprisingly, Okinawans also value many of the attributes of home and neighborhood as the Americans surveyed. Yards are important, but they do not need to be the size of polo fields. Single-family homes are desirable, but need not be set back behind a moat of concrete paving and grass. In light of the increasing reliance on privatization, and to see how Okinawan developers build their neighborhoods, analyzing a private housing development near the base provides a point of comparison. One local developer, for example, took a 9.6-acre site adjacent to the Pacific Ocean that had been an industrial area and converted it into a neighborhood with 125 homes (Figure 8.6, top). The priorities were single homes with small private yards, parking attached to the unit, convenience to nearby markets and offices, and individualized designs.

Sociologist Eyal Ben-Ari suggests that there are two primary types of postwar residential settlements in Japan. The first involves the infilling

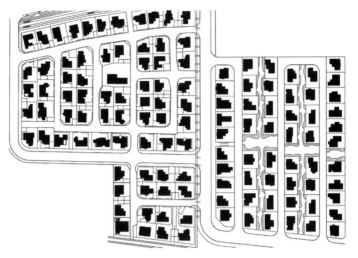

Chatan-cho Site Plan

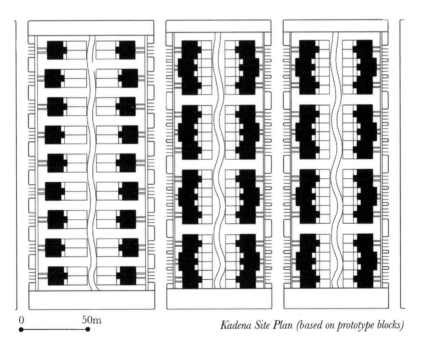

0   50m

Kadena Site Plan (based on prototype blocks)

Figure 8.6. Accommodating family housing: At Chatan-cho, just a few kilometers from the main gate of Kadena Air Base, a local developer built single-family homes at nearly twice the density of the military's proposed plan for sixplexes. These two plans, drawn at the same scale, show two approaches to family housing.

of older rural villages or hamlets situated near urban centers. The second sites new housing estates of either apartment blocks or individual homes. These individual homes are typically two-story detached dwellings and are characteristic of many newer residential areas in Japan.[63] The Chatan-cho development analyzed here is an example of this type of settlement pattern. Ironically, the attributes considered important by the developer were the same attributes the Americans wanted but did not get. The private developer at Chatan-cho built about the same number of single-family homes in an area that is 40 percent smaller than what the American designers proposed for typical blocks of sixplexes (Figure 8.6, bottom). This resulted in almost double the net density at Chatan-cho: nineteen dwelling units per acre compared to ten dwelling units per acre. And in Chatan-cho, the developer built all single-family homes on a smaller site area and at greater densities than what the experts from the United States proposed for Kadena Air Base.

At Kadena, the survey respondents wanted visual privacy first, followed by parking adjacent to the unit. With large common back yards, which the designers proposed to fill with curvilinear pedestrian pathways, the Kadena plan offered no privacy on any side to the residents. Front yards are open to the street, side yards are shared or nonexistent, and rear yards are common and made even less private by the public pathways. Chatan-cho residents, in contrast, get their own home on their own lot with small, private back yards or sideyards and parking close to the front doors (Figure 8.8). The site is a short walk to public transit as well as numerous markets and shops, which is one reason why residents of the development can get by with fewer cars than their American neighbors. To get anywhere on-base, driving is the norm.

The only similarity between the two developments is in paved area per residential unit. Chatan-cho has about 4 percent more than the Kadena proposal, which some engineers would argue increases the cost of development. But this would be more than offset by the added expense of extending utility lines an extra forty-one feet per unit as measured from the street centerline to the face of each unit. From an aesthetic point of view, the Chatan-cho homes exhibit some variety. On the base, "cookie cutter" is a charitable description of the designs.

Cloaked under the cover of a "survey," the designers were free to create yet another example of suburbia at the expense of Japanese land. The consulting team called their questionnaire a "User Preference Survey."

	Kadena Air Base	Chatan-cho
Dwelling Unit (DU)		
Number of Housing Units	132	125
Single Family	0	100%
Duplex	27%	0
Sixplex	73%	0
Size (gross square feet) (average)	1,773	1,164
Number of Bedrooms (mode)	3	3
Number of Floors (mode)	2	2
Lot		
Lot size (sf) (average)	4,453	1,961
Front setback (feet) (average)	43	4
Rear setback (ft) (average)	49	6
Side setbacks (ft) (average)	0	5
Lot Coverage (average)	20%	30%
Lot Floor Area Ratio (average)	0.40	0.59
Off-street Parking (mode)	2	1
Car to Door distance (ft) (average)	30	5
Neighborhood		
Block Size (sq ft) (mode)	195,000	14,400
Block Dimensions (ft) (mode)	300 x 650	80 x 180
Gross Site Area (acres)	16.2	9.6
Gross Density (du/gross acre)	8	13
Net Site Area (not including roads)	13.5	6.7
Net Density (du/net acre)	10	19
Paving width (ft)	25	20
Paving length (ft)	4,658	5,841
Paving area (sf)	118,182	115,862
Paving per unit (sf)	895	926
Intersections	8	20
Utility Lateral Run per unit (ft)	55	14

Figure 8.7. Comparing housing, Okinawa. From author's fieldwork, 2002.

While it did reveal preferences for single-family homes with private yards in neighborhoods close to working and shopping areas, it could not overcome the entrenched attitudes of either the design team, who misread its results, or the installation commander, who wanted more green space. While the project's rendering (Figure 8.9) shows off the "green space" of the common backyard, it does not show the excessively deep front yards (ten times deeper than the development at Chatan-cho). A view of the front yard would have been quite unflattering. It would show front yards of little value adjacent to streets that serve as parking lots. While one

Figure 8.8. At Chatan-cho, carports are on one side of each unit—a necessary amenity given the frequent rains on Okinawa. A landscaped pedestrian walk with entry courts and gardens for each unit is on the other side.

can certainly question the wisdom of building single-family homes in an area as densely populated as Okinawa, this example shows that the U.S. military could have done just that in an area substantially smaller than what they proposed for sixplexes.

The Futenma Relocation

The construction of new housing at Kadena, paid for by the government of Japan following the SACO recommendations, was only one element of the overall realignment and reduction process on Okinawa. While Americans were to benefit through $2 billion for new homes, the Japanese were to benefit through the closure of Futenma Marine Corps Air Station, located in the middle of a densely populated commercial and residential area of Ginowan city on land owned by 2,000 Okinawans.[64] The 1,188-acre outpost takes up one quarter of Ginowan, a city of over 82,000 in an area of 4,821 acres, which results in a population density for Ginowan of 5,633 people per square kilometer.[65] This is almost five times higher than nearby Kadena Air Base. As one analyst described the situation, "It is a little as if one carved runways into, say, downtown Baltimore."[66] While descriptive of the current situation, this statement obscures the fact that the base largely preceded Ginowan's growth. As Mike Millard notes,

Figure 8.9. Kadena Housing Redevelopment Plan. From U.S. Air Force.

the pattern [on Okinawa] for the past 50 years has been for the civilian population to build up around the bases, so that with the passage of time military installations are always located in dangerous places, surrounded by schools, hospitals, and residential areas, and ripe for disaster.[67]

This is not a new experience for imperial powers. David Peers notes that in the nineteenth century, the British located their cantonments at some distance from nearby towns, but local authorities failed to prevent "merchants and cultivators from infiltrating into the intervening lands."[68] But, in India, the British did not have jets flying overhead, accidentally dropping their bombs or fuel tanks. Today, "encroachment" makes for very dangerous conditions. The development that has closed in on Futenma is a pattern similar to what occurs at bases in the United States. But at Futenma, as is the case at many overseas outposts, the United States does not control all the land in the clear zones. These are the areas most prone to damage in airfield accidents. Regarding construction at U.S. bases in Okinawa, Mike Kleeman, a U.S. engineer who has worked at Kadena Air Base, said, "The biggest issue here is encroachment."[69] The potential for loss of life makes encroachment a very serious matter. In the United States, the military does not allow any development in the clear zone. But at Futenma, the United States cannot prohibit the construction of homes, schools, offices, and shopping areas inside the 3,000-foot clear zones at either end of the runway on land that it does not control.

According to former governor Masahide Ota, the presence of American outposts has distorted the urbanization process and has led to "erratic sprawl" in places like Ginowan.[70] Unlike U.S. sprawl, Okinawa's version is of dense, two- and three-story development hugging the base perimeter (Figure 8.10). In the United States, a base with encroachment this severe, where helicopters crash into school buildings, is a base that would find itself on the closure list. But this is not the case in Japan. The United States has agreed to close Futenma only after the Japanese build a replacement facility.

The SACO report called for the replacement to be an offshore air base, located off the east coast of the main island of Okinawa.[71] Under the plan, over 2,500 personnel would have transferred to the floating air base or other sites up to an hour away, where housing, shopping, and medical facilities would be located.[72] Additionally, about seventy aircraft from Futenma would have moved to the floating airfield and its 4,200-foot runway. This is less than half the length of Futenma's 9,000-foot

Figure 8.10. Futenma Marine Corps Air Station. From Government Accountability Office.

runway and, according to a GAO study of the proposal, was too short for operating the Marines' MV-22 at maximum weight.[73]

Additionally, the "sea-based facility" or SBF as the Japanese press dubbed the proposal, would have a 10,000-pound ammunition storage area under the steel runway, making it an attractive target for sea-based terrorists. Under the SACO agreement, the Japanese would have designed, built, and paid for the SBF following planning guidance issued by the United States. Recognizing the complexity of the endeavor, the United States asked the Japanese to establish a Project Management Office, which would be similar to what NATO and the United States formed to oversee Aviano 2000. Such an office would have a challenging task building a facility that U.S. Navy officials have described as "at the edge of technical feasibility."[74] In addition to the estimated $4-billion construction cost and ten-year projected construction schedule, the GAO identified serious technical limitations to the proposal:

> The sea-based facility would have to survive natural events such as typhoons, which strike within 180 nautical miles of Okinawa Island an average of four times per year. Also, structural issues pose technological challenges. The sea-based facility would have to be invulnerable to sinking or capsizing and resume normal operations within 24 to 48 hours after an aircraft crash, an accident involving ordnance aboard the facility, or an attack in wartime or by terrorists.[75]

In addition to these substantial challenges, the GAO concluded that annual operations and maintenance costs would be over seventy times more expensive at the SBF than at Futenma ($200 million versus $2.8 million).[76] Engineers studied several options for the SBF, including a pontoon-type facility with maintenance, storage, and personnel support functions below the deck. The GAO report noted that no nation has built a floating structure of this size. Another option was a pile-supported facility with 7,000 piles driven into a fragile coral reef (Figure 8.11).

Significant international opposition formed to protest the ambitious proposal. Several hundred Japanese and U.S. scientists from the Center for Biological Diversity stated, "The proposal site is known to be particularly rich in biological diversity and [is] the primary remaining habitat for the critically endangered Okinawa dugong [saltwater manatee] and numerous threatened species."[77] Similarly, 889 people from eighty-three countries attended a coral reef symposium on Okinawa in 2004 and issued a statement calling for the proposal's cancellation.[78] The SBF proposal

Figure 8.11. Two proposals for a sea-based facility designed to replace Futenma Marine Corps Air Station. Technical, environmental, and fiscal challenges put a halt to these proposals, but the United States has continued to look for ways to minimize engagement with "host" nations. From Government Accountability Office.

demonstrated how spillover can extend underwater. The proposal also affected local politics. On December 28, 1999, the Japanese Diet offered almost $95 million in economic aid to the city of Nago if they would support the plan. This was a large sum for a town with a population of 55,000.[79] Under Japanese land-use law, since the floating base would connect to Nago via a causeway, Nago could reject the plan. Eleven days earlier, 59 percent of Nago's voters opposed the plan; 23 percent were in favor. Some in favor, though, liked the idea of placing the Marines in quarantine, on a floating island.[80] This "economic aid" ushered in a wave of offers from other municipalities on Okinawa, eager to offer up sites for the U.S. military in exchange for cash.[81] The offer persuaded the Nago City Council to support the plan by a vote of 17 to 10.[82] After several years of study, in 2002, Nago citizens reelected its pro-SBF mayor, Tateo Kishimoto.[83] His opponent, urban planner Yasuhiro Miyagi, threatened to withdraw support for the proposal.[84]

Throughout the controversy, the United States maintained its position that it was up to the Japanese to find a site and build a replacement for Futenma. Given the problems with the proposal, the United States eventually agreed to a scaled back plan in October 2005 that called for the Futenma mission to relocate to Camp Schwab, an existing U.S. base located in a rural section of Okinawa.[85] But this plan required reclamation of areas of Oura Bay, which presented another set of environmental problems. Other ideas have included relocating some Marines to more remote locations in Japan or even to Australia.[86]

In addition to relocating Marines from Futenma, the United States agreed in principle to relocate up to 7,000 Marines from other installations on Okinawa to Guam. The practical problem, though, has been funding relocation costs. The United States wanted Japan to fund 75 percent of the estimated $10 billion cost, but officials in Japan were not willing to commit to such an enormous bill.[87] Regardless of the eventual fate of Okinawa's Marines, the status of the SACO recommendations is not encouraging. While the government of Japan has funded substantial reconstruction at Kadena Air Base and several other U.S. installations targeted for expansion under SACO, the United States has yet to give back any significant amount of land.

Avoiding Contact

In 1998 Sgt. Timothy Woodland raped a twenty-four-year-old Okinawan woman in the parking lot of a dance club in an area called "American Village." This hybrid district has a towering neon-outlined Ferris wheel overlooking places like Club America and the America Hotel.[88] Flashing Coca-Cola ads and McDonald's golden arches beckon the thirsty and hungry for a taste of America. Using San Diego's Sea Port village as a model, former Chatan-cho mayor Choichi Hentona led the effort to convert the land, which the U.S. military abandoned, into American Village. "The entire district is designed to create an American atmosphere," Hentona said. "People who come to this district can enjoy a touch of America. When the rape incident took place, I felt like our dream had been shattered."[89] By removing Americans from the area, the United States might minimize the chances of a repeat incident. The governments of Japan and the United States have yet to lift the burden on Okinawa. Despite a multibillion-dollar "sympathy budget" and relocation proposals put forth by SACO, little off-base has changed. While SACO funds are paying for $2 billion worth of new homes on America's Okinawan outposts, the other part of the deal, the closure of Futenma Marine Corps Air Station, has stalled. The Futenma relocation exemplifies the new American Empire's shift, for many reasons, to a policy of avoidance.

Relocating the U.S. military to deserts or to isolated islands (artificial or real) in order to be "safe" from terrorism is only one justification for policies of avoidance. These moves are also ways to remove American soldiers from places like American Village. One former Marine officer stationed on Okinawa, Robert Hamilton, makes the case against these moves. He argues,

> Currently on Okinawa, serious and committed young Americans who have volunteered to serve in their nation's armed forces are increasingly being viewed as mercenaries to be isolated and caged away from the local populace in peacetime, and only to be let loose in times of military emergency.[90]

If the U.S. military cannot trust these young soldiers to live in peace with their neighbors, how can the military trust them to wield weapons of mass destruction? Even some Okinawans recognize the value of cultural exchange. Naohiro Tsutsumi, Ministry of Foreign Affairs Okinawa Liaison Office deputy chief, argues, "Coming into contact with a different culture will help [U.S. soldiers] adjust and blend into the local community."[91] Retreating to an Australian desert or some form of sea-based facility will preclude this kind of contact.

Conclusion

Avoidance: The New Imperial Land Use Model

The first plane slammed into the North Tower at 8:46 A.M. The second plane struck the South Tower sixteen minutes later. Soon after, half a world away, military police began knocking on doors. "Get your family together, pack one bag for each person, and get on the bus," one police officer told Sgt. Michael Nutter. He was living with his wife, In Suk, and their four sons in Air Force Village, a housing area about twenty minutes by foot from Osan Air Base in South Korea. "We're moving you on the base."[1] That morning, U.S. military police worldwide gave the same order to hundreds of families living off-base. The heavily loaded buses brought the shocked and terrified families to the bases where commanders thought they could better protect their troops. September 11 marked a tipping point in the imperial approach.

Until the nineteenth century, most imperial powers implemented policies of assimilation (and in some extreme cases outright annihilation). Colonizers consumed the cultures of the colonized. They would transform languages, legal structures, and building practices, by force if needed. In the twentieth century the model changed, however, when imperial powers encountered stiff resistance; association became the norm. They reluctantly acknowledged the cultural practices of the colonized and integrated them into the imperial model when it suited the imperial power. In the twenty-first century, I argue that the new model is neither assimilation nor association; rather, the new American Empire practices avoidance.

The Roman Empire practiced policies of assimilation that set the standard for almost two thousand years. They built massive public works for their newly acquired subjects and hoped that the locals would eventually assimilate into the Roman Empire.[2] Spanish, British, and French empires followed the Roman example and used educational policies, religious institutions, monetary systems, and political structures to subjugate and absorb local cultures. In Spain's "new world," the *Laws of the Indies* established both the legal justification and the practical methods for assimilation. Catholicism came with grand plazas in an effort that recognized the importance of the built environment in the process of cultural domination. Several hundred years later, the British tried similar methods. Through the Cantonment Acts, the British Army regulated everything across the Indian subcontinent, from land use to prostitution. In North Africa, the French and Italians practiced assimilation policies as well. In nineteenth-century Algiers, the French demolished whole sections of the existing city and widened streets to facilitate the movement of their military, tactics Haussmann also employed in Paris.[3] At the same time, the Japanese followed a similar model in their conquest of Okinawa in 1879 and Korea in 1910. The Japanese Imperial Army called the process *doka seisaku,* whereby one nation attempts to make the lifestyles and ideologies of the colonized the same as the colonizer. The Japanese dictated language and educational policies. They censored religious dance dramas thought to be injurious to public morals. And they discouraged traditional forms of dress.[4]

But assimilation policies began to weaken in the face of stiff resistance, and "association" became the norm. This was the case with both the French and Italians in North Africa in the late nineteenth and early twentieth centuries.[5] No longer was the idea to remake the colonized, as Edward Said has argued, but to recognize "immutable characteristics of which required separation and subservience."[6] This effort at orientalizing the other, at collapsing their urban form traditions into essentialized principles, was the prerogative of the colonizer. The American Empire practiced its own form of association throughout the twentieth century. The United States established military bases in capital cities like Madrid, Tokyo, and Seoul, but there was no attempt to forcibly change the material cultures of the colonized. There was no imposition of an official language or curtailment of indigenous religions. The power differential was obvious nonetheless, reflected in economic directives, constitutional schemes, and land-use policies. American soldiers enforced "free markets" and capitalism, they wrote constitutions, and they defined entire countries. To do all of this, they maintained sizable standing armies in these countries for extended periods. But American soldiers engaged with their local settings. Many of them lived off-base, in locally designed and locally built neighborhoods. They dined at restaurants on- and off-base run by local entrepreneurs. They shopped at small Base Exchanges and nearby markets.

This pattern has changed. However, September 11 was not the starting point of this change. Rather, it was more like a shock that spurred action on stalled projects and instilled a sense of urgency into the representatives of the new American Empire. The starting point was the 1996 bombing of Khobar Towers in Saudi Arabia that killed nineteen U.S. airmen. This tragic event convinced the secretary of defense to "retire" a promising general officer for failing to protect his troops from a known threat. After this incident, the U.S. military relocated its 6,000 soldiers from Khobar to a vacant airfield in the open desert of Saudi Arabia. In six weeks, American engineers turned the unused base into a major military compound the size of metropolitan Chicago.[7] In congressional testimony three months after the Khobar Towers bombing, former secretary of defense William Perry previewed the new policy of avoidance:

> We now know that we face an unprecedented threat. We must fundamentally rethink our approach to force protection. First, we are relocating. The location at Khobar Towers made defense against such an attack almost impossible. Therefore we are moving our combatant forces to the Prince Sultan Air Base, whose remote location permits much more extensive security protection against terrorist attack.[8]

While the United States would not withdraw from Saudi Arabia at the time, it certainly could retreat to the desert. The image of the world's only superpower hastily relocating to the desert symbolized to some a new imperial weakness. At the same time, the military implemented sweeping policies that called for extensive "standoff" or setbacks between buildings, cars, and base boundaries. The car bomb was the most feared threat. Will relocating to the hinterlands or enforcing larger standoff requirements make the U.S. military safer? In Graham Greene's Vietnam, the threat came from hundreds of bicycle pumps converted into small plastic bombs. Will bikes be the next vector to eliminate? Is it possible to avoid all probable threats and remain an effective military force? This could be a never-ending exercise in avoidance.

Setbacks are not the only significant change resulting from a policy of avoidance. Shopping malls and grocery stores on-base have doubled and tripled in size, obviating the need for trips beyond the main gate. Franchised restaurants have replaced local establishments on-base and reduced the demand for dining off-base. New hotels have been built on-base, thus eliminating the need to send visiting soldiers to hotels off-base. Osan Air Base in South Korea, for example, recently built a 350-room, $26-million hotel for just this purpose.[9] Similar projects are underway at other U.S. outposts. In addition, in South Korea alone, the United States is spending more than $100 million on fitness centers, ballfields, and clubs designed to keep Americans occupied on-base.[10] In South Korea and Japan, the host governments have committed several billion dollars to build more housing on-base so that soldiers no longer have to live in "vulnerable" neighborhoods off-base. Moreover, the United States is relocating entire military bases from capital cities to more remote areas. One must wonder if the mayor of Tokyo will succeed in his demands that Yokota Air Base follow suit. The United States was even willing to move an entire airfield to a $4-billion floating island, provided someone else paid for its construction.

American planners are isolating bases from local areas and segregating buildings on those bases from each other in short-sighted policies aimed at avoiding the next car bomb. The result is less a military base than a prison. "The American presence overseas is increasingly armed, in uniform and behind barbed wire and high walls," argues historian Michael Ignatieff. "This sort of projection of power, hunkered down against attack, can earn the United States fear and respect, but not admiration and affection."[11] Since the American Empire now operates preemptively, advocating "shock and awe" over dialogue and empathy, the admiration of other nations is apparently of little concern.

> A mysterious change seems to come over Americans when they go to a foreign land. They isolate themselves socially. They live pretentiously. They're loud and ostentatious. Perhaps they're frightened and defensive; or maybe they're not properly trained and make mistakes out of ignorance.
> —William Lederer and Eugene Burdick, *The Ugly American*

I end where I began, in the Blackhawk above Kadena Air Base. After taking several rolls of pictures, through the static and roar of the rushing wind and whine of the turbine, I instructed the pilot to return the helicopter to the base. Once back on the ground, I began to process more than the film. If our encounters with others tell us as much about ourselves as the other, what does this tell us about American soldiers living abroad? In defense of the United States, the military has imposed on the globe the single-family home and the shopping mall. Americans seem to be saying, "I will live in a suburb regardless of how valuable or how limited your land is. I will live the way I want, build the way I want, and act the way I want. I have my rules, and they apply whether I'm in Kadena or Kansas, so don't make me change them for you."

What can we learn about America from the way it builds its outposts? Americans working for the DoD isolate themselves in sprawling suburbs. They are frightened of the next terrorist. They are defensive and want to hold on to what they have. They follow rules that mimic the cultural landscapes of suburbia. They live under an all-consuming corporate military complex that insists on conformity. Their demands for bigger houses, more baseball fields, and bigger standoff distances result in ever-greater requirements for land. But these demands are fueled less by an individual soldier's desire than by the collusion between corporate America and the military's leadership. This is a new form of the military-industrial complex, where the military has even started to privatize its outposts. Commercial interests have signed on in unprecedented ways to extend their reach under the guise of national security and in the service of capital accumulation. We can see how this complex uses built form to create the familiar in unfamiliar terrain. But the brothels and bars just outside the gates undercut a suburban ethos. Outside of their "suburbia," soldiers and their superiors have created a second space, a gendered and sexualized space where the power equation is clear.

Over 100 years ago, Joseph Chamberlain declared,

> The British Empire is based upon a community of sacrifice. Whenever that is lost sight of, then, indeed, I think we may expect to sink into oblivion like the empires of the past, which . . . after having exhibited to the world evidences of their power and strength, died away regretted by none, and leaving behind them a record of selfishness only.[12]

Sacrifice, however, is rarely popular in an age of prosperity. As Francis Fukuyama has suggested, such times "encourage preoccupation with one's own petty affairs and allow people to forget that they are parts of larger communities."[13] Whether in Japan or South Korea, the United States has exploited tragic crimes and avoidable accidents to justify its imperial reach. It has transformed local pressures to consolidate and reduce forces into a jackpot: a chance to modify the built environment using other people's land and money, an opportunity to extend its culture of consumption.

In the *Ugly American*, Ambassador Gilbert MacWhite requests modifications to American policies in the fictitious country of Sarkhan as a way of making U.S. action more humane:

- I request that every American (and his dependents) sent to Sarkhan be required to be able to both read and speak Sarkhanese.
- I request that no American employee be allowed to bring his dependents to Sarkhan unless he is willing to serve here for at least two years. If he does bring his family, it should be the understanding they will not be given luxurious quarters, but will live in housing which is normal to the area; their housing should certainly not be more luxurious than they are able to afford in America. They should also subsist on food available in local stores—which are wholesome and ample.
- I request that the American commissary and PX be withdrawn from Sarkhan, and that no American supplies be sold except for toilet articles, baby food, canned milk, coffee, and tobacco.
- I request that Americans not be allowed to bring their private automobiles to this country. All of our official transportation should be done in official automobiles. Private transportation should be taxi, pedicab, or bicycle.[14]

In the story, Ambassador MacWhite sent his requests to the U.S. secretary of state and waited three weeks for a reply:

Reply negative to all suggestions in your handwritten note. Such actions even though they have merit are highly impractical. We would not be able to get Americans to serve overseas under these conditions. Please return continental United States first available transportation. Anticipate substantial replacement of your present staff.[15]

Like the fictional secretary of state, the U.S. military wants its outposts to be as attractive as possible to the men and women tasked to defend the homeland from a distance. These landscapes reflect underlying cultural, political, and economic values. The 2002 U.S. *National Security Strategy* claimed, "The presence of American forces overseas is one of the most profound symbols of the U.S. commitments to allies and friends."[16] I would add that America's outposts are as much symbols of American power as the tanks and warplanes. Designers help produce these places by following familiar modes of practice. They write and apply rigid rules based on the logic of capital and the emotion of fear.

These rules standardize design processes and built environments across the globe. And they demand more land regardless of the sociopolitical cost. While Americans may discount the cost of land, especially given its abundance in the homeland, land use is a significant concern of residents in places like Japan, South Korea, and Italy, who are stuck with absorbing America's spillover. When 1,200 South Koreans were asked what the United States could do first to improve the situation in South Korea, 45 percent wanted the United States to use less land. Next, at 19 percent, was better education and improved regulations for the soldiers.[17] But for a nation like the United States that measures land in 43,560-square-foot increments, appreciating the perspectives of other nations that have measured land in 35.5-square-foot increments is a difficult endeavor.

One could use numerous adjectives for today's empire: *arrogant, supersized, extravagant,* and *isolated,* to name a few. There is another adjective that Pentagon strategists disdain: *entangled.* This is yet another justification for avoidance. American policymakers do not want their war-fighting options limited. The United States wants to avoid global alliances, dismiss concerns of long-standing allies, and isolate its soldiers from the very people they are presumably defending. Since the 1990s, both Bush administrations concluded that they had little freedom to act unilaterally, even though George W. Bush has done just that.[18] Military analyst Adam Siegel notes that "host" nations have placed a myriad of constraints on U.S. power, including denying war planes the right to fly over their airspace, restricting use of U.S. bases on their soil to specific purposes, or establishing limits on the types of personnel and weapons at American outposts.[19] Admittedly, there are some restrictions, like Turkey's refusal to support offensive operations against Iraq, but the United States has demonstrated the capacity to work around these "constraints."

Strategists in the DoD have been busy inventing ways out of the need for alliances so that they can continue acting unilaterally and using preemptive military force. The second Bush administration's realignment policy for Eastern Europe was one element. It rewarded more-compliant nations with military bases and their economic benefits. Relocating the remaining soldiers in South Korea away from the heavily armed DMZ was another element designed in part to free the hand of military planners, who would not have as much concern about instant retaliatory strikes on soldiers within artillery distance of the North Korean army. Safely out of the way, U.S. soldiers could be less limited in their options for dealing with North Korea. Seoul, however, remains in the deadly middle, which may be one reason why South Korea has planned to relocate its national government to a new capital city.

In one important respect, the United States has had an incoherent approach to this realignment. In Asia, military planners have tried to increase the number of family members that can accompany U.S. soldiers. Given the advantages in terms of crime reduction and retention of highly trained personnel, this was a valid goal. But to achieve this goal, the United States wanted more land to build its sprawling compounds. The United States apparently could not figure out how to accommodate more families without getting more land. But annexing this land has been controversial and has led to more calls for U.S. withdrawal from disaffected residents of the "host" nations. On the other hand, in Eastern Europe, the outposts have been "remote" assignments with few amenities and no families. The results seem predictable: more crime and dysfunction will inevitably lead to another round of costly reconstruction.

These one-sided realignments and regular rebuilding efforts may be coming to an end. New technologies may offer U.S. military planners even greater freedom to plan their devastating wars. In 2004 U.S. president George W. Bush said that the United States will "take advantage of twenty-first-century military technologies to rapidly deploy increased combat power."[20] Some of these "technologies" will minimize the need for overseas bases. For instance, the United States is developing a robotic hypersonic aircraft that could attack targets anywhere in the world within two hours of taking off from a remote base in the United States. With a top speed of up to eight times the speed of sound and a 20,000-mile range, the plane would free the military from having to rely on overseas air bases, according to the Defense Advanced Research Projects Agency.[21] While the plane may be twenty years away, the Pentagon already employs pilotless drones like the Global Hawk and Predator. Engineers from defense contractor Lockheed have even estimated that operating a squadron of F-16s costs five times more than a similar force of drones.[22] This may be one way to reduce the financial burdens of empire. All of this adds up to what could be an unfortunate irony: the U.S. abandonment of its outposts may make the world less safe. By being freed from the entanglements of Status of Forces agreements and base use restrictions, as limited as they are, an aggressive administration may find unilateral wars even easier to execute. For now, the United States is bloating its remaining overseas bases, but in the distant future, it appears the United States may favor complete disengagement so that it may exert its power by remote control.

During a 2002 visit to Okinawa, Gen. Michael J. Williams, former deputy Marine Corps commandant, stated, "We are committed to make our presence as inoffensive as it can possibly be."[23] But by demanding even more land for its outposts, this commitment is largely superficial. In many ways, the United States is responding to local concerns by retreating into increasingly isolated compounds. The never-ending spillover wears down America's allies and has been successfully exploited to justify this new retreat. But withdrawing into heavily fortified bubbles will further exacerbate the tensions between the world's only superpower and its increasingly wary allies.

While land-use policies are not the most pressing concern for an administration bent on spreading democracy, they do reflect larger patterns of isolation and disregard. Whether rebuilding Iraq or redesigning Aviano, the United States could well afford to listen to the cultures outside the walls of its outposts. Edward Said has reminded empires that "domination breeds resistance, and that the violence inherent in the imperial contest—for all its occasional profit or pleasure—is an impoverishment for both sides."[24] The United States has made its new land grab when its troops are increasingly unwelcome in the very nations hosting them, which requires new investments and new strategies regarding military bases. The United States has mothballed many of its outposts in "unsupportive" nations like Saudi Arabia and Turkey and closed bases in Western Europe where the environmental and political constraints are too demanding for a DoD in search of its own version of freedom—freedom to plan and execute its war plans without interference from the "host" nations. Hence, the United States has shifted to building new bases in Eastern Europe while expanding and relocating bases in parts of Asia.

While today's empire desires implicit control over global affairs, it need not have explicit control over entire countries. Rather, to project its power, it wants secluded and self-contained outposts strategically located across the planet. Locked into their version of suburbia, with its low-slung homes, oversized shopping centers, and franchised restaurants set amid a heavily manicured landscape, American soldiers need not be bothered with learning the language, cultures, or customs of their hosts. In the end, the land-use patterns that support this type of avoidance significantly increase the social and political cost of empire's reach.

On Methods

While taking field measurements of block and street patterns in a South Korean neighborhood near Osan Air Base, a middle-aged man in impeccably tailored black slacks and a crisp white shirt stopped me in the middle of a quiet street. He abruptly asked if I was an intelligence officer. I assured him I was just an architect and researcher interested in the development of the nearby air base. He did not seem to believe me. Another young man was more specific and wanted to know if I was in the CIA, despite my faded jeans and T-shirt.

Wherever I went and whenever I would ask South Koreans questions about the U.S. military bases, the responses were always positive. The bases were good for the economy; they protected South Korea from North Korea; they brought in a unique cultural mix. Never did I hear any negative comments about Americans or their bases. This was despite a survey of 1,200 South Koreans that found 41.5 percent wanted a reduction of U.S. troops compared to only 39.3 percent who wanted the U.S. forces to remain as is.[1] Where were the opponents of these bases? Looking back, I attribute this to the fact that, even though I was not in a uniform, I was seen as a representative of the U.S. military. Why else would a white American male be wandering around neighborhoods near the bases asking questions and making maps? Given a cultural desire not to offend, I believe those that I talked with would likely say positive things regardless of their true feelings.

Back in the United States, some of my colleagues would joke about my "hidden CIA connections." I am in good company, however. "I write as a double agent," Graham Greene has said. "Novelists and spies share some of the same gifts and instincts...in a sense a writer is a double agent, he may have a wicked character, but he has a feeling of sympathy for the wicked character."[2] My wicked character is the American outpost. But I am sympathetic to it nonetheless. Greene, however, went too far. After meeting Fidel Castro or Nikita Khrushchev, he would file secret reports with British Intelligence. While the U.S. military will certainly weigh in on the topics discussed in this report, there is nothing secret in this study. As with most institutions, the U.S. military exists not as an abstract force acting without human direction. Rather, it consists of individuals making decisions, solving and creating problems, struggling with heavy workloads and ethical dilemmas. The individuals with whom I have worked in the course of this project have been supportive as well as skeptical. They knew I would challenge their assumption that the United States is a benevolent empire but spent time debating with me anyway.

Research Method

My initial goal of completing an ethnography, with a local informant versed in the sociospatial life of a base and willing to let me enter into his or her cultural milieu, was hopelessly naïve. I at first had a few basic questions: How do local residents live with imperial spillover? In what ways do the bases affect their daily lives? At their most basic level, we can consider ethnographies as a means to develop a deeper understanding of cultural practices, social norms, and political structures. Ethnographies rely less on observation and more on a researcher's analysis of the descriptions made by members of the culture studied. Ethnographies began as anthropologists embarked on a worldwide study and cataloging of "foreign" cultures. To do this, however, has typically required an extended period in the field during which researchers immerse themselves in the culture under study and gain access to reliable informants. Traditionally, this has involved a rather detailed period of participant-observation.[3]

Early ethnographic projects, like Margaret Mead's 1920s study of Samoan psychosexual development and William F. Whyte's study of a "street corner society," followed this model and relied heavily on the currency of the moment and the veracity of the informants.[4] These scholars queried their informants and studied their settings with little concern about larger structural or historic forces. Other scholars have highlighted the limitations of these single-site ethnographies, which include a potentially problematic reliance on a few informants, an inability to place the findings within a larger sociopolitical context, and a difficulty in moving beyond the personal to what Marcus terms "the distanced social." This is ethnography's "double bind."[5] Namely, by focusing on individual cases, early ethnographers failed to contextualize projects in larger sociocultural, political, and economic concerns. Numerous scholars have questioned the wisdom of relying too heavily on informants. For example, Derek Freeman forcefully claims that Mead's informants essentially conducted an elaborate hoax.[6]

Since one key goal of ethnographies is to study a culture from an insider's or *emic* point of view, the ethnographer coming from the outside will necessarily rely on the testimony of informants. Moreover, the problematic relationship between observed and observer that is potentially present on single-site studies can raise questions about reliability (would the findings be at least similar if another informant was selected?) and validity (is social hierarchy really what is being measured or is it another as yet unknown phenomena?). As Lewis Dexter notes, "The informant's statement represents merely the perception of the informant, filtered and modified by cognitive and emotional reactions and reported through personal verbal usages."[7] This is a serious limitation to a pure ethnographic approach. Multisited ethnographies begin to overcome these limitations and can help scholars locate their projects within a larger sociocultural and political context. Such comparative research can uncover previously hidden agencies operating within the ethnographic site.

Nevertheless, traditional ethnographies, whether single or multisited, may still suffer the fate that befell Herbert Gans's study of Levittown.[8] Gans left no room for any significant action by the state or even the forces of late capitalism (in Gans's view the developer, Levitt, was responding simply to demand). The work of many more recent scholars convincingly demonstrates that not only is there room for such institutional action, but those institutions create their own space for intervention for their own reasons.[9] Sociologist Mark Gottdiener challenges scholars to acknowledge "that spatial forms are contingent products of the dialectical articulation between action and structure."[10] The actions are what people at America's outposts do (i.e., policies they write, plans they produce) and the structure is an inherited sociospatial framework.

Due to the limitations and challenges of the traditional ethnographic approach, especially when applied to my case, different questions and more tailored methods were in order. One such method pioneered by Dorothy Smith is the institutional ethnography.[11] As Marie Campbell and Frances Gregor note, "Institutional ethnographers are attempting to explicate everyday experiences and people's accounts of them, not just collect and describe them."[12] My new questions—how did these outposts emerge and what does this tell us about Americans working at them—required this translocal explication. Institutional ethnographies use standard ethnographic methods of participant-observation, interviews, and textual analysis to research institutional settings, their policies, their practices, and their impacts on everyday actions. Institutional ethnographies can uncover the "ruling apparatus" by which professionals reproduce power relations through their everyday practices and decision-making structures. What I found most appealing about institutional ethnography as a method is that its aim is not to produce an account from the insiders' perspectives. Rather, it is ultimately an account about people and the policies that structure their actions. In this way, my work combines the emic perspective with the *etic* or external perspective.[13]

In addition to this institutional focus, whereby I seek to uncover the processes and practices employed by the U.S. military in the development of overseas bases, I also incorporate an autoethnographic approach. Autoethnography, like descriptive ethnography, studies a culture, its social structures, and patterns of behavior by placing the researcher within the cultural context under study. Specific research techniques can include participant-observation, formal and informal interviews, surveys, and questionnaires. But autoethnography abandons the standard conception of participant-observation that accepts a researcher's short-term participation with a group under study. Rather, autoethnography requires long-standing membership. The emphasis is not on one's own life story but on an ethnography of one's own culture.[14]

The concept of autoethnography, defined by anthropologists as studies of their "own people," emerged out of anthropology in the mid-1970s as a way of addressing the limitations of reliability, voice, and access presented by standard participant-observation. The key feature, according to anthropologist David Hayano, is that the autoethnographer "possesses the qualities of often permanent self-identification with a group and full internal membership, as recognized both by themselves and the people of whom they are a part."[15] Author and anthropologist Deborah Reed-Danahay adds, "One of the main characteristics of an autoethnographic perspective is that the autoethnographer is a boundary-crosser, and the role can be characterized as that of a dual identity."[16]

There can be no doubt that I have crossed multiple boundaries in this study: geographical, political, and professional. Of particular relevance to this study is the fact that I worked in the U.S. Air Force for nine years on active duty and I have been in the Air Force Reserves for nearly ten years. Due to my familiarity with the culture and language of the military, this method can overcome one of the significant critiques of standard ethnographies, which argues researchers have difficulty in communicating in and understanding the vernacular language.[17] This is obviously the case with the military. Its language is rife with acronyms, jargon, and double-speak. But accessing this discourse and making it accessible were key components of my research project. With my clear insider status as an architect and planner with the U.S. military and with my outsider status as an academic, I created a research method that combined autoethnography with institutional ethnography. Additionally, the focused use of multiple sites helped uncover common practices and polices used in the production of military installations. In the end, I have combined multiple methods into what is essentially an institutional autoethnography.

Research Strategy

As Lawrence Vale suggests, "we can . . . learn much about a political regime by observing closely what it builds."[18] Using several case studies, I have attempted to anchor geopolitics to the social production and physical consumption of space. Planners are using familiar modes of practice to create familiar models of spatial development. Moreover, the Department of Defense exploits geopolitical events, from rapes in Okinawa to September 11, to justify the building and expansion of America Towns across the globe. My research did change direction because of the September 11 attacks and the ensuing wars. Before September 11, there was considerable talk of shutting down bases not only in Europe but in Asia as well. Closing overseas outposts following battle was a normal tactic for America. For example, since 1990, the United States has reduced or closed operations at nearly 1,000 overseas locations, a nearly 60 percent reduction from the Cold War peak.[19] I had been analyzing some bases that would likely have shut down and, hence, I considered my work to be a historical study.

After the attacks, however, geopolitics intervened and the funding spigot opened fast and wide and shows no sign of damping down. At every base I studied, expansion, not reduction, was the new mantra. I must admit, however, that the specific outposts I studied did not emerge from a systematic master research plan beyond what I have just described. I became acquainted with the case-study sites while on active duty. My first overseas assignment was a short visit to Aviano Air Base to make repair recommendations for a series of failed roofs. While there, I saw the regrettable plans for the Zappala area. Shortly after my time at Aviano, the Air Force sent me to bases in Japan and then to bases in Korea to prepare various development plans.

Since 1989 I have been to nearly every major overseas Air Force base and have seen the same development patterns employed. I have visited Army, Navy, and Marine installations as well and can safely claim that America's military installations in Asia, Europe, and across the United States look remarkably alike, despite different "host-nation" cultures, climates, and geographies. Over time, I became more concerned about the nature of development on these bases. When I left active duty, many of these locations continued to be of interest to me, and I went back to them numerous times. Over the course of this six-year study, I have been to the case-study bases in Asia and Europe multiple times. After a visit, I would return home, consider what I had found, then go back to each base with even more questions. Because of this long-term commitment, at times it seemed I knew more about the bases than the newly assigned officers or civilians who I was interviewing. In a geopolitical coincidence, the very bases I ended up studying are the ones that the United States slated to become the hubs of a realigned empire. While many bases in Europe and Asia will be closing, the five bases analyzed in this study will remain open. All five case-study sites are also "enduring" locations that will grow rather than shrink because of a global realignment of U.S. forces announced in August 2004. Perhaps this study will make some rethink their imperial ambitions.

Throughout this study, I have relied on stories told to me by all types of employees of the Department of Defense, from active-duty officers to "host-nation" civilians. They have been generous with their time and with their ideas. Given the sensitivity of the subject, I have used pseudonyms for everyone I interviewed. However, I have tried to rely as much as possible on published comments. Where my own interviews overlapped with published material, I have used the latter for this study. In using these published accounts, I have not changed any names. Other data sources I have used are publicly available and unclassified.

I used three levels of data in this study: personal accounts, published documents, and environmental images. The research was neither exclusively qualitative nor quantitative. My own survey of architects and planners working for the U.S. military gave me insight into the consensus around current problems in the planning of military bases.[20] The survey also revealed a disconnect between opinions and actual projects. Additionally, in over 100 interviews, I heard revealing, informative, and troubling personal accounts. I heard these stories at America's outposts, at international conferences, at restaurants, and in shopping centers. My extensive search of articles in newspaper archives and government publications recovered many other perspectives. Of course, all these sources have their own slant. Perhaps the most biased were the aggressively named base newspapers like Osan's *MiG Alley Flyer,* Kadena's *Shogun,* Kunsan's *Wolf Pack Warrior,* and Aviano's *Vigileer.* These regularly published papers presented the "party line." With a much more balanced perspective, I found the independent newspaper *Stars and Stripes* to be quite helpful. In the last few years they have published critical accounts of the military's actions overseas. Other sources outside the United States included the *Japan Times, Okinawa Times, Korea Herald,* and *Korea Times.* I clearly benefited from the imperial legacy of English as a global language. These papers are all available in English. What I uncovered was empire's long and well-documented paper trail of authority.

Stories collected from my own interviews and from published accounts helped me develop an understanding of the way these bases are created, in the terms of their creators, and to learn how they are perceived by those living on and around them, also in their own terms. These personal views also helped me map out the contested nature and entangled constructions of imperial outposts. This approach gave me multiple perspectives. The compartmentalized nature of the military necessitated this broad view. For instance, one person may know all about noise pollution but little about the building process.

However, researchers bring power into the settings they are studying. Given my rank as an officer in the Air Force Reserves, this could be a potential problem. I tried to deal with this in two ways. First, while obvious, I stressed that I was not in any way acting in a supervisory capacity over those I interviewed. They were free to share with me as much or as little as they felt appropriate. Second, I confirmed my status as an outsider by letting people know I was approaching this from my perspective as a university researcher, not as an Air Force officer. Surprisingly, the mere mention of this put people at ease. Many would then sit back in their chair and proceed to talk at length with little prompting. It was as if I gave them academic freedom, free from reprisal, to discuss their ideas and concerns. These unstructured interviews followed the model established by James Spradley which calls for an opening "grand tour" question.[21] I would first ask people to describe their job or role on the base and perhaps have them show me around their home, office, or work site. From here, many questions would emerge out of the conversations. Questions led to even more questions until, all too frequently, our time ran out.

However, these conversations did not fully reveal the connections between people and their sociospatial settings. For this, I employed both archival and graphic research. I reviewed master plans and architectural designs, scrutinized base maps, and surveyed the built environment on and around America's outposts. Counting cars, measuring streets, and drafting floor plans were tedious but essential work. I also produced and studied aerial photographs and made figure-ground drawings. The figure-ground or black plan is an abstraction of urban form used for spatial analysis. This type of plan has a rich tradition in urban analysis and can trace its origins back to the maps of Rome developed in 1748 by Giambattista Nolli. Today's scholars have also used figure-ground plans to study more abstract morphology, or settlement patterns, of various cultures.[22] However, seen alone, they can be limiting. To enhance the relevancy of figure-ground plans, I have added to the graphic analysis a discussion of the third dimension. Building heights (primarily measured in number of floors), lot coverage (the amount of lot covered by building), and floor-area-ratio (the amount of total floor space divided by the lot area) enhance comparative analysis. Moreover, my use of photographs supports Dolores Hayden's claim that low-level aerial photography is "useful for capturing the scale of recent development in relation to older patterns."[23] These photos and the abstracted figure-ground drawings clarified the contrasts between each outpost and its neighbor. These methods helped me connect geographically distant personal and political actions with specific built environments. Taken together, figure-ground plans, quantitative analysis, archival research, and ethnographic narratives help complete our understanding of the sociospatial world.

This project exposes my position at the border. I wear the military uniform at times, but I am also an academic. Given these positions, I cannot eliminate my presence from the research. My "location" in the world of military planning provides a basis for entry and gives me an ability to see the institutional structures at work, but it also makes any objective research impossible. What is more relevant is the realization that the personal is political, as feminist scholars consistently point out. This includes my own work. My positions became the basis for structuring this research. Dorothy Smith suggests that researchers focus on puzzles encountered in everyday life.[24] I discovered the puzzle when I took the photos from the Blackhawk helicopter. The day before the photo shoot, the base planner was complaining about the lack of available land for construction. But I could not reconcile his opinion with the view from above. This puzzle led to my research. As an academic, I was able to develop a research agenda based on my own experiences. As an architect, I knew where to go for the answers. As an officer, I could go there.

One evening, while on a research visit to South Korea, I was with a group looking for an authentic Korean restaurant. We had already tried a Thai place—twice—and we found a passable Chinese restaurant. But our last experience with Korean food was not that great—the bulgogi had more fat than meat and I was left picking through the kimchi to find some chopped radish that was edible. Fortunately, I like steamed rice. Some soldiers at the nearby Osan Air Base told us about a thatched-roof place with great food but warned us that it was on "the other side of the tracks." They did not go into detail with us about this so we set out to find it. After we crossed "the tracks" about a half-mile down the main street from the base, the din from the bars died down and the street just emptied out. We then took a right turn and walked up a small, dimly lit road and spotted a rather authentic-looking thatched roof hut with a steeply pitched hip roof, deep overhangs, and traditional silk banners on the porch columns. And the thatch was real.

We ducked to make it under the intricately carved porch beams and walked through a lovely beaded entryway. The slight jingle of the beads as we passed by announced our presence and an elegantly dressed host materialized from behind a wood paneled wall. He quietly directed us to a large booth with a deep grill in the middle. After the obligatory delivery of OBs (Korean beer), for which I am always thankful, he brought several types of meat to grill over the nicely matured charcoal and began quite a show. With his long stainless steel tongs, he effortlessly reached over our shoulders and grilled up mouthwatering bulgogi with perfectly marinated beef. The grilled garlic, onions, and peppers added a robust flavor. We even needed more kimchi. I was, however, having some difficulty wrapping my lettuce leaves around the bulgogi, but with what appeared to be effortless precision, the host delicately finished constructing my bulgogi wrap with his tongs. He walked away with an ever so slight smile. Throughout the meal, the four officers at the table shared their thoughts about living and working overseas.

Afterwards, we began our walk back to the base. I asked Maj. Elaine Johnston, the chief of Osan's Engineering Flight at the time, who had been stationed at the base for almost two years, about the "other side of the track" comment. She replied, "The Fire Department hasn't approved for use any restaurants or bars over here because they can't accept thatched roofs—especially ones without a sprinkler system. So these places are supposed to be off-limits because we can't guarantee your safety." Well, if thatch roofs would fail the inspection, I wonder what the fire chief would say if he saw the grills at every table. I am surprised we made it through the night without the U.S. stamp of approval on the place.

After we crossed the tracks, everything immediately changed. The light levels, noise, and even the pedestrian count increased dramatically. The bars were coming to life. And it was almost 11 P.M. In the space of a mere twenty feet, we stepped out of yesterday's Korea into America's Korea. After walking past the bars packed with soldiers out for a good time, after passing the icons of a globalizing world—McDonald's and Burger King, 7–11 and Subway—we made it to the main gate of Osan Air Base. After a quick flash of our identification cards, the heavily armed security police waved us into Korea's America.

On the one hand, critics may charge me with complicity in the imperial project. With my identification card and easy access to bases across the globe, this view may be understandable. On the other hand, supporters of empire can accuse me of criticizing that same project. I am not endorsing the status quo. There is some truth on both sides. Yes, I believe in the value of military readiness, because, unfortunately, the world is not a utopia. Moreover, the study and modification of the bases U.S. soldiers occupy is as appropriate a function for an academic/architect as the study and modification of suburbia and its ills. Because we have reservations with institutions does not justify abandoning them. While faculty at the University of California, for example, may be opposed to the fact that their institution has run the primary nuclear weapons labs at Los Alamos and Livermore since their inception, they do not abandon their positions with the university. They remain engaged but critical. That is my hope—that I can participate in but challenge the military and its policies. I respect those from all sides who may argue that this is a naïve hope. But until the academy disowns me or the military fires me, I will continue to occupy my outpost at the border of academia and empire.

Notes

Introduction

1. Andrew Bacevich argues that "openness" has replaced containment as the justification for American foreign policy. The goals of this strategy include the expansion of free markets, the liberalization of trade, and the advancement of U.S. interests worldwide. See Bacevich, *American Empire*. For discussion of the economic and political motivations behind America's wars in Iraq and Afghanistan, see Tremblay, *The New American Empire*. For a fascinating look at the lives of the soldiers who implement this grand strategy on the ground, see Kaplan, *Imperial Grunts*. Also see Bacevich, ed., *The Imperial Tense*.

2. See Johnson, *The Sorrows of Empire*. For bases in central and eastern Asia, see Mann, *Incoherent Empire*.

3. On the political left, see Chomsky, *Hegemony or Survival*; Khalidi, *Resurrecting Empire*; and Roy, *An Ordinary Person's Guide to Empire*. On the political right, see Barnett, *The Pentagon's New Map*; D'Souza, *What's So Great about America?*; and Ferguson, *Colossus*.

4. One notable exception is Neil Smith. His analysis of the influence of Isaiah Bowman, a man Smith refers to as President Franklin Roosevelt's geographer, shows how empires underpin their ambitions with a "hidden geography." For the twentieth-century American empire, Bowman's example reveals that America could build its empire out of maps rather than actual places. Cartographic domination of space rather than actual control of large swaths of foreign land became the American model. Once the United States could map and measure independent nations, officials could then watch over these nations, which may require economic, political, or military control. See Smith, *American Empire*.

5. See Kim Ji-ho, "U.S. Military Causes Problems to Residents."

6. On Chinatowns see Yip, "California Chinatowns." Also see Mitchell, "Global Diasporas and Traditional Towns"; Lu, "The Changing Landscape of Hybridity." On Japantowns, see Laguerre, *The Global Ethnopolis*. For a report on Los Angeles' Koreatown, see Navarro, "It's Koreatown, Jake."

7. Cited in Low, *Behind the Gates,* 232.

8. An outpost, according to the *American Heritage Dictionary,* is a "detachment of troops stationed at a distance from the main unit of forces." *The American Heritage Dictionary,* 2nd college edition.

9. For a discussion of soft power, see Nye, *Soft Power.*

10. Data from www.globalsecurity.org.

11. For a discussion of future outposts in Iraq and Central Asia, see Kleveman, *The New Great Game.*

12. Vlahos, "Analysts Ponder U.S. Basing in Iraq."

1. Empires across Time

1. AlSayyad, *Cities and Caliphs.*

2. Nuttall, "Royal Ordinances," 254.

3. Reed, "From Suprabarangay to Colonial Capital."

4. Chopra, "Pondicherry."

5. Jonathan Barnett claims Haussmann widened existing streets, realigned main avenues, and sliced the elegant, tree-lined boulevards through the dense urban fabric of Paris to improve everyday traffic flow through the city. Would, he seems to ask, the military really need such elegant streets? See Barnett, *Introduction to Urban Design.* Another view, taken by historian Mark Girouard, sees the project in primarily economic terms. "The expenditure" he writes, "was an investment, recoverable from raising tax revenues and increased property values." He leaves out of his analysis any discussion regarding the military utility of Haussmann's efforts. See Girouard, *Cities and People.* That some scholars could ignore the military usefulness of the project is surprising. The belief that the new streets improved traffic flow, increased tax assessments, and invigorated a shopping culture but did not in any way enhance the military's mobility in a city rife with tension seems implausible.

6. See Carmona, *Haussmann.* Carmona argues that creating accessible routes for the army was a concern of both Haussmann and his contemporaries who knew that "two overturned carriages, a cable, a few chairs, and mattresses were enough for a barricade that could hold at bay the best troops in the regular army" (143). Architectural historian Spiro Kostof reminds doubters that Haussmann's *percées* or cuts obviously frustrated the participants in the *Commune* uprising of 1871 since the revolution's strongholds were in areas where Haussmann did not intervene. See Kostof, *The City Assembled.*

7. For a detailed description of the event leading up to the mutiny and the resulting retribution see Ferguson, *Empire.*

8. Peers, "Imperial Vice."

9. Ferguson, *Empire.*

10. Cited in Lamprakos, "Le Corbusier and Algiers," 188.

11. Fuller, "Building Power."

12. Rabinow, *French Modern.*

13. Wycherley, *How the Greeks Built Cities.*

14. Mumford, *The City in History;* Palladio cited on p. 369.

15. Nuttall, "Royal Ordinances," 251. For a description of the planning of Manila under Spanish rule, see Reed, "From Suprabarangay to Colonial Capital."

16. In Algiers, for instance, architectural historian Michele Lamprakos argues that the "configuration of the city came to summarize the colonial relationship, with the poor, densely populated alleyways of the old city, or Casbah, standing in dramatic contrast to the wide modern boulevards of the European district." Lamprakos, "Le Corbusier and Algiers," 183.

17. Rabinow, "Colonialism, Modernity."

18. For the case of Pondicherry, see Chopra, "Pondicherry." For the Italians in Ethiopia, see Fuller, "Building Power." And for the case of the Victoria Memorial in Calcutta, see Ferguson, *Empire*.

19. Fuller, "Building Power," 477.

20. Peers, "Imperial Vice."

21. Rabinow, *French Modern*.

22. Chopra, "Pondicherry."

23. King, "Values, Science, and Settlement."

24. The memo is reprinted in Kaminsky, "Morality Legislation and British Troops," 79.

25. Her Majesty's Stationary Office, *Statistical Abstract Relating to British India from 1894–95 to 1903–04: Sickness, Mortality, and Invaliding in European Army* (1905).

26. Dyer, "The Black Hand of Authority in India," 30.

27. Ibid.

28. For accounts of the events surrounding the Cantonment Acts, see Levine, "Rereading the 1890s." Also see Kaminsky, "Morality Legislation and British Troops." Kaminsky believes the Cantonment Acts reduced the rates of infection. Government records show a drop—from 1896 to 1902 infection rates dropped by 48 percent, from 522 to 281 per 1,000 troops. However, other factors were also at work that Kaminsky ignores. For one, between those same years British troop strength in India dropped by over 18 percent, from 75,349 to 61,528—see Her Majesty's Stationary Office, *Statistical Abstract Relating to British India from 1894–95 to 1903–04: Age of Men of All Arms Serving in India* (1905).

29. See Said, *Culture and Imperialism*. Also see Mann, *Incoherent Empire*.

30. Her Majesty's Stationary Office, *Statistical Abstract Relating to British India from 1894–95 to 1903–04: Established Strength of European and Native Armies in British India* (1896).

31. Ferguson, *Empire*.

32. Killingray, "Guardians of Empire."

33. British historian Niall Ferguson points out that "out of an army of 70,000 British soldiers, 4,830 would die each year and 5,880 hospital beds would be occupied by those incapacitated by illness. Since it cost £100 to recruit a soldier and maintain him in India, Britain was thereby losing more than £1 million a year. Given that a similar force might have cost around £200,000 stationed in Europe, the extra £800,000 had to be regarded as a kind of tropical service premium." Ferguson, *Empire*, 173. In his 392-page history of imperial Britain, Ferguson did not address the causes of this premium. It is as if the heat and humidity of the tropics killed Britain's finest. The omission by Ferguson of the debates swirling around the Cantonment Acts and the rates of venereal disease among British soldiers is a striking reminder that the historians doing the writing can construct the very histories about which they are writing. Clearly, the official support of prostitution and its spatial needs in the cantonments would not add to Ferguson's thesis that the British Empire

was "a good thing." For the soldiers who contracted deadly diseases or for women working as prostitutes in the cantonments and cholera camps of the British Army, it was most certainly not a good thing.

2. Pax Americana

1. For the concept of "invited empire," see Lundestad, *The American Empire and Other Studies*. For "informal empire," refer to Louis and Hull, *The "Special Relationship."* Also see Johnson, *Blowback*.

2. Areas based on author's calculations.

3. If one accepts Jane M. Jacobs definition that colonialism is the exercise of power over a separate group of people and their territories, then these outposts qualify, at least in part, as a continuation of the colonial enterprise. See Jacobs, *Edge of Empire*.

4. C. T. Sandars calls America's approach the "leasehold empire," distinguishable from previous empires in that U.S. bases are located in sovereign states and operate according to Status of Forces agreements. See Sandars, *America's Overseas Garrisons*. Despite these agreements, negotiated under the influence of unequal power relationships, the temporary ceding of sovereignty over even a small piece of land (as is the case when land is occupied by the U.S. military) raises questions of access, control, and dominance.

5. See Barber, *Jihad vs. McWorld*; Giddens, *Runaway World*.

6. See Friedman, "Hybridization of Roots and the Abhorrence of the Bush." Also see Beck, *What Is Globalization?*

7. See Bauman, *Globalization*. Also see Welsh, "Transculturality."

8. The Air Force has since changed the title of its strategic vision from "Global Power–Global Reach" to "Global Engagement." With the multiplicity of meanings of "engage," from its military angle as in "engaged in battle" to its reference to occupy as in "the writing of this book engages most of my time," the change may be appropriate.

9. The White House, *National Security Strategy*, 6; U.S. Department of Defense, *Quadrennial Defense Review Report*.

10. Sanger and Filkins, "U.S. Is Pessimistic Turks Will Accept Aid Deal on Iraq."

11. Mann, *Incoherent Empire*.

12. O'Sullivan, "Annexation," 5.

13. Roosevelt, *Winning of the West*, 119.

14. White House, *National Security Strategy*, 2.

15. For a history of Fort Leavenworth, see Hunt, Lorence, and Bundel, *History of Fort Leavenworth*. For the Presidio of San Francisco, see Thompson and Woodbridge, *Presidio of San Francisco*. Other historical works that reference U.S. Army posts include Brandes, *Frontier Military Posts of Arizona*, and Hunt, *Army of the Pacific*. Unfortunately, these studies do not provide significant details on the settlement patterns of army posts. This is a topic worthy of further research.

16. Mahan, *Influence of Sea Power*.

17. The suspect charge that the USS *Maine* was sunk by a Spanish mine in 1898 mirrors the controversial 2002 claim that Iraq purchased aluminum tubes to help make nuclear weapons. In both cases, government officials used questionable evidence to justify a policy that, in the end, resulted in a substantial increase in the number of

U.S. military bases overseas. See Barstow, Broad and Gerth, "How the White House Embraced Disputed Arms Intelligence."

18. See Hendrickson, *The Spanish-American War*. Also see Johnson, *Sorrows of Empire*.

19. Greider, *Fortress America*.

20. Cited in Sandars, *America's Overseas Garrisons,* 148.

21. Architectural historian Jeffrey Cody discusses how the U.S. Army led the way in exporting American building practices to its new territories. See Cody, *Exporting American Architecture*.

22. Conrad, *Nostromo,* 77.

23. Marx and Engels, *Manifesto of the Communist Party,* 6.

24. White House, *National Security Strategy,* 3.

25. Nye, "Propaganda Isn't the Way: Soft Power."

26. Greene, *The Quiet American,* 32.

27. Ibid., 51. The novel exposes the "third force" for none other than a CIA-funded paramilitary group.

28. For the Anti-imperialist League, see the Library of Congress Web page at http://www.loc.gov/rr/hispanic/1898/league.html. Notable members included Mark Twain and William James. For the more recent American Empire Project, see www.americanempireproject.com.

29. See chapter 3 for descriptions of these events and the U.S. response.

30. For details on the protests following the rape, see Johnson, "The 1995 Rape Incident and the Rekindling of Okinawan Protest."

31. Cited in Smith, "Inertia on Display," 42.

32. Sandars, *America's Overseas Garrisons*.

33. White House, "President Bush Announces Major Combat Operations in Iraq Have Ended."

34. VandeHei, "Bush Says U.S. Troops Will Stay in Iraq Past '08."

35. See U.S. Department of Defense, Office of the Deputy Under Secretary of Defense, *Base Structure Report,* FY2006. For numbers of deployed personnel by country, see U.S. Department of Defense, *Worldwide Manpower Distribution by Geographical Area*.

36. Johnson, *Sorrows of Empire*. Johnson shows how the number is actually low since it does not include temporary sites in the Middle East and Central Asia.

37. See Harkavy, *Bases Abroad;* Sandars, *America's Overseas Garrisons;* and Blaker, *United States Overseas Basing*.

38. Refer to Part III of this study for details on the diplomatic initiatives concerning military bases in South Korea and Japan.

39. U.S. Department of Defense, *Construction Programs: Fiscal Year 2007*.

40. Zakaria, "The Arrogant Empire."

41. Office of Management and Budget, *Budget Summary* (2006).

42. Barringer, "Strategic Importance of the Philippines."

43. For an extensive discussion of "rent" and other monetary matters, see Harkavy, *Bases Abroad*.

44. Blaker, *United States Overseas Basing*. Permission costs include both economic and security assistance.

45. U.S. Department of Defense, *Report on Allied Contributions to the Common Defense*.

46. For a transcript of the speech, see White House, "President Bush Announces Major Combat Operations in Iraq Have Ended."

47. Cited in Schrader, "Pentagon Plans Major Shift of Troops Throughout Asia."

48. Giordono, "S. Korea to Set Aside Land for Base Growth."

49. Schrader, "Pentagon Plans Major Shift of Troops Throughout Asia." Also see "U.S. Embarks on Global Shuffle of Military Forces."

50. White House, "President Speaks at V.F.W. Convention."

51. For the concept of tripwire, see Bandow, *Tripwire*.

52. Kirk and Fisher, "Army."

53. Kirk, "U.S. Pushing Realignment of Troops in South Korea."

54. U.S. Congressional Budget Office, *Options for Changing the Army's Overseas Basing*.

55. Liewer, "Study Weighs Costs," 3.

56. Choi Soung-ah, "Troop Removal May Increase Chances of War."

57. French, "Official Says U.S. Will Reposition Its Troops in South Korea."

58. Editorial, "Misconceived Military Shuffle."

59. Niringiye, "Mission."

60. Giordono, "Base Shift Report Garners Little Reaction in the Pacific." The last major shift in military strength on South Korea occurred in 1971, when the Army deactivated 18,000 soldiers.

61. Embassy of the Republic of Korea, "Osan-Pyeongtaek to Become Hub of USFK."

62. U.S. Congressional Budget Office, *Options for Changing the Army's Overseas Basing*.

63. Shimoyachi, "Pullout of U.S. Forces Could Skip Japan."

64. Deguchi, "Base Foes Dismayed at Kadena's Longevity."

65. See Kleveman, *New Great Game*.

66. Cited in Rizzo, "Romania Moving Closer to Base Access Deal with U.S."

67. Beale, "U.S. Gets Deal on Kyrgyz Air Base."

68. Coon, "Treaty with Romania Will Allow U.S. Forces to Use Bases."

69. For Bush's remarks on cost savings, see White House, "President Speaks at V.F.W. Convention." Also see Spencer, *Statement of Jack Spencer*.

70. U.S. Congressional Budget Office, *Options for Changing the Army's Overseas Basing*.

71. Cited in McEntee, "Reduction Plan Likely Won't Affect Already Transformed USAFE."

72. Giordono, "Base Shift Report Garners Little Reaction in the Pacific."

3. Spillover

1. Ota, "Governor of Okinawa at the Supreme Court of Japan," 5.

2. Sandars, *America's Overseas Garrisons*. The number of Okinawans that died represented 20 percent of the total population and equaled the number that died in Hiroshima and Nagasaki combined.

3. Ota, "Re-Examining the History of the Battle of Okinawa," 18.

4. House Armed Services Committee, *Report of a Special Subcommittee*. For a discussion of the Bolivian connection, see Amemiya, "Reinventing Population Problems in Okinawa."

5. House Armed Services Committee, *Report of a Special Subcommittee.*

6. Ota, "Governor of Okinawa at the Supreme Court of Japan," 4.

7. House Armed Services Committee, *Report of a Special Subcommittee.*

8. Ibid.

9. Ota, "Governor of Okinawa at the Supreme Court of Japan."

10. Sebald, *Emperor of Japan's Opinion Concerning the Future of the Ryukyu Islands;* MacArthur, "Memorandum on Concept Governing Security in Postwar Japan"; Sandars, *America's Overseas Garrisons,* 158; Ogden, Civil Administration Proclamation No. 26; Eisenhower, Executive Order 10713 Providing for Administration of the Ryukyu Islands.

11. This takes the concept of environmental justice to another level. For a discussion of the concept, see Bullard, *Dumping in Dixie.*

12. Yamamoto, *A Report on Aircraft Noise as a Public Health Problem in Okinawa.*

13. Francis, "Women and Military Violence."

14. Cited in Kirk and Choe Song-won, "Kunsan Noise Plaintiffs Win Damages."

15. Tomoaki Takakura, "Japanese Court Orders Noise Pollution Compensation"; "Tokyo High Court Grants Residents Living near U.S. Air Base Monetary Compensation"; Chiyomi Sumida, "Futenma Noise Suit Names Base Commander"; Allen and Chiyomi Sumida, "Okinawans Say Aircraft Noise Is Increasing."

16. U.S. Department of Defense Office of the Deputy Under Secretary of Defense, *Base Structure Report,* 2004.

17. Specht, "Some Misawa Merchants Weigh Moving to Avoid Noise."

18. Specht, "Residents near Ripsaw Gunnery Range Have Decided to Relocate."

19. Cited in Specht, "Some Misawa Merchants Weigh Moving to Avoid Noise."

20. Cited in Allen and Chiyomi Sumida, "Noise from Kadena Exercise Rankles Town."

21. Cited in Murakami, "Kadena Air Base Noise Stirs Memories of War."

22. Cited in Specht, "Misawa F-16 Drops Tanks, Training Missiles on Farm."

23. "The Downside of U.S. Bases"; Johnson, *Of Sex, Okinawa, and American Foreign Policy;* "Crimes Committed and Incidents Concerning U.S. Military on Okinawa," *Okinawa Times,* October 12, 1995; Millard, "Okinawa"; Sandars, *America's Overseas Garrisons;* Bongioanni, "Okinawa Officials Protest Latest F-15 Crash"; Lea, "U.S. Pilot Dies as F-16 Crashes into South Korean Rice Paddy"; Specht, "One Pilot Missing after U.S. F-16 Jets Collide Off Japan"; Specht, "Misawa F-16 Drops Tanks, Training Missiles on Farm"; Specht and Kusumoto, "Misawa Farmer Settles with Air Force"; Specht, Sekioka, and Chida, "Misawa Officials Criticize Safety Record of Air Force's F-16s"; Bongioanni, "Gregson Apologizes for Okinawa Plane Mishaps, Promises Remedies"; Bongioanni and Sekioka, "Okinawan Leaders Express Concerns about Falling Jet Parts"; Bongioanni, "Okinawa Governor Urges Tokyo to Pressure U.S. to Ground Jets"; Fisher and Choe Song-won, "Pilot Rescued from Sea after F-16 Crash Off Korea"; Flack, "U-2 Plane Crashes in South Korea"; Specht, "Report Finds Engine Failure Caused F-16 Crash near Misawa Air Base"; Allen and Chiyomi Sumida, "Helicopter Crash Provides Spark for Opponents of Futenma Base"; Zimmerman, "Two F-15s Make Contact During Training Mission Off Okinawa."

24. Cited in Specht, Sekioka, and Chida, "Misawa Officials Criticize Safety Record of Air Force's F-16s."

25. Specht, "Misawa Sinks Wells to Gauge Spread of Underground Fuel Spill from 45 Years Ago"; Specht and Chida, "Officials Say Underground Jet Fuel Plume Poses

No Hazard at Misawa"; Flack, "Osan Emergency Workers Respond to Base Fuel Spill"; Lee Jae-hee, "Seoul City to Investigate Contaminated Spring Water."

26. Lea, "Korean Groups Demand USFK Leader's Resignation."

27. Lea, "Ambassador Offers Regrets for Seoul Chemical Dumping."

28. Cited in Lea, "U.S. Forces Korea Launches Environmental Protection Program."

29. Bongioanni, "As Okinawa Landfill Space Dwindles, Recycling Is Urged"; Gittler, "Illegal Dumping a Big Mess for Bases"; Allen, "Bases Push Residents to Change Trash Habits"; Kulman, "Our Consuming Interest."

30. For a discussion of crimes committed by members of the U.S. military, see Johnson, *Of Sex, Okinawa, and American Foreign Policy.*

31. Kim Ji-ho, "GIs Chalk Up 32 Billion Won in Damages"; Hwang Jang-jin, "Koreans Handled 5.5% of Crimes Committed by U.S. Soldiers."

32. Jones, Letter to the editor. General Jones was the commandant of the Marine Corps when he wrote the letter in response to an article about American crime in Okinawa.

33. Cited in Botting, "Waging War on the U.S. Presence."

34. Allen and Chiyomi Sumida, "Okinawa."

35. Yoo Yong-won, "U.S. Soldiers Avoid Service in Korea: Research."

36. Johnson, *Sorrows of Empire,* 202.

37. Enloe, *Bananas, Beaches, and Bases,* 71–72.

38. One officer told me that she was compelled to ask her commanding officer for permission to get pregnant while stationed in South Korea. His approval was needed to authorize use of a hospital with a maternity ward off-base. He approved and "turned ten shades of red." Leslie Triano, personal interview, May 20, 2004 (hereafter Triano interview).

39. Gottdiener, *Social Production of Urban Space.*

40. Cited in Bongioanni, "Servicemembers on Okinawa Are Fighting a Battle of Public Perception."

41. Ibid.

42. Cynthia Enloe's contributions have been profound. She has shown how prostitution is not simply an issue about disease control, nor is it strictly a woman's issue. Rather, it is a practice that links the personal world of women struggling to survive with the international world of nations competing for power. See Enloe, *Bananas, Beaches, and Bases,* "A Feminist Perspective on Foreign Military Bases," and "It Takes Two." Other scholars have added their voices to the subject. Bearing some resemblance to the efforts of Alfred Dyer and his Christian audience in the 1890s, the work of Brenda Stoltzfus, a member of the Mennonite Central Committee working in the Philippines, helped set the stage for the involvement of several women's organizations as well as the National Council of Churches. The oral histories and photographic essays that resulted from the work of Stoltzfus and her colleague Saundra Sturdevant exposed the complex network supporting camptown life. See Sturdevant and Stoltzfus, *Let the Good Times Roll.* Katharine Moon focused on the transnational policies and practices that underpin U.S.-Korea relations regarding prostitution. See Moon, *Sex among Allies.*

43. In a disturbing novel by Martin Limón, Itaewon is the setting for the murder of Miss Pak Ok-suk, a local bar girl. The vicious murder in the novel is not much different from the actual murder of a twenty-six-year-old prostitute in 1992. Limón shows us how power and prestige play out in the nightclubs and neighborhoods of

Itaewon. Throughout the novel, Limón helps us see how the presumed barriers of the garrison give way to internationalized conflicts of class, gender, and race in the camptown. See Limón, *Jade Lady Burning.*

44. McMichael, "Sex Slaves and the U.S. Military."

45. Cited in Norgen, "Patrol Keeps Night Life Safe at Osan."

46. Architects and planners advancing the agenda of "new urbanism" claim that Americans will only walk five minutes or 1,250 feet before getting in a car. I find this simplistic. If the walk is pleasant, past storefronts, under shade trees, and with a friend, many people will walk longer than five minutes. But if it is across a Wal-Mart parking lot, dodging SUVs and supersized shopping carts, a five-minute walk is far too long. For a primer on new urbanism see Duany, Plater-Zyberk, and Speck, *Suburban Nation.*

47. Lea and Bae Gi-chul, "South Koreans Worry Business Will Suffer If G.I. Tours Change."

48. Heldman, *Itaewon, South Korea.*

49. For an account of the USS *Pueblo* incident, see Lerner, *The Pueblo Incident.*

50. Kalani O'Sullivan, personal communication, September 7, 2004.

51. Moon, *Sex among Allies.*

52. Yuh Ji-yeon, *Beyond the Shadow of Camptown,* 23–24.

53. See Jackson, *Crabgrass Frontier;* Gottdiener, *Social Production of Urban Space;* and Wiewel and Persky, eds., *Suburban Sprawl.*

54. O'Sullivan, personal communication.

55. "Off-Limits."

56. Childs and Chiyomi Sumida, "Courtesy Patrols Start This Weekend on Okinawa."

57. Foucault, *Discipline and Punish,* 201.

58. Demick, "Off-Base Behavior in Korea."

59. O'Sullivan, *Off-Base Issues.*

60. As of 2001, women working as prostitutes at A-Town were examined weekly and required to register with South Korean authorities. If a woman did not have a "health card," that meant she either tested positive on the check or was not registered at all. The Town Patrol and the base hospital gave out condoms free of charge. See "Sexually Transmitted Diseases."

61. Wooten, "Follow the Rules and Survive in A-Town."

62. Dan Edwards, personal interview, August 19, 2003.

63. James Wolfe, personal interview, May 23, 2003.

64. Anne Wirth, personal interview, June 11, 2003 (hereafter Wirth interview).

65. Monty Green, personal interview, March 24, 2003.

66. O'Sullivan, *Off-Base Issues.*

67. Kim Yong-si, personal interview, March 28, 2003.

68. Svoboda, "Supporting the Troops."

69. Flack and Choe Song-won, "S. Korean Merchants, Fearing Protesters Will Scare Off Clients, Defend U.S. Bases."

70. Ananya Roy refers to the idea that resistance ties expressions of freedom together with the unveiling of power relationships. See Roy, *City Requiem, Calcutta.*

71. Cited in Flack and Choe Song-won, "S. Korean Merchants, Fearing Protesters Will Scare Off Clients, Defend U.S. Bases."

72. Cited in ibid.

73. U.S. Department of State, *Trafficking in Persons Report.*

74. McMichael, "Sex Slaves and the U.S. Military."

75. Sims, "A Hard Life for Amerasian Children."

76. Johnson, *Of Sex, Okinawa, and American Foreign Policy.*

4. Homeward Bound

1. Bernard Lightle, personal interview, May 12, 2004.

2. Beck, *What Is Globalization?*

3. Barber, *Jihad vs. McWorld.*

4. Allen and Chiyomi Sumida, "City Mayors Ask Kadena to Cancel Thunderbirds F-16 Aerial Demonstration."

5. Cited in Bongioanni, "Total Base Effort Is Required to Pull Off Americafest at Kadena."

6. Allen and Chiyomi Sumida, "City Mayors Ask Kadena to Cancel Thunderbirds F-16 Aerial Demonstration"; Fisher, "Thunderbirds a Roaring Success."

7. On Okinawa, as of 2004 the United States controlled 20 percent of the ground and 100 percent of the airspace. See "Kadena Cut Causes Naha Hemorrhage."

8. Choe Song-won and Giordono, "South Koreans Get Look at U.S. Air Base."

9. Barber, *Jihad vs. McWorld.*

10. Becker, "Confused Coastals Give Midwest a Bad Rap."

11. Rapoport, "On Cultural Landscapes."

12. I am grateful to Dr. Mark Labberton, senior pastor at First Presbyterian Church of Berkeley, for conceptualizing American culture in this way. Mark Labberton, personal communication, October 17, 2004.

13. Triano interview.

14. Elizabeth Brown, personal interview, May 20, 2004. For a variety of perspectives on hybrid urbanism, see the contributions in AlSayyad, ed., *Hybrid Urbanism.*

15. Ron Walker and Daniel Fallino, personal interviews, June 5, 2003.

16. Mike Kleeman, personal interview, June 5, 2003. Number of civilian employees at Kadena in 2003 from U.S. Department of Defense Office of the Deputy Under Secretary of Defense, "Base Structure Report," 2003.

17. Lisa Prater, personal communication, September 12, 2004 (hereafter Prater interview).

18. Katie Murrey, personal interview, July 12, 2001 (hereafter Murrey interview).

19. Dana Willis, personal interview, July 27, 2003.

20. Han C. H., personal interview, May 19, 2004; Ed Hilt, personal interview, July 15, 2002; Kelly Portal, personal interview, July 28, 2002.

21. Hugh MacBride, personal interview, June 9, 2003 (hereafter MacBride interview).

22. Scott Jansen, personal interview, June 9, 2003.

23. Given the parking lots and green space in both developments, densities of the towers, built at twelve units per acre, were still less than the density of Misawa City's three-story morphology, built at fifteen to twenty units per acre. The townhomes on the base were built at four units per acre.

24. Victor Lee, personal interview, January 15, 2004 (hereafter Lee interview).

25. Marty Holland, personal interview, September 20, 2004 (hereafter Holland interview); Schutz, *Phenomenology of the Social World*, 74.

26. Veblen, *Theory of the Leisure Class;* Gottdiener, *Social Production of Urban Space,* 94. Margaret Crawford has highlighted the link between consumption and control in America's shopping malls. They are places designed specifically to breed desire through their merchandising decisions, layouts, and marketing campaigns. See Crawford, "The World in a Shopping Mall."

27. Zukin, *The Cultures of Cities,* 208; Kulman, "Our Consuming Interest"; Hayden, *Building Suburbia.*

28. Army and Air Force Exchange Service, *Annual Report;* Wal-Mart, *Annual Report* (2002).

29. See Zukin, *Cultures of Cities;* Gottdiener, *Social Production of Urban Space;* and Davis, *City of Quartz.*

30. Susan Brown, personal interview, June 9, 2003. Cinnabon is a new arrival on Air Force bases and is doing quite well. Opening overseas franchises is part of their "aggressive" "multi-unit territory development" plan, which sounds more like a military campaign than a bakery promotion. See their website at http://www.cinnabon .com/international/index.html.

31. Misawa City had a population of 42,800 in 2004 (source: http://www .world-gazetteer.com/d/d_jp_ao.htm). Misawa Air Base had a population of 4,634 (source: U.S. Department of Defense Office of the Deputy Under Secretary of Defense, "Base Structure Report," 2004).

32. Susan Brown interview.

33. Murrey interview.

34. Matthew Dalton, personal interview, June 5, 2003.

35. Lee Suk-bok, *Impact of U.S. Forces in Korea,* 79.

36. Wells, "Command Referral System Tool in Fight"; Barber, *Jihad vs. McWorld,* 16. On the concept of "corporate globalization" see Roy, *An Ordinary Person's Guide to Empire.*

37. Lederer and Burdick, *The Ugly American,* 80.

38. Huddy, "Overseas Commissaries Offer Servicemembers a Taste of Home."

39. Defense Commissary Agency, 2004.

40. Svan and Liewer, "Unpaid Baggers at Commissaries Offer Services with a Smile."

41. Cited in Huddy, "Overseas Commissaries Offer Servicemembers a Taste of Home."

42. Fisher, "Kunsan Commissary to Expand Size, Inventory."

43. Cited in Tyler, "Many Shoppers Feel Right at Home."

44. Cited in Oliva, "Chili's Restaurant to Serve up Spice."

45. Svan, "AF Services Official."

46. Lea and Bae Gi-chul, "Local Governments Seek Subsidies." Most South Korean golf courses are located outside urban areas, which require a time-consuming commute.

47. Chris Rodgers, personal interview, March 27, 2003 (hereafter Rodgers interview).

48. Jeff Kessling, personal interview, May 17, 2004.

49. Fisher, "Golf Course Renovations Fit Base to a Tee."

50. Lea and Gi-chul, "Local Governments Seek Subsidies."

51. Gerald Hillyard, personal interview, May 14, 2004.

52. Lee interview.

53. Hildegard Stetler, personal interview, November 14, 2004 (hereafter Stetler interview).

54. See the Armed Forces Recreation Center Web site at http://www.armymwr .com/portal/travel/recreationcenters/.

55. See "AFRC Takes Bookings for New Resort Hotel." Also see Coon, "Troops on R&R Are Priority at Edelweiss Lodge."

56. Stetler interview.

57. Dale Sherman, personal interview, November 16, 2004 (hereafter Sherman interview).

58. Harris, "Americans Make the Most of Recreation Options."

59. See Okinawa Convention and Visitors Bureau, http://www.ocvb.or.jp/ (cited May 12, 2003).

60. Hurst, "Okuma!"

61. Size of Okuma from Workman, "Kadena Services Getaway Resort Is Second to None."

62. Lee interview.

63. Cited in "Ishihara Rants after Tour of U.S. Military Park."

64. Lee interview.

65. Cited in Toshi Maeda and Sumiko Oshima, "Base Not Ishihara's Only Target."

66. From http://www.374th-services.org/tamarec/tamarec.htm (cited October 5, 2003).

67. Kathryn Woodward argues that identity is marked through symbols and "recovery of the past . . . is part of the process of constructing identity." See Woodward, "Concepts of Identity and Difference," 9.

68. See Hall, "Cultural Identity and Diaspora." Also see Woodward, "Concepts of Identity and Difference."

69. Hall, "Cultural Identity and Diaspora."

70. Judith Butler has highlighted the performative aspects of identity. Identity is not given; rather it is a performance using a variety of symbols. Butler considers the production of gender a performance. Gender is an act that people rehearse, script, and stage. If this is the case, then the rules that govern the concept of gender are not given. Rules, like a script, can change for the next show or they can rerun forever. These rules rely on the continual reenactment by the very people on the stage. See Butler, "Performative Acts and Gender Constitution."

71. Neil Leach, paper presented at the International Association for the Study of Traditional Environments, Hong Kong, 2002.

72. For a description of Seaside, see Katz, *The New Urbanism*. Also see AlSayyad, *Cinematic Urbanism*.

73. Blakely and Snyder, *Fortress America*.

74. For discussions of suburbia's sociospatial problems, see Kunstler, *The Geography of Nowhere;* Duany, Plater-Zyberk, and Speck, *Suburban Nation;* and Langdon, *A Better Place to Live*. For a discussion of the history of suburbanization, see Jackson, *Crabgrass Frontier,* and Archer, *Architecture and Suburbia*. And for a discussion of the political ramifications of a suburban nation, see Thomas, *The United States of Suburbia*. For a discussion of the economic impact of sprawling suburbs, see

Burchell, Downs, Mukherji, and McCann, *Sprawl Costs.* For a discussion of the environmental impact, see the Sierra Club, "Sprawl." Sprawl does have some supporters. At least one scholar has highlighted the mobility and privacy benefits of sprawling suburbs. See Bruegmann, *Sprawl.*

75. King, *Spaces of Global Cultures.* Greig Crysler has argued that cities stretch across nations as diaspora cultures spread across the globe. See Crysler, *Writing Spaces.*

76. Kay, *Asphalt Nation.* See page 130.

77. Harris, "Parking Problems on Bases across Europe."

78. Ibid.

79. Adams, *The Hitchhiker's Guide to the Galaxy.*

80. Kelbaugh, "Into the Abyss," 49.

81. From "Song of the Open Road" in Whitman, *Leaves of Grass.*

82. Cited in Harris, "Parking Problems on Bases across Europe."

83. Howard Nicchols, personal interview, March 28, 2003.

84. Zukin, *Landscapes of Power.*

85. U.S. Air Force, "Air Force Family Housing Guide." The guide specifies housing densities by location: overseas and dense metropolitan areas; highly developed urban areas; and suburban areas and rural areas. Most stateside bases fall under the "suburban" classification.

86. MacBride interview.

87. Pollan, "Grass Gardens," 9.

88. As Dolores Hayden notes, "Downing's obsession with setting a suburban residence behind a wide swath of lawn . . . [is] still part of suburban house design today." See Hayden, *Building Suburbia,* 27.

89. See Jackson, *Crabgrass Frontier.*

90. Many franchises copyright their architecture to protect their "distinctive" images. See Schlosser, *Fast Food Nation.*

91. Whitaker, *Architecture and the American Dream.*

92. Cited in Schlosser, *Fast Food Nation,* 47.

93. Ivan Louden, personal interview, August 2, 2004 (hereafter Louden interview).

94. For a history of the concept of zoning as it pertains to the United States, see Barnett, *Introduction to Urban Design.*

95. Oscar Perman, personal interview, October 4, 2004 (hereafter Perman interview).

96. Jamal Stevenson, personal interview, May 21, 2004.

97. Holland interview.

98. National Public Radio, "Today's U.S. Military," January 11, 2004. African Americans make up 23 percent of the U.S. military and only 12.3 percent of the U.S. population as a whole. U.S. Census Bureau, *Statistical Abstract of the United States* (2000). "Service Demographics Offer Snapshot of Force"; Peers, "Imperial Vice."

99. Henry Keller, personal interview, May 14, 2004; Galen Cranz, personal communication, December 8, 2004; Perman interview.

100. Solomon, *Global City Blues,* 102.

101. For a discussion of company towns, see Crawford, *Building the Working-man's Paradise.* For a discussion of gated communities, see Blakely and Snyder, *Fortress America,* and Low, *Behind the Gates.*

102. Homi Bhabha suggests there is an in-between space, a "third space" or borderland that cultures inhabit where "the contaminated yet connective tissue between cultures" makes definite boundaries between cultures impossible. See Bhabha, "Culture's In-Between," 54.

103. AlSayyad, "Hybrid Culture/Hybrid Urbanism," 7.

104. See Broudehoux, "Learning from Chinatown." Also see Fuchs and Herbert, "A Colonial Portrait of Jerusalem."

105. Jacobs, *Edge of Empire,* 27.

106. Valerie Jansen, personal interview, June 13, 2003.

107. Ibid.

108. Zukin, *Landscapes of Power,* 136.

109. Edwards, personal interview, August 19, 2003.

110. Reprinted from Hana Kusumoto and Tyler, "Iwakuni Runway Project Revs Local Interest."

111. Chris Wallace, interview with Colin Powell on *Fox News Sunday,* June 13, 2004.

5. Ruling the World

1. For a discussion of social ontology, see Campbell and Gregor, *Mapping Social Relations.*

2. Anderson, *Imagined Communities,* 5; Campbell and Gregor, *Mapping Social Relations,* 33; Lefebvre, *Production of Space,* 75, 374.

3. Fisher, "Agency Streamlines Korea Map-Ordering."

4. Anderson, *Imagined Communities,* 173.

5. Cited in Smith, *American Empire,* 147.

6. Barnett, *Introduction to Urban Design.*

7. The Air Force developed the concept of airfield clear zones in the 1970s, when airplanes were crashing into buildings and other obstructions near the runway. Engineers created scatter plots locating where all aircraft hit and where parts were landing. These plots led to the clear zone at each end of a runway of 3,000 feet by 3,000 feet. In addition, the plots led to a lateral clear zone of 1,000 feet along the runway. Holland interview.

8. Larry Ferman, personal interview, March 27, 2003 (hereafter Ferman interview).

9. Mike Ramirez, personal interview, October 1, 2004.

10. Lefebvre, *Production of Space,* 146.

11. As of March 31, 2001, 17.2 percent of Air Force officers were women and 19.4 percent of enlisted were women. For the military as a whole, 14.5 percent of officers were women and 14.7 percent of enlisted were women. See U.S. Department of Defense, Defense Manpower Data Center.

12. Naomi Blaser, personal interview, August 6, 2004 (hereafter Blaser interview).

13. Holland interview.

14. Lee interview.

15. Holland interview.

16. Ibid.

17. Ibid.

18. Ibid.

19. For a discussion of the "circulation of elites" among the Department of Defense and the private sector, see Johnson, *Sorrows of Empire*.

20. Cody, *Exporting American Architecture.*

21. Troy Halpin, personal interview, March 25, 2003.

22. Lovelace, *Harland Bartholomew*, 4.

23. Jamal Stevenson, personal interview, March 28, 2003 (hereafter Stevenson interview).

24. Lee interview.

25. I will discuss this survey and the resulting plan in detail in chapter 8.

26. Holland interview.

27. For a discussion of the FHA planning guides, see Southworth and Ben-Joseph, *Streets and the Shaping of Towns and Cities.*

28. United States Air Force, *Air Force Family Housing Guide,* 1995, 35.

29. Ibid., 2004, 66.

30. Ibid., 68.

31. Sharon Johnston, personal interview, December 5, 2003.

32. Szegedy-Maszak, "Where Size Matters."

33. Hefemeister, "Dorms 4 Airmen."

34. Ibid.

35. Burgess, "Survey."

36. King, "Values, Science, and Settlement."

37. Yoo Yong-won, "Soldiers Have No Elbow Room."

38. Edward Piekarczyk, personal interview, May 17, 2004.

39. Juan Morales, personal interview, June 11, 2003.

40. Cited in Banda, "New Dormitory Standard Means Bigger Rooms."

41. Wickwire, "Recent Facility Evaluation."

42. Scott Jansen interview.

43. U.S. Air Force, *Architectural Compatibility Guide,* 2.

44. Ibid., 11.

45. Chang Hee-seung, "Osan Air Base Architectural Compatibility Plan," 5.

46. Han Y. T., personal interview, March 28, 2003 (hereafter Han Y. T. interview).

47. Zukin, *Landscapes of Power,* 259.

48. Fuller, "Building Power."

49. Said, "Representing the Colonized," 100.

50. Kanno, "Creech's 'Five-P's' Alive and Well at Osan."

51. Braider, "Geoquiz."

52. Barnett, *Introduction to Urban Design,* 229.

53. Rodgers interview.

54. Triano interview.

55. Carl Bristol, personal interview, March 27, 2003.

56. See Said, *Culture and Imperialism.*

57. Lederer and Burdick, *The Ugly American,* 276.

58. Jorge Cuellar, personal interview, May 15, 2002.

59. Stevenson interview.

60. Rodgers interview.

61. Wirth interview.

62. Nicole Davidson, personal interview, August 6, 2004.

63. Sennett, "Growth and Failure," 18.

64. Kim R. I., personal interview, May 16, 2002.

65. Han Y. T. interview.

66. Cited in McEntee, "Programs to Improve USAFE."

67. See Carmona, *Haussmann.*

68. Dishner, conference presentation.

69. Holland interview.

70. Ibid.

71. Hart and Spivak, *An Elephant in the Bedroom,* 69.

72. Stevenson interview.

73. Gilroy, "Diaspora and the Detours of Identity."

74. Anthony King argues, "What increasingly occurs in the public domain of architecture is that the meanings and interpretations of the powerful proliferate, meanings created not simply by those with economic and political power, but by those of the managerial and professional elite, including the architect-planner." See King, "Rethinking Colonialism," 344.

75. Dishner, conference presentation.

76. Garamone, *DoD's Privatized Housing Program Hits High Gear.*

77. Grier, "Ellsworth Fraud Case Settled."

78. DuBois, *Statement before the Subcommittee on Readiness of the House Armed Services Committee* (March 13, 2003).

79. Dishner, "Congressional Testimony, 2000."

80. U.S. Air Force Center for Environmental Excellence, *United States Air Force Housing Privatization.*

81. Markusen, Campbell, Hall, and Deitrick, *The Rise of the Gunbelt.*

82. U.S. Army, *Army's Residential Communities Initiative Information Paper.*

83. Garamone, "New BAH Rates among Largest in History." Also see Dishner, "Congressional Testimony, 2000."

84. Garamone, "New BAH Rates among Largest in History."

85. Dishner, "Congressional Testimony, 2000."

86. Blaser interview.

87. U.S. House of Representatives Armed Services Committee, *Military Installations and Facilities Subcommittee Hearings.*

88. Hayden, *Building Suburbia,* 9.

89. Lefebvre, *Production of Space.*

90. See Jackson, *Crabgrass Frontier.*

91. Zukin, *Landscapes of Power.* Zukin refers to suburban developments in the United States and the power imbalance in favor of private developers rather than public interests.

92. Louden interview.

93. Ibid.

94. Filkins, "2 Bombers Kill 5 in Guarded Area in Baghdad."

95. Harris, "Five Killed by Two Blasts in Green Zone."

96. Trowbridge, "Rodriguez Offers Details of Mosul Dining Hall Attack."

97. "Fast Facts." Size of Khobar Tower bomb from U.S. Federal Bureau of Investigation, *Khobar Towers Indictment.*

98. King, "Values, Science, and Settlement."

99. Branch, *An Atlas of Rare City Maps.*

100. See Peers, "Imperial Vice."

101. See Dudley, "Sprawl as Strategy." Also see O'Mara, *Cities of Knowledge.*

102. Flint, "Sept. 11 Pushes Firms to Suburbs."

103. Cohen, *Personal Accountability for Force Protection at Khobar Towers.*

104. Cited in Kohn, "The Early Retirement of Gen. Ronald R. Fogleman."

105. Ellin, *Postmodern Urbanism,* 145. Ellin argues that in the postmodern world, form follows function, finance, and fear. She links the growing trend toward privatization of public space to the increasing fear of uncontrolled urban life.

106. U.S. Air Force, "Installation Force Protection Guide," 14.

107. See Newman, *Defensible Space.* Also see Jacobs, *The Death and Life of Great American Cities.*

108. Perman interview.

109. This is comparable to a story Mike Davis tells in *City of Quartz.* The Los Angeles Police Department had a representative on design review boards and advised city agencies on security issues, which in one case led to the demolition of the last public toilet in L.A.'s Skid Row. With its fortified architecture and high-technology surveillance systems, Davis argues that the correct place name is *Fortress L.A.* See Davis, *City of Quartz.*

110. Holland interview.

111. Kirk, "Korean News Report." Those wanting entry are not terrorists; rather, they are South Koreans who want to gamble on American bases. One report found that tens of thousands of dollars are flowing into U.S. coffers from the gambling machines without taxes being paid to the South Korean government.

112. U.S. Department of Defense, "Minimum Standards for Antiterrorism Standards," 1–6.

113. Stevenson interview.

114. This quote is from a planner who participated in my 2004 survey of planners and architects working for the U.S. military.

115. The Crime Prevention Through Environmental Design (CPTED) movement believes that proper physical design can lead to a reduction in crime. Adherents to the philosophy have their own international organization, hold regular conferences, publish a journal, and monitor a registration program for professionals. They also lobby municipalities to adopt CPTED ordinances that require designs that maximize the ability for natural surveillance, provide natural access control, and allow for territorial reinforcement. See http://www.cpted.net.

116. Giordono, "S. Korea to Set Aside Land for Base Growth."

117. Wayne Kennedy and Dean Jackson, personal interviews, October 6, 2004.

118. Childs, Lea, and Svan, "Overseas Bases One of the Safest Places to Live."

119. U.S. Green Building Council, "LEED Rating System Version 2.0." The U.S. Green Building Council developed the LEED criteria to quantify "sustainability" as it pertains to construction design and practices. Compliance is measured in six primary categories and points are given if a particular project meets specified criteria. Since the LEED criteria give only one point out of a total 69 points for channeling construction to areas developed at 60,000 square feet per acre, the U.S. military can easily make up that one point using other means. For example, they can hire a LEED

certified professional to write up a compliance plan (one point) or use paint that minimizes emissions of volatile organic compounds (one point).

120. Boyer, *Dreaming the Rational City*, 60.
121. Foucault, *Discipline and Punish*, 200.

6. Reinforcing the Southern Flank

1. See Sandars, *America's Overseas Garrisons;* and Lehrer, "Dirty Bomb Arrest."
2. Wald, "U.S. Maps Become Legal Issue in Alpine Cable Accident."
3. For a detailed history of the events in Spain and Italy, see Sandars, *America's Overseas Garrisons.*
4. Perman interview.
5. U.S. Air Force, "Design Awards Program Annual Report," 12.
6. Lundy, lecture at the Air Force Institute of Technology.
7. See U. S. Congress, House of Representatives, *To Prohibit the Construction of Facilities.*
8. Roberts, "Aviano 2000 in Full Throttle."
9. Population of the base from Weslowski, "Aviano Today."
10. U.S. Congress, House of Representatives, *Statement of Major General Eugene A. Lupia.*
11. Roberts, "Aviano 2000 in Full Throttle"; Weslowski, "Aviano Today"; Arana-Barradas, "Aviano Renaissance"; Kozaryn, *Clinton Salutes U.S., Allied Troops.*
12. Cited in Harris, "Retiring Colonel Says Aviano Is Part of His Soul."
13. Cited in Roberts, "Aviano 2000 in Full Throttle."
14. "U.S. Expanding NATO Base in Italy."
15. Harris, "Aviano 2000 Projects"; Arana-Barradas, "Aviano Renaissance"; Weslowski, "Aviano Today."
16. Harris, "First of New Aviano Dorms Almost Ready for Occupation"; Harris, "New Mini-Mall Big Hit with Aviano Shoppers"; Kosowatz, "Aviano Air Base Falls Into Step under Central Line of Command"; Weslowski, "Aviano Today"; Harris, "Airmen Feasting at New Club, Lodge in Aviano"; Kunich, "New Base Exchange, Commissary Open at Aviano"; Harris, "Aviano Projects Set to Reach New Milestones"; Harris, "Ambitious Aviano 2000 Program Enters Heavy Construction Stage"; Coon, "8 Aviano Firefighters Extend 'Resting Period' Strike Time."
17. Cited in Kosowatz, "Aviano Air Base Falls Into Step under Central Line of Command."
18. Cited in Weslowski, "Aviano Today," 7, 8.
19. Kosowatz, "Winging It Home at Aviano Air Base."
20. Rizzo, "Spain Lifts Hurdles to NATO Funding of Aviano Projects."
21. Weslowski, "Aviano Today," 8.
22. Kunich, "Aviano School Opening Is Way Behind Schedule."
23. Cited in Harris, "Contractor for Aviano School Is Fired."
24. Cited in Cobb, "Construction, Renovations Add Sparkle."
25. Cited in Harris, "Aviano School Opens Its Doors."
26. Cited in Weslowski, "Aviano Today," 8.
27. Arana-Barradas, "Aviano Renaissance."
28. Cited in Harris, "Aviano 2000 Reviewed."

29. U.S. Air Force, "General Plan Study for Aviano Air Base, Italy," 4–6.

30. Ibid., 4–11.

31. It is interesting that people at the bases refer to the AAFES organization by the name of its location. It is as if "Dallas" speaks like the "Pentagon" speaks. When news reports begin, "The Pentagon says . . . ," it is a convenient way to depersonalize the process and strip agency from people who actually make the decisions.

32. Arana-Barradas, "Aviano Renaissance."

33. Giuseppe Falino, personal communication, October 3, 2004.

34. From the *Aviano Air Base Architectural Compatibility Guide*, 2004, 61.

35. Andrea Nicolleta, Gill Sanchez, and Patricia Yates, personal interviews, November 16, 2004.

36. Danilo Columbrano, personal interview, November 16, 2004.

37. Jason Pell, personal interview, September 10, 2003.

38. Ibid.

39. Cited in Harris, "Aviano's Long Housing Nightmare Easing as Construction Projects Are Completed."

40. U.S. Air Force, "Notice of Request for Proposal—Aviano Housing Initiative."

41. Arthur Andersen, "Aviano Housing Initiative."

42. Ibid.

43. Drigo, "Project Narrative for U.S. Air Force Design Awards Program."

44. Sherman interview.

45. Will Febig, personal communication, September 14, 2004.

46. Prater interview.

47. For a discussion of European sprawl, see Marshall, "Eurosprawl."

7. Rewarding Realignment

1. See Kirk, "2nd U.S. Sergeant Is Cleared in the Death of 2 Korean Girls"; Brooke, "First of 2 GIs on Trial in Deaths of 2 Korean Girls Is Acquitted." Also see Ray, "Higher-Ups Put Safety Second."

2. For a history of the formation of South Korea, see Lee Suk-bok, *The Impact of U.S. Forces in Korea*. Major Rusk would later become secretary of state under President Kennedy.

3. Cited in Sandars, *America's Overseas Garrisons*, 183.

4. U.S. Department of Defense Office of the Deputy Under Secretary of Defense, "Base Structure Report," 2006.

5. Kim Mun-hee, "Will American GIs Pack up and Go Home?"

6. Woo-Cumings, "South Korean Anti-Americanism."

7. Cited in Na Jeong-ju, "Media Reps Focus on Anti-U.S. Feelings."

8. "Rising Anti-American Sentiment"; Sanger, "South Korean Leader Wants U.S. Troops to Stay, for Now"; Kim, "Will American GIs Pack up and Go Home?"; Kirk, "Kim Affirms Importance of USFK."

9. U.S. Forces Korea, *USFK Press Release No. 021004*.

10. Cited in ibid. Army General Thomas Schwartz compared LPP with BRAC in that both plans have as a fundamental goal the elimination of excess bases. See Burgess, "U.S., S. Korea Set to OK Plan to Consolidate American Military Facilities."

11. Nam Chang-hee, "Relocating USFK Bases: Background and Implications."

12. U.S. Forces Korea, *USFK PAO.*

13. Cited in Fisher, "U.S., S. Korea Sign Pact to Reduce Bases."

14. "South Korea Chooses New Capital Site."

15. "Land Purchasing for Base Relocation to Start Next Year"; Wilson, *Executive Summary Land Partnership Plan.* Yoo Yong-won, "80% of Yongsan Base to Be Returned." Yoo reports on a $3 billion cost. Joseph Giordono reports on up to a $4 billion cost; see "Completion of Yongsan Garrison Move Pushed to 2008." Choe Song-won and Kirk, "Report: U.S. Could Pull out of Seoul Entirely"; "New Sites Proposed for USFK Housing."

16. Burgess, "U.S., S. Korea Set to OK Plan to Consolidate American Military Facilities."

17. Choe and Kirk, "Report: U.S. Could Pull out of Seoul Entirely."

18. Cited in Giordono, "Completion of Yongsan Garrison Move Pushed to 2008."

19. Fisher, "Giving Back Land."

20. Giordono, "S. Korea to Set Aside Land for Base Growth."

21. Nam, "Relocating USFK Bases: Background and Implications."

22. Korea Central News Agency, *U.S. "Return" of Its Bases Dismissed as Hypocritical.*

23. Report is available at Green Korea United, *Report on Land Readjustment Plan.*

24. Cited in Fisher, "Commander Proud of Improving Life in Korea's Area IV."

25. Fisher, "Giving Back Land."

26. "USFK To Regroup Troops into 7 Areas of the Country."

27. Yoo, "U.S. Soldiers Avoid Service in Korea: Research."

28. Cited in Childs, "GIs, Spouses See Need for Plan to Improve, Expand Housing in S. Korea."

29. See U.S. GAO, *Basing Uncertainties Necessitate Reevaluation of U.S. Construction Plans in South Korea.*

30. Childs, "GIs, Spouses See Need for Plan to Improve, Expand Housing in S. Korea"; cited in Lea, "New Osan Commander Hopes More Families Are in S. Korea Base's Future"; Yoo Yong-won, "U.S.-Korea Meet on Base Housing Plan."

31. Kirk, "General: Despite Housing Conditions, Many in USFK Taking Bonus to Stay."

32. Cited in Lea, "U.S. Seeking Proposals from Korean Developers."

33. Reported in Lea, "Mission, Aesthetics Balancing out as Improvements Abound at Humphreys." Also see Lea, "Camp Humphreys Master Plan"; Kirk, "Work Starts on New Commissary"; and Fisher, "New Bowling Alley Opens at Camp Humphreys."

34. Cited in Lee Tae-hun, "Gyeonggi Governor Embraces Troop Relocation."

35. Han interview.

36. Seo Soo-min, "Expansion Plan for Osan Sparks Controversy."

37. Ibid.

38. Kim Kwang-tae, "U.S. Base Expansion Could Force Evictions."

39. Seo, "Expansion Plan for Osan Sparks Controversy."

40. U.S. Department of Defense Office of the Deputy Under Secretary of Defense, "Base Structure Report," 2006.

41. Stevenson interview.

42. Lea, "Construction Boom Is On at Osan."

43. For a detailed history of Osan Air Base, see "Base, Korean Culture Tied from Beginning."

44. U.S. Department of Defense, *2000 Report to Congress: Military Situation on the Korean Peninsula.*

45. Fisher, "U.S., S. Korea Sign Pact to Reduce Bases; Troop Levels Not Affected."

46. Bristol.

47. When the Korean National Housing Corporation (KNHC) built Sochong Air Force Village in 1986, all the units had two bedrooms and one bathroom. After construction, the Air Force decided they wanted some four-bedroom units so the KNHC demolished party walls between 150 two-bedroom units to create 75 four-bedroom units. To increase the profitability of the property, after the Air Force vacated the site, the new developer added the walls back. The result was 75 more units and a density of 33 units per acre.

48. United States Air Force, "Osan Air Base Housing Plan," 4.

49. Andrea White, personal interview, March 28, 2003.

50. Hwang Y. C., personal interview, March 28, 2002.

51. Jeff Kessling, personal interview, May 17, 2004. The Air Force has sixty-eight golf courses worldwide. Osan's is not only the most profitable but it is the most played, with more rounds of golf than any other Air Force course. The profits are returned to the base to support a variety of community services and subsidize other commercial establishments managed by the Services Squadron on the base. But the course cannot make it on U.S. personnel alone; Korean employees play more rounds than members of the U.S. military.

52. U.S. Air Force, "Osan Air Base Housing Plan," 17.

53. Hee K. Y., personal interview, May 24, 2004.

54. I am grateful for the assistance of Whitney Wang who translated the sales brochure for Hyunjin Ville from Korean to English.

55. See Lee Sang-hae, "Continuity and Consistence of the Traditional Courtyard House Plan."

56. Rodgers interview.

57. Ibid.

58. Fisher, "Huge One-Stop Shopping Mall Being Built at Osan."

59. Stevenson interview.

60. Kessling.

61. Kennedy and Jackson interviews.

62. Yoo Yong-won, "USFK Presents 'Good Neighbor' Program."

63. Vince Martinez, personal interview, May 14, 2004.

8. Reacting to Rape

1. Jameson, "People's Rally of October 21, 1995." When the three men were released, they received dishonorable discharges from the U.S. military.

2. Eckert, "Okinawans Want Reduction of U.S. Base."

3. Cited in Allen and Chiyomi Sumida, "Pre-Summit Protestors Demand U.S. Withdrawal from Okinawa."

4. Mikanagi, "Okinawa."

5. U.S. Department of State, "Transcript: Kartman, Campbell Discuss U.S.-Japan '2+2' Meeting."

6. Shunji Taoka, "Is This Base Really Necessary?"

7. U.S. GAO, *Overseas Presence: Issues Involved in Reducing the Impact of the U.S. Military Presence on Okinawa,* 22.

8. Cliff, Tangredi, and Wormuth, *Q.D.R. 2001 Strategy Driven Choices for America's Security.*

9. U.S. Department of Defense, *Quadrennial Defense Review Report.*

10. Taoka, "Is This Base Really Necessary?" Also see Mochizuki, "Japan-U.S. Relations Chair in Memory of Gaston Sigur Inaugural Lecture."

11. Masaru Honda, "Sympathy Budget to Be Reduced 1.2% for First Cutback."

12. Ibid.

13. Cited in ibid.

14. Cited in Kozaryn, *U.S. Leaders Call for Japan's Support.*

15. Definition of "sympathy" from the *American Heritage Dictionary,* 2nd college edition.

16. Ramsey, *District Supports U.S. Force in Japan.*

17. Svan, "New Yokota Community Center Scheduled to Open Its Door in October."

18. U.S. Forces Japan, *Public Website.*

19. Son Jeong-mi, "Shinsegae's E-Mart Makes Foray into the Chinese Market."

20. Government of Japan Ministry of Foreign Affairs, *The Japan-U.S. Special Action Committee (SACO) Interim Report.*

21. Allen and Chiyomi Sumida, "Japan Defense Minister Visits Okinawa to Address 'Military Related Problems.'" The Okinawa Prefecture encompasses 554,750 acres, and the island of Okinawa represents 53 percent of that area or 294,017 acres.

22. Chalmers Johnson has argued that the Japanese have discriminated against Okinawans ever since the annexation of Okinawa. See Johnson, *Sorrows of Empire.*

23. Ota, "Governor of Okinawa at the Supreme Court of Japan," 5.

24. For a discussion the Okinawan leases, see Johnson, *Blowback.*

25. Allen, "Papers Bolster Evidence of Secret Okinawa Deal."

26. For a discussion of this law, see John Purves, "Island of Military Bases: A Contemporary Political and Economic History of Okinawa" (International University of Japan, 1995).

27. "Scandal over Base Lease Payments."

28. "Legal Basis Given to Lease for Bases."

29. "Landowner Visits Property on Base."

30. "Legal Basis Given to Lease for Bases."

31. Purves, "Island of Military Bases."

32. "The Okinawa Referendum."

33. "Okinawa to Vote on Base Presence." Base employment is a prized job. Salaries are 1.2 to 1.5 times higher than comparable work outside the base, and workers have very predictable hours. In 2002, 22,234 people applied for 562 openings. As of March 31, 2003, 8,768 Japanese employees worked on the island's twenty-three U.S. military installations. See Chiyomi Sumida, "Applications Pour in for Base Jobs in Okinawa." Also see Chiyomi Sumida, "Okinawa Sees Big Hole in Job Base If Marines Leave."

34. Cited in Millard, "Okinawa," 100.

35. In 2001 Okinawa's unemployment rate was 8.4 percent while Japan's overall rate was just 4.5 percent. Annual per capita income (1999) in Okinawa was $20,000 while Japan's overall per capita income was $28,500. See Toshi Maeda, "Economic Disparities, Bases Frustrate Okinawa."

36. Government of Japan, *Okinawa Prefecture Population Data;* U.S. Census Bureau, *Statistical Abstract of the United States.* Areas of towns occupied by base from U.S. Air Force, *18th Wing Administrative Plan 545, Spill Prevention and Response Plan.* Area of Kadena from U.S. Department of Defense Office of the Deputy Under Secretary of Defense, "Base Structure Report," 2004 (hereafter U.S. DoD, "Base Structure Report").

37. Rapoport, *House Form and Culture.* My own research supports Rapoport's views on crowding and privacy regulation. Every informant I interviewed in this study acknowledged the importance of controlling access to his or her own space.

38. For a description of U.S. street morphologies since the 1900s, see Southworth and Owens, "The Evolving Metropolis."

39. Francis, "Women and Military Violence," 202.

40. U.S. GAO, *Overseas Presence.*

41. "Final SACO Report Announced."

42. Cited in Lee, "U. S. Returns More Land to Okinawa."

43. Cited in "Final SACO Report Announced."

44. John Purves, personal communication, September 12, 2004.

45. U.S. DoD, *Base Structure Report,* 2004.

46. Allen, "Okinawa Might Build School on MCCS Golf Course Site."

47. Murrey interview. Captain Murrey explained how the local mayors, under Japanese law, can approve or reject construction projects. If they do reject a proposal, the United States can appeal to prefectural authorities or the Government of Japan.

48. Allen and Chiyomi Sumida, "Mayor OKs Navy Ramp Move at Kadena."

49. U.S. Air Force, "General Plan Study for Kadena Air Base, Japan."

50. Ramsey, *District Supports U.S. Force in Japan.*

51. Ibid.

52. Ryan Martini, personal interview, June 10, 2003.

53. U.S. Air Force, "General Plan Study for Kadena Air Base, Japan."

54. Science Applications International Corporation, "Okinawa Housing Requirements and Market Analysis," 1-1.

55. Ibid., 1-1.

56. GRW Engineers, "Survey of User Perceptions: Kadena Air Base," November 18, 1997.

57. Ibid., 3-1.

58. Ibid., 3-14.

59. Ibid., 3-6.

60. U.S. Air Force, "General Plan Study for Kadena Air Base, Japan."

61. Berkeley has fifty-two parks and a total of 46,875 households (sources: City of Berkeley website and U.S. Census Bureau).

62. U.S. Air Force, "General Plan Study for Kadena Air Base, Japan."

63. See Ben-Ari, *Changing Japanese Suburbia.*

64. U.S. GAO, *Overseas Presence.*

65. Size of Futenma from U.S. DoD, "Base Structure Report," 2004. Size and population of Ginowan from Government of Japan, *Okinawa Prefecture Population Data.*

66. Smith, "Inertia on Display," 284.

67. Millard, "Okinawa," 101.

68. Peers, "Imperial Vice," 33.

69. Kleeman interview.

70. Ota, "Re-Examining the History of the Battle of Okinawa."

71. Special Action Committee Okinawa, *The SACO Final Report on Futenma Air Station*.

72. Allen and Chiyomi Sumida, "Frustration Reigns over Futenma's Future."

73. U.S. GAO, *Overseas Presence*.

74. Ibid., 32.

75. Ibid., 38.

76. Ibid.

77. Allen and Chiyomi Sumida, "Group Says Offshore Base to Replace Futenma Would Endanger Coral Reefs."

78. Ibid.

79. Allen, "Nago, Okinawa Mayoral Election Focusing on U.S. Air Station Proposal."

80. Johnson, "Further Nago Notes."

81. McCormack and Yonetani, "The Okinawan Summit Seen from Below."

82. "Nago City Council Accepts Main Base."

83. "Fukudo Hails Election Results."

84. Allen, "Nago, Okinawa Mayoral Election Focusing on U.S. Air Station Proposal."

85. Allen and Chiyomi Sumida, "Mayoral Election Could Be Key to Japan Realignment Plan."

86. "Official: U.S. Wants Base Talks with Japan." Also see Schrader, "Pentagon Plans Major Shift of Troops Throughout Asia."

87. "Relocation of U.S. Troops Hits Snag."

88. Woodland was sentenced by a Japanese court to two years and eight months of hard labor. For a discussion of how Woodland's race (he is African American) affected his sentencing, see Cullen, "Sex and Racism in Okinawa." Cullen's article is sympathetic to Woodland's case. She notes that the victim dated Woodland and was a *kokujo*, one of many Japanese women who congregate around Okinawa's bars looking for African American men to date. She also argues that Woodland's race, not his nationality, led to his conviction. She reports that between 1972 and 2001, U.S. soldiers represented 4 percent of Okinawa's population and committed 1.7 percent of the crimes on the island.

89. Cited in Oliva, "Chatan Mayor, Council Want Curfew for Servicemembers."

90. Cited in Millard, "Okinawa," 102.

91. Cited in Allen and Chiyomi Sumida, "Crimes Tied to U.S. Military Drop on Okinawa."

Conclusion

1. Cited in Lea, "Military Families in S. Korea Deal with Displacement."

2. Mann, *Incoherent Empire*, 97.

3. Hamadeh, "Creating the Traditional City."

4. Rabson, "Assimilation Policy in Okinawa."

5. For the French, see Rabinow, *French Modern*. Also see Hamadeh, "Creating the Traditional City." For the Italian case, see Fuller, "Building Power."

6. Said, *Culture and Imperialism,* 170.

7. Johnson, *The Sorrows of Empire.*

8. Senate Armed Services Committee, *Opening Statement by Secretary of Defense William Perry,* September 18, 1996.

9. Tougaw, "51st C.E.S. Breaks New Ground for Office Dormitory." In an example of transnational urbanism, of what goes on over "there" affects over "here," the hotel built at Osan in 2002 has become the standard for hotels at all Air Force bases, affecting proposed projects as far away as Altus, Oklahoma, and Pittsburgh, Pennsylvania.

10. Flack, "Drinking Problems Decrease in Korea."

11. Ignatieff, "The American Empire."

12. Cited in Ferguson, *Empire,* 248.

13. Fukuyama, "The End of America's Exceptionalism."

14. Lederer and Burdick, *The Ugly American,* 268.

15. Ibid., 270.

16. The White House, *The National Security Strategy of the United States of America,* 29.

17. Kim, "U.S. Military Causes Problems to Residents: Survey."

18. Zakaria, "Arrogant Empire," 21.

19. Siegel, "Base Access Constraints and Crisis Response."

20. White House, *President Speaks at V.F.W. Convention.*

21. Bridges, "U.S. Working to Develop New Generation of Attack Planes."

22. Greider, *Fortress America.*

23. Cited in Allen and Chiyomi Sumida, "General Visits with Okinawa Governor."

24. Said, *Culture and Imperialism,* 288.

Appendix

1. Kim, "U.S. Military Causes Problems to Residents: Survey."

2. Cited in Simon, "Centennial for Author Graham Greene."

3. Burawoy, *Ethnography Unbound.*

4. See Mead, *Coming of Age in Samoa.* Also see Whyte, *Street Corner Society.*

5. Marcus, *Ethnography through Thick and Thin,* 12, 15.

6. Freeman, *Margaret Mead and Samoa.*

7. Dexter, *Elite and Specialized Interviewing,* 120.

8. Gans, *The Levittowners.*

9. See Harvey, *The Urban Experience.* Also see Lefebvre, *The Production of Space.*

10. Gottdiener, *The Social Production of Urban Space,* 199.

11. Smith, *Texts, Facts and Femininity.*

12. Campbell and Gregor, *Mapping Social Relations,* 86.

13. For a presentation of the emic and etic conceptual models, see Pike, *Language in Relation to a Unified Theory of the Structure of Human Behavior.*

14. Reed-Danahay, ed., *Auto Ethnography.*

15. Hayano, "Auto-Ethnography," 99, 100.

16. Reed-Danahay, ed., *Auto Ethnography,* 3.

17. See Agar, *Professional Stranger.* Also see Spradley, *Participant Observation.*

18. Vale, "Designing National Identity," 316.

19. House Armed Services Committee, *Statement before the Subcommittee on Readiness by Raymond F. Dubois Deputy Under Secretary of Defense (Installations and Environment)* (March 18, 2003).

20. I invited 180 participants via email to take the web-based survey. The known response rate was just under 80 percent (143). Since the survey was openly available for thirty days on the web, there may have been people who were informed of it and participated in it anonymously without notifying me. In the survey, 86.7 percent worked for the U.S. military, 4.9 percent worked for consulting firms, and 8.4 percent were retired military/consultants; 31.5 percent were planners, 42.7 percent were architects, and 12.6 percent were civil engineers; 13.2 percent were other (mechanical engineers, electrical engineers, landscape architects, etc.); 79.7 percent were currently working in the United States, and 20.3 percent were working overseas.

21. Spradley, *The Ethnographic Interview.*

22. Jacobs, *Great Streets.*

23. Hayden, *Building Suburbia,* 22. Hayden uses the aerial photographs of Alex MacLean in her study of suburban developments in the United States.

24. Smith, *The Everyday World as Problematic.*

Bibliography

Adams, Douglas. *The Hitchhiker's Guide to the Galaxy.* London: Heinemann, 1995.

"AFRC Takes Bookings for New Resort Hotel." *Stars and Stripes,* November 27, 2003.

Agar, Michael. *Professional Stranger: An Informal Introduction to Ethnography.* Orlando, Fla.: Academic Press, 1980.

Allen, David. "Bases Push Residents to Change Trash Habits." *Stars and Stripes,* July 5, 2004.

———. "Japan's Defense Chief Visits U.S. Bases on Okinawa." *Stars and Stripes,* December 29, 2000.

———. "Nago, Okinawa Mayoral Election Focusing on U.S. Air Station Proposal." *Stars and Stripes,* February 2, 2002.

———. "Okinawa Might Build School on MCCS Golf Course Site." *Stars and Stripes,* December 7, 2002.

———. "Papers Bolster Evidence of Secret Okinawa Deal." *Stars and Stripes,* July 3, 2002.

Allen, David, and Chiyomi Sumida. "City Mayors Ask Kadena to Cancel Thunderbirds F-16 Aerial Demonstration after Helo Accident." *Stars and Stripes,* August 26, 2004.

———. "Crimes Tied to U.S. Military Drop on Okinawa." *Stars and Stripes,* July 24, 2004.

———. "Frustration Reigns over Futenma's Future." *Stars and Stripes,* April 19, 2004.

———. "General Visits with Okinawa Governor, Hears Call for Troop Reduction." *Stars and Stripes,* June 15, 2002.

———. "Group Says Offshore Base to Replace Futenma Would Endanger Coral Reefs." *Stars and Stripes,* July 8, 2004.

———. "Helicopter Crash Provides Spark for Opponents of Futenma Base." *Stars and Stripes,* August 19, 2004.

———. "Japan Defense Minister Visits Okinawa to Address 'Military Related Problems.'" *Stars and Stripes,* August 26, 2001.

———. "Mayor OKs Navy Ramp Move at Kadena." *Stars and Stripes,* August 5, 2003.

———. "Mayoral Election Could Be Key to Japan Realignment Plan." *Stars and Stripes,* January 18, 2006.

———. "Noise from Kadena Exercise Rankles Town." *Stars and Stripes,* August 27, 2003.

———. "Okinawa: Crimes by Americans on Rise." *Stars and Stripes,* September 15, 2002.

———. "Okinawans Say Aircraft Noise Is Increasing; Officials File Protests." *Stars and Stripes,* September 30, 2002.

———. "Pre-Summit Protestors Demand U.S. Withdrawal from Okinawa." *Stars and Stripes,* July 17, 2000.

AlSayyad, Nezar. *Cinematic Urbanism: A History of the Modern from Reel to Real.* New York: Routledge, 2006.

———. *Cities and Caliphs: On the Genesis of Arab Muslim Urbanism.* New York: Greenwood Press, 1991.

———. "Hybrid Culture/Hybrid Urbanism: Pandora's Box of the 'Third Place.'" In *Hybrid Urbanism,* ed. AlSayyad, 2–18.

———, ed. *Hybrid Urbanism: On the Identity Discourse and the Built Environment.* Westport, Conn.: Praeger, 2001.

Amemiya, Kozy. "Reinventing Population Problems in Okinawa: Emigration as a Tool of American Occupation." JPRI Working Paper No. 90. Japan Policy Research Institute, November 2002.

Anderson, Benedict. *Imagined Communities: Reflections on the Origin and Spread of Nationalism.* London: Verso, 1991.

Arana-Barradas, Louis. "Aviano Renaissance." *Airman Magazine,* November 2000.

Archer, John. *Architecture and Suburbia: From English Villa to American Dream House, 1690–2000.* Minneapolis: University of Minnesota Press, 2005.

Army and Air Force Exchange Service. *Annual Report 2002* (accessed October 5, 2004), http://www.aafes.com/pa/annual02.pdf.

Arthur Andersen. "Aviano Housing Initiative: Northern Italy." August 28, 1997. On file at Aviano Air Base.

Aviano Air Base Architectural Compatibility Guide, 2004.

Bacevich, Andrew. *American Empire: The Realities and Consequences of U.S. Diplomacy.* Cambridge: Harvard University Press, 2002.

———, ed. *The Imperial Tense.* Chicago: Ivan R. Dee, 2003.

Banda, Sara. "New Dormitory Standard Means Bigger Rooms." *MiG Alley Flyer,* November 8, 2002.

Bandow, Doug. *Tripwire: Korea and U.S. Foreign Policy in a Changed World.* Washington, D.C.: Cato Institute, 1996.

Barber, Benjamin R. *Jihad vs. McWorld.* New York: Ballantine Books, 1996.

Barnett, Jonathan. *Introduction to Urban Design.* New York: Harper and Row, 1982.

Barnett, Thomas. *The Pentagon's New Map: War and Peace in the Twenty-first Century.* New York: Putnam, 2004.

Barringer, Philip. "The Strategic Importance of the Philippines." In *U.S. Bases Overseas: Negotiations with Spain, Greece, and the Philippines,* ed. John W. McDonald and Diane Bendahmane, 117–20. San Francisco: Westview Press, 1990.

Barstow, David, William J. Broad, and Jeff Gerth. "How the White House Embraced Disputed Arms Intelligence." *New York Times,* October 3, 2004, 1.

"Base, Korean Culture Tied from Beginning." *MiG Alley Flyer,* October 6, 2000.

Bauman, Zygmunt. *Globalization: The Human Consequences.* New York: Columbia University Press, 1998.

Beale, Jonathan. "U.S. Gets Deal on Kyrgyz Air Base," BBC News, October 11, 2005 (accessed January 15, 2006), http://news.bbc.co.uk/2/hi/asia-pacific/4332234.stm.

Beck, Ulrich. *What Is Globalization?* Cambridge: Polity Press, 2000.

Becker, T. J. "Confused Coastals Give Midwest a Bad Rap." *Chicago Tribune,* June 13, 2004.

Ben-Ari, Eyal. *Changing Japanese Suburbia: A Study of Two Present-Day Localities.* London: Kegan Paul International, 1991.

Bhabha, Homi K. "Culture's In-Between." In *Questions of Cultural Identity,* ed. Stuart Hall and Paul du Gay, 53–60. London: Sage, 1996.

Blakely, Edward James, and Mary Gail Snyder. *Fortress America: Gated Communities in the United States.* Washington, D.C.: Brookings Institution Press, 1997.

Blaker, James R. *United States Overseas Basing: An Anatomy of the Dilemma.* New York: Praeger, 1990.

Bongioanni, Carlos. "As Okinawa Landfill Space Dwindles, Recycling Is Urged." *Stars and Stripes,* February 6, 2003.

———. "Gregson Apologizes for Okinawa Plane Mishaps, Promises Remedies." *Stars and Stripes,* May 2, 2002.

———. "Okinawa Governor Urges Tokyo to Pressure U.S. to Ground Jets." *Stars and Stripes,* August 30, 2002.

———. "Okinawa Officials Protest Latest F-15 Crash." *Stars and Stripes,* August 23, 2002.

———. "Servicemembers on Okinawa Are Fighting a Battle of Public Perception." *Stars and Stripes,* August 7, 2001.

———. "Total Base Effort Is Required to Pull Off Americafest at Kadena." *Stars and Stripes,* June 29, 2001.

Bongioanni, Carlos, and Naoko Sekioka. "Okinawan Leaders Express Concerns about Falling Jet Parts." *Stars and Stripes,* April 27, 2002.

Botting, Geoff. "Waging War on the U.S. Presence: Is the U.S. Military in Japan Getting a Fair Deal?" *Japan Times,* September 9, 2003.

Boyer, M. Christine. *Dreaming the Rational City: The Myth of American City Planning.* Cambridge: MIT Press, 1997.

Braider, Jackson. "Geoquiz." In *The World on BBC News,* broadcast December 8, 2004.

Branch, Melville C. *An Atlas of Rare City Maps: Comparative Urban Design, 1830–1842.* New York: Princeton Architectural Press, 1978.

Brandes, Ray. *Frontier Military Posts of Arizona.* Globe, Ariz.: D. S. King, 1960.

Bridges, Andrew. "U.S. Working to Develop New Generation of Attack Planes." *San Francisco Chronicle,* November 28, 2003.

Brooke, James. "First of 2 GIs on Trial in Deaths of 2 Korean Girls Is Acquitted." *New York Times,* November 21, 2002, A9.

Broudehoux, Anne-Marie. "Learning from Chinatown: The Search for a Modern Chinese Architectural Identity, 1911–1998." In *Hybrid Urbanism,* ed. AlSayyad, 156–80.

Bruegmann, Robert. *Sprawl: A Compact History.* Chicago: University of Chicago Press, 2005.

Bullard, Robert. *Dumping in Dixie: Race, Class, and Environmental Quality.* Boulder, Colo.: Westview Press, 1990.

Burawoy, Michael. *Ethnography Unbound: Power and Resistance in the Modern Metropolis.* Berkeley: University of California Press, 1991.

Burchell, Robert, Anthony Downs, Sahan Mukherji, and Barbara McCann. *Sprawl Costs: Economic Impacts of Unchecked Development.* Washington, D.C.: Island Press, 2005.

Burgess, Lisa. "Survey: Airmen Say Air Force a Good Place to Work." *Stars and Stripes,* June 12, 2003.

———. "U.S., S. Korea Set to OK Plan to Consolidate American Military Facilities." *Stars and Stripes,* March 6, 2002.

Butler, Judith. "Performative Acts and Gender Constitution: An Essay in Phenomenology and Feminist Theory." In *Performing Feminisms: Feminist Critical Theory and Theatre,* ed. Sue-Ellen Case, 270–82. Baltimore: Johns Hopkins University Press, 1990.

Campbell, Marie, and Frances Gregor. *Mapping Social Relations: A Primer in Doing Institutional Ethnography.* Aurora, Ont.: Garamond Press, 2002.

Carmona, Michel. *Haussmann: His Life and Times, and the Making of Modern Paris.* Chicago: I. R. Dee, 2002.

Chang, Hee-seung. "Osan Air Base Architectural Compatibility Plan." 51st Civil Engineering Squadron, U.S. Air Force, 2003.

Childs, Jan, Jim Lea, and Jennifer Svan. "Overseas Bases One of the Safest Places to Live." *Stars and Stripes,* August 25, 2002.

Childs, Jan Wesner. "GIs, Spouses See Need for Plan to Improve, Expand Housing in S. Korea." *Stars and Stripes,* July 23, 2001.

Childs, Jan Wesner, and Chiyomi Sumida. "Courtesy Patrols Start This Weekend on Okinawa." *Stars and Stripes,* September 1, 2000.

Choe, Song-won, and Joseph Giordono. "South Koreans Get Look at U.S. Air Base." *Stars and Stripes,* December 10, 2003.

Choe, Song-won, and Jeremy Kirk. "Report: U.S. Could Pull Out of Seoul Entirely." *Stars and Stripes,* November 22, 2003.

Choi, Soung-ah. "Troop Removal May Increase Chances of War." *Korea Herald,* May 21, 2004.

Chomsky, Noam. *Hegemony or Survival: America's Quest for Global Dominance.* New York: Henry Holt, 2003.

Chopra, Preeti. "Pondicherry: A French Enclave." In *Forms of Dominance,* ed. Nezar AlSayyad, 83–107. Brookfield, Vt.: Avebury, 1992.

Cliff, Roger, Sam J. Tangredi, and Christine E. Wormuth. *Q.D.R. 2001 Strategy Driven Choices for America's Security: The Future of U.S. Overseas Presence,* National Defense University, 2000 (accessed October 15, 2004), http://www.ndu.edu/inss/press/QDR_2001/sdcascont.html.

Cobb, Sean. "Construction, Renovations Add Sparkle to DODDS-Europe School Grounds." *Stars and Stripes,* August 15, 2002.

Cody, Jeffrey W. *Exporting American Architecture, 1870–2000.* New York: Routledge, 2002.

Cohen, William. *Personal Accountability for Force Protection at Khobar Towers.* U.S. Department of Defense, July 31, 1997 (accessed October 8, 2004), http://www.defenselink.mil/pubs/khobar/.

Conrad, Joseph. *Nostromo.* 1904; New York: Modern Library, 1983.

Coon, Charlie. "8 Aviano Firefighters Extend 'Resting Period' Strike Time." *Stars and Stripes*, August 8, 2003.

———. "Treaty with Romania Will Allow U.S. Forces to Use Bases." *Stars and Stripes*, December 6, 2005.

———. "Troops on R&R Are Priority at Edelweiss Lodge." *Stars and Stripes*, September 15, 2004.

Crawford, Margaret. *Building the Workingman's Paradise: The Design of American Company Towns*. London: Verso, 1995.

———. "The World in a Shopping Mall." In *Variations on a Theme Park: The New American City and the End of Public Space*, ed. Michael Sorkin, 3–30. New York: Hill and Wang, 1992.

"Crimes Committed and Incidents Concerning U.S. Military on Okinawa." *Okinawa Times*, October 12, 1995.

Crysler, C. Greig. *Writing Spaces: Discourses of Architecture, Urbanism, and the Built Environment, 1960–2000*. London: Routledge, 2003.

Cullen, Lisa Takeuchi. "Sex and Racism in Okinawa." *Time* 158, no. 8 (August 27, 2001).

D'Souza, Dinesh. *What's So Great about America?* New York: Penguin Books, 2003.

Davis, Mike. *City of Quartz: Excavating the Future in Los Angeles*. New York: Vintage Books, 1992.

Defense Commissary Agency, 2004 (accessed October 5, 2004), http://www.commissaries.com/insidedeca.htm.

Deguchi, Tomohiro. "Base Foes Dismayed at Kadena's Longevity." *Japan Times*, March 4, 2004.

Demick, Barbara. "Off-Base Behavior in Korea: By Allowing GIs to Patronize Certain Clubs, the U.S. Military Is Seen as Condoning the Trafficking of Foreign Women for Prostitution." *Los Angeles Times*, September 26, 2002, A-1.

Dexter, Lewis. *Elite and Specialized Interviewing*. Evanston, Ill.: Northwestern University Press, 1970.

Dishner, Jimmy. Conference presentation at the American Planning Association Annual Conference (Federal Planning Division). San Diego, 1997.

———. "Congressional Testimony, 2000." Office of the Undersecretary of Defense, Installations and Environments (accessed July 7, 2004), http://www.acq.osd.mil/housing/ctoo_dishner.htm.

"The Downside of U.S. Bases: A Day of Sorrow Forty Years Later." *Okinawa Times*, July 3, 1999.

Drigo, Roberto. "Project Narrative for U.S. Air Force Design Awards Program." 2001.

Duany, Andres, Elizabeth Plater-Zyberk, and Jeff Speck. *Suburban Nation: The Rise of Sprawl and the Decline of the American Dream*. New York: North Point Press, 2000.

DuBois, Raymond. *Statement before the Subcommittee on Readiness of the House Armed Services Committee*, March 13, 2003 (accessed July 7, 2004), Office of the Undersecretary of Defense for Acquisition, Technology, and Logistics, http://www.acq.osd.mil/ie/irm/irm_library/HASC%20MilCon%20Testimony_04budget.doc.

Dudley, Michael. "Sprawl as Strategy: City Planners Face the Bomb." *Journal of Planning Education and Research* 21 (2001): 52–63.

Dyer, Alfred S. "The Black Hand of Authority in India." *The Sentinel* 2, no. 10 (1888): 19–21.

Eckert, Paul. "Okinawans Want Reduction of U.S. Base." Reuters, October 21, 1995.

Eisenhower, Pres. Dwight D. Executive Order 10713 Providing for Administration of the Ryukyu Islands, June 5, 1957 (accessed August 12, 2003), http://www.niraikanai.wwma.net/pages/archive/eisen.html.

Ellin, Nan. *Postmodern Urbanism*. Cambridge, Mass.: Blackwell, 1996.

Embassy of the Republic of Korea. "Osan-Pyeongtaek to Become Hub of USFK," 2004 (accessed October 1, 2004), http://www.koreaemb.org/archive/2003/04/foreign/foreign7.asp.

Enloe, Cynthia. *Bananas, Beaches, and Bases: Making Feminist Sense of International Politics*. Berkeley: University of California Press, 1990.

———. "A Feminist Perspective on Foreign Military Bases." In *The Sun Never Sets . . . Confronting the Network of Foreign U.S. Military Bases*, ed. Joseph Gerson and Bruce Birchard, 95–106. Boston: South End Press, 1991.

———. "It Takes Two." In *Let the Good Times Roll,* ed. Sturdevant and Stoltzfus, 22–27.

"Fast Facts: Big Truck Bomb Strikes." Fox News Channel, 2004 (accessed October 4, 2004), http://www.foxnews.com/story/0,2933,128610,00.html.

Ferguson, Niall. *Colossus: The Price of America's Empire*. New York: Penguin Press, 2004.

———. *Empire: The Rise and Demise of the British World Order and the Lessons for Global Power*. London: Basic Books, 2002.

Filkins, Dexter. "The Reach of War: Insurgents; 2 Bombers Kill 5 in Guarded Area in Iraq's Capital." *New York Times,* October 15, 2004, A-1.

"Final SACO Report Announced." *Okinawa Times,* December 9, 1996.

Fisher, Franklin. "Agency Streamlines Korea Map-Ordering." *Stars and Stripes,* June 8, 2003.

———. "Commander Proud of Improving Life in Korea's Area IV." *Stars and Stripes,* July 9, 2002.

———. "Giving Back Land." *Stars and Stripes,* July 17, 2001.

———. "Golf Course Renovations Fit Base to a Tee." *Stars and Stripes,* July 20, 2002.

———. "Huge One-Stop Shopping Mall Being Built at Osan." *Stars and Stripes,* October 24, 2003.

———. "Kunsan Commissary to Expand Size, Inventory." *Stars and Stripes,* April 17, 2004.

———. "New Bowling Alley Opens at Camp Humphreys." *Stars and Stripes,* April 6, 2004.

———. "Thunderbirds a Roaring Success." *Stars and Stripes,* September 21, 2004.

———. "U.S., S. Korea Sign Pact to Reduce Bases; Troop Levels Not Affected." *Stars and Stripes,* March 21, 2002.

Fisher, Franklin, and Choe Song-won. "Pilot Rescued from Sea after F-16 Crash Off Korea." *Stars and Stripes,* September 11, 2003.

Flack, T. D. "Drinking Problems Decrease in Korea." *Stars and Stripes,* December 29, 2002.

———. "Osan Emergency Workers Respond to Base Fuel Spill." *Stars and Stripes,* January 16, 2003.

———. "U-2 Plane Crashes in South Korea." *Stars and Stripes,* January 28, 2003.

Flack, T. D., and Choe Song-won. "S. Korean Merchants, Fearing Protesters Will Scare Off Clients, Defend U.S. Bases." *Stars and Stripes,* May 10, 2003.

Flint, Anthony. "Sept. 11 Pushes Firms to Suburbs." *Boston Globe,* August 18, 2002, A1.

Foucault, Michel. *Discipline and Punish: The Birth of the Prison.* Translated by Alan Sheridan. 2nd ed. New York: Random House, 1995.

Francis, Carolyn Bowen. "Women and Military Violence." In *Okinawa: Cold War Island,* ed. Chalmers Johnson, 189–204. Cardiff, Calif.: Japan Policy Research Institute, 1999.

Freeman, Derek. *Margaret Mead and Samoa: The Making and Unmaking of an Anthropological Myth.* Cambridge: Harvard University Press, 1983.

French, Howard. "Official Says U.S. Will Reposition Its Troops in South Korea." *New York Times,* June 3, 2003, A-6.

Friedman, Jonathan. "The Hybridization of Roots and the Abhorrence of the Bush." In *Spaces of Culture,* ed. M. Featherstone and S. Lash, 230–56. London: Sage, 1999.

Fuchs, Ron, and Gilbert Herbert. "A Colonial Portrait of Jerusalem: British Architecture in Mandate-Era Palestine." In *Hybrid Urbanism,* ed. AlSayyad, 83–108.

"Fukudo Hails Election Results." *Japan Times,* February 5, 2002.

Fukuyama, Francis. "The End of America's Exceptionalism." *Financial Times,* September 16, 2001.

Fuller, Mia. "Building Power: Italy's Colonial Architecture and Urbanism, 1923–1940." *Cultural Anthropology* 3, no. 4 (1988): 455–87.

Gans, Herbert. *The Levittowners: Ways of Life and Politics in a New Suburban Community.* New York: Pantheon Books, 1967.

Garamone, Jim. *DoD's Privatized Housing Program Hits High Gear.* Department of Defense American Forces News Service, February 16, 1999 (accessed October 4, 2004), http://www.dod.gov/news/Feb1999/n02161999_9902162.html.

———. "New BAH Rates among Largest in History." *MiG Alley Flyer,* January 12, 2001.

Giddens, Anthony. *Runaway World: How Globalization Is Reshaping Our Lives.* New York: Routledge, 2000.

Gilroy, Paul. "Diaspora and the Detours of Identity." In *Identity and Difference,* ed. Kathryn Woodward, 299–343. London: Sage, 1997.

Giordono, Joseph. "Base Shift Report Garners Little Reaction in the Pacific." *Stars and Stripes,* May 21, 2004.

———. "Completion of Yongsan Garrison Move Pushed to 2008." *Stars and Stripes,* July 26, 2004.

———. "S. Korea to Set Aside Land for Base Growth." *Stars and Stripes,* August 21, 2004.

Girouard, Mark. *Cities and People: A Social and Architectural History.* New Haven: Yale University Press, 1985.

Gittler, Juliana. "Illegal Dumping a Big Mess for Bases." *Stars and Stripes,* August 8, 2004.

Gottdiener, Mark. *The Social Production of Urban Space.* 2nd ed. Austin: University of Texas Press, 1994.

Graham, Bradley. "Army Plans to Keep Iraq Troop Level through '06." *Washington Post,* January 25, 2006, A1.

Green Korea United. *Report on Land Readjustment Plan 2002* (accessed October 5, 2004), http://www.korea.army.mil/LPP/LPPHomepage.asp.

Greene, Graham. *The Quiet American.* New York: Viking Press, 1956.

Greider, William. *Fortress America: The American Military and the Consequences of Peace.* New York: Public Affairs, 1998.

Grier, Peter. "Ellsworth Fraud Case Settled." *Air Force Magazine: Journal of the Air Force Association* 83, no. 5 (1999).

GRW Engineers. "Kadena Air Base Housing Redevelopment Plan." Kadena Air Base, 1997.

———. "Survey of User Perceptions: Kadena Air Base." Kadena Air Base, November 18, 1997.

Hall, Stuart. "Cultural Identity and Diaspora." In *Identity and Difference,* ed. Kathryn Woodward, 51–59. London: Sage, 1997.

Hamadeh, Shirine. "Creating the Traditional City: A French Project." In *Forms of Dominance,* ed. Nezar AlSayyad, 241–59. Brookfield, Vt.: Avebury, 1992.

Harkavy, Robert E. *Bases Abroad: The Global Foreign Military Presence.* Oxford: Oxford University Press, 1989.

Harris, Emily. "Five Killed by Two Blasts in Green Zone." *All Things Considered.* National Public Radio, October 14, 2004.

Harris, Kent. "Airmen Feasting at New Club, Lodge in Aviano." *Stars and Stripes,* November 25, 2003.

———. "Ambitious Aviano 2000 Program Enters Heavy Construction Stage." *Stars and Stripes,* August 31, 2001.

———. "Americans Make the Most of Recreation Options near Camp Darby." *Stars and Stripes,* May 12, 2002.

———. "Aviano 2000 Projects: 97 Down, Two to Go." *Stars and Stripes,* December 7, 2005.

———. "Aviano 2000 Reviewed." *Stars and Stripes,* November 21, 2002.

———. "Aviano Projects Set to Reach New Milestones." *Stars and Stripes,* August 18, 2002.

———. "Aviano School Opens Its Doors." *Stars and Stripes,* September 4, 2002.

———. "Aviano's Long Housing Nightmare Easing as Construction Projects Are Completed." *Stars and Stripes,* December 8, 2001.

———. "Contractor for Aviano School Is Fired." *Stars and Stripes,* September 7, 2000.

———. "First of New Aviano Dorms Almost Ready for Occupation." *Stars and Stripes,* June 12, 2002.

———. "New Mini-Mall Big Hit with Aviano Shoppers." *Stars and Stripes,* May 31, 2004.

———. "Parking Problems on Bases across Europe." *Stars and Stripes,* January 3, 2003.

———. "Retiring Colonel Says Aviano Is Part of His Soul." *Stars and Stripes,* June 6, 2005.

Hart, Stanley I., and Alvin L. Spivak. *The Elephant in the Bedroom: Automobile Dependence and Denial—Impacts on the Economy and Environment.* Pasadena, Calif.: New Paradigm Books, 1993.

Harvey, David. *The Urban Experience.* Baltimore: Johns Hopkins University Press, 1989.

Hayano, David. "Auto-Ethnography: Paradigms, Problems, and Prospects." *Human Organization* 38, no. 1 (1979): 99–104.

Hayden, Dolores. *Building Suburbia: Green Fields and Urban Growth, 1820–2000.* New York: Pantheon Books, 2003.

Hefemeister, Rod. "Dorms 4 Airmen: Housing Design Features Private Bed, Bath, and Communal Kitchen." *Air Force Times,* September 15, 2003.

Heldman, Keven. "Itaewon, South Korea. On the Town with the U.S. Military." Korea Web Weekly, 1996 (accessed October 5, 2004), http://www.kimsoft.com/korea/us-army.htm.

Hendrickson, Kenneth E. *The Spanish-American War.* Westport, Conn.: Greenwood Press, 2003.

Her Majesty's Stationary Office. *Statistical Abstract Relating to British India from 1894–95 to 1903–04: Age of Men of All Arms Serving in India* 1905 (accessed October 5, 2004), http://dsal.uchicago.edu/digbooks/digpager.html?BOOKID=statistical_1894&object=228.

———. *Statistical Abstract Relating to British India from 1894–95 to 1903–04: Established Strength of European and Native Armies in British India* 1896 (accessed October 5, 2004), http://dsal.uchicago.edu/digbooks/digpager.html?BOOKID=Statistics_1885&object=243.

———. *Statistical Abstract Relating to British India from 1894–95 to 1903–04: Sickness, Mortality, and Invaliding in European Army* 1905 (accessed October 5, 2004), http://dsal.uchicago.edu/digbooks/digpager.html?BOOKID=statistical_1894&object=235.

Honda, Masaru. "Sympathy Budget to Be Reduced 1.2% for First Cutback; Bureaucrats Lead Diplomacy for Fine-Tuning." *Asahi Shimbun,* July 23, 2000.

Huddy, Doug. "Overseas Commissaries Offer Servicemembers a Taste of Home." *Stars and Stripes,* December 16, 2001.

Hunt, Aurora. *The Army of the Pacific.* Mechanicsburg, Pa.: Stackpole Books, 2004.

Hunt, Elvid, Walter Ernest Lorence, and Charles Michael Bundel. *History of Fort Leavenworth, 1827–1937.* 2nd ed. Fort Leavenworth, Kan.: Command and General Staff School Press, 1937.

Hurst, Rob. "Okuma!" *Venture Magazine,* July 2001.

Hwang, Jang-jin. "Koreans Handled 5.5% of Crimes Committed by U.S. Soldiers." *Korean Herald,* July 27, 2002.

Ignatieff, Michael. "The American Empire: The Burden." *New York Times,* January 5, 2003, 22.

"Ishihara Rants after Tour of U.S. Military Park." *Japan Times,* September 17, 1999.

Jackson, Kenneth T. *Crabgrass Frontier: The Suburbanization of the United States.* New York: Oxford University Press, 1985.

Jacobs, Allan B. *Great Streets.* Cambridge: MIT Press, 1993.

Jacobs, Jane. *The Death and Life of Great American Cities.* New York: Vintage Books, 1961.

Jacobs, Jane M. *Edge of Empire: Postcolonialism and the City.* London: Routledge, 1996.

Jameson, Sam. "People's Rally of October 21, 1995." *Los Angeles Times,* October 22, 1995.

Japan, Government of. *Okinawa Prefecture Population Data* 2000 (accessed October 1, 2004), http://web-japan.org/stat/category_01.html.

———. Ministry of Foreign Affairs. *The Japan-U.S. Special Action Committee (SACO) Interim Report, 1996* (accessed June 17, 2003), http://www.mofa.go.jp/region/n-america/us/security/seco.html.

Johnson, Chalmers. "The 1995 Rape Incident and the Rekindling of Okinawan Protest against the American Bases." In *Okinawa: Cold War Island,* ed. Chalmers Johnson, 109–29. Cardiff, Calif.: Japan Policy Research Institute, 1999.

———. *Blowback: The Costs and Consequences of American Empire.* New York: Metropolitan Books, 2000.

———. "Further Nago Notes." Japan Policy Research Institute Critique 7, no. 2 (February 2000).

———. *The Sorrows of Empire: Militarism, Secrecy, and the End of the Republic.* New York: Metropolitan Books, 2004.

Johnson, Sheila K. *Of Sex, Okinawa, and American Foreign Policy.* Japan Policy Research Institute, Occasional Paper No. 23, September 2001.

Jones, General James L. Letter to the editor. *Los Angeles Times,* July 22, 2001.

"Kadena Cut Causes Naha Hemorrhage." *Okinawa Times,* November 10, 1999.

Kaminsky, Arnold. "Morality Legislation and British Troops in Late Nineteenth-Century India." *Military Affairs* 43, no. 2 (1979): 78–84.

Kanno, Neil. "Creech's 'Five-P's' Alive and Well at Osan." *MiG Alley Flyer,* January 11, 2002.

Kaplan, Robert D. *Imperial Grunts: The American Military on the Ground.* New York: Random House, 2005.

Katz, Peter. *The New Urbanism: Toward an Architecture of Community.* New York: McGraw-Hill, 1993.

Kay, Jane Holtz. *Asphalt Nation: How the Automobile Took over America, and How We Can Take It Back.* New York: Crown, 1997.

Kelbaugh, Doug. "Into the Abyss." *Urban Land,* June 1999, 46–49.

Khalidi, Rashid. *Resurrecting Empire: Western Footprints and America's Perilous Path in the Middle East.* Boston: Beacon Press, 2004.

Killingray, David. "Guardians of Empire." In *Guardians of Empire: The Armed Forces of the Colonial Powers, c. 1700–1964,* ed. David Killingray and David Omissi, 1–24. Manchester: Manchester University Press, 1999.

Kim, Ji-ho. "GIs Chalk Up 32 Billion Won in Damages." *Korea Herald,* January 31, 2003.

———. "U.S. Military Causes Problems to Residents: Survey." *Korea Herald,* December 18, 2002.

Kim, Kwang-tae. "U.S. Base Expansion Could Force Evictions." *Eugene Register Guard,* March 19, 2006.

Kim, Mun-hee. "Will American GIs Pack up and Go Home?" *Korea Economic Report* 18, no. 3 (2003): 14–20.

King, Anthony. "Rethinking Colonialism." In *Forms of Dominance,* ed. Nezar AlSayyad, 339–55. Brookfield, Vt.: Avebury, 1992.

———. *Spaces of Global Cultures: Architecture, Urbanism, Identity.* London: Routledge, 2004.

———. "Values, Science, and Settlement: A Case Study in Environmental Control." In *The Mutual Interaction of People and Their Built Environment,* ed. Amos Rapoport, 365–89. Paris: Mouton, 1976.

Kirk, Don. "2nd U.S. Sergeant Is Cleared in the Death of 2 Korean Girls." *New York Times,* November 22, 2003.

———. "U.S. Pushing Realignment of Troops in South Korea." *New York Times,* June 1, 2003.

Kirk, Jeremy. "General: Despite Housing Conditions, Many in USFK Taking Bonus to Stay." *Stars and Stripes,* April 7, 2004.

———. "Kim Affirms Importance of USFK." *Stars and Stripes,* January 5, 2003.

———. "Korean News Report: Bribes Can Produce Access to U.S. Facilities." *Stars and Stripes,* February 2, 2001.

———. "Work Starts on New Commissary, Barracks in S. Korea." *Stars and Stripes,* December 12, 2003.

Kirk, Jeremy, and Franklin Fisher. "Army: No Timetable for South Korea Move." *Stars and Stripes,* June 10, 2003.

Kirk, Jeremy, and Choe Song-won. "Kunsan Noise Plaintiffs Win Damages." *Stars and Stripes,* January 30, 2004.

Kleveman, Lutz. *The New Great Game: Blood and Oil in Central Asia.* New York: Atlantic Monthly Press, 2003.

Kohn, Richard. "The Early Retirement of Gen. Ronald R. Fogleman, Chief of Staff, United States Air Force." *Aerospace Power Journal* 15, no. 1 (Spring 2001).

Korea Central News Agency. *U.S. "Return" of Its Bases Dismissed as Hypocritical,* 2002 (accessed October 5, 2004), http://www.kcna.co.jp/contents/27.htm#3.

Kosowatz, John. "Aviano Air Base Falls Into Step under Central Line of Command." *Engineering News Record,* July 22, 2002.

———. "Winging It Home at Aviano Air Base." *Engineering News Record,* July 22, 2002.

Kozaryn, Linda D. *Clinton Salutes U.S., Allied Troops.* American Forces Information Service, 1999 (accessed October 5, 2004), http://www.defense.gov/news/Jun1999/n06231999_9906236.html.

———. *U.S. Leaders Call for Japan's Support.* United States Department of Defense American Forces Information Service, March 17, 2000 (accessed October 15, 2004), http://www.defense.gov/news/Mar2000/n03172000_20003171.html.

Kostof, Spiro. *The City Assembled: The Elements of Urban Form through History.* London: Thames and Hudson, 1992.

Kulman, Linda. "Our Consuming Interest." *U.S. News and World Report,* June 28, 2004.

Kunich, Gary. "Aviano School Opening Is Way Behind Schedule." *Stars and Stripes,* August 15, 2000.

———. "New Base Exchange, Commissary Open at Aviano." *Stars and Stripes,* November 8, 2000.

Kunstler, James Howard. *The Geography of Nowhere.* New York: Simon and Schuster, 1993.

Kusumoto, Hana, and Greg Tyler. "Iwakuni Runway Project Revs Local Interest." *Stars and Stripes,* October 12, 2003.

Laguerre, Michel. *The Global Ethnopolis: Chinatown, Japantown and Manilatown in American Society.* New York: St. Martin's Press, 2000.

Lamprakos, Michele. "Le Corbusier and Algiers: The Plan Obus as Colonial Urbanism." In *Forms of Dominance,* ed. Nezar AlSayyad, 183–210. Brookfield, Vt.: Avebury, 1992.

"Land Purchasing for Base Relocation to Start Next Year." *Korea Times,* October 5, 2003.

"Landowner Visits Property on Base; Thorny Legal Question Remains." *Okinawa Times*, May 20, 1996.

Langdon, Philip. *A Better Place to Live: Reshaping the American Suburb.* New York: HarperPerennial, 1995.

Lea, Jim. "Ambassador Offers Regrets for Seoul Chemical Dumping." *Stars and Stripes*, July 25, 2000.

———. "Camp Humphreys Master Plan Includes New Shopping Facilities, Family Housing." *Stars and Stripes*, April 11, 2001.

———. "Construction Boom Is On at Osan; Mall, Hotel among $106M in Improvements." *Stars and Stripes*, June 30, 2001.

———. "Korean Groups Demand USFK Leader's Resignation." *Stars and Stripes*, July 16, 2000.

———. "Military Families in S. Korea Deal with Displacement from Off-Base Homes." *Stars and Stripes*, September 15, 2001.

———. "Mission, Aesthetics Balancing Out as Improvements Abound at Humphreys." *Stars and Stripes*, June 30, 2001.

———. "New Osan Commander Hopes More Families Are in S. Korea Base's Future." *Stars and Stripes*, April 30, 2002.

———. "U.S. Forces Korea Launches Environmental Protection Program." *Stars and Stripes*, June 22, 2001.

———. "U.S. Pilot Dies as F-16 Crashes into South Korean Rice Paddy." *Stars and Stripes*, June 14, 2001.

———. "U.S. Seeking Proposals from Korean Developers to Build Camp Humphreys Housing Area." *Stars and Stripes*, December 18, 2001.

Lea, Jim, and Bae Gi-chul. "Local Governments Seek Subsidies for Lost Revenue Blamed on Military." *Stars and Stripes*, June 21, 2001.

———. "South Koreans Worry Business Will Suffer If GI Tours Change." *Stars and Stripes*, December 21, 2001.

Leach, Neil. "Belonging." Paper presented at the International Association for the Study of Traditional Environments, Hong Kong, 2002.

Lederer, William J., and Eugene Burdick. *The Ugly American.* New York: Norton, 1958.

Lee, Jae-hee. "Seoul City to Investigate Contaminated Spring Water near U.S. Military Base." *Korea Herald*, July 6, 2002.

Lee, May. "U. S. Returns More Land to Okinawa." CNN, April 15, 1996 (accessed November 1, 2004), http://www.cnn.com/WORLD/9604/15/perry.japan/.

Lee, Sang-hae. "Continuity and Consistency of the Traditional Courtyard House Plan in Modern Korean Dwellings." *Traditional Dwellings and Settlements Review* 3, no. 1 (1991).

Lee, Suk-bok. *The Impact of U.S. Forces in Korea.* Washington, D.C.: National Defense University Press, 1987.

Lee, Tae-hun. "Gyeonggi Governor Embraces Troop Relocation." *Chosun Ilbo*, June 17, 2003.

Lefebvre, Henri. *The Production of Space.* Translated by Donald Nicholson-Smith. Cambridge, Mass.: Blackwell, 1991.

"Legal Basis Given to Lease for Bases." *Okinawa Times*, April 19, 1997.

Lehrer, Jim. "Dirty Bomb Arrest." *Newshour* (PBS), June 10, 2002 (accessed October 6,

2004), http://www.pbs.org/newshour/bb/terrorism/jan-june02/dirtybomb_6–10
.html.

Lerner, Mitchell B. *The Pueblo Incident: A Spy Ship and the Failure of American Foreign Policy.* Lawrence: University Press of Kansas, 2002.

Levine, Philippa. "Rereading the 1890s: Venereal Disease as 'Constitutional Crisis' in Britain and British India." *Journal of Asian Studies* 55, no. 3 (1996): 585–612.

Liewer, Steve. "Study Weighs Costs, Benefits of Options in Shifting U.S. Forces Overseas." *Stars and Stripes,* May 19, 2004.

Limón, Martin. *Jade Lady Burning.* New York: Soho Press, 1992.

Louis, William Roger, and Hedley Bull. *The "Special Relationship": Anglo-American Relations since 1945.* New York: Oxford University Press, 1986.

Lovelace, Eldridge. *Harland Bartholomew: His Contributions to American Urban Planning.* Urbana: University of Illinois Department of Urban and Regional Planning, 1993.

Low, Setha M. *Behind the Gates: Life, Security, and the Pursuit of Happiness in Fortress America.* New York: Routledge, 2003.

Lu, Duanfang. "The Changing Landscape of Hybridity: A Reading of Ethnic Identity and Urban Form in Vancouver." *Traditional Dwellings and Settlements Review* 11, no. 2 (2000): 19–28.

Lundestad, Geir. *The American Empire and Other Studies of U.S. Foreign Policy in a Comparative Perspective.* Oxford: Oxford University Press, 1990.

Lundy, Jack. "Comprehensive Planning." Lecture at the Air Force Institute of Technology, August 2, 2004.

MacArthur, General Douglas. "Memorandum on Concept Governing Security in Postwar Japan," 1950 (accessed August 12, 2003), http://www.niraikanai.wwma .net/pages/archive/mac.html.

Maeda, Toshi. "Economic Disparities, Bases Frustrate Okinawa." *Japan Times,* March 29, 2002.

Maeda, Toshi, and Sumiko Oshima. "Base Not Ishihara's Only Target." *Japan Times,* June 28, 1999.

Mahan, Alfred T. *The Influence of Sea Power Upon History, 1660–1783.* London: S. Low Marston, 1890.

Mann, Michael. *Incoherent Empire.* London: Verso, 2003.

Marcus, George. *Ethnography through Thick and Thin.* Princeton, N.J.: Princeton University Press, 1998.

Markusen, Ann, Scott Campbell, Peter Hall, and Sabina Deitrick. *The Rise of the Gunbelt: The Military Remapping of Industrial America.* New York: Oxford University Press, 1991.

Marshall, Alex. "Eurosprawl." *Metropolis* 14, no. 6 (January/February 1995).

Marx, Karl, and Frederick Engels. *Manifesto of the Communist Party.* Translated by Samuel Moore (1888). Moscow: Progress Publishers, 1969.

McCormack, Gavan, and Julia Yonetani. "The Okinawan Summit Seen from Below." *Japan Policy Research Institute Working Paper,* no. 71 (September 2000).

McEntee, Marni. "Programs to Improve USAFE Begin with Bettering the Look of Its Bases." *Stars and Stripes,* December 14, 2003.

———. "Reduction Plan Likely Won't Affect Already-Transformed USAFE." *Stars and Stripes,* August 19, 2004.

McMichael, William H. "Sex Slaves and the U.S. Military." *Air Force Times,* August 19, 2002.

Mead, Margaret. *Coming of Age in Samoa: A Psychological Study of Primitive Youth for Western Civilizations.* New York: Morrow, 1961.

Mikanagi, Yumiko. "Okinawa: Women, Bases, and U.S.-Japan Relations." *International Relations of the Asia-Pacific* 4 (2004): 97–111.

Millard, Mike. "Okinawa: Then and Now." In *Okinawa: Cold War Island,* ed. Chalmers Johnson, 93–108. Cardiff, Calif.: Japan Policy Research Institute, 1999.

"Misconceived Military Shuffle" (editorial). *New York Times,* August 17, 2004.

Mitchell, Katharyne. "Global Diasporas and Traditional Towns: Chinese Transnational Migration and the Redevelopment of Vancouver's Chinatown." *Traditional Dwellings and Settlements Review* 11, no. 2 (2000): 7–18.

Mochizuki, Mike M. "Japan-U.S. Relations Chair in Memory of Gaston Sigur Inaugural Lecture." Sigur Center for Asian Studies, George Washington University, Washington, D.C., 1999.

Moon, Katharine H. S. *Sex among Allies: Military Prostitution in U.S.-Korea Relations.* New York: Columbia University Press, 1997.

Mumford, Lewis. *The City in History: Its Origins, Its Transformation, and Its Prospects.* New York: Harcourt Brace, 1961.

Murakami, Asako. "Kadena Air Base Noise Stirs Memories of War." *Japan Times,* July 20, 2000.

Na, Jeong-ju. "Media Reps Focus on Anti-U.S. Feelings." *Korea Times,* January 9, 2003.

"Nago City Council Accepts Main Base." *Okinawa Times,* December 25, 1999.

Nam, Chang-hee. "Relocating USFK Bases: Background and Implications." *East Asian Review* 15, no. 3 (2003).

National Public Radio. "Who Is Serving in the Military." *Talk of the Nation,* March 11, 2003.

Navarro, Mireya. "It's Koreatown, Jake." *New York Times,* August 8, 2004.

"New Sites Proposed for USFK Housing." *Korea Times,* December 18, 2001.

Newman, Oscar. *Defensible Space: Crime Prevention through Urban Design.* New York: Macmillan, 1972.

Niringiye, Zac. "Mission: A Journey of Conversion. A Lecture at the First Presbyterian Church of Berkeley." Berkeley, Calif., October 3, 2004.

Norgen, John. "Patrol Keeps Night Life Safe at Osan." *MiG Alley Flyer,* May 19, 2000.

Nuttall, Zelia. "Royal Ordinances Concerning the Laying Out of New Towns." *Hispanic American Historical Review* 5, no. 2 (1922): 249–54.

Nye, Joseph, Jr. "Propaganda Isn't the Way: Soft Power." *International Herald Tribune,* July 10, 2003.

———. *Soft Power: The Means to Success in World Politics.* New York: Public Affairs, 2004.

"Off-Limits." *Wolf Pack Warrior,* July 13, 2001.

Office of Management and Budget. *Budget Summary,* 2004 (accessed October 5, 2004), http://www.whitehouse.gov/omb/budget/fy2004/summary.html.

"Official: U.S. Wants Base Talks with Japan." *Air Force Times,* August 2, 2004.

Ogden, Maj. Gen. David. Civil Administration Proclamation No. 26. December 5, 1953 (accessed August 12, 2003), http://www.niraikanai.wwma.net/pages/archive/caproc26.html.

"The Okinawa Referendum." *Okinawa Times,* September 10, 1996.

"Okinawa to Vote on Base Presence." *Okinawa Times,* September 2, 1996.

Oliva, Mark. "Chatan Mayor, Council Want Curfew for Servicemembers, More Safety Patrols." *Stars and Stripes,* July 14, 2001.

———. "Chili's Restaurant to Serve Up Spice at Okinawa Base." *Stars and Stripes,* October 3, 2002.

O'Mara, Margaret. *Cities of Knowledge: Cold War Science and the Search for the Next Silicon Valley.* Princeton, N.J.: Princeton University Press, 2004.

O'Sullivan, John. "Annexation." *United States Magazine and Democratic Review* 17, no. 85 (1845): 5–9.

O'Sullivan, Kalani. "Off-Base Issues: Prostitution and A-Town." 2003 (accessed May 6, 2004), http://kalaniosullivan.com/KunsanAB/8thFW/howitwasb11d6.html.

Ota, Masahide. "Governor of Okinawa at the Supreme Court of Japan." *Ryukyuanist,* no. 35 (1996).

———. "Re-Examining the History of the Battle of Okinawa." In *Okinawa: Cold War Island,* ed. Chalmers Johnson, 13–37. Cardiff, Calif.: Japan Policy Research Institute, 1999.

Peers, Douglas M. "Imperial Vice: Sex, Drink, and the Health of British Troops in North Indian Cantonments, 1800–1858." In *Guardians of Empire: The Armed Forces of the Colonial Powers c. 1700–1964,* ed. David Killingray and David E. Omissi, 25–52. Manchester: Manchester University Press, 1999.

Pike, Kenneth. *Language in Relation to a Unified Theory of the Structure of Human Behavior.* The Hague: Mouton, 1967.

Pollan, Michael. "Grass Gardens." *Sanctuary: Journal of the Massachusetts Audubon Society* (May/June 1995).

Purves, John. "Island of Military Bases: A Contemporary Political and Economic History of Okinawa." Master's thesis, International University of Japan, 1995.

Rabinow, Paul. "Colonialism, Modernity: The French in Morocco." In *Forms of Dominance,* ed. Nezar AlSayyad, 167–82. Brookfield, Vt.: Avebury, 1992.

———. *French Modern: Norms and Forms of the Social Environment.* Cambridge: MIT Press, 1989.

Rabson, Steve. "Assimilation Policy in Okinawa: Promotion, Resistance, and 'Reconstruction.'" In *Okinawa: Cold War Island,* ed. Chalmers Johnson, 133–48. Cardiff, Calif.: Japan Policy Research Institute, 1999.

Ramsey, Maureen. *District Supports U.S. Force in Japan.* Japan Engineer District, U.S. Army Corps of Engineers, 2000 (accessed April 14, 2003), http://www.hq.usace.army.mil/cepa/pubs/juloo/story10.htm.

Rapoport, Amos. *House Form and Culture.* Englewood Cliffs, N.J.: Prentice-Hall, 1969.

———. "On Cultural Landscapes." *Traditional Dwellings and Settlements Review* 3, no. 2 (1992): 33–47.

Ray, Joshua C. "Higher-Ups Put Safety Second: Letter to the Editor." *Stars and Stripes,* November 22, 2003.

Reed, Robert. "From Suprabarangay to Colonial Capital." In *Forms of Dominance,* ed. Nezar AlSayyad, 45–81. Brookfield, Vt.: Avebury, 1992.

Reed-Danahay, Deborah, ed. *Auto Ethnography: Rewriting the Self and the Social.* New York: Berg, 1997.

"Relocation of U.S. Troops Hits Snag." *Register-Guard,* March 27, 2006, A2.

"Rising Anti-American Sentiment." *Korea Times,* May 3, 2002.

Rizzo, Russ. "Romania Moving Closer to Base Access Deal with U.S." *Stars and Stripes,* July 25, 2005.

———. "Spain Lifts Hurdles to NATO Funding of Aviano Projects." *Stars and Stripes,* April 8, 2005.

Roberts, Chuck. "Aviano 2000 in Full Throttle." *Airman Magazine,* April 2004.

Roosevelt, Theodore. *The Winning of the West.* 1894; New York: G. P. Putnam's Sons, 1989.

Roy, Ananya. *City Requiem, Calcutta: Gender and the Politics of Poverty.* Minneapolis: University of Minnesota Press, 2003.

Roy, Arundhati. *An Ordinary Person's Guide to Empire.* Cambridge, Mass.: South End Press, 2004.

Said, Edward W. *Culture and Imperialism.* New York: Random House, 1993.

———. "Representing the Colonized: Anthropology's Interlocutors." *Critical Inquiry* 15 (1989): 205–25.

Sandars, C. T. *America's Overseas Garrisons: The Leasehold Empire.* Oxford: Oxford University Press, 2000.

Sanger, David. "South Korean Leader Wants U.S. Troops to Stay, for Now." *New York Times,* May 13, 2003, A20.

Sanger, David, and Dexter Filkins. "U.S. Is Pessimistic Turks Will Accept Aid Deal on Iraq." *New York Times,* February 20, 2003, A1.

"Scandal over Base Lease Payments." *Okinawa Times,* March 16, 2002.

Schlosser, Eric. *Fast Food Nation: The Dark Side of the All-American Meal.* New York: Perennial, 2002.

Schrader, Esther. "Pentagon Plans Major Shift of Troops Throughout Asia." *Pittsburgh Post Gazette,* June 1, 2003.

Schutz, Alfred. *The Phenomenology of the Social World.* London: Heinemann, 1972.

Science Applications International Corporation. "Okinawa Housing Requirements and Market Analysis: 2003–2008." 2003.

Sebald, W. J. "Emperor of Japan's Opinion Concerning the Future of the Ryukyu Islands," 1947 (accessed August 12, 2003), http://www.niraikanai.wwma.net/pages/archive/emp2.html.

Sennett, Richard. "Growth and Failure: The New Political Economy and Its Culture." In *Spaces of Culture: City, Nation, World,* ed. Scott Lash and Mike Featherstone, 14–26. London: Sage, 1999.

Seo, Soo-min. "Expansion Plan for Osan Sparks Controversy." *Korea Times,* April 28, 2003.

"Service Demographics Offer Snapshot of Force." *Hilltop Times,* August 2, 2001.

"Sexually Transmitted Diseases." *Wolf Pack Warrior,* July 13, 2001.

Shimoyachi, Nao. "Pullout of U.S. Forces Could Skip Japan: Presence May Actually Increase." *Japan Times,* August 18, 2004.

Siegel, Adam. "Base Access Constraints and Crisis Response." *Air and Space Power Chronicles* (1996) (accessed August 12, 2004), http://www.airpower.maxwell.af.mil/airchronicles/apj/wsiegl.htm.

Sierra Club. "Sprawl: The Dark Side of the American Dream." San Francisco: Sierra Club, 1998 (accessed July 11, 2006), http://www.sierraclub.org/sprawl/report98/report.asp.

Simon, Scott. "Centennial for Author Graham Greene." *Weekend Edition,* NPR, October 2, 2004.

Sims, Calvin. "A Hard Life for Amerasian Children." *New York Times,* July 23, 2000, I-10.

Sitte, Camillo. *The Art of Building Cities.* Translated by C. T. Stewart. 1879; New York: Reinhold, 1945.

Smith, Dorothy. *The Everyday World as Problematic: A Feminist Sociology.* Boston: Northeastern University Press, 1987.

———. *Texts, Facts, and Femininity: Exploring Relations of Ruling.* London: Routledge, 1990.

Smith, Neil. *American Empire: Roosevelt's Geographer and the Prelude to Globalization.* Berkeley: University of California Press, 2003.

Smith, Patrick. "Inertia on Display." In *Okinawa: Cold War Island,* ed. Chalmers Johnson, 283–99. Cardiff, Calif.: Japan Policy Research Institute, 1999.

Solomon, Daniel. *Global City Blues.* Washington, D.C.: Island Press, 2003.

Son, Jeong-mi. "Shinsegae's E-Mart Makes Foray into the Chinese Market." *Chosun Ilbo,* June 17, 2004.

"South Korea Chooses New Capital Site." BBC, August 11, 2004 (accessed August 12, 2004), http://news.bbc.co.uk/2/hi/asia-pacific/3554296.stm.

Southworth, Michael, and Eran Ben-Joseph. *Streets and the Shaping of Towns and Cities.* New York: McGraw-Hill, 1997.

Southworth, Michael, and Peter Owens. "The Evolving Metropolis: Studies of Community, Neighborhood, and Street Form at the Urban Edge." *Journal of the American Planning Association* (1993): 271–87.

Specht, Wayne. "Misawa F-16 Drops Tanks, Training Missiles on Farm." *Stars and Stripes,* November 10, 2001.

———. "Misawa Sinks Wells to Gauge Spread of Underground Fuel Spill from 45 Years Ago." *Stars and Stripes,* July 11, 2001.

———. "One Pilot Missing after U.S. F-16 Jets Collide Off Japan." *Stars and Stripes,* November 14, 2000.

———. "Report Finds Engine Failure Caused F-16 Crash near Misawa Air Base." *Stars and Stripes,* November 21, 2003.

———. "Residents Near Ripsaw Gunnery Range Have Decided to Relocate." *Stars and Stripes,* May 11, 2002.

———. "Some Misawa Merchants Weigh Moving to Avoid Noise against Losing Business." *Stars and Stripes,* February 8, 2002.

Specht, Wayne, and Hiroshi Chida. "Officials Say Underground Jet Fuel Plume Poses No Hazard at Misawa." *Stars and Stripes,* March 30, 2001.

Specht, Wayne, and Hana Kusumoto. "Misawa Farmer Settles with Air Force." *Stars and Stripes,* October 20, 2002.

Specht, Wayne, Naoko Sekioka, and Hiroshi Chida. "Misawa Officials Criticize Safety Record of Air Force's F-16s; Urge Removal." *Stars and Stripes,* April 28, 2002.

Special Action Committee Okinawa. *The SACO Final Report on Futenma Air Station,* December 2, 1996 (accessed May 15, 2004), http://www.niraikanai.wwma.net/pages/archive/21296.html.

Spencer, Jack. Statement before the Overseas Basing Commission, September 1, 2004 (accessed January 20, 2006), http://www.heritage.org/Research/NationalSecurity/tst090104a.cfm.

Spradley, James. *The Ethnographic Interview.* New York: Holt, Rinehart, Winston, 1979.
———. *Participant Observation.* New York: Holt, Rinehart, 1980.
Sturdevant, Saundra Pollock, and Brenda Stoltzfus. *Let the Good Times Roll: Prostitution and the U.S. Military in Asia.* New York: New Press, 1992.
Sumida, Chiyomi. "Applications Pour in for Base Jobs in Okinawa." *Star and Stripes,* June 11, 2002.
———. "Futenma Noise Suit Names Base Commander." *Stars and Stripes,* November 1, 2002.
———. "Okinawa Sees Big Hole in Job Base If Marines Leave." *Stars and Stripes,* June 8, 2003.
Svan, Jennifer. "AF Services Official: Yokota to Get Chili's." *Stars and Stripes,* October 31, 2003.
———. "New Yokota Community Center Scheduled to Open Its Door in October." *Stars and Stripes,* June 22, 2001.
Svan, Jennifer, and Steve Liewer. "Unpaid Baggers at Commissaries Offer Services with a Smile . . . But Tips Are Appreciated." *Stars and Stripes,* December 16, 2001.
Svoboda, Andrew. "Supporting the Troops." *Wolf Pack Warrior,* January 17, 2003.
Szegedy-Maszak, Mariane. "Where Size Matters." *U.S. News and World Report,* June 28, 2004.
Takakura, Tomoaki. "Japanese Court Orders Noise Pollution Compensation for Residents Living near U.S. Air Base." *Mainichi Daily News,* May 23, 1998.
Taoka, Shunji. "Is This Base Really Necessary?" *Japan Policy Research Institute Critique* 7, no. 2 (February 2000).
Thomas, G. Scott. *The United States of Suburbia.* Amherst, N.Y.: Prometheus Books, 1998.
Thompson, Erwin N., and Sally Byrne Woodbridge. *Presidio of San Francisco: An Outline of Its Evolution as a U.S. Army Post, 1847–1990.* Special History Study. Denver: U.S. Dept. of the Interior National Park Service, 1992.
"Tokyo High Court Grants Residents Living Near U.S. Air Base Monetary Compensation." *Mainichi Daily News,* August 2, 1999.
Tougaw, Travis. "51st C.E.S. Breaks New Ground for Office Dormitory." *MiG Alley Flyer,* April 26, 2002.
Tremblay, Rodrique. *The New American Empire.* Haverford, Pa.: Infinity, 2004.
Trowbridge, Gordon. "Rodriguez Offers Details of Mosul Dining Hall Attack." *Army Times,* August 19, 2005.
Tyler, Greg. "Many Shoppers Feel Right at Home in Overseas Commissaries." *Stars and Stripes,* December 16, 2001.
United Kingdom Trade and Investment Council. "Automotive Industry Market in South Korea," 2003 (accessed October 12, 2004), http://www.trade.uktradeinvest.gov.uk/automotive/south_korea/profile/overview.shtml.
U.S. Air Force. "18th Wing Administrative Plan 545, Spill Prevention and Response Plan," 2003 (accessed November 17, 2003), http://216.33.118.202/EPSData/USAF/Synopses/642/F62321–03-S-Q246/SampleofKadenaSPRP.doc.
———. *Air Force Family Housing Guide.* 1995 and 2004.
———. *Architectural Compatibility Guide,* 1998 (accessed March 16, 2004), http://www.afcee.brooks.af.mil/dc/dcd/arch/ACguide/liveACG/index.htm.
———. "Aviano Air Base Planning Assistance Team Study." Aviano Air Base, 1985.

———. "Design Awards Program Annual Report." U.S. Air Force Center for Environmental Excellence, 1990.

———. "General Plan Study for Aviano Air Base, Italy." Aviano Air Base, 1996.

———. "General Plan Study for Kadena Air Base, Japan." Kadena Air Base, 1998.

———. "Installation Force Protection Guide." U.S. Air Force Center for Environmental Excellence, 1997.

———. "Notice of Request for Proposal—Aviano Housing Initiative." Aviano Air Base, 1996.

———. "Osan Air Base Housing Plan." Osan Air Base, 1999.

———. Center for Environmental Excellence. "United States Air Force Housing Privatization," 2004 (accessed October 5, 2004), http://www.afcee.brooks.af.mil/dc/dcp/news/.

U.S. Army. "Army's Residential Communities Initiative Information Paper," 2004 (accessed September 17, 2004), http://www.rci.army.mil/programinfo/RCI_Program_Information_Paper_August_2004.pdf.

U.S. Census Bureau. *Statistical Abstract of the United States*, 2000 (accessed August 6, 2004), http://www.census.gov/prod/2001pubs/statab/sec05.pdf.

U.S. Congressional Budget Office. "Options for Changing the Army's Overseas Basing," 2004 (accessed July 7, 2004), http://www.cbo.gov/ftpdocs/54xx/doc5415/05-03-ArmyOBasing.pdf.

U.S. Department of Defense. "Minimum Standards for Antiterrorism Standards for Buildings. Unified Facilities Criteria 4–010–01." Washington, D.C., 2002.

———. "National Defense Budget Estimates for the Fiscal Year 2004 Budget," 2003 (accessed October 5, 2004), http://www.dod.mil/comptroller/defbudget/fy2004/.

———. "Quadrennial Defense Review Report," September 30, 2001 (accessed October 5, 2004), http://www.loyola.edu/dept/politics/intel/qdr2001.pdf.

———. "Report on Allied Contributions to the Common Defense," 2003 (accessed October 5, 2004), http://www.defenselink.mil/pubs/allied_contrib2003/allied2003.pdf.

———. "2000 Report to Congress: Military Situation on the Korean Peninsula," 2000 (accessed October 5, 2004), http://www.defenselink.mil/news/Sep2000/korea09122000.html.

———. "Worldwide Manpower Distribution by Geographical Area," 2003 (accessed October 5, 2004), http://web1.whs.osd.mil/mmid/M05/m05sep03.pdf.

———, Office of the Deputy Under Secretary of Defense. *Base Structure Report*. Washington D.C., 2000–2006.

U.S. Department of State. *Trafficking in Persons Report*, 2002 (accessed October 5, 2004), http://www.state.gov/documents/organization/10815.pdf.

———. "Transcript: Kartman, Campbell Discuss U.S.-Japan '2+2' Meeting," 1996 (accessed March 5, 2002), http://usinfo.state.gov/regional/ea/easec/japansc7.htm.

"U.S. Embarks on Global Shuffle of Military Forces." *Japan Times*, June 15, 2003.

"U.S. Expanding NATO Base in Italy." Associated Press, January 30, 2000.

U.S. Federal Bureau of Investigation. "Khobar Towers Indictment," June 21, 2001 (accessed October 7, 2004), http://www.fbi.gov/pressrel/pressrel01/khobar.htm.

U.S. Forces Korea. "USFK PAO Release on Land Partnership Program," January 31, 2002 (accessed October 5, 2004), http://www.korea.army.mil/LPP/LPPHomepage.aspm.

———. USFK Press Release No. 021004, 2004 (accessed July 7, 2004), http://www.korea.army.mil/pao/news/021004.htm.

"USFK to Regroup Troops into 7 Areas of the Country." *Seoul Yonhap,* January 11, 2002.

U.S. GAO. "Basing Uncertainties Necessitate Reevaluation of U.S. Construction Plans in South Korea," 2003 (accessed June 16, 2004), http://www.gao.gov/new.items/d03643.pdf.

———. "Overseas Presence: Issues Involved in Reducing the Impact of the U.S. Military Presence on Okinawa," 1998 (accessed June 16, 2004), http://www.gao.gov/archive/1998/ns98066.pdf.

U.S. Green Building Council. "LEED Rating System Version 2.0." Washington, D.C., 2001.

U.S. Congress. House Armed Services Committee. "Report of a Special Subcommittee of the Armed Services Committee," 1955 (accessed October 17, 2003), http://www.niraikanai.wwma.net/pages/archive/price.html.

———. "Statement before the Subcommittee on Readiness by Raymond F. Dubois, Deputy Under Secretary of Defense (Installations and Environment)," March 18, 2003 (accessed October 5, 2004), http://www.house.gov/hasc/openingstatementsandpressreleases/108thcongress/03–03–18dubois.html.

U.S. Congress. House of Representatives. "Statement of Major General Eugene A. Lupia," March 2, 1999 (accessed September 17, 2002), http://www.house.gov/hasc/testimony/106thcongress/99–03–02lupia.htm.

———. "To Prohibit the Construction of Facilities for the Purpose of Relocating Functions of the Department of Defense Located at Torrejón Air Base, Madrid, Spain, to Crotone, Italy, or Any Other Location Outside the United States." 101, HR 3948.

———. Armed Services Committee. *Military Installations and Facilities Subcommittee Hearings,* March 9, 2000.

———. Senate Armed Services Committee. Opening Statement by Secretary of Defense William Perry, September 18, 1996 (accessed June 11, 2006), http://www.defenselink.mil/Releases/Release.aspx?ReleaseID=1042.

Vale, Lawrence. "Designing National Identity: Post-Colonial Capitols as Intercultural Dilemmas." In *Forms of Dominance,* ed. Nezar AlSayyad, 315–38. Brookfield, Vt.: Avebury, 1992.

VandeHei, Jim. "Bush Says U.S. Troops Will Stay in Iraq Past '08." *Washington Post,* March 22, 2006, A01.

Veblen, Thorstein. *The Theory of the Leisure Class.* New York: Macmillan, 1899.

Vlahos, Kelley Beaucar. "Analysts Ponder U.S. Basing in Iraq." *Fox News,* November 1, 2004.

Wal-Mart. *Annual Report.* 2002.

Wald, Matthew. "U.S. Maps Become Legal Issue in Alpine Cable Accident." *New York Times,* March 13, 1999.

Wallace, Chris. Interview with Colin Powell on *Fox News Sunday,* June 13, 2004 (accessed October 5, 2004), http://www.state.gov/secretary/rm/33476.htm.

Wells, Robbie. "Command Referral System Tool in Fight to Keep Duty-Free Goods Out of Wrong Hands in Korea." *MiG Alley Flyer,* December 21, 2001.

Welsh, Wolfgang. "Transculturality: The Puzzling Form of Cultures Today." In *Spaces of Culture: City, Nation, World,* ed. Scott Lash and Mike Featherstone, 194–213. London: Sage, 1999.

Weslowski, Jim. "Aviano Today." *Air Force Civil Engineer Magazine* (Fall/Winter 2002): 4–9.

Whitaker, Craig. *Architecture and the American Dream.* New York: Clarkson Potter, 1996.

White House. "The National Security Strategy of the United States of America," September 17, 2002 (accessed October 5, 2004), http://www.whitehouse.gov/nsc/nss.pdf.

———. "President Bush Announces Major Combat Operations in Iraq Have Ended," May 1, 2003 (accessed October 5, 2004), http://www.whitehouse.gov/news/releases/2003/05/iraq/20030501–15.html.

———. "President Speaks at V.F.W. Convention," August 16, 2004 (accessed October 5, 2004), http://www.whitehouse.gov/news/releases/2004/08/20040816-12.html#.

Whitman, Walt. *Leaves of Grass.* Philadelphia: David McKay, 1900.

Whyte, William. *Street Corner Society: The Social Structure of an Italian Slum.* Chicago: University of Chicago Press, 1943.

Wickwire, Karin. "Recent Facility Evaluation, 1,400 Bed-Shortage Could Mean Up to 17 New Buildings." *Stars and Stripes,* September 8, 2000.

Wiewel, Wim, and Joseph J. Persky, eds. *Suburban Sprawl: Private Decisions and Public Policy.* Armonk, N.Y.: M. E. Sharpe, 2002.

Wilson, Daniel. "Executive Summary Land Partnership Plan," January 31, 2002 (accessed October 5, 2004), http://www.korea.army.mil/LPP/LPPHomepage.asp.

Woo-Cumings, Meredith. "South Korean Anti-Americanism." Japan Policy Research Institute Working Paper no. 93, July 2003.

Woodward, Kathryn. "Concepts of Identity and Difference." In *Identity and Difference,* ed. Woodward, 7–50. London: Sage, 1997.

Wooten, Greg. "Follow the Rules and Survive in A-Town." *Wolf Pack Warrior,* September 5, 1997.

Workman, Chevon DuBois. "Kadena Services Getaway Resort Is Second to None" (April). U.S. Air Force Services News and Views, 2003 (accessed October 5, 2004), http://www.afsv.af.mil/NWVW/NWVWApril03/Art64.htm.

Wycherley, Richard E. *How the Greeks Built Cities: The Relationship of Architecture and Town Planning to Everyday Life in Ancient Greece.* New York: W. W. Norton, 1962.

Yamamoto, Dr. Takeo. "A Report on Aircraft Noise as a Public Health Problem in Okinawa." Research Study Committee of Aircraft Noise Influences to Health, March 1999 (accessed April 14, 2003), http://www.jca.ax.apc.org/%7eseiu/hitotsubo_kanto/Stat.Okinawa/PH9803E.html#anchor798332.

Yip, Christopher. "California Chinatowns: Built Environments Expressing the Hybridized Culture of Chinese Americans." In *Hybrid Urbanism,* ed. AlSayyad, 67–82.

Yoo, Yong-won. "80% of Yongsan Base to Be Returned." *Chosun Ilbo,* September 25, 2003.

———. "Soldiers Have No Elbow Room." *Chosun Ilbo,* March 5, 2003.

———. "U.S. Soldiers Avoid Service in Korea: Research." *Chosun Ilbo,* January 22, 2002.

———. "USFK Presents 'Good Neighbor' Program." *Chosun Ilbo,* March 6, 2003.

———. "U.S.-Korea Meet on Base Housing Plan." *Chosun Ilbo,* December 12, 2001.

Yuh, Ji-yeon. *Beyond the Shadow of Camptown: Korean Military Brides in America.*
  New York: New York University Press, 2002.
Zakaria, Fareed. "The Arrogant Empire." *Newsweek,* March 24, 2003, 17–20.
Zimmerman, Fred. "Two F-15s Make Contact During Training Mission Off Okinawa."
  Stars and Stripes, October 6, 2004.
Zukin, Sharon. *The Cultures of Cities.* Cambridge, Mass.: Blackwell, 1995.
———. *Landscapes of Power: From Detroit to Disney World.* Berkeley: University of
  California Press, 1991.

Index

Mark L. Gillem is assistant professor of architecture and landscape architecture at the University of Oregon. He is also an architect and planner, and he served as an officer on active duty in the United States Air Force for nine years.